THE COLLECTED PLAYS OF
W. SOMERSET MAUGHAM

VOL. III

By W. SOMERSET MAUGHAM

LIZA OF LAMBETH
MRS. CRADDOCK
THE MOON AND SIXPENCE
OF HUMAN BONDAGE
THE TREMBLING OF A LEAF
ON A CHINESE SCREEN
THE PAINTED VEIL
THE CASUARINA TREE
ASHENDEN
THE GENTLEMAN IN THE PARLOUR
CAKES AND ALE
THE FIRST PERSON SINGULAR
THE NARROW CORNER
AH KING
ALTOGETHER (*Collected Short Stories*)
DON FERNANDO
COSMOPOLITANS
THEATRE
THE SUMMING UP
CHRISTMAS HOLIDAY
THE MIXTURE AS BEFORE
BOOKS AND YOU
UP AT THE VILLA
STRICTLY PERSONAL
THE RAZOR'S EDGE
THEN AND NOW
HERE AND THERE (*Collection of Short Stories*)
CREATURES OF CIRCUMSTANCE
CATALINA
QUARTET (*Four Short Stories with Film Scripts*)
TRIO (*Three Short Stories with Film Scripts*)
ENCORE (*Three Short Stories with Film Scripts*)
A WRITER'S NOTEBOOK

The Collected Plays

VOL. I: LADY FREDERICK
MRS. DOT
JACK STRAW
PENELOPE
SMITH
THE LAND OF PROMISE

VOL. 2: OUR BETTERS
THE UNATTAINABLE
HOME AND BEAUTY
THE CIRCLE
THE CONSTANT WIFE
THE BREADWINNER

VOL. 3: CÆSAR'S WIFE
EAST OF SUEZ
THE SACRED FLAME
THE UNKNOWN
FOR SERVICES RENDERED
SHEPPEY

THE COLLECTED
❖ PLAYS ❖

of

W. SOMERSET
MAUGHAM

VOL. III

WILLIAM HEINEMANN LTD
MELBOURNE :: LONDON :: TORONTO

9999014891

THE COLLECTED PLAYS
FIRST PUBLISHED 1931
REPRINTED 1952

PRINTED IN GREAT BRITAIN
AT THE WINDMILL PRESS
KINGSWOOD, SURREY

THE COLLECTED PLAYS OF W. SOMERSET MAUGHAM

—

CÆSAR'S WIFE

EAST OF SUEZ

THE SACRED FLAME

THE UNKNOWN

FOR SERVICES RENDERED

SHEPPEY

PREFACE

Cæsar's Wife was suggested by Madame de Lafayette's *La Princesse de Clèves*. It is one of the most exquisite novels that has ever been written. Short though it is and written in the restrained manner of the time, for it is contemporary with the tragedies of Racine, it is in the grand style. The theme is tragic, the triumph of will over passion, and it is unfolded with a delicate subtlety that was new to fiction. Indeed, it is according to the critics with this little book that the psychological novel was born. The story is not very well known, I think, to English readers of the present day, so that I may be forgiven, perhaps, if I briefly narrate it. Monsieur de Clèves had fallen in love with his wife at first sight, but was well aware that she had for him no more than affection; but his respect and admiration for her were so great that when, inviting his aid in her distress, she told him that she loved another, he accepted her confession with sympathy. The drama lies in the effort of Monsieur de Clèves to overcome his jealousy and in his wife's to master her passion. It is beautiful to see the skill with which Madame de Lafayette depicts the gradual disintegration of this great gentleman's character. He has the decorum of the *grand siècle*, that lively sense of what he owes his own dignity, and something of that stoical heroism which his contemporaries learnt from Corneille or which he discovered in the world around him; he is exasperated at his inability to crush a vice that he despises, but human nature is too strong for him, and by degrees he becomes mean, petty, suspicious and irritable. The situation is unfolded with sobriety, the tone is never raised above that seemly to persons of good breeding; there is no vehemence, and the expression of the most violent emotion is kept within the bounds of propriety. But the emotion is deep and true.

I thought that it would be interesting to treat this theme
in a modern way. I had been often reproached for writing
only about unpleasant people, and though I did not think
the reproach justified, I was not averse from trying to write
a play in which all the characters were estimable. I thought
it possible to devise a piece in which the persons were
virtuous without being insipid and in which duty and honour
triumphed over temperament. But it was not in my plan
to make my hero succumb feebly to a passion he disdained.
Monsieur de Clèves, making too great a demand on human
nature, fails in a dozen small ways; it is true to life, but, such
is our own weakness, it makes him in the end somewhat
antipathetic. You would sooner he committed some act
of violence than be so weakly querulous. It is exasperating
that against all reason he should be convinced of his wife's
infidelity and go catch a fever and die. He had not indeed
the strength of character to play the heroic part for which
he had cast himself. I did not see why a man should not
play it to the end if he had courage, tolerance and self-
control; but tolerance and self-control are virtues that the
old learn, they seldom come naturally to the young; so I
made my hero an elderly man. This further explained and
excused the wife's infatuation for the pleasant young secretary. I had always felt it a weakness in Madame de Clèves,
with her good sense, excellent upbringing and sound
principles, that she should so casually fall for the flighty
handsome young man who was the Duc de Nemours. This
happens every day, but it is not satisfactory in fiction. And
since honour, which was a reasonable motive for action in
the seventeenth century and which, I suppose, is nothing
more than self-respect, would in these days fail to convince,
I brought in patriotism to help me to make Violet's abnega-
tion reasonable. By doing this, of course, I limited the
success of the play to this country, since patriotism is a
motive that does not travel; it is faintly ridiculous to a
German or an American that an Englishman should make
sacrifices for England. *Cæsar's Wife* will to me remain a

pleasing memory for the beautiful performance that Miss Fay Compton gave in the part of Violet. The gesture with which she held out her arms to her lover after she had sent him away for good and all and he had miserably gone, had a grace tenderness and beauty the like of which I have never before or since seen on the stage.

East of Suez purports to be a play of spectacle. I had long wanted to try my hand at something of the sort and a visit to China presented me with an appropriate setting. The bare bones of a story that I had for twenty years from time to time turned over in my mind, recurred to me. It seemed very well suited to my purpose. I kept my ears open and from this person and that heard little incidents that fitted in with my scheme and gave it the fullness, colour and variety that it needed. For the first and only time in my career as a dramatist I wrote the scenario which the professors of play-writing teach their pupils to do. It is a practice in which I have always felt there is great danger. For one thing, it is very difficult to hold in the mind's eye the whole development of a play; the imagination (mine, at least) provides you only with the important scenes, the beginning, the curtains of the acts, and the end, it leaves out the necessary scenes of transition, the scenes of preparation, and the scenes necessary to the mechanism of the play; these passages will in a scenario generally be set down per-functorily, to make it coherent, and when you come to write your play you will very likely find that the fact of having written them down cramps you. Having forced your imagination to work by an effort of will, it fails then to work with proper freedom. It seems to me better to keep your general idea in your head, with your theme and your chief scenes fluid, as they must be before they are set down in black and white, and trust to the natural development by which, if you have the dramatic instinct, one scene leads to the next. A scenario seems also to paralyse the amiable and useful little imp that dwells in your fountain pen and does for you all your best writing. The prudent writer gives him his head and if the little fellow has a mind to write something quite different from what he intended, knows that it is only common sense to yield. After all it is to this wily sprite that is due whatever merit the ignorant ascribe to the unimportant instrument who holds the pen. But the story of *East of Suez* was so complicated that I thought it necessary to construct a very detailed scenario. I must admit that it made the subsequent writing an easy matter. In a play of this sort, in which exotic and beautiful scenery is used to divert the eye and crowds to give movement and colour, it is evident that the spectacle should be an integral part of the theme. Looking back, I realise that in my inexperience I did not always adhere to the canon and in this edition I have omitted a marriage procession which I inserted because I thought this common sight in a Chinese city picturesque and amusing, but which had nothing to do with my story. On the other hand, I cannot think that anyone who saw the play will have forgotten the thrill and strangeness of the mob of Chinese, monks and neighbours, who crowded in when the wounded man was brought in after the attempted assassination in the fourth scene. With their frightened gestures and their low, excited chatter they produced an effect of great dramatic tension.

In *The Sacred Flame* I attempted a greater elaboration of dialogue than I had been in the habit of using. In certain passages I tried, quite deliberately, to make my characters use not the words and expressions that they would have used in real life on the spur of the moment and in the give and take of conversation, but words and expressions that they might have used if they had had time to set their thoughts in order. Several very good critics blamed my dialogue for being 'literary', more suitable to a novel than to the stage, and I realised myself, on hearing it with an audience, that it was sometimes none too easy to speak. I did not insist. I was in the position of the tenant of a house whose lease is running out; even though he finds certain things about it inconvenient, it is not worth his while to attempt structural alterations. In the plays I wrote later I reverted to the naturalistic dialogue that seems to comply with the requirements of the present day.

Nevertheless I have a feeling that I was on the right track, and I will ask the reader to have patience with me while I discuss for a little this matter of dialogue. Mr. St. John Ervine once wrote a little book called *How to Write a Play*. Mr. Ervine is a dramatist as well as a critic and his book is pithy and sensible. It is one that any writer for the theatre can study with profit. He has some interesting things to say about dialogue and especially about Mr. Noel Coward's. He finds it commonplace and dull. He contends that the dramatist should "heighten and lengthen and deepen the common speech and yet have it seeming to be the common speech".

Now dialogue has long been growing more naturalistic and it was inevitable that some dramatist would eventually write it in a way that exactly copied the average talk, with its hesitations, mumblings and repetitions, of average people. I do not suppose anyone can do this with more brilliant accuracy than Mr. Coward. It adds to the difficulty of the author's task; for it is evident that when he represents dull and stupid people they will be as stupid and dull on the stage as in real life and they will bore us in the same way. Moreover, when the writer who confines himself to naturalistic dialogue exposes his theme or joins together the various parts of his story (and I should think it was impossible to write a play in which certain explanations of no interest in themselves can be avoided) he will only with difficulty hold the attention of the audience. He will certainly do this more easily if he can bring himself to glid the pill. The dramatist thus limits himself to characters that are in themselves exciting and amusing and to a theme that is from the beginning of the first act to the end of the last naturally absorbing. It is asking a great deal. I may point out in passing that as Ibsen's dialogue grew more naturalistic he was led to deal with more and more abnormal characters.

But I do not think there is so much difference between Mr. Coward's practice and Mr. Ervine's theory as Mr. Ervine seems to think. One seeks to reproduce dialogue; the other to represent it. Mr. Ervine tells us that the talk of the characters in a play must be "selected and manipulated and trimmed". "The sentences," he goes on, "must not be too well or preciously written: they must not be grammatical, and yet they must not be too ungrammatical." The idea is the same, and it seems to me that if Mr. Coward tightened up his dialogue a little there would be nothing in it that Mr. Ervine could legitimately complain of. First of all, let me hazard a suggestion that the current fashion to be slangy, brief and incoherent has blinded the dramatists to the fact that a great many people do talk grammatically, do choose their words, and do make use of well-turned phrases. My impression is that if Mr. Ervine read a shorthand report of his own conversation over the luncheon table he would be surprised to find how bookish it was. The present mode in dialogue debars the writer from introducing into his play people who express themselves in an educated manner. It may be true that the English are tongue-tied, but are they so tongue-tied as the dramatists nowadays pretend? Listen to the conversation of barristers, doctors, politicians, parsons, and you will find that they speak quite naturally in a way that on the stage would certainly be thought stilted. Stage dialogue has been simplified out of all relation with life but that of the cocktail bar. It is a pity. The fashion of today prevents any reference on the stage to the great subjects of human life and the most profound thoughts of human beings. It is to this, I think, that may be ascribed the childishness with which the continental critics often charge the English drama. It does not seem to me that the French and German dramatists make so great a distinction as we do between the spoken and the written word. It gives them the opportunity to treat of psychological states as we, trammelled by realism, may not. The cinema has done so many things better than the spoken drama can do them that it has made it futile for the spoken drama to attempt them. The spoken drama, if it is going to survive, must surely look for its material in places where the pictures cannot compete with it. They have made physical action more than a trifle tame, but the drama depends on action, and so it looks as though the drama must henceforward deal with action that is purely spiritual. But if he is going to seek to represent states of mind and affections of the soul, the dramatist handicaps himself unnecessarily if he confines himself to the baldness of contemporary speech. I do not see why he should not put into the mouths of his characters, not what they would naturally say in the circumstances, but what they would say if they knew how to put into words their true and considered thoughts. It is probable that for a moment an audience used to naturalistic dialogue would think the words strange, but an audience can be coaxed or driven to accept any formula. Representation is merely an æsthetic procedure like another: naturalism is no more to be preferred to formalism than a leg of mutton to a sirloin of beef. Now that naturalistic dialogue has been carried as far as it can go I cannot but think it might be worth while to try a dialogue that does not reproduce the conversation of the day and only vaguely represents it, but is deliberately and significantly formal.

But I know that reason has little effect on men; if you wish to turn them from an evil course you must appeal to their emotions. I would beg the tender-hearted reader therefore to consider the hard life that is led by a character in a play. We happy-go-lucky persons who live in the world surrender to one impulse after another, but to him no such freedom is permitted. Necessity holds him in an iron grasp. He cannot go for a walk without a sound dramatic reason, he cannot leave a room till his presence is no longer required, nay, he may not even move from one chair to another without a convincing motive. If he has a revolver in the drawer of his desk he is almost bound to shoot himself with it. A pain in the first act is fairly certain to kill him in the last. If there is a mill-stream or a lake in the vicinity he is sure to throw himself in it, and if he climbs a mountain or a steeple, he will undoubtedly break his neck. If he backs a horse it is certain to lose and a flutter on the Stock Exchange will inevitably ruin him. However upright his principles, should chance throw him on a desert island or the break-down of his car lead him to a strange hotel and there is a woman there, even though he has never set eyes on her before, he cannot but have intimate relations with her. The consequences will be disastrous. He is the natural prey of the adventurer and the blackmailer. Nor must he expect a happy life at home. If his wife is old she will bully or bore him, and if she is young will be grossly unfaithful to him. The joys of parenthood are denied him, for the birth-rate among dramatis personæ makes the French appear wildly prolific; but should he have a son he will be a thorn in his flesh, he will either forge a cheque, get a servant girl into trouble or at the best tell his unhappy father in no uncertain terms where he gets off. The most he can hope of a daughter is that she will marry someone he does not approve of; it is much more likely that she will be seduced and then exultingly refuse to be made an honest woman.

I do not deny that the advance of civilisation has brought some alleviation to his lot. He can now have a girl to tea in his rooms without hopelessly compromising her, he can even kiss a pretty woman in a public place with the certainty that no one will come by and discover him, and he can leave indiscreet letters anywhere he likes without danger of their being found. Whenever he urgently wants to see someone he can be sure that he will walk in; he can call up a friend on the telephone without any fear of finding the number engaged, and indeed the person with whom he wishes to speak is pretty certain to be waiting for the call with the receiver in his hand; if he rings the bell a servant answers it with a celerity the rest of us can only marvel at, and should he want a cup of tea or a whisky and soda it is brought him in the twinkling of an eye. Finally, if he desires to smoke, his cigarette case is always provided with cigarettes and his lighter never fails to work. Nevertheless, these are but trivial compensations for a life of trouble. In past times the person of a play purged your soul and mine of pity and terror by declaiming at considerable length in verse, blank or otherwise, and so enabled us to consider the misfortunes of our friends and neighbours without undue concern; for this the best critics assert is the purpose of tragedy. But even this solace is now denied him. It may be that he may now talk to us only in prose, but that he should be confined to unfinished sentences, phrases not grammatical enough to offend our ears, interjections, expletives, shrugs of the shoulder and waves of the hand, is monstrous inhumanity.

When *For Services Rendered* was about to be produced and I mentioned to an interviewer that it was the last play but one that I proposed to write, I was much surprised to find that this matter, which I supposed of concern only to myself, aroused nearly as much interest as if a well-known prize-fighter had announced his intention of retiring from the ring. For a week, from dawn till dewy eve, I received in my parlour a succession of gentlemen of the Press from all parts of the world; they came from the furthest Hebrides, they came from Sydney, Australia and from Toronto, Canada, they came from Buenos Ayres (known to us film fans for its connection with the White Slave Traffic) and from Buda Pesth in Hungary, celebrated for Tzigane orchestras and the aperient water of Hunyadi Jànos; and, if I may express myself in the vernacular, I spilt the beans. I was rung up from the offices of great newspapers that till then had never communicated with me but to ask me what I ate for breakfast or what was my opinion of the Modern Girl and invited, sometimes for nothing and sometimes for fifteen, twenty or even thirty guineas, my bitter tale to tell. I could not but wish that I had kept my own counsel or that I had sworn my first interviewer to secrecy. I found it very boring to repeat the same thing a dozen times to a dozen interviewers. Nor were they anxious that I should; each wanted an exclusive story. Some time ago an ingenious person induced a number of authors to write a story on a plot that he provided and the readers were expected to be amused by seeing how different authors dealt with the same idea. I had to make all the different stories on the same plot myself.

What I had to say really was very simple. For some years I had had in mind the four plays with which I proposed to finish my career as a practising dramatist. I was prepared to write them only on this account, for I did not think any of them was likely to succeed and I knew how difficult it was for a dramatist to recover a popularity that he had lost. I was much surprised that *The Sacred Flame* and *The Breadwinner* had a considerable success. I expected nothing of *For Services Rendered*. During the rehearsals of this piece I amused myself by devising the way in which it might have been written to achieve popularity. Any dramatist will see how easily the changes could have been made. The characters had only to be sentimentalised a little to affect their behaviour at the crucial moments of the play and everything might have ended happily. The audience could have walked out of the theatre feeling that war was a very unfortunate business, but that notwithstanding God was in his heaven and all was right with the world; there was nothing to fash oneself about and haddock *a la crème* and a dance would finish the evening very nicely. But it would not have been the play I wished to write.

The Unknown was produced immediately after the First World War, and the circumstances of the time helped it to a certain success. I could not anticipate it, for in performance it turned out to have an error of construction that I had not seen. I took up again in it an idea I had used many years before in a forgotten novel called *The Hero* and the drama I saw in my mind's eye lay in the conflict between two persons who loved one another and were divided by the simple piety of the one and the lost faith of the other. But to my surprise it appeared in representation that the drama lay in the arguments on one side and the other, and not at all in the personal relations of the characters. The result was that the play came to an end with the second act; the third consequently was meaningless and there was no trick or device I could think of that could make it significant.

Sheppey puzzled a good many of the critics. Some of them, strangely ignorant of the principles of the drama, reproached me because I had set a problem and had not solved it. The dramatist takes a situation and wrings out of it all the dramatic value he can. *Sheppey* does not set out to be a problem play; I should describe it as a sardonic comedy. When I wrote it I was aware that the last scene might displease. It seemed to me to be in the same vein as the rest of the play, and I did not think I was asking an audience to accept too much when I set before them an hallucination of Sheppey's disordered brain. But it would be foolish not to recognise that they were as puzzled as the critics. I grew conscious that I was no longer in touch with the public that patronises the theatre. This happens in the end to most dramatists and they are wise to accept the warning. It is high time for them then to retire.

I did so with relief. For some years I had found it increasingly irksome to confine myself within the necessary limits of dramatic convention. With a greater knowledge of men, with the toleration and perhaps wisdom that the passing years have brought me, I found it difficult to draw characters as decided and precise as the stage demands. The first rule of drama is to stick to your point, but when your experience is wide every idea that comes to you has so many ramifications that the temptation to follow them is tedious to resist. I have hinted in this preface how tiresome I find this representative dialogue that enables you to represent so little. The dialogue of the present day is a sort of spoken shorthand by means of which the listener must guess at the thoughts and emotions of the persons of the play. When you consider the complexity of human nature it is hard to resist the feeling that the characters themselves that can be represented on the stage have little more sub-

stance than mathematical symbols. Everything must be
taken from them but what is useful to get on with your play.
Nor, if you have any independence of temper, can you
reconcile yourself to the interposition between you and your
audience of the actors and the producer. You cannot have
that intimate relation there is between the writer of a book
and his reader. The placing of a play on the stage is a business of its own and there are few dramatists, unless they have
been actors, who can do it satisfactorily. But the producer
very naturally looks upon a play as a means to exercise his
own creative activity, and it is very seldom that he has the
artistic integrity to confine himself to a faithful interpreta-
tion. It may be a better play that he produces than the
author wrote, but it is a different one. A bad, a vain
producer can do terrible things. Because he is not a man of
many ideas he attaches undue importance to any he has.
Every dramatist has suffered from the bits of business a
producer has invented and insists on keeping at whatever
cost of probability or of dramatic effect. It is often said that
a good actor can bring out of a character far more than the
author ever put in it, and this is doubtless true, though it is
more often the case that a bad actor brings out far less; but I
do not know that this is a matter on which the author must
necessarily congratulate himself. I once saw Mrs. Patrick
Campbell give a magnificent performance of Hedda Gabler,
but I think it would have driven Ibsen to distraction. She
put so much into the part that he had never thought of that
the character he had drawn was entirely obliterated. I
should not like these remarks to be taken as a mark of
ingratitude to the actors and actresses who have acted in my
plays. To take only the plays in this volume, I can say that
I have never seen such a moving performance as that of
Haidee Wright in *The Unknown*, and that of Miss Flora
Robson in *For Services Rendered*. My earlier plays owed
much of their success to the deft comedy of Marie
Tempest and to the great and versatile gifts of Irene
Vanbrugh. I have spoken in a previous preface of Miss Fay

Compton. I know how much I am indebted to Miss Gladys Cooper. She is as beautiful now as when she first went on the stage, and she has become an actress of extraordinary variety, emotional force and sensitiveness. She can play nothing without distinction.

Though in this edition I have included only such of my plays as I have wished for one reason or another to reprint, I have written nearly thirty. There is no subject, however hackneyed, calf-love, jealousy, the ill-assorted marriage, the relation between fathers and sons, that the writer cannot deal with as though it had never been dealt with before, but there is no subject that he can deal with more than once with profit and there are some that his own idiosyncrasies for ever debar him from. The material is inexhaustible, but the writer can only deal with it so far as his personality reaches, and eventually, though the mine remains as rich as ever for others, for him it is worked out. Play-writing is a young man's job. A play demands actuality. Though its theme may be of permanent value, it seems essential to dress it in the mode of the moment. Not only must the dramatist follow the changes of habit, observing for example how the automatic telephone has displaced the old-fashioned one and the phonograph the piano, but he must be alive to the changes of convention, the changes in vocabulary and the changes in the ephemeral thoughts that influence the motives and actions of people. All this the young writer does instinctively, because he is part of the change himself, but the older one only with labour. It is difficult for him to take any interest in these trivial matters: nor does it seem very fitting that he should. I do not know whether it is more tedious to see a play written now in the manner of a generation back or whether it is more painful to see one written by an elderly man determined to be up to date.

Most ideas that come to the writer come to him in terms of the medium he is in the habit of using; if he is a dramatist in play form; if a novelist or a short story writer as novels or short stories. If he is all three they come in the medium in which he is interested at the time. Speaking for myself I know that when I was interested in play-writing I would get ideas for a good many more plays than I cared to write; and then, when I was engaged in writing short stories, ideas used to occur to me in that form. The fact that so many of them have been turned into plays, successful or otherwise, seems to show that they might just as easily have come to me as plays in the first case. I think there are very few ideas that can be treated only in one way. If one had come to me that clamoured to be written as a play I suppose I should have written it, but with the last play in this volume I did in point of fact end my career as a professional dramatist.

I hope the reader will not accuse me of stupid egotism if I hazard the suggestion that the form of drama that I knew is destined to end very soon, and of course I do not mean for any such foolish reason as that I ceased to write. Realistic drama in prose is a form of art, though a minor one, and a minor art, responding to a particular state in civilisation, is likely to perish with a change in that state. The history of prose drama is short. It seems to have sprung into life here and there, during the sixteenth century, in rude farces like those played by Tabarin in a booth to attract customers for his quack medicines. In Spain it quickly achieved uncommon merit in the racy plays of Lope de Rueda, but was killed by the greater attractiveness to the public of verse. It was raised to a form of art by Molière, flourished with his reflected light in the comedies of the Restoration, and was practised with elegance by Marivaux and Beaumarchais in the France of the eighteenth century; it throve with increasing luxuriance in France during the next hundred years, and was cultivated by a long series of men of talent. It reached its utmost height in the solid work of Ibsen. It seems to me that Ibsen brought the realistic prose drama to such perfection as it is capable of, and in the process killed it. His plays seem stagy enough now; *When We Dead Awaken*, which many good judges think an important work, is a piece of theatrical clap-trap that you cannot believe in for a moment; but it was his influence that finally stripped the drama of those elements of recreation which, in my opinion, are essential to it. The dramatists have wilfully cast aside the ornaments that made their plays an entertainment for the eye and ear. The desire for verisimilitude has resulted in an intolerable dullness. Realism, where realism is out of place, has forced the dramatists in order to hold the attention of their audience to resort to themes outside the normal run of life, and so is responsible for the plays of murder and detection that give, with all their absurdities, the opportunity for thrilling incident.

The great dramatists of the past sacrificed truth of characterisation and probability of incident to situation, which (to my mind, rightly) they considered the essence of drama. But the interest of the present day is in the analysis of character. I think this is something new, and points to a change of civilisation, and this, as I suggested just now, entails the death of a form of art that was sustained by it. The characters of the older fiction were static; Balzac and Dickens told you all about their persons when they first brought them before your notice, and they remained unaltered, whatever happened to them and however long a period elapsed, till their authors had finished with them. This view of human nature evidently suited the prepossessions of the time, and it was perfectly convenient to the playwright. It enabled him to make his characters consistent and distinct. But the characters of fiction now are diverse and unstable. It has been found that the novelist can get all the excitement of a tale of adventure by the gradual disclosure of a person's character; in other cases he is concerned to show the changes in it that are occasioned by lapse of time and the circumstances of life. He examines, sometimes naïvely, sometimes subtly, the contradictions of human nature, and his readers are ready to take an interest in the complexity of the man in the street. All this is very difficult for the dramatist to deal with, and he has discarded the two devices, the soliloquy and the aside, by which he might have achieved at least some success. The burden is thrown upon the actors to translate into flesh and blood the conventional hieroglyphs which are all the dramatist can provide them with. It is too great a burden. The spectator no longer believes in the persons that are set before him.

But my melancholic prognosis applies only to the modern realistic prose drama. I do not mean of course that the drama can die. Its long history shows that like music, painting, architecture and poetry it responds to a permanent need of the human race. But when a form of art has reached what perfection it is capable of and then decays there is nothing to do but return to its origins. You have an example in sculpture at the present day which is finding a new inspiration in the wood-carving of the negroes and in the stone work of the Mayan and Peruvian craftsmen. The early drama amused the eye with spectacle and dancing and the ear with verse and music. I think the modern playwright would do well to call in these allied arts to his help. I do not suppose blank verse can profitably be used again, but a quick, running metre like that used by the old Spanish dramatists, though with less frequent rhymes, may well be acceptable, not only to the 'chosen few', but to the public at large. A long tirade in verse, as everyone knows who has seen a play of Racine, has apart from the sense, by its volume of rhythmical sound, a very high dramatic value. I do not see why music should not be used, as in the old melodramas, to prepare a mood or emphasise an emotion. There is no need to remark on the diverting effect of beautiful scenes and gay costumes or on the agreeableness of good dancing. An ingenious dramitist should be able to make all these an integral part of his play. With such pleasant means of recreation he may render attractive that drama of the soul which, as I have suggested, seems the natural development forced upon him by the success of the cinema.

But I would not condemn the dramatist to occupy himself only with high and serious matters. Cómedy also has its claims. It has been greatly hampered by the demand for verisimilitude. My good fortune has brought me in contact with most of the celebrated wits of my day; and I have noticed that they sparkle but intermittently; no one in private life shines so continuously as a witty character should in a play, he is never so pointed, finished and apt; the conversation of a comedy is artificial in its essence, and to take pains to make it resemble the conversation of real life is absurd. The aim of comedy is not to represent life, but amusingly to comment on it. There is no valud reason why farce should not enter into it. In practice it is almost impossible to hold the attention of an audience for two hours and a half with pure comedy. But when the humours grow broad the critics shake their heads and, mildly or acrimoniously, regret the introduction of horse-play. I think they make a mistake. Comedy, depending as it does on wit, appeals only to the intellect; that is not enough: farce appeals to the belly. The great comic writers of the past felt no fear of it, and I would have the comic writers of the future feel no fear of it either, but use it, as freely as Aristophanes and Molière, whenever it suits their purpose. They must not mind if the very superior look down their noses. They can always console themselves with the recollection that Walter Pater laughed consumedly at *The Magistrate.**

*The prefaces to these volumes were written for the Collected Edition of my plays that was published in 1931. In a book I wrote later, *The Summing Up*, I repeated a certain amount of what I had already said in them.   W.S.M.

CÆSAR'S WIFE

A COMEDY
in Three Acts

CHARACTERS

Sir Arthur Little, K.C.B., K.C.M.G.
Ronald Parry
Henry Pritchard
Richard Appleby, M.P.
Osman Pasha
Violet
Mrs. Etheridge
Mrs. Pritchard
Mrs. Appleby

An English Butler; Native Servants; an Arab Gardener.

———

The scene is laid in Cairo, in the house and garden of the British Consular Agent.

CÆSAR'S WIFE

THE FIRST ACT

SCENE: *The morning-room in the Consular Agent's house at Cairo. The windows are Arabic in character and so are the architraves of the doors, but otherwise it is an English room, airy and spacious. The furniture is lacquer and Chippendale, there are cool chintzes on the chairs and sofas, cut roses in glass vases, and growing azaleas in pots; but here and there an Eastern antiquity, a helmet and a coat of mail, a piece of woodwork, reminds one of the Mussulman conquest of Egypt; while an ancient god in porphyry, graven images in blue pottery, blue bowls, recall an older civilisation still.*

When the curtain rises the room is empty, the blinds are down so as to keep out the heat, and it is dim and mysterious. A SERVANT *comes in, a dark-skinned native in the gorgeous uniform, red and gold, of the Consular Agent's establishment, and draws the blinds. Through the windows is seen the garden with palm-trees, oranges and lemons, tropical plants with giant leaves; and beyond, the radiant blue of the sky. In the distance is heard the plaintive, guttural wailing of an Arab song. A* GARDENER *in a pale blue gaberdine passes with a basket on his arm.*

SERVANT: Es-salâm 'alêkum (Peace be with you).

GARDENER: U'alêkum es-Salâm warahmet Allâh wa barakâta (And with you be peace and God's mercy and blessing).

> [*The* SERVANT *goes out. The* GARDENER *stops for a moment to nail back a straggling creeper and then goes on his way. The door is opened.* MRS. APPLEBY *comes in with* ANNE ETHERIDGE *and they are followed immediately by* VIOLET. ANNE *is a woman of forty, but handsome still, very pleasant and sym-*

pathetic; she is a woman of the world, tactful and self-controlled. She is dressed in light, summery things. MRS. APPLEBY *is an elderly, homely woman, soberly but not inexpensively dressed. The wife of a North-country manufacturer, she spends a good deal of money on rather dowdy clothes.* VIOLET *is a very pretty young woman of twenty. She looks very fresh and English in her muslin frock; there is something spring-like and virginal in her appearance, and her manner of dress is romantic rather than modish. She suggests a lady in a Gainsborough portrait rather than a drawing in a paper of Paris fashions. Luncheon is just finished and when they come in the women leave the door open for the men to follow.*

MRS. APPLEBY: How cool it is in here! This isn't the room we were in before lunch?

ANNE: No. They keep the windows closed and the blinds drawn all the morning so that it's beautifully cool when one comes in.

MRS. APPLEBY: I suppose we shan't feel the heat so much when we've been here a few days.

ANNE: Oh, but this is nothing to what you'll get in Upper Egypt.

VIOLET: [*As she enters.*] Is Mrs. Appleby complaining of the heat? I love it.

ANNE: Dear Violet, wait till May comes and June. You don't know how exhausting it gets.

VIOLET: I'm looking forward to it. I think in some past life I must have been a lizard.

MRS. APPLEBY: I dare say the first year you won't feel it. I have a brother settled in Canada, and he says the first year people come out from England they don't feel the cold anything like what they do later on.

ANNE: I've spent a good many winters here, and I always make a point of getting away by the fifteenth of March.

MRS. APPLEBY: Oh, are you staying as late as that?

ANNE: Good gracious, no. You make Lady Little's heart positively sink.

VIOLET: Nonsense, Anne, you know we want you to stay as long as ever you can.

ANNE: I used to have an apartment in Cairo, but I've given it up now and Lady Little asked me to come and stay at the Agency while I was getting everything settled.

MRS. APPLEBY: Oh, then you knew Sir Arthur before he married?

ANNE: Oh, yes, he's one of my oldest friends. I can't help thinking Lady Little must have great sweetness of character to put up with me.

VIOLET: Or you must be a perfect miracle of tact, darling.

MRS. APPLEBY: My belief is, it's a little of both.

ANNE: When Arthur came to see me one day last July and told me he was going to marry the most wonderful girl in the world, of course I thought good-bye. A man thinks he can keep his bachelor friendships, but he never does.

MRS. APPLEBY: His wife generally sees to that.

VIOLET: Well, I think it's nonsense, especially with a man like Arthur who'd been a bachelor so long and naturally had his life laid out before ever I came into it. And besides, I'm devoted to Anne.

ANNE: It's dear of you to say so.

VIOLET: I came here as an absolute stranger. And after all, I wasn't very old, was I?

MRS. APPLEBY: Nineteen?

VIOLET: Oh, no, I was older than that. I was nearly twenty.

MRS. APPLEBY: [*Smiling.*] Good gracious!

VIOLET: It was rather alarming to find oneself on a sudden the wife of a man in Arthur's position. I was dreadfully self-conscious; I felt that everybody's eyes were upon me.

And you don't know how easy it is to make mistakes in a country that's half Eastern and half European.

ANNE: To say nothing of having to deal with the representatives of half a dozen Great Powers all outrageously susceptible.

VIOLET: And, you know, there was the feeling that the smallest false step might do the greatest harm to Arthur and his work here. I had only just left the schoolroom and I found myself almost a political personage. If it hadn't been for Anne I should have made a dreadful mess of things.

ANNE: Oh, I don't think that. You had two assets which would have made people excuse a great deal of inexperience, your grace and your beauty.

VIOLET: You say very nice things to me, Anne.

MRS. APPLEBY: Your marriage was so romantic, I can't see how anyone could help feeling very kindly towards you.

VIOLET: There's not much room for romance in the heart of the wife of one of the Agents of the foreign Powers when she thinks she hasn't been given her proper place at a dinner party.

MRS. APPLEBY: I remember wondering at the time whether you weren't a little overcome by all the excitement caused by your marriage.

VIOLET: I was excited too, you know.

MRS. APPLEBY: Everyone had always looked upon Sir Arthur as a confirmed bachelor. It was thought he cared for nothing but his work. He's had a wonderful career, hasn't he?

VIOLET: The Prime Minister told me he was the most competent man he'd ever met.

ANNE: I've always thought he must be a comfort to any Government. Whenever anyone has made a hash of things he's been sent to put them straight.

VIOLET: Well, he always has.

MRS. APPLEBY: Mr. Appleby was saying only this morning he was the last man one would expect to marry in haste.

VIOLET: Let's hope he won't repent at leisure.

ANNE: [Smiling.] Mrs. Appleby is dying to know all about it, Violet.

MRS. APPLEBY: I'm an old woman, Lady Little.

VIOLET: [Gaily.] Well, I met Arthur at a week-end party. He'd come home on leave and all sorts of important people had been asked to meet him. I was frightened out of my life. The duchesses had strawberry leaves hanging all over them and they looked at me down their noses. And the Cabinet Ministers' wives had protruding teeth and they looked at me up their noses.

ANNE: What nonsense you talk, Violet!

VIOLET: I was expecting to be terrified of Arthur. After all, I knew he was a great man. But you know, I wasn't a bit. He was inclined to be rather fatherly at first, so I cheeked him.

ANNE: I can imagine his surprise. No one had done that for twenty years.

VIOLET: When you know Arthur at all well you discover that when he wants anything he doesn't hesitate to ask for it. He told our hostess that he wanted me to sit next to him at dinner. That didn't suit her at all, but she didn't like to say no. Somehow people don't say no to Arthur. The Cabinet Ministers' wives looked more like camels than ever, and by Sunday evening, my dear, the duchesses' strawberry leaves began to curl and crackle.

ANNE: Your poor hostess, I feel for her. To have got hold of a real lion for your party and then have him refuse to bother himself with anybody but a chit of a girl whom you'd asked just to make an even number!

MRS. APPLEBY: He just fell in love with you at first sight?

VIOLET: That's what he says now.

MRS. APPLEBY: Did you know?

VIOLET: I thought it looked very like it, you know, only it
was so improbable. Then came an invitation from a
woman I only just knew for the next week-end, and she
said Arthur would be there. Then my heart really did
begin to go pit-a-pat. I took the letter in to my sister and
sat on her bed and we talked it over. "Does he mean to
propose to me," I said, "or does he not?" And my sister
said: "I can't imagine what he sees in you. Will you
accept him if he does?" she asked. "Oh, no," I said.
"Good heavens, why he's twenty years older than I am!"
But of course I meant to all the time. I shouldn't have
cared if he was a hundred, he was the most wonderful
man I'd ever known.

MRS. APPLEBY: And did he propose to you that week-end,
when he'd practically only seen you once before?

VIOLET: I got down in the afternoon and he was there
already. As soon as I swallowed a cup of tea he said:
"Come out for a walk." Well, I'd have loved a second
cup, but I didn't like to say so, so I went. But we had a
second tea in a cottage half an hour later, and we were
engaged then.

> [APPLEBY *comes in with* OSMAN PASHA. MR. APPLEBY
> *is a self-made man who has entered Parliament; he is
> about sixty, grey-bearded, rather short and stout, with
> some accent in his speech, shrewd, simple and good-
> natured. He wears a blue serge suit.* OSMAN PASHA
> *is a swarthy, bearded Oriental, obese, elderly but
> dignified; he wears the official frock-coat of the
> Khedivial service and a tarbush.*

APPLEBY: Sir Arthur is coming in one moment. He is
talking to one of his secretaries.

VIOLET: Really, it's too bad of them not to leave him alone
even when he's snatching a mouthful of food.

OSMAN PASHA: Vous permettez que j'apporte ma cigarette,
chère Madame.

VIOLET: Of course. Come and sit here, Pasha.

APPLEBY: I wanted to tell his Excellency how interested I am in his proposal to found a technical college in Cairo, but I can't speak French.

VIOLET: Oh, but his Excellency understands English perfectly, and I believe really he talks it as well as I do, only he won't.

OSMAN PASHA: Madame, je ne comprends l'anglais que quand vous le parlez, et tout galant homme sait ce que dit une jolie femme.

ANNE: [*Translating for the* APPLEBYS.] He says he only understands English when Lady Little speaks it, and every nice man understands what a pretty woman says.

VIOLET: No one pays me such charming compliments as you do. You know I'm learning Arabic.

OSMAN PASHA: C'est une bien belle langue, et vous, Madame vous avez autant d'intelligence que de beauté.

VIOLET: I have a Copt who comes to me every day. And I practise a little with your brother, Anne.

ANNE: [*To* MRS. APPLEBY.] My brother is one of Sir Arthur's secretaries. I expect it was he that Mr. Appleby left with Sir Arthur.

VIOLET: If it is I shall scold him. He knows quite well that he has no right to come and bother Arthur when he's in the bosom of his family. But they say he's a wonderful Arabic scholar.

OSMAN PASHA: Vous parlez de M. Parry? Je n'ai jamais connu un Anglais qui avait une telle facilité.

ANNE: He says he's never known an Englishman who speaks so well as Ronny.

VIOLET: It's a fearfully difficult language. Sometimes my head seems to get tied up in knots.

[*Two* SAISES *come in, one with a salver on which are coffee cups and the other bearing a small tray on which is a silver vessel containing Turkish coffee. They go round*

*giving coffee to the various people, then wait in silence.
When* SIR ARTHUR *comes in they give him his coffee
and go out.*

ANNE: It's wonderful of you to persevere.

VIOLET: Oh, you know, Ronny's very encouraging. He
says I'm really getting on. I want so badly to be able to
talk. You can't think how enthusiastic I am about
Egypt. I love it.

OSMAN PASHA: Pas plus que l'Egypte vous aime, Madame.

VIOLET: When we landed at Alexandria and I saw that blue
sky and that coloured, gesticulating crowd, my heart
leapt. I knew I was going to be happy. And every day
I've loved Egypt more. I love its antiquities, I love the
desert and the streets of Cairo and those dear little
villages by the Nile. I never knew there was such beauty
in the world. I thought you only read of romance in
books; I didn't know there was a country where it sat by
the side of a well under the palm trees, as though it were
at home.

OSMAN PASHA: Vous êtes charmante, Madame. C'est un
bien beau pays. Il n'a besoin que d'une chose pour
qu'on puisse y vivre.

ANNE: [*Translating.*] It's a beautiful country. It only wants
one thing to make it livable. And what is that, your
Excellency?

OSMAN PASHA: La liberté.

APPLEBY: Liberty?

[ARTHUR *has come in when first* VIOLET *begins to speak of
Egypt and he listens to her enthusiasm with an
indulgent smile. At the Pasha's remark he comes
forward.* ARTHUR LITTLE *is a man of forty-five,
alert, young in manner, very intelligent, with the
urbanity, self-assurance, tact, and resourcefulness of the
experienced diplomatist. Nothing escapes him, but he
does not often show how much he notices.*

ARTHUR: Egypt has the liberty to do well, your Excellency. Does it need the liberty to do ill before it loses the inclination to do it?

VIOLET: [*To* MRS. APPLEBY.] I hope you don't mind Turkish coffee?

MRS. APPLEBY: Oh, no, I like it.

VIOLET: I'm so glad. I think it perfectly delicious.

ARTHUR: You have in my wife an enthusiastic admirer of this country, Pasha.

OSMAN PASHA: J'en suis ravi.

ARTHUR: I've told Ronny to come in and have a cup of coffee. [*To* ANNE.] I thought you'd like to say how d'you do to him.

ANNE: Are you very busy to-day?

ARTHUR: We're always busy. Isn't that so, Excellency?

OSMAN PASHA: En effet, et je vous demanderai permission de me retirer. Mon bureau m'appelle.

> [*He gets up and shakes hands with* VIOLET.

VIOLET: It was charming of you to come.

OSMAN PASHA: Mon Dieu, Madame, c'est moi qui vous remercie de m'avoir donné l'occasion de saluer votre grâce et votre beauté.

> [*He bows to the rest of the company.* ARTHUR *leads him towards the door and he goes out.*

ANNE: You take all these compliments without turning a hair, Violet.

ARTHUR: [*Coming back.*] You know, that's a wonderful old man. He's so well-bred, he has such exquisite manners, it's hard to realise that if it were possible he would have us all massacred to-morrow.

APPLEBY: I remember there was a certain uneasiness in England when you recommended that he should be made Minister of Education.

ARTHUR: They don't always understand local conditions in England. Osman is a Moslem of the old school. He has a bitter hatred of the English. In course of years he has come to accept the inevitable, but he's not resigned to it. He never loses sight of his aim.

APPLEBY: And that is?

ARTHUR: Why, bless you, to drive the English into the sea. But he's a clever old rascal, and he sees that one of the first things that must be done is to educate the Egyptians. Well, we want to educate them too. I had all sorts of reforms in mind which I would never have got the strict Mohammedans to accept if they hadn't been brought forward by a man whose patriotism they believe in and whose orthodoxy is beyond suspicion.

ANNE: Don't you find it embarrassing to work with a man you distrust?

ARTHUR: I don't distrust him. I have a certain admiration for him, and I bear him no grudge at all because at the bottom of his heart he simply loathes me.

APPLEBY: I don't see why he should do that.

ARTHUR: I was in Egypt for three years when I was quite a young man. I was very small fry then, but I came into collision with Osman and he tried to poison me. I was very ill for two months, and he's never forgiven me because I recovered.

APPLEBY: What a scoundrel!

ARTHUR: He would be a little out of place in a Nonconformist community. In the good old days of Ismael he had one of his wives beaten to death and thrown into the Nile.

APPLEBY: But is it right to give high office to a man of that character?

ARTHUR: They were the manners and customs of the times.

MRS. APPLEBY: But he tried to kill you. Don't you bear him any ill will?

ARTHUR: I don't think it was very friendly, you know, but after all no statesman can afford to pay attention to his private feelings. His duty is to find the round peg for the round hole and put him in.

ANNE: Why does he come here?

ARTHUR: He has a very great and respectful admiration for Violet. She chaffs him, if you please, and the old man adores her. I think she's done more to reconcile him to the British occupation than all our diplomacy.

MRS. APPLEBY: It must be wonderful to have power in a country like this.

VIOLET: Power? Oh, I haven't that. But it makes me so proud to think I can be of any use at all. I only wish I had the chance to do more. Since I've been here I've grown very patriotic.

> [RONALD PARRY *comes in. He is a young man, very good-looking, fresh and pleasant, with a peculiar charm of manner.*

ARTHUR: Ah, here is Ronny.

RONNY: Am I too late for my cup of coffee?

VIOLET: No, it will be brought to you at once.

RONNY: [*Shaking hands with* VIOLET.] Good morning.

VIOLET: This is Mr. Parry. Mr. and Mrs. Appleby.

RONNY: How d'you do?

ARTHUR: Now, Ronny, don't put on your Foreign Office manner. Mr. and Mrs. Appleby are very nice people.

MRS. APPLEBY: I'm glad you think that, Sir Arthur.

ARTHUR: Well, when you left your cards with a soup ticket from the F.O. my heart sank.

APPLEBY: There, my dear, I told you he wouldn't want to be bothered with us.

ARTHUR: You see, I expected a pompous couple who knew all about everything and were going to tell me exactly how Egypt ought to be governed. A Member of

Parliament doesn't inspire confidence in the worried bosom of a Government official.

VIOLET: I don't know if you think you're putting Mr. and Mrs. Appleby at their ease, Arthur.

ARTHUR: Oh, but I shouldn't say this if I hadn't been most agreeably disappointed.

MRS. APPLEBY: I never forget the days when Mr. Appleby used to light the kitchen fire himself and I used to do the week's washing every Monday morning. I don't think we've changed much since then, either of us.

ARTHUR: I know, and I'm really grateful to the Foreign Office for having given you your letter.

MRS. APPLEBY: It's been a great treat to us to come and see you. And it's done my heart good to see Lady Little. If you don't mind my saying so she's like a spring morning and it makes one glad to be alive just to look at her.

VIOLET: Oh, don't!

ARTHUR: I'm inclined to feel very kindly to everyone who feels kindly towards her. You must enjoy yourselves in Upper Egypt and when you come back to Cairo you must let us know.

APPLEBY: I'm expecting to learn a good deal from my journey.

ARTHUR: You may learn a good deal that will surprise you. You may learn that there are races in the world that seem born to rule and races that seem born to serve; that democracy is not a panacea for all the ills of mankind, but merely one system of government like another, which hasn't had a long enough trial to make it certain whether it is desirable or not; that freedom generally means the power of the strong to oppress the weak, and that the wise statesman gives men the illusion of it but not the substance—in short, a number of things which must be very disturbing to the equilibrium of a Radical Member of Parliament.

ANNE: On the other hand, you'll see our beautiful Nile and the temples.

ARTHUR: And perhaps they'll suggest to you that however old the world is it's ever young, and that when all's said and done the most permanent on the face of the earth is what seems the most transitory—the ideal.

APPLEBY: Fanny, it looks to me as though we'd bitten off as big a piece of cake as we can chew with any comfort.

MRS. APPLEBY: Oh, well, we'll do our best. And though I never could do arithmetic I've always thought perhaps one might be saved without. Good-bye, Lady Little, and thank you for having us.

VIOLET: Good-bye.

> [*There are general farewells and they go to the door.* RONNY *opens it for them. They go out.*]

RONNY: I forgot to tell you, sir, Mrs. Pritchard has just telephoned to ask if she can see you on a matter of business.

ARTHUR: [*With a grim smile.*] Say I'm very busy to-day, and I regret exceedingly that it will be quite impossible for me to see her.

RONNY: [*With a twinkle in his eye.*] She said she was coming round at once.

ARTHUR: If she's made up her mind to see me at all costs she might have saved herself the trouble of ringing up to find out if it was convenient.

ANNE: Your sister is a determined creature, Arthur.

ARTHUR: I know. I have some authority in the affairs of this country, but none over dear Christina. I wonder what she wants.

VIOLET: Let us hope for the best.

ARTHUR: I've noticed that whenever anyone wants to see me very urgently it's never to give me anything. When Christina wants to see me urgently my only safety is in instant flight.

VIOLET: You must be nice to her, Arthur. If you're not she'll only take it out of me.

ARTHUR: It's monstrous, isn't it?

VIOLET: After all, she kept house for you for ten years. Admirably, mind you.

ARTHUR: Admirably. She has a genius for order and organisation in the house. Everything went like clockwork. She never wasted a farthing. She saved me hundreds of pounds. She led me a dog's life. I've come to the conclusion there's nothing so detestable as a good housekeeper.

VIOLET: How fortunate you married me, then! But you can't expect her to see that point of view. It's very hard for her to be turned out of this very pleasant billet, and it's natural that when you won't do something she asks you she should put it down to my influence.

ANNE: It must have been a very difficult position for you.

VIOLET: I did all I could to make her like me. I did feel rather like a usurper, you know. I tried to make her see that I didn't at all want to put on airs.

ARTHUR: Fortunately she's taken it very well. I confess I was a little nervous when she told me she meant to stay on in Egypt to be near her son.

ANNE: It would be a detestable person who didn't like Violet, I think.

ARTHUR: Detestable. I should have no hesitation in having him deported.

RONNY: I think I'd better be getting back to my work.

ANNE: Oh, Ronny, would you like me to come and help you with your packing?

VIOLET: [To RONNY.] Are you going somewhere?

RONNY: I'm leaving Cairo.

ANNE: Didn't you know? Ronny has just been appointed to Paris.

VIOLET: Is he going to leave Egypt for good?

> [*She is taken aback by the news. She clenches her hand on the rail of a chair;* ARTHUR *and* ANNE *notice the little, instinctive motion.*

RONNY: I suppose so.

VIOLET: But why was it kept from me? Why have you been making a secret of it?

ARTHUR: Darling, no one's been making a secret of it. I—I thought Anne would have told you.

VIOLET: Oh, it doesn't matter at all, but Ronny has been in the habit of doing all sorts of things for me. It would have been convenient if I'd been told that a change was going to be made.

ARTHUR: I'm very sorry. It was only arranged this morning. I received a telegram from the Foreign Office. I thought it would interest Anne, so I sent Ronny along to tell her.

VIOLET: I hate to be treated like a child.

> [*There is a moment's embarrassment.*

ANNE: It was stupid of me. I ought to have come and told you. I was so pleased and excited that I forgot.

VIOLET: I don't quite know why you should have been so excited.

ANNE: It will be very nice for me to have Ronny so near. You see, now I've given up my flat I shan't come to Egypt very often and I should never have seen Ronny. I can run over to Paris constantly. Besides, it's a step, isn't it? And I want to see him an Ambassador before I die.

VIOLET: I don't see what good it will do him in Paris to speak Arabic like a native.

ARTHUR: Oh, well, that is the F.O. all over. The best Persian scholar in the Service has spent the last six years in Washington.

RONNY: It's been a great surprise for me. I expected to remain in Egypt indefinitely.

VIOLET: [*Recovering herself.*] I expect you'll have a very good time in Paris. When do you go?

RONNY: There's a boat the day after to-morrow. Sir Arthur thought I'd better take that.

VIOLET: [*Scarcely mistress of herself.*] As soon as that! [*Recovering, gaily.*] We shall miss you dreadfully. I can't imagine what I shall do without you. [*To* ANNE.] You can't think how useful he's been to me since I came here.

RONNY: It's very kind of you to say so.

VIOLET: He's invaluable at functions and things like that. You see, he knows where everyone should sit at dinner. And at first he used to coach me with details about various people so that I shouldn't say the wrong thing.

ARTHUR: If you had you'd have said it so charmingly that no one would have resented it.

VIOLET: I'm so afraid that the man who takes Ronny's place will refuse to write my invitations for me.

ARTHUR: It's not exactly the duty of my secretaries.

VIOLET: No, but I do hate doing it myself. And Ronny was able to imitate my handwriting.

ARTHUR: I'm sure he could never write as badly as you.

VIOLET: Oh, yes, he could. Couldn't you?

RONNY: I managed to write quite enough like you for people not to notice the difference.

VIOLET: You know, there are thirty-two invitations to do now.

ANNE: Why don't you send cards?

VIOLET: Oh, I think a letter is so much more polite. Somehow I don't feel old enough to ask people to dine with me in the third person.

RONNY: I'll come and do them the moment Sir Arthur can let me go.

ARTHUR: You'd better do them before Violet goes out.

VIOLET: That'll be very soon. The Khedive's mother has asked me to go and see her at half-past three. I'll get the list now, shall I? I don't think I'll wait for Christina. If she wants to see you on business I dare say she'd rather I wasn't there.

ARTHUR: Very well.

VIOLET: [*To* RONNY.] Will you come here when you're ready?

RONNY: Certainly.

[She goes out.

ARTHUR: Have you finished that report yet?

RONNY: Not quite, sir. It will be ready in ten minutes.

ARTHUR: Put it on my desk.

RONNY: All right, sir.

> [*Exit.* ARTHUR *and* ANNE *are left alone. He looks at her reflectively.*]

ARTHUR: Violet is very sensitive to anything that might be considered a slight.

ANNE: It's very natural, isn't it? A high-spirited girl.

ARTHUR: She likes me to tell her my arrangements. It gives her a little feeling of importance to know things before other people.

ANNE: Oh, of course. I quite understand. I should do the same in her place.

ARTHUR: I ought to have remembered and told her that Ronny was going. She was just a little vexed because she thought I'd been fixing things up behind her back.

ANNE: Yes, I know. It would naturally put her out for a moment to learn on a sudden that one of the persons she'd been thrown in contact with was going away.

ARTHUR: [*With a twinkle in his eye.*] I'm wondering if I must blame you for the loss of an excellent secretary.

ANNE: Me?

ARTHUR: I don't know why the F.O. should suddenly have made up their minds that your brother was wanted in Paris. Have you been pulling strings?

ANNE: [*Smiling.*] What a suspicious nature you have!

ARTHUR: Anne, own up.

ANNE: I thought Ronny was getting into a groove here. There didn't seem to be much more for him to do than he has been doing for some time. If you *will* have the truth, I've been moving heaven and earth to get him moved.

ARTHUR: How deceitful of you not to have said a word about it!

ANNE: I didn't want to make him restless. I knew he'd be mad to go to Paris. I thought it much better not to say anything till it was settled.

ARTHUR: D'you think he's mad to go to Paris?

ANNE: [*Fencing with him.*] Any young man would be.

ARTHUR: I wonder if he'd be very much disappointed if I made other arrangements.

ANNE: What do you mean, Arthur? You wouldn't prevent him from going when I've done everything in the world to get him away.

ARTHUR: [*Abruptly.*] Why should you be so anxious for him to go?

[*She looks at him for an instant in dismay.*

ANNE: Good heavens, don't speak so sharply to me. I told Violet just now. I wanted him to be more get-at-able. I think he stands a much better chance of being noticed if he's in a place like Paris.

ARTHUR: [*With a smile.*] Ah, yes, you said you were coming less frequently to Egypt than in the past. It might be worth while to keep Ronny here in order to tempt you back.

ANNE: Egypt isn't the same to me that it was.

ARTHUR: I hope my marriage has made no difference to our friendship, Anne. You know how deeply I value it.

ANNE: You used to come and see me very often. You knew I was discreet and you used to talk over with me all sorts of matters which occupied you. I was pleased and flattered. Of course I realised that those pleasant conversations of ours must stop when you married. I only came here this winter to collect my goods and chattels.

ARTHUR: You make me feel vaguely guilty towards you.

ANNE: Of course you're nothing of the sort. But I don't want Violet to feel that I am making any attempt to—to monopolise you. She's been charming to me. The more I know her the more delightful I find her.

ARTHUR: It's very nice of you to say so.

ANNE: You know I've always had a great admiration for you. I'm so glad to see you married to a girl who's not unworthy of you.

ARTHUR: I suppose it was a dangerous experiment for a man of my age to marry a girl of nineteen.

ANNE: I think one can admit that. But you've always been one of the favourites of the gods. You've made a wonderful success of it.

ARTHUR: It needs on a husband's part infinite tact, patience, and tolerance.

ANNE: You have the great advantage that Violet is genuinely in love with you.

ARTHUR: I suppose only a fatuous ass would confess that a beautiful girl was in love with him.

ANNE: You make her very happy.

ARTHUR: There's nothing I wouldn't do to achieve that. I'm more desperately in love with Violet even than when I first married her.

ANNE: I'm so glad. *I* want nothing but your happiness.

ARTHUR: Here is Christina.

> [*The door opens as he says these words and an English* BUTLER *ushers in* MRS. PRITCHARD. *She is a tall, spare woman, with hair turning grey, comely, upright in her carriage, with decision of character indicated by every gesture; but though masterful and firm to attain her ends, she is an honest woman, direct, truthful and not without humour. She is admirably gowned in a manner befitting her station and importance.*

BUTLER: Mrs. Pritchard.

> [*Exit.*

ARTHUR: I knew it was you, Christina. I felt a sense of responsibility descend upon the house.

CHRISTINA: [*Kissing him.*] How is Violet?

ARTHUR: Lovely.

CHRISTINA: I was inquiring about her health.

ARTHUR: Her health is perfect.

CHRISTINA: At her age one's always well, I suppose. [*Kissing* ANNE.] How d'you do? And how are you, my poor Arthur?

ARTHUR: You ask me as though I was a doddering old gentleman, crippled with rheumatism. I'm in the best of health, thank you very much, and very active for my years. [CHRISTINA *has seen a flower on the table that has fallen from a bowl, and picks it up and puts it back in its place*.] Why do you do that?

CHRISTINA: I don't like untidiness.

ARTHUR: I do.

> [*He takes the flower out again and places it on the table.*

CHRISTINA: I was expecting to find you in your office.

ARTHUR: Do you think I'm neglecting my work? I thought it more becoming to wait for you here.

CHRISTINA: I wanted to see you on a matter of business.

ARTHUR: So I understood from your message. I feel convinced you're going to put me in the way of making my fortune.

ANNE: I'll leave you, shall I?

CHRISTINA: Oh, no, pray don't. There's not the least reason why you shouldn't hear what it's all about.

ARTHUR: You're not going to make my fortune after all. You're going to ask me to do something.

CHRISTINA: What makes you think that?

ARTHUR: You want a third person present to be witness to my brutal selfishness when I refuse. I know you, Christina.

CHRISTINA: [*Smiling.*] You're much too sensible to refuse a perfectly reasonable request.

ARTHUR: Let us hear it. [*She sits down on the sofa. The cushions have been disordered by people sitting on them and she shakes them out, and pats them and arranges them in their place.*] I wish you'd leave the furniture alone, Christina.

CHRISTINA: I cannot make out what pleasure people take in seeing things out of their proper place.

ARTHUR: You're very long in coming to the point.

CHRISTINA: I hear that the Khedive has quarrelled with his secretary.

ARTHUR: You're a marvellous woman, Christina. You get hold of all the harem gossip.

CHRISTINA: It's true, isn't it?

ARTHUR: Yes. But I only heard of it myself just before luncheon. How did it come to your ears?

CHRISTINA: That doesn't matter, does it? I have a way of hearing things that may be of interest to me.

ARTHUR: I'm afraid I'm very dense, but I don't see how it can be of any particular interest to you.

CHRISTINA: [*Smiling.*] Dear Arthur. The Khedive has asked you to recommend him an English secretary.

ANNE: Has he really? That's a change. He's never had an English secretary before.

ARTHUR: Never.

ANNE: It's a wonderful opportunity.

ARTHUR: If we get the right man he can be of the greatest possible help. If he's tactful, wise, and courteous, there's no reason why in time he shouldn't attain very considerable influence over the Khedive. If we can really get the Khedive to work honestly and sincerely with us, instead of hampering us by all kinds of secret devices, we can do miracles in this country.

ANNE: What a splendid chance for the man who gets the job!

ARTHUR: I suppose it is. If he has the right qualities he may achieve anything. And after all, it's a splendid chance to be able to render such great service to our own old country.

CHRISTINA: Has the Khedive given any particulars about the sort of man he wants?

ARTHUR: He naturally wants a young man and a good sportsman. It's important that he should be able to speak Arabic. But the qualifications which will satisfy the Khedive are nothing beside those which will satisfy me. The wrong man may cause irreparable damage to British interests.

CHRISTINA: Have you thought that Henry would be admirably suited?

ARTHUR: I can't say I have, Christina.

CHRISTINA: He's young and he's very good at games. He speaks Arabic.

ARTHUR: Quite well, I believe. I think he's very well suited to the post he has. It would be a pity to disturb him when he's just got at home with the work.

CHRISTINA: Arthur, you can't compare a very badly paid

job in the Ministry of Education with a private secretaryship to the Khedive.

ARTHUR: The best job for a man is the one he's most fitted
to do.

CHRISTINA: You've got no fault to find with Henry. He's a
very good worker, he's honest, industrious and pains-
taking.

ARTHUR: You don't praise a pair of boots because you can
walk in them without discomfort; if you can't you chuck
them away.

CHRISTINA: What d'you mean by that?

ARTHUR: The qualities you mention really don't deserve any
particular reward. If Henry hadn't got them I'd fire him
without a moment's hesitation.

CHRISTINA: I have no doubt you'd welcome the opportunity.
It's the greatest misfortune of Henry's life that he
happens to be your nephew.

ARTHUR: On the other hand, it's counterbalanced by his
extraordinary good luck in being your son.

CHRISTINA: You've stood in his way on every possible
occasion.

ARTHUR: [Good-humouredly.] You know that's not true,
Christina. I've refused to perpetrate a number of
abominable jobs that you've urged me to. He's had his
chances as everyone else has. You're an admirable
mother. If I'd listened to you he'd be Commander-in-
Chief and Prime Minister by now.

CHRISTINA: I've never asked you to do anything for Henry
that wasn't perfectly reasonable.

ARTHUR: It's evident then that we have different views
upon what is reasonable.

CHRISTINA: I appeal to you, Anne: do you see any objection
to suggesting Henry to the Khedive as a private secretary?

ARTHUR: I knew that's what she wanted you here for, Anne,
to be a witness to my pig-headed obstinacy.

CHRISTINA: Don't be absurd, Arthur. I'm asking Anne for an unprejudiced opinion.

ARTHUR: Anne is unlikely to have an opinion of any value on a matter she knows nothing about.

ANNE: [*With a chuckle.*] That is a very plain hint that I can't do better than hold my tongue. I'll take it, Christina.

CHRISTINA: It's so unreasonable of you Arthur. You won't listen to any argument.

ARTHUR: The only one you've offered yet is: here's a good job going, Henry's your nephew, give it him. My dear, don't you see the Khedive would never accept such a near relation of mine?

CHRISTINA: I don't agree with you at all. The fact of his asking you to recommend an English secretary shows that he wants to draw the connection between you and himself closer. After all, you might give the boy a chance.

ARTHUR: This is not an occasion when one can afford to give a chance. It's hit or miss. If the man I choose is a failure the Khedive will never ask me to do such a thing for him again. I can't take any risks.

CHRISTINA: Will you tell me what qualifications Henry lacks to make him suitable for the post?

ARTHUR: Certainly. It's true he speaks Arabic, but he doesn't understand the native mind. Grammars can't teach you that, my dear, only sympathy. He has the mind of an official. I often think that you must have swallowed a ramrod in early life and poor Henry was born with a foot-rule in his inside.

CHRISTINA: I am not amused, Arthur.

ARTHUR: I have no doubt in course of time he'll become a very competent official, but he'll never be anything else. He lacks imagination, and that is just as necessary to a statesman as to a novelist. Finally he has no charm.

CHRISTINA: How can you judge? You're his uncle. You might just as well say I have no charm.

ARTHUR: You haven't. You're an admirable woman, with all the substantial virtues which make you an ornament to your sex, but you have no charm.

CHRISTINA: [*With a grim smile.*] I should be a fool if I expected you to pay me compliments, shouldn't I?

ARTHUR: You would at all events be a woman who is unable to learn by experience.

CHRISTINA: Besides, I don't agree with you. I think Henry has charm.

ARTHUR: Why do we all call him Henry? Why does Henry suit him so admirably? If he had charm we would naturally call him Harry.

CHRISTINA: Really, Arthur, it amazes me that a man in your position can be influenced by such absurd trifles. It's so unfair, when a boy has a dozen solid real virtues that you should refuse to recommend him for a job because he hasn't got in your opinion a frivolous, unsubstantial advantage like charm.

ARTHUR: Unsubstantial it may be, but frivolous it certainly isn't. Believe me, charm is the most valuable asset that any man can have. D'you think it sounds immoral to say it compensates for the lack of brains and virtue? Alas! it happens to be true. Brains may bring you to power, but charm enables you to keep it. Without charm you will never lead men.

CHRISTINA: And do you imagine you're likely to find a young Englishman who's a sportsman and an Arabic scholar, who has tact, imagination, sympathy, wisdom, courtesy and charm?

ANNE: If you do, Arthur, I'm afraid he won't remain here very long, because I warn you, I shall insist on marrying him.

ARTHUR: It's not so formidable as it sounds. I'm going to suggest Ronny.

CHRISTINA: [*Astounded.*] Ronald Parry! That's the very last person I should have thought you'd be inclined to suggest.

ARTHUR: [*Sharply.*] Why?

ANNE: [*With dismay.*] You don't really mean that, Arthur?

ARTHUR: Why not?

CHRISTINA: [*To* ANNE.] Didn't you know?

ANNE: It's the last thing that would ever have entered my head.

CHRISTINA: I thought you'd made all arrangements for sending him away.

ARTHUR: I made no arrangements at all. I received a telegram from the F.O. saying that he'd been appointed to Paris.

ANNE: [*After a very short pause.*] Don't you think you'd better leave it at that?

ARTHUR: No, I don't. I'm going to wire to London explaining the circumstances and suggesting that I think him very suitable for the post that's just offered itself.

ANNE: [*Trying to take it lightly.*] I feel rather aggrieved, after all the efforts I've made to get him appointed to Paris.

CHRISTINA: Oh, he owes that to you, does he? You thought it would be better for him to leave here?

ARTHUR: [*Deliberately.*] I don't quite understand what you're driving at, Christina.

CHRISTINA: [*Taking him up defiantly.*] I cannot imagine anyone more unsuitable than Ronald Parry.

ARTHUR: That is for me to judge, isn't it?

ANNE: Perhaps the Foreign Office will say they see no reason to change their mind.

ARTHUR: I don't think so.

ANNE: Have you told Ronny?

ARTHUR: No, I thought it unnecessary till I'd found out whether the Khedive would be willing to take him.

CHRISTINA: I'm amazed, Arthur. When Henry told me Ronald Parry was going I couldn't help thinking it was very desirable.

ARTHUR: Why?

[*She looks at him, about to speak, then hesitates. She does not dare, and resolves to be silent.* ANNE *comes to the rescue.*

ANNE: Christina knows that I shall be very little in Egypt in future and how fond Ronny and I are of one another. We naturally want to be as near each other as we can.

CHRISTINA: [*With a chuckle.*] It really amuses me that you should refuse to give a good job to Henry because you've made up your mind to give it to Ronald Parry.

[ARTHUR *walks up to her deliberately and faces her*.

ARTHUR: If you've got anything to say against him say it.

[*They stare at one another for a moment in silence.*

CHRISTINA: If you have nothing against him there's no reason why I should.

ARTHUR: I see. I have a good deal to do this afternoon. If you have nothing more to say to me I'd like to get back to my work.

CHRISTINA: Very well, I'll go.

ARTHUR: You won't stop and see Violet?

CHRISTINA: I don't think so, thank you.

[*She goes out. He opens the door for her.*

ANNE: Why didn't you tell me just now that you'd decided to keep Ronny in Cairo?

ARTHUR: I thought it was unnecessary till everything was settled. I daresay you'll be good enough to hold your tongue about it.

ANNE: Have you definitely made up your mind?

ARTHUR: Definitely.

> [*They look at one another steadily.*

ANNE: I think I'll go up to my room. I keep to my old habit of a siesta after luncheon.

ARTHUR: I wish I could get Violet to take it.

ANNE: She's so young, she doesn't feel the need of it yet.

ARTHUR: Yes, she's so young.

> [ANNE *goes out. For a moment* ARTHUR *gives way to discouragement. He feels old and tired. But he hears a footstep and pulls himself together. He is his usual self, gay, gallant and humorous, when* VIOLET *enters the room.*

VIOLET: I saw Christina drive away. What did she want?

ARTHUR: The earth.

VIOLET: I hope you gave it her.

ARTHUR: No, I'm trying to get the moon for you just now, darling, and I thought if I gave her the earth it really would upset the universe a little too much.

VIOLET: I thought I'd better do these invitations before I dressed.

ARTHUR: You're not going to put on a different frock to go and have tea with the Khedive's mother? You look charming in that.

VIOLET: I think it's a little too young. It was all right for the morning.

ARTHUR: Of course you are older this afternoon, that's quite true.

VIOLET: Can you spare Ronny just now?

ARTHUR: [*After an instant's pause.*] Yes, I'll send him to you at once.

VIOLET: [*As he is going.*] I shall be back in time to give you your tea.

ARTHUR: That will be very nice. Good-bye till then.

[*He goes out. She is meditative. She gives a slight start as* RONNY *comes in.*

VIOLET: I hope I haven't torn you away from anything very important.

RONNY: I was only typing a very dull report. I'd just finished it.

VIOLET: You mustn't ever bother about me if it's not convenient, you know.

RONNY: I shan't have much chance, shall I?

VIOLET: No. . . . Look, here's the list.

[*She hands him a sheet of paper on which names are scribbled, and he reads it.*

RONNY: It looks rather a stodgy party, doesn't it? I see you've crossed my name out.

VIOLET: It's not much good asking you when you won't be here. Whom d'you advise me to ask in your place?

RONNY: I don't know. I hate the idea of anyone being asked in my place. Shall I start on them at once?

VIOLET: If you don't mind. I have to go out, you know.

[*He sits down at a writing table.*

RONNY: I'll start on those I dislike least.

VIOLET: [*With a chuckle.*] Don't you remember when Arthur said I must ask the Von Scheidleins how we hated to write them a civil letter?

RONNY: [*Writing.*] Dear Lady Sinclair.

VIOLET: Oh, she asked me to call her Evelyn.

RONNY: Hang! I'll have to start again.

VIOLET: It always makes me so uncomfortable to address fat old ladies by their Christian names.

RONNY: I'll end up "yours affectionately," shall I?

VIOLET: I suppose you're awfully excited at the thought of going?

RONNY: No.

VIOLET: It's a step for you, isn't it? I . . . I ought to congratulate you.

RONNY: You don't think I want to go, do you? I hate it.

VIOLET: Why?

RONNY: I've been very happy here.

VIOLET: You knew you couldn't stay here for the rest of your life.

RONNY: Why not?

VIOLET: [*With an effort at self-control.*] Who is the next person on the list?

RONNY: [*Looking at it.*] Will you miss me at all?

VIOLET: I suppose I shall at first.

RONNY: That's not a very kind thing to say.

VIOLET: Isn't it? I don't mean to be unkind, Ronny.

RONNY: Oh, I'm so miserable!

[*She gives a little cry and looks at him. She presses her hands to her heart.*

VIOLET: Let us go on with the letters.

[*Silently he writes. She does not watch him, but looks hopelessly into space. She is unable to restrain a sob.*

RONNY: You're crying.

VIOLET: No, I'm not. I'm not. I swear I'm not. [*He gets up and goes over to her. Her looks into her eyes.*] It came so suddenly. I never dreamt you'd be going away.

RONNY: Oh, Violet!

VIOLET: Don't call me that. Please, don't.

RONNY: Did you know that I loved you?

VIOLET: How should I know? Oh, I'm so unhappy. What have I done to deserve it?

RONNY: I couldn't help loving you. It can't matter if I tell you now. It's the end of everything. I don't want to go without your knowing. I love you. I love you. I love you.

VIOLET: Oh, Ronny!

RONNY: It's been so wonderful, all these months. I've never known anyone to come up to you. Everything you said pleased me. I loved the way you walk, and your laugh, and the sound of your voice.

VIOLET: Oh, don't!

RONNY: I was content just to see you and to talk with you and to know you were here, near me. You've made me extraordinarily happy.

VIOLET: Have I? Oh, I'm so glad.

RONNY: I couldn't help myself. I tried not to think of you. You're not angry with me?

VIOLET: I can't be. Oh, Ronny, I've had such a rotten time. It came upon me unawares, I didn't know what was happening. I thought I only liked you.

RONNY: Oh, my dearest! Is it possible . . .?

VIOLET: And when it struck me—oh, I was so frightened. I thought it must be written on my face and everyone must see. I knew it was wrong. I knew I mustn't. I couldn't help myself.

RONNY: Oh, say it, Violet. I want to hear you say it: "I love you."

VIOLET: I love you. [*He kneels down before her and covers her hands with kisses.*] Oh, don't, don't!

RONNY: My dearest. My very dearest.

VIOLET: What have I done? I made up my mind that no one should ever know. I thought then it wouldn't matter. It needn't prevent me from doing my duty to Arthur. It didn't interfere with my affection for him. I didn't see how it could hurt anyone if I kept my love for you locked up in my heart, tightly, and it made me so happy. I rejoiced in it.

RONNY: I never knew. I used to weigh every word you said to me. You never gave me a sign.

VIOLET: I didn't know it was possible to love anybody as I love you, Ronny.

RONNY: My precious!

VIOLET: Oh, don't say things like that to me. It breaks my heart. I wouldn't ever have told you only I was upset by your going. If they'd only given me time to get used to the thought I wouldn't . . . I wouldn't make such a fool of myself.

RONNY: You can't grudge me that little bit of comfort.

VIOLET: But it all came so suddenly, the announcement that you were going and your going. I felt I couldn't bear it. Why didn't they give me time?

RONNY: Don't cry, my dearest, it tortures me.

VIOLET: This is the last time we shall be alone, Ronny. I couldn't let you go without . . . oh, my God, I can't bear it.

RONNY: We might have been so happy together, Violet. Why didn't we meet sooner? I feel we're made for one another.

VIOLET: Oh, don't talk of that. D'you suppose I haven't said to myself: "Oh, if I'd only met him first"? Oh, Ronny, Ronny, Ronny!

RONNY: I never dared to think that you loved me. It's maddening that I must go. It's horrible to think of leaving you now.

VIOLET: No, it's better. We couldn't have gone on like that. I'm glad you're going. It breaks my heart.

RONNY: Oh, Violet, why didn't you wait for me?

VIOLET: I made a mistake. I must pay for it. Arthur's so good and kind. He loves me with all his heart. Oh, what a fool I was! I didn't know what love was. I feel that my life is finished, and I'm so young, Ronny.

RONNY: You know I'd do anything in the world for you.

VIOLET: My dear one. [*They stand face to face, looking at one another wistfully and sadly.*] It's no good, Ronny, we're both making ourselves utterly miserable. Say good-bye to me and let us part. [*He draws her towards him.*] No, don't kiss me. I don't want you to kiss me. [*He takes her in his arms and kisses her passionately.*] Oh, Ronny, I do love you so. [*At last she tears herself away from him. She sinks into a chair. He makes a movement towards her.*] No don't come near me now. I'm so tired.

[*He looks at her for a moment, then he goes back to the table and sits down to write the letters. Their eyes meet slowly.*

RONNY: It's good-bye, then?

VIOLET: It's good-bye.

[*She presses her hands to her heart as though the aching were unendurable. He buries his head in his hands.*

END OF THE FIRST ACT

THE SECOND ACT

The scene is the garden of the Consular Agent's residence. It is an Eastern garden with palm-trees, magnolias, and flowering bushes of azaleas. On one side is an old Arabic well-head decorated with verses from the Koran; a yellow rambler grows over the ironwork above. Rose-trees are in full bloom. On the other side are basket chairs and a table. At the bottom of the garden runs the Nile and on the farther bank are lines of palm-trees and the Eastern sky. It is towards evening and during the act the sun gradually sets.

The table is set out with tea-things. ANNE is seated reading a book. The gardener in his blue gaberdine, with brown legs and the little round cap of the Egyptian workman, is watering the flowers. CHRISTINA comes in.

ANNE: [*Looking up, with a smile.*] Ah, Christina!

CHRISTINA: I was told I should find you here. I came to see Violet, but I hear she hasn't come back yet.

ANNE: She was going to see the Khedive's mother.

CHRISTINA: I think I'll wait for her.

ANNE: Would you like tea? I was waiting till Violet came in. I expect she's been made to eat all sorts of sweet things and she'll want a cup of tea to take the taste out of her mouth.

CHRISTINA: No, don't have it brought for me. . . . I can never quite get over being treated as a guest in the house I was mistress of for so many years. [*To the GARDENER.*] Imshi (Get out).

GARDENER: Dêtak sa 'ideh (May thy night be happy).

[*He goes out.*

ANNE: Your knowledge of Arabic is rather sketchy, Christina.

CHRISTINA: I never see why I should trouble myself with strange languages. If foreigners want to talk to me they can talk to me in English.

ANNE: But surely when we're out of our own country we're foreigners.

CHRISTINA: Nonsense, Anne, we're English. I wonder Arthur allows Violet to learn Arabic. I can't help thinking it'll make a bad impression on the natives. *I* managed this house on fifty words of Arabic.

ANNE: [*Smiling.*] I'm convinced that on a hundred you'd be prepared to manage the country.

CHRISTINA: I don't think you can deny that I did my work here competently.

ANNE: You're a wonderful housekeeper.

CHRISTINA: I have common sense and a talent for organisation. [*Pursing her lips.*] It breaks my heart to see the way certain things are done here now.

ANNE: You must remember Violet is very young.

CHRISTINA: Much too young to be a suitable wife for Arthur.

ANNE: He seems to be very well satisfied, and after all he is the person most concerned.

CHRISTINA: I know. His infatuation is—blind, don't you think?

ANNE: [*Coolly.*] I think it's very delightful to see two people so much in love with one another.

CHRISTINA: D'you know that I used to be fearfully jealous of you, Anne?

ANNE: [*Amused.*] I know that you thoroughly disliked me, Christina. You didn't trouble to hide it.

CHRISTINA: I was always afraid that Arthur would marry you. I didn't want to be turned out of this house. I suppose you think that's horrid of me.

ANNE: No, I think it's very natural.

CHRISTINA: I didn't see why Arthur should marry. I gave him all the comforts of home life. And I thought it would interfere with his work. Of course I knew that he liked you. I suffered agonies when he used to go and dine with you quietly. [*With a sniff.*] He said it rested him.

ANNE: Perhaps it did. Did you grudge him that?

CHRISTINA: I knew you were desperately in love with him.

ANNE: Need you throw that in my face now? Really, I haven't deserved it.

CHRISTINA: My dear, I wish he had married you. It never struck me he'd marry a girl twenty years younger than himself.

ANNE: He never looked upon me as anything but a friend. I don't suppose it occurred to him for an instant that my feeling might possibly be different.

CHRISTINA: It was stupid of me. I ought to have given him a hint.

ANNE: [*With a smile.*] You took care not to do that, Christina. Perhaps you knew that was all it wanted.

CHRISTINA: [*Reflectively.*] I don't think he's treated you very well.

ANNE: Nonsense. A man isn't obliged to marry a woman just because she's in love with him. I don't see why loving should give one a claim on the person one loves.

CHRISTINA: You would have made him a splendid wife.

ANNE: So will Violet, my dear. Most men have the wives they deserve.

CHRISTINA: I marvel at your kindness to her. You're so ᵗolerant and sympathetic, one would never imagine she's robbed you of what you wanted most in the world.

ANNE: I shouldn't respect myself very much if I bore her the shadow of a grudge. I'm so glad that she's sweet and charming and ingenuous; it makes it very easy to be fond of her.

CHRISTINA: I know. I wanted to dislike her. But I can't really. There is something about her which disarms one.

ANNE: Isn't it lucky? It's a difficult position. That irresistible charm of hers will make everything possible. After all, you and I can agree in that we both want Arthur to be happy.

CHRISTINA: I wonder if there's much chance of that.

[ANNE *looks at her for a moment inquiringly,* and CHRISTINA *coolly returns the stare.*

ANNE: Why did you come here this afternoon, Christina?

CHRISTINA: [*With a faint smile.*] Why did you take so much trouble to get your brother moved to Paris?

ANNE: Good heavens, I told you this morning.

CHRISTINA: D'you think we need make pretences with one another?

ANNE: I don't think I quite understand.

CHRISTINA: Don't you? You wanted Ronny to leave Egypt because you know he's in love with Violet.

[*For a moment* ANNE *is a little taken aback, but she quickly recovers herself.*

ANNE: He's very susceptible. He's always falling in and out of love. I had noticed that he was attracted, and I confess I thought it better to put him out of harm's way.

CHRISTINA: How cunning you are, Anne! You won't admit anything till you're quite certain the person you're talking to knows it. You know as well as I do that Violet is just as much in love with him.

ANNE: [*Much disturbed.*] Christina, what are you going to do? How could I help knowing? You've only got to see the way they look at one another. They're sick with love.

c

CHRISTINA: What did Arthur expect? I've never seen a couple more admirably suited to one another.

ANNE: I thought no one knew but me till this morning, when you were talking to Arthur. Then I thought you must know too. My heart was in my mouth, I was afraid you were going to tell him. But you didn't, and I thought I'd been mistaken.

CHRISTINA: You didn't give me credit for very nice feeling, Anne. Because I didn't act like a perfect beast you thought I must be a perfect fool.

ANNE: I know how devoted you are to your son. I didn't believe you'd stick at anything when his interests were at stake. I'm sorry, Christina.

CHRISTINA: Pray don't apologise. I didn't know it myself. It was on the tip of my tongue to tell Arthur, but I simply couldn't. I couldn't do anything so shabby.

ANNE: Oh, Christina, we mustn't ever let him know, we can't make him so miserable. It would break his heart.

CHRISTINA: Well, what is to be done?

ANNE: Heaven knows. I've been racking my brains. I can think of nothing. I'd arranged everything so beautifully. And now I'm helpless. I thought even of going to Ronny and asking him to refuse any job that will keep him here. But Arthur looks upon it as so important. He'll insist on Ronny's accepting unless his reasons for going are—what's the word I want?

CHRISTINA: Irrefutable. It seems very hard that my boy should be done out of such a splendid chance by Ronny. Except for your brother I'm sure Arthur would give it to Henry.

ANNE: [*Diplomatically.*] I know he has the highest opinion of Henry's abilities.

CHRISTINA: You can't expect me to sit still and let things go on.

ANNE: Arthur is perfectly unconscious. He thinks Violet is as much in love with him as he is with her. You couldn't be so cruel as to hint anything to him.

CHRISTINA: How you adore him, Anne! You may set your mind at rest. I'm not going to say a word to Arthur. I'm going to speak to Violet.

ANNE: [*Frightened.*] What are you going to say?

CHRISTINA: I'm going to ask her to do all she can to persuade Arthur to give Henry the job. And then Ronny can go to Paris.

ANNE: You're not going to tell her you know?

CHRISTINA: [*Deliberately.*] If it's necessary she must make Ronny refuse the appointment. He must invent some excuse that Arthur will accept.

ANNE: But it's blackmail.

CHRISTINA: I don't care what it is.

> [VIOLET *comes in. She wears an afternoon gown, picturesque and simple, yet elegant enough for the visit she has been paying. She has a large hat, which she presently removes.*

ANNE: Here is Violet.

VIOLET: Oh, you poor people, haven't you had any tea?

ANNE: I thought we'd wait till you came back. It'll come at once now.

VIOLET: How are you, Christina? How is Henry? [*They kiss one another.*] I've not seen him for days.

CHRISTINA: He's coming to fetch me presently.

VIOLET: I shall tell him he neglects me. He's the only one of my in-laws I'm not a little afraid of.

CHRISTINA: He's a good boy.

VIOLET: He has a good mother. I thought it would be such fun having a nephew several years older than myself, but he won't treat me as an aunt. He will call me Violet. I tell him he ought to be more respectful.

[*Meanwhile* SERVANTS *have brought the tea.*

CHRISTINA: What have you been doing this afternoon?

VIOLET: Oh, I went to see the Khedive's mother. She made me eat seventeen different things and I feel exactly like a boa-constrictor. [*Looking at the cakes and scones.*] I'm afraid there's not a very nice tea.

CHRISTINA: So I notice.

VIOLET: [*With a smile.*] I suppose I couldn't persuade you to pour it out.

CHRISTINA: [*Gratified.*] Certainly, if you wish it.

[*She sits down in front of the teapot and pours out cups of tea.* ARTHUR *comes in.*

ARTHUR: Hulloa, Christina, are you pouring out the tea?

CHRISTINA: Violet asked me to.

VIOLET: If only I weren't here it would be quite like old times.

ARTHUR: I understand you want to see me, Violet.

VIOLET: Oh, I hope you haven't come out here on purpose. I sent the message that I wished to have a word with you when convenient, but I didn't want to hurry you. I was quite prepared to go to you.

ARTHUR: That sounds very formidable. I had a few minutes to spare while some letters were being prepared for me to sign. But in any case I'm always at your service.

VIOLET: The Khedive's mother has asked me to talk to you about a man called Abdul Said.

ARTHUR: Oh!

VIOLET: She thought if I put the circumstances before you . . .

ARTHUR: [*Interrupting.*] What has he got to do with her?

VIOLET: He's been employed for years on an estate of hers up the Nile. His mother was one of her maids. It appears she gave her a dowry when she married.

ARTHUR: [*Smiling.*] I see. I gathered that Abdul Said had powerful influence somewhere or other.

CHRISTINA: Who is this man, Arthur?

ARTHUR: He's been sentenced to death for murder. It was a perfectly clear case, but there was a lot of perjury and we had some difficulty in getting a conviction. What has the Princess asked you to do?

VIOLET: She explained the whole thing to me, and then she asked if I wouldn't intercede with you. I promised to do everything I could.

ARTHUR: You shouldn't have done that. The old lady knows quite well an affair of this sort is no business of yours. I wish you'd told her so.

VIOLET: Arthur, what could I do? His wife was there, and his mother. If you'd seen them. . . . I couldn't bear to look at their misery and do nothing. I said I was sure that when you knew all the facts you'd reprieve the man.

ARTHUR: It's not in my power to do anything of the sort. The prerogative of mercy is with the Khedive.

VIOLET: I know, but if you advise him to exercise it he will. He's only too anxious to, but he won't move without your advice.

ARTHUR: It's monstrous of the Princess to try and make use of you in this way. She prepared a complete trap for you.

ANNE: What did the man do exactly?

ARTHUR: It's rather a peculiar case. Abdul Said had a difference of opinion with an Armenian merchant and shortly after his only son fell ill and died. He took it into his head that the Armenian had cast the evil eye on him, and he took his gun, waited for his opportunity, and shot the Armenian dead. The man isn't a criminal in the ordinary sense of the word, but we can't afford to make exceptions. If we did there'd be a crop of murders with the same excuse. I looked into the case this morning and I see no reason to advise the Khedive to interfere with the course of justice.

VIOLET: This morning? When you came in to luncheon full of spirits, laughing and chaffing, had you just sent a man to his death? How horribly callous!

ARTHUR: I'm sorry you should think that. I give every matter my closest attention, and when I've settled it to the best of my ability I put it out of my mind. I think it would be just as unwise to let it affect me as for a doctor to let himself be affected by his patients' sufferings.

VIOLET: It seems to me horrible to slaughter that wretched man because he's ignorant and simple-minded. Don't you see that for yourself?

ARTHUR: I'm afraid I'm not here to interpret the law according to my feelings but according to its own spirit.

VIOLET: It's easy to talk like that when you haven't got any feeling one way or the other. Don't you realise the misery of that man condemned to die for what he honestly thought was a mere act of justice? I wish you'd seen the agony of those poor women. And now they're more or less happy because I promised to help them. The Princess told them I had influence with you. If she only knew!

ARTHUR: You should never have been put in such a position. It was grossly unfair. I'll take care that nothing of the sort occurs again.

VIOLET: D'you mean to say you'll do nothing? Won't you even go into the matter again—with a little sympathy?

ARTHUR: I can't!

VIOLET: It's the first thing I've ever asked you, Arthur.

ARTHUR: I know. I'm only sorry that I must refuse you.

VIOLET: This is the first sentence of death in Egypt since our marriage. Don't you know what it would mean to me to think I'd saved a man's life? The Khedive is waiting to sign the reprieve. It only requires a word from you. Won't you say it? I feel that the gratitude of these poor women may be like a blessing on us.

ARTHUR: My dear, I think my duty is very clear. I must do it.

VIOLET: It's clear because all that grief means nothing to you. What do you care if a man is hanged whom you've never even seen? I wonder if you'd find it so easy to do your duty in a matter that affected you. If it meant misery or happiness to you. It's easy to do one's duty when one doesn't care.

ARTHUR: You're quite right. That is the test: if one can do one's duty when it means the loss of all one holds dear and valuable in the world.

VIOLET: I hope you'll never be put to it.

ARTHUR: [With a chuckle.] My dear, you say that as though you hoped precisely the contrary.

VIOLET: Must I write to the Princess and say I was entirely mistaken, and I have no more influence over you than a tripper at Shepheard's Hotel?

ARTHUR: I'd sooner you didn't write to her at all. I will have a message conveyed which you may be sure will save you from any humiliation.

VIOLET: [Icily.] I'm afraid you have a lot of business; you mustn't let me keep you.

[He looks at her reflectively for a moment and then goes out. There is an awkward silence.

VIOLET: Those good people we had to luncheon to-day would be amused to see what the power amounts to that they congratulated me on.

CHRISTINA: There's very little that Arthur would refuse you. He'd do practically anything in the world to please you.

VIOLET: It'll be a long time before I ask him to do anything else.

CHRISTINA: Don't say that, Violet. Because I came here to-day on purpose to ask you to use your influence with him.

VIOLET: You see how much I have.

CHRISTINA: That was a matter of principle. Men are always funny about principles. You can never get them to understand that circumstances alter cases.

VIOLET: Arthur looks upon me as a child. After all, it's not my fault that I'm twenty years younger than he is.

CHRISTINA: I want your help so badly, Violet. And you know, the fact that Arthur has just refused to do something for you is just the reason that will make him anxious to do anything you ask now.

VIOLET: I don't want to expose myself to the humiliation of another refusal.

CHRISTINA: It's so important to me. It may mean all the difference to Henry's future.

VIOLET: [*With a change of manner, charmingly.*] Oh! I'd love to do anything I could for Henry.

CHRISTINA: The Khedive has asked Arthur for an English secretary. It seems to me that Henry has every possible qualification, but you know what Arthur is; he's terrified of the least suspicion of favouring his friends and relations.

VIOLET: My dear Christina, what can I do? Arthur would merely tell me to mind my own business.

CHRISTINA: He wants to give the post to Ronald Parry. . . .

VIOLET: [*Quickly.*] Ronny? But Ronny's going to Paris. It's all arranged.

CHRISTINA: It was. But Arthur thinks it essential that he should stay in Egypt.

VIOLET: Did you know this, Anne?

ANNE: Not till just now.

VIOLET: Does Ronny know?

ANNE: I don't think so.

> [VIOLET *is aghast. She does all she can to hide her agitation. The two women watch her,* CHRISTINA *with cold curiosity,* ANNE *with embarrassment.*

VIOLET: I'm . . . I'm awfully surprised. It's only an hour or two ago that Ronny and I bade one another a pathetic farewell.

CHRISTINA: Really? But there was never any talk of his going till the day after to-morrow. You were in a great hurry with your leave-takings.

VIOLET: I thought he'd be busy packing and that I mightn't have another chance.

CHRISTINA: You've been so intimate, I'm sure he would have been able to snatch a moment to say good-bye to you and Arthur before his train started.

> [VIOLET *does not quite know what this speech means. She gives* CHRISTINA *a look.* ANNE *comes to the rescue quickly.*

ANNE: Ronny has been acting as Violet's secretary to a certain extent. I expect they had all sorts of little secrets together that they wanted to discuss in private.

CHRISTINA: Of course. That's very natural. [*With great friendliness.*] If I thought I were robbing you of anyone who was indispensable to you I wouldn't ask you to put in a good word for Henry. But, of course, if Ronald became the Khedive's secretary he couldn't exactly continue to write letters and pay bills for you, could he?

VIOLET: I'm rather taken aback. I'd got it fixed in my head that Ronny was going.

CHRISTINA: I can promise you that in helping Henry you're

not doing any harm to Ronald. Anne is very anxious that he should leave Egypt. Isn't that so?

ANNE: In a way. Henry is proposing to spend the rest of his official life in Egypt. An appointment like this is naturally more important to him than it would be to Ronny, who is by way of being a bird of passage.

CHRISTINA: Exactly. Ronny has had his experience here. If he stayed longer it would only be waste of time. Anne naturally wants to have him near her. I daresay she's a little afraid of his getting into mischief here.

ANNE: I don't know about that, Christina.

CHRISTINA: My dear, you know how susceptible he is. There's always the possibility that he'll fall in love with someone who isn't very desirable.

VIOLET: I've got an awful headache.

CHRISTINA: Why don't you take a little aspirin? I'm quite sure that if you set your mind to it you can persuade Arthur to give the job to Henry. And that would settle everything.

VIOLET: And if I can't persuade him?

CHRISTINA: Then you must put it to Ronny.

VIOLET: I?

CHRISTINA: You see, if he refused the appointment and left Egypt, then I'm convinced Arthur would accept Henry.

VIOLET: Why should I put it to Ronny?

CHRISTINA: [Pleasantly.] You've been so very friendly, haven't you? If you suggested to him that . . . he's standing in Henry's way . . .

VIOLET: I should have thought it was for Anne to do that.

CHRISTINA: How simple-minded you are! A man will often do for a pretty woman what he won't do for his sister.

VIOLET: You want me to make him go?

CHRISTINA: Don't you think yourself that would be the very best thing . . . for all parties?

[VIOLET *and* CHRISTINA *look steadily at one another.*
VIOLET sinks her eyes. She knows that CHRISTINA
is aware of her love. She is terrified. RONALD *comes*
in. He is in the highest spirits.

RONNY: I've been sent to have a cup of tea. Sir Arthur is
coming along in a minute. I've got some news. I'm
staying in Egypt. Isn't it splendid?

[VIOLET *gives a little gasp.*

VIOLET: Is it settled then?

RONNY: Did you know? I thought it would be a surprise.

VIOLET: No. I've just heard.

RONNY: Isn't it magnificent?

CHRISTINA: You're very changeable. It's only a few months
ago that you were constantly telling Henry you'd had
enough of the country.

RONNY: Never. I love it. I should like to stay here all my
life.

CHRISTINA: Fancy that!

RONNY: [*Addressing himself to* VIOLET.] It would be madness to leave a place where you're so happy, wouldn't
it? I feel so intensely alive here. It's a wonderful
country. One lives every minute of the day.

CHRISTINA: You're so enthusiastic. One would almost think
you'd fallen in love.

VIOLET: Ronny is naturally enthusiastic.

RONNY: [*To* CHRISTINA.] And why shouldn't I have fallen
in love?

CHRISTINA: Won't you tell us whom with?

RONNY: [*With a chuckle.*] I was only joking. Isn't it enough
to have a splendid job in a country where there's so
much hope? Sir Arthur has given me a marvellous
opportunity. It'll be my fault if I don't make the most
of it.

CHRISTINA: [*Dryly.*] Shall I give you a cup of tea?

RONNY: [*Chaffing her.*] D'you think I want calming down? I feel like a prisoner who was going to be hanged and has just had a free pardon. I don't want to be calmed down. I want to revel in my freedom.

CHRISTINA: All that means, I take it, that you don't want tea.

RONNY: It's no good trying to snub me. I'm unsnubable to-day. You haven't congratulated me, Anne.

ANNE: My dear, you've been talking nineteen to the dozen. I've not had the chance to get a word in edgeways.

RONNY: [*To* VIOLET.] Will you put my name back on your list for that dinner? It would have broken my heart to miss it.

VIOLET: Your official position rather alters things, doesn't it? I would never dare to ask you now just to make an even number.

RONNY: Oh, well, I'm sending out the invitations. I shall write a formal letter to myself, explaining the circumstances, and I daresay I shall see my way to accept.

CHRISTINA: Dear Ronald, you might be eighteen.

> [ARTHUR *comes in with* HENRY PRITCHARD. *This is* CHRISTINA'S *son, a pleasant, clean young man, but in no way remarkable.*

ARTHUR: Henry tells me he's come to fetch you away, Christina.

CHRISTINA: So you lose not a moment in bringing him here.

ARTHUR: Really, Christina, you do me an injustice. I can't bear to think you should be parted from your precious boy an instant longer than necessary.

HENRY: [*Shaking hands with* VIOLET.] How is my stately aunt?

VIOLET: Merry and bright, thank you.

HENRY: You know I'm having a birthday soon, don't you?

VIOLET: What of it?

HENRY: I've always been given to understand that aunts give their nephews ten shillings on their birthday.

VIOLET: Do they? I am glad. I'd love to press ten shillings into your willing hand.

HENRY: Holloa, Ronny. Lucky devil. I congratulate you.

RONNY: That's awfully good of you, old man.

ARTHUR: On what? Christina!

CHRISTINA: I told Henry. I didn't think it would matter, I thought it better that he should know.

HENRY: I say, Uncle Arthur, I'm afraid mother has been giving you a rotten time. It's not my fault, you know.

ARTHUR: What isn't?

HENRY: Well, when mother told me at luncheon that the Khedive had applied for an English secretary, I saw by the beady look in her eye that if I didn't get the job she was going to make things unpleasant for somebody.

CHRISTINA: Really, Henry, I don't know what you mean.

HENRY: Well, mother, you're an old dear . . .

CHRISTINA: Not so old either.

ARTHUR: Certainly not, Henry. Let us have none of your nonsense.

HENRY: But you know perfectly well that you'd cheerfully bring the British Empire tumbling about our ears if you could get me a good fat billet by doing so.

ARTHUR: Out of the mouths of babes and sucklings . . .

CHRISTINA: You've got no right to say that, Henry. I've never asked anything for you that it wasn't practically your right to have.

HENRY: Well, mother, between you and me I don't mind telling you that Ronny is much more suited to this particular job than I am. Only a perfect fool would have hesitated, and for the honour of the family we can't suspect Uncle Arthur of being that.

ARTHUR: You see what comes of bringing up a boy properly, Christina; you've made him a decent fellow in spite of yourself.

CHRISTINA: You're a tiresome creature, Henry, but I'm attached to you. You may kiss me.

HENRY: Come along, Mother. I'm not going to kiss you in public.

CHRISTINA: [*Getting up.*] Well, good-bye, Violet. Don't forget our little conversation, will you?

VIOLET: Good-bye. Good-bye, Henry.

CHRISTINA: [*To* ANNE.] Why don't you come for a little drive with us? It's such a beautiful evening.

ANNE: Will you take me? I think I'd like it. It won't take me a minute to put on my hat.

[*She gets up. They start to walk towards the house.*

CHRISTINA: [*Putting up her cheek.*] Good-bye, Arthur.

ARTHUR: Oh, I'll just come along and put you in your carriage. You shan't say that I don't treat you with the ceremony due to your importance.

[*They saunter off.* VIOLET *and* RONNY *are left alone.*

VIOLET: You're coming back, Arthur?

ARTHUR: Oh, yes, in a minute.

[*Exit.*

RONNY: [*Under his breath.*] Violet.

VIOLET: Be quiet.

RONNY: Isn't it ripping? I could hardly prevent myself from letting them see how much I loved you.

VIOLET: You didn't. Christina suspected before and now you've told her in plain words.

RONNY: [*Gaily.*] That's only your fancy. You think because it's plain to you it must be plain to anybody else.

VIOLET: I've never before had anything to hide. D'you think I like it?

RONNY: And even if she does know, what does it matter? It does her no harm. . . . And how could anyone help loving you?

VIOLET: [*Quickly.*] Take care what you say.

RONNY: No one can hear. To look at us anyone would think we were discussing the political situation.

VIOLET: You're cunning, Ronny.

RONNY: I love you. I love you. I love you.

VIOLET: For God's sake don't keep on saying it. I'm so ashamed.

RONNY: [*Astonished.*] What about?

VIOLET: Just now, this afternoon, I would never have said what I did only I thought you were going. I wasn't myself then, Ronny. I ought never to have . . .

RONNY: Thank God you did. You can't grudge me the happiness you gave me. You can't take it away from me now. I know you love me. I hold the sun and the moon in my hands and all the stars of heaven.

VIOLET: [*Desperately.*] What are we going to do? Oh, it's not fair to me.

RONNY: It's done now. You can't unsay it. Each time I look at you I shall remember. I've held you in my arms and kissed your lips. You can never take that away from me. And I needn't go. I shall see you constantly. Oh, I'm so happy.

[*She walks up and down for a moment, trying to control herself, then she makes up her mind: she stops and faces him.*

VIOLET: I want you to go, Ronny. I want you to make some excuse and refuse the appointment here.

RONNY: No, I can't leave you now.

VIOLET: I beseech you to go.

RONNY: Do you want me to?

VIOLET: Yes.

RONNY: Give me your hand, then.

VIOLET: Why?

RONNY: Give me your hand. [*She gives it him and he holds it.*] Say you love me, Violet.

VIOLET: No.

RONNY: How cold your hand is!

VIOLET: Let me go.

RONNY: D'you really want me to go?

VIOLET: You know I don't. I adore you. It'll kill me if you go. [*He bends down and passionately kisses her hand.*] Ronny, Ronny, don't! What are you doing? [*She tears her hand away. She is trembling with emotion. He is white and cold with passion. They sit opposite one another for a while in silence.*] What a punishment! When you told me this afternoon that you loved me I thought I'd never been happy in my life before, and though it tore my heart to think that you must go I felt—oh, I don't know— as though my joy was so overwhelming, there was no room in my heart for anything else. And now I'm wretched, wretched.

RONNY: But why? Darling! My darling, we were going to be parted, and now we're going to be together. Can anything matter beside that?

VIOLET: It's all so hopeless.

RONNY: It needn't be.

VIOLET: How can it be anything else?

RONNY: I don't love you for a day or a week, Violet; I love you for always.

VIOLET: Whatever happens, I'm going to try to do my duty to Arthur.

RONNY: I'm not seeking to prevent you. What am I asking for? I only want to see you. I want to know that I'm close to you. I want to touch your hand. I want to think of you. What harm can that do you?

VIOLET: If I were my own mistress I could laugh and let you do as you choose. But I'm not. I'm bound to you hand and foot. It's torture to me. And the worst of it is I love my bonds. I can't wish to be without them. I'm at your mercy, Ronny. I love you.

RONNY: Oh, but that's enough for me. I swear to you I don't want you to do anything that you'll ever regret.

VIOLET: If it could only be taken out of our hands. If something would only happen.

RONNY: What can happen?

VIOLET: Perhaps the Khedive will change his mind. Perhaps the Foreign Office will say you must go to Paris.

RONNY: Would you be pleased? Violet, I want so little from you. How can it hurt you to give me that? Let us give ourselves a chance to be happy.

VIOLET: We shall never be happy. Never. The only thing we can do is to part, and I can't let you go. I can't. I can't. It's asking too much of me.

RONNY: I love you with all my heart and soul. I didn't know it was possible to love anyone as I love you.

[ARTHUR *is heard gaily whistling to himself*.

VIOLET: There's Arthur!

RONNY: [*Quickly.*] Shall I go?

VIOLET: Yes. No. Have we got to hide ourselves? Has it come to that already? Oh, I hate myself.

[ARTHUR *comes in*.

VIOLET: [*Brightly.*] You're very gay this afternoon, Arthur. One doesn't often hear you whistle.

ARTHUR: D'you think it's unbecoming to my years or to my dignity?

VIOLET: Shall I give you a cup of tea?

ARTHUR: To tell you the honest truth that is what I came here for.

VIOLET: And I was flattering myself it was for the pleasure of my company.

ARTHUR: Ronny, will you find out if it would be convenient for the Khedive to see me at eleven o'clock to-morrow?

RONNY: Very good, sir.

[*He goes out.*

VIOLET: What have you to see the Khedive about—if it isn't a secret?

ARTHUR: Not at all. I'm merely going to place before him Ronny's name.

VIOLET: Then the matter's not definitely settled yet?

ARTHUR: Not formally. I've not had the reply yet to my telegram to the Foreign Office, and I've not had the Khedive's acceptance of my suggestion.

VIOLET: But supposing the Foreign Office say they think he'd better go to Paris after all?

ARTHUR: I think it's most unlikely. They know by now that the man on the spot is the best judge of the circumstances, and I've accustomed them to giving me a free hand.

VIOLET: And you think the Khedive will raise no objection?

ARTHUR: He knows Ronny a little and likes him. I think he'll be delighted with my choice.

[*There is a pause.* ARTHUR *drinks his tea. There is no sign that he is conscious of* VIOLET'S *agitation. She is tortured by indecision.*

VIOLET: Arthur, I'm sorry if I was cross just now about Abdul Said. It was stupid of me to interfere with something that wasn't my business.

ARTHUR: Oh, my dear, don't say that. I'm sorry I couldn't do what you wanted.

VIOLET: I made myself needlessly disagreeable. Will you forgive me?

ARTHUR: Darling, don't reproach yourself. That's more than I can bear. There's nothing to forgive.

VIOLET: I owe so much to you. I hate to think that I was horrid.

ARTHUR: You don't owe anything to me at all. And you're incapable of being horrid.

> [*He seizes her hands and is about to kiss them, when she draws them abruptly away.*]

VIOLET: No, don't kiss my hands.

ARTHUR: Why not?

> [*He is surprised. For an instant she is taken aback. He looks at her hands and she withdraws them as though he could see on them the kisses which* RONNY, *a few minutes before, had pressed on them.*]

VIOLET: [*With the faintest laugh of embarrassment.*] If you want to kiss me I prefer you to kiss my cheeks.

ARTHUR: That is evidently what they're made for.

> [*He does not attempt to kiss them. She gives him a quick glance and looks away.*]

VIOLET: Arthur, I'm afraid Christina will be awfully disappointed at Henry's not getting that job.

ARTHUR: Let us hope she will bear her disappointment with as much fortitude as I do.

VIOLET: I don't think she's entirely given up hope that you will change your mind.

ARTHUR: [*With a chuckle.*] I'm sure of that. I don't expect to have much peace till the matter is officially settled. That is why I mean to settle it quickly.

VIOLET: What is your objection to Henry?

ARTHUR: None. He's not such a good man as Ronald Parry, that's all.

VIOLET: The last time there was a good job going Henry just missed getting it.

ARTHUR: Henry is one of those men who would do very well for a job if there weren't always somebody just a little bit better applying at the same time.

VIOLET: Christina thinks you're so anxious not to favour him because he's your nephew that you are positively biased against him.

ARTHUR: Christina, like the majority of her sex, has an unerring eye for the discreditable motive.

VIOLET: She blames me because you won't help Henry. She thinks it's because I'm jealous of her.

ARTHUR: How exactly like her! The best mother and the most unreasonable woman I've ever known.

VIOLET: [*Forcing the words out.*] It would be a great pleasure to me if you could change your mind and let Henry have the post instead of Ronald Parry.

ARTHUR: Oh, my dear, don't ask me to do that. You know how I hate refusing to do anything you wish.

VIOLET: Anne is so anxious that Ronny should go to Paris. He's made all his preparations, don't you think you might just as well let him go?

ARTHUR: I'm afraid I don't. I want him here.

VIOLET: It would be such a joy to me if I could go and tell Christina that you'd consented. It would make such a difference to me, you see. I want her to be fond of me, and I know she'd never forget if I'd been able to do her a good turn like that. Oh, Arthur, won't you?

ARTHUR: Darling, I'm afraid I can't.

VIOLET: I promise I'll never ask you anything again as long as I live if you'll only do this for me. It means so much to me. You don't know how much.

ARTHUR: I can't, Violet.

VIOLET: Won't you talk it over with Anne?

ARTHUR: To tell you the truth, I don't think it's any business of hers.

VIOLET: [*Hesitatingly.*] Is it due to her influence that Ronald was appointed to Paris?

ARTHUR: Why?

VIOLET: I want to know. If she's been pulling strings to get him moved I suppose it's for some reason. He was very comfortable here. It's not often you find a secretary who exactly suits you.

ARTHUR: Well, yes, it was her doing. She tells me she doesn't mean to come to Egypt so much as in the past and wants her brother nearer to her.

VIOLET: If she wants to see much of her brother she let him choose rather an unfortunate profession. . . . I wonder she didn't tell you the truth.

ARTHUR: [*Quickly.*] I'm convinced she did. I thought her explanation very natural. I'm sorry it's necessary for me to interfere with her plans.

VIOLET: I'm sure she wouldn't mind my telling you why she's so anxious Ronny should leave Egypt. She thinks he's in love with a married woman and it seems desirable to get him away. Perhaps she didn't want to tell you. I fancy she's been very uneasy about it.

ARTHUR: I daresay it's only a momentary infatuation. Let us hope he will get over it quickly. I can't lose a useful public servant because he happens to have formed an unfortunate attachment.

VIOLET: I'm afraid I'm not explaining myself very well· Ronny is desperately in love. There's no other way of putting it. You *must* let him go. After all, you're very fond of him, you've known him since he was a small boy; it isn't as though he were a stray young man sent you by the Foreign Office. You can't be entirely in-different to him. Perhaps his welfare is at stake. Don't you think it's wiser—it's only kind—to send him out of harm's way?

ARTHUR: My dear, you know that I—Arthur Little—would do anything to please you and that I care very much for the happiness of Anne and the welfare of Ronald Parry. But, you see, I'm an official too, and the official can't do all sorts of things that the man would be very glad to.

VIOLET: How can you separate the official and the man? The official can't do things that the man disapproves.

ARTHUR: Ah! that's a point that has been discussed ever since states came into being. Are the rules of private morality binding on the statesman? In theory most of us answer yes, but in practice very few act on that principle. In this case, darling, it hardly applies. I see no conflict between the man and the official.

VIOLET: You think it doesn't really concern you, Arthur?

ARTHUR: I've not said that. But I'm not going to let an appeal to my emotions interfere with my judgment. I think I understand the situation. I'm not proposing to change my mind. I shall present Ronny's name to the Khedive to-morrow.

VIOLET: D'you think me very stupid, Arthur?

ARTHUR: Not at all, darling. Only a clever woman could achieve your beauty.

VIOLET: Then doesn't it occur to you that if I've made such a point of Ronny's going it must be for some very good reason?

ARTHUR: [*With a quick look at her.*] Don't you think we'd better leave that subject alone, darling?

VIOLET: I'm afraid you'll think it silly and vain of me to say so, but I think you should know that—that Ronny's in love with me. That is why I want him to go.

ARTHUR: It's very natural that he should be in love with

you. I'm always surprised that everybody else isn't. I don't see how I can prevent that except by taking you to live in the depths of the Sahara.

VIOLET: Don't make light of it, Arthur. It wasn't very easy for me to tell you.

ARTHUR: How do you wish me to take it? I can't blame Ronald. He's by way of being a gentleman. I've been good to him. He'll make the best of a bad job.

VIOLET: D'you mean to say that it makes no difference to you?

ARTHUR: This secretaryship is a stepping-stone to a very important position. You're not going to ask me to rob him of it because he's done something so very natural as to fall in love with the most charming woman in Egypt? I imagine that all my secretaries will fall in love with you. Poor devils, I don't see how they can be expected to help it.

VIOLET: You drive me mad. It's so serious, it's so tremendously serious, and you have the heart to make little jokes about it.

ARTHUR: [Gravely.] Has it ever struck you that flippancy is often the best way of dealing with a serious situation? Sometimes it's really too serious to be taken seriously.

VIOLET: What do you mean by that?

ARTHUR: Nothing very much. I was excusing myself for my ill-timed jests.

VIOLET: You're determined to keep Ronny here?

ARTHUR: Quite. [There is a pause. ARTHUR gets up and puts his hand on her shoulder.] I don't think there's anything more to say. If you will forgive me I will get back to the office.

VIOLET: No, don't go yet, Arthur. There's something more I want to say to you.

ARTHUR: Will you allow me to advise you not to? It's so easy to say too much; it's never unwise to say too little. I beseech you not to say anything that we should both of us regret.

VIOLET: You think it's unimportant if Ronny loves me, because you trust me implicitly.

ARTHUR: Implicitly.

VIOLET: Has it never occurred to you that I might be influenced by his love against my will? Do you think it's so very safe?

ARTHUR: If I allowed any doubt on that matter to enter my head I should surely be quite unworthy of your affection.

VIOLET: Arthur, I don't want to have any secrets from you.

ARTHUR: [*Trying to stop her.*] Don't, Violet. I don't want you to go on.

VIOLET: I must now.

ARTHUR: Oh, my dear, don't you see that things said can never be taken back. We may both know something . . .

VIOLET: [*Interrupting.*] What do you mean?

ARTHUR: But so long as we don't tell one another we can ignore it. If certain words pass our lips then the situation is entirely changed.

VIOLET: You're frightening me.

ARTHUR: I don't wish to do that. Only you can tell me nothing that I don't know. But if you tell me you may do irreparable harm.

VIOLET: D'you mean to say you know? Oh, it's impossible. Arthur, Arthur, I can't help it. I must tell you. It burns my heart. I love Ronny with all my body and soul.

[*There is a pause while they look at one another.*

ARTHUR: Did you think I didn't know?

VIOLET: Then why did you offer him the job?

ARTHUR: I had to.

VIOLET: No one could have blamed you if you had suggested Henry.

ARTHUR: My dear, I'm paid a very considerable salary. It would surely be taking money under false pretences if I didn't do my work to the best of my ability.

VIOLET: It may mean happiness or misery to all three of us.

ARTHUR: I must take the risk of that. You see, Ronny is cut out for this particular position. It's only common honesty to give it him.

VIOLET: Don't you love me any more?

ARTHUR: Don't ask me that, Violet. You know I love you with all my heart.

VIOLET: Then I can't understand.

ARTHUR: You don't think I want him to stay, do you? When the telegram came from the Foreign Office ordering him to Paris my middle-aged heart simply leapt for joy. Do you think I didn't see all the advantages he had over me? He seemed to have so much to offer you and I so little.

VIOLET: Oh, Arthur!

ARTHUR: But if he went away I thought presently you'd forget him. I thought if I were very kind to you and tolerant, and if I asked nothing more from you than you were prepared to give, I might in time make you feel towards me, not love perhaps, but tenderness and affection. That was all I could hope for, but that would have made me very happy. Then the Khedive asked for an English secretary, and I knew Ronny was the only man for it. You see, I've been at this work so long, the official in me makes decisions almost mechanically.

VIOLET: And supposing they break the heart of the man in you?

ARTHUR: [*Smiling.*] By a merciful interposition of Providence we all seem to have just enough strength to bear the burdens that are placed on us.

VIOLET: D'you think so?

ARTHUR: You, like the rest of us, Violet.

VIOLET: How long have you known I loved him?

ARTHUR: Always. I think perhaps I knew before you did.

VIOLET: Why didn't you do something?

ARTHUR: Will you tell me what there was to do?

VIOLET: Aren't you angry with us?

ARTHUR: I should be a fool to be that. It seems to me so natural, so horribly natural. He's young and nice-looking and cheery. It seems to me now inevitable that you should have fallen in love with him. You might be made for one another.

VIOLET: Oh, do you see that?

ARTHUR: It had struck you too, had it? I suppose it's obvious to anyone who takes the trouble to think about it. [*She does not answer.*] Haven't you wished with all your heart that you'd met him first? Don't you hate me now because I married you? [*She looks away.*] My dear child, I'm so sorry for you. I've been very grateful for your kindness to me during the last month or two. I've seen you try to be loving to me and affectionate. I've been so anxious to tell you not to force yourself, because I understood and you mustn't be unhappy about me. But I didn't know how. I could only make myself as little troublesome as possible.

VIOLET: You've been immensely good to me, Arthur.

ARTHUR: That's the least you had a right to expect of me. I did you a great wrong in marrying you. I knew you didn't love me. You were dazzled by the circumstances. You didn't know what marriage was and how irksome it must be unless love makes its constraints sweeter than freedom. But I adored you. I thought love would come. With all my heart I ask you to forgive me.

VIOLET: Oh, Arthur, don't talk like that. You know I was so happy to marry you. I thought you wonderful, I was so excited and flattered—I thought that was love. I never knew that love would come like this. If I'd only known what to expect I could have fought against it. It took me unawares. I never had a chance. It wasn't my fault, Arthur.

ARTHUR: I'm not blaming you, darling.

VIOLET: It would be easier for me if you did.

ARTHUR: It's just bad luck. Bad luck? I might have expected it.

VIOLET: Still, I'm glad I've told you. I hated having a secret from you. It's better that we should be frank with one another.

ARTHUR: If I can help you in any way I'm glad too that you've told me.

VIOLET: What is to be done?

ARTHUR: There's nothing to be done.

VIOLET: Arthur, until to-day Ronny and I have never exchanged a word that anyone might not have heard. I was happy to be with him, I knew he liked me, I was quite satisfied with that. But when I heard that he was going away suddenly everything was changed. I felt I couldn't bear to let him go. Oh, I'm so ashamed, Arthur.

ARTHUR: Dear child!

VIOLET: I don't know how it happened. He told me he loved me. He didn't mean to. Don't think he's been disloyal to you, Arthur. We were both so upset. It was just as much my fault as his. I couldn't help letting him see how much he meant to me. We thought we were never going to see one another again. He took me in his arms and held me in them. I was so happy and so miserable. I never thought life could mean so much.

ARTHUR: And just now when you were alone he kissed your hands.

VIOLET: How do you know?

ARTHUR: When I wanted to kiss them you withdrew them. You couldn't bear that I should touch them. You felt on them still the pressure of his lips.

VIOLET: I couldn't help it. He was beside himself with joy because he needn't go. I don't want to love him, Arthur. I want to love you. I've tried so desperately hard.

ARTHUR: My dear, one either loves or one doesn't. I'm afraid trying doesn't do much good.

VIOLET: If he stays here I shall have to see him constantly. I shan't have a chance to get over it. Oh, I can't. I can't. It's intolerable. Have pity on me.

ARTHUR: I'm afraid you'll be very unhappy. But you see, something more than your happiness is at stake. A little while ago you said you wanted to do more for your country than you did. Does it strike you that you can do something for it now?

VIOLET: I?

ARTHUR: We all want to do great and heroic things, but generally we can only do very modest ones. D'you think we ought to shirk them?

VIOLET: I don't understand.

ARTHUR: Ronny can be of infinite value here. You can't help your feelings for him. I can't bring myself to blame you. But you are mistress of your words and your actions. What are we to do? You wouldn't wish me to resign when my work here is but half done. We must make the best of the position. Remember that all of us here, you more than most women, because you're my wife, work for the common cause by our lives and the example we set. At all costs we must seem honest, straightforward, and without reproach. And one finds by experience that it's much less trouble to be a thing than only to seem it. There's only one way in which we can avoid reproach and that is by being irreproachable.

VIOLET: You mean that it's necessary for the country that Ronny and you should stay here? And if my heart breaks it doesn't matter. I thought I was doing so much in asking you to send him away. Don't you know that with all my heart I wanted him to stay? D'you know what I feel, Arthur? I can't think of anything else. I'm obsessed by a hungry longing for him. Till to-day I could have borne it. But now . . . I feel his arms about me every moment, and his kisses on my lips. You can't know the rapture and the torture and the ecstasy that consume me.

ARTHUR: Oh, my dear, do you think I don't know what love is?

VIOLET: I want to do the right thing, Arthur, but you mustn't ask too much of me. If I've got to treat him as a casual friend, I can't go on seeing him. I can't, Arthur, I can't! If he must stay then let me go.

ARTHUR: Never! I think, even if it weren't necessary, I should make him stay now. You and I are not people to run away from danger. After all, we're not obliged to yield to our passions—we can control them if we want to. For your own sake you must stay, Violet.

VIOLET: And if I break, I break.

ARTHUR: It's only the worthless who are broken by unhappiness. If you have faith and courage and honesty, unhappiness can only make you stronger.

VIOLET: Have you thought of yourself, Arthur? What will you feel when you see him with me? What will you suspect when you're working in your office and don't know where I am?

ARTHUR: I shall know that you are unhappy, and I shall feel the most tender compassion for you.

VIOLET: You're exposing me to a temptation that I want with all my heart to yield to. What is there to hold me back? Only the thought that I must do my duty to you. What is there to reward me? Only the idea that perhaps I'm doing a little something for the country.

ARTHUR: I put myself in your hands, Violet. I shall never suspect that you can do anything, not that I should reproach you for—I will never reproach you—but that you may reproach yourself for.

[*A pause.*

VIOLET: Just now, when we were talking of Abdul Said, I asked if you could do your duty when it was a matter that affected you, if it meant misery or happiness to you, I said.

ARTHUR: My dear, duty is rather a forbidding word. Let us say that I—want to earn my screw.

VIOLET: You must have thought me very silly. I said I hoped you'd never be put to the test, and the test had come already, and you never hesitated.

ARTHUR: These things are very much a matter of habit, you know.

VIOLET: What you can do I can do too, Arthur—if you believe in me.

ARTHUR: Of course I believe in you.

VIOLET: Then let him stay. I'll do what I can.

[RONNY *comes in*.

RONNY: The Khedive was engaged when I rang up. But I left the message and the answer has just come through. He will be pleased to see you, sir, at eleven o'clock.

ARTHUR: That will do admirably. Ronny must lunch with us to-morrow, Violet. We'll crack a bottle to celebrate his step!

END OF THE SECOND ACT

THE THIRD ACT

The scene shows part of the garden and a verandah at the Consular Agent's house. Coloured lanterns are fixed here and there. It is night, and in the distance is seen the blue sky bespangled with stars. At the back of the verandah are the windows of the house gaily lit. Within a band is heard playing dance music. VIOLET *is giving a dance. Everyone who appears is magnificently gowned.* VIOLET *is wearing all her pearls and diamonds.* ARTHUR *has across his shirt-front the broad riband of an order. It is the end of the evening. Various people are seated on the verandah, enjoying the coolness. They are* MR. *and* MRS. APPLEBY, CHRISTINA *and* ARTHUR.

APPLEBY: Well, my dear, I think it's about time I was taking you back to your hotel.

ARTHUR: Oh, nonsense! It's when everybody has gone that a dance really begins to get amusing.

CHRISTINA: That's a pleasant remark to make to your guests.

MRS. APPLEBY: I'm really ashamed to have stayed like this to the bitter end, but I do love to see the young folk enjoying themselves.

ARTHUR: Ah! you have learnt how to make the most of advancing years. The solace of old age is to take pleasure in the youth of those who come after us.

CHRISTINA: I don't think you're very polite, Arthur.

MRS. APPLEBY: Bless your heart, I know I'm not so young as I was.

ARTHUR: Do you mind?

MRS. APPLEBY: Me? Why should I? I've had my day and

I've enjoyed it. It's only fair to give others a chance now.

CHRISTINA: I'm sure you enjoyed your trip up the Nile.

MRS. APPLEBY: Oh, we had a wonderful time.

ARTHUR: And what conclusions did you come to, Mr. Appleby? I remember that you were looking for instruction as well as amusement.

APPLEBY: I didn't forget what you told me. I just kept my ears open and my mouth shut.

ARTHUR: A capital practice, not much favoured by democratic communities.

APPLEBY: But I came to one very definite conclusion, for all that.

ARTHUR: What was it?

APPLEBY: In fact, I came to two.

ARTHUR: That's not so satisfactory—unless they contradicted one another; in which case I venture to suggest that you have grasped at all events the elements of the Egyptian problem.

APPLEBY: The first is that you're the right man in the right place.

ARTHUR: Christina would never admit that. She has known for many years that she could manage Egypt far better than I do.

CHRISTINA: I don't deny that for a minute. I think on the whole women are more level-headed than men. They're not swayed by emotion. They're more practical. They know that principle must often yield to expediency, and they can do the expedient without surrendering the principle.

ARTHUR: You make my head whirl, Christina.

APPLEBY: I had the opportunity of seeing a good many different sorts of people. I never heard a reasonable complaint against you. Some of them didn't like you

D

personally, but they looked up to you, and they believed in you. I asked myself how you managed it.

MRS. APPLEBY: I told him that it's because you're human.

ARTHUR: Christina thinks it very bad for me to hear pleasant things said of me.

CHRISTINA: Christina doesn't know what her brother would do if he hadn't got an affectionate sister to gibe at.

APPLEBY: It must be a great satisfaction to you to see the country becoming every year more prosperous and contented.

ARTHUR: What was the second conclusion you came to?

APPLEBY: I'm coming to that. Most of us are torn asunder as it were by a conflict of duties. This and that urgently needs to be done, and if you put one thing right you put something else wrong. We all want to do for the best, but we don't exactly know what the best is. Now, you've got your duty clearly marked out before you, if you take my meaning; you're young.

ARTHUR: Youngish.

APPLEBY: You've made a success of your job and of your life. It's not all of us who can say that. My second conclusion is that you must be the happiest man alive.

MRS. APPLEBY: I'm glad he's got that off his chest. He's been dinning it into my ears for the last ten days. My impression is that he fell in love with Lady Little that day he lunched here six weeks ago.

ARTHUR: I'm not going to blame him for that. Everybody does. . . . It was a wise old fellow who said that you must count no man happy till he's dead. [CHRISTINA *gives him a look, and puts her hand affectionately on his arm. He quickly withdraws it.*] Here is Violet.

[*She comes in on* HENRY PRITCHARD'S *arm and sinks into a chair.*

VIOLET: I'm absolutely exhausted. I feel that in another minute my legs will drop off.

ARTHUR: Do take care, darling, that would be so disfiguring.

VIOLET: Oh, I'd still dance on the stumps.

ARTHUR: When are you going to send that unfortunate band away?

VIOLET: Oh, we must have one more dance. After all, it's our last ball of the season. And now that everyone has gone I needn't be dignified any more. There's no one but Henry and Anne and Ronny. We've just had a gorgeous one-step, haven't we, Henry?

HENRY: Gorgeous. You're a ripping dancer.

VIOLET: My one accomplishment. [*The band is heard beginning a waltz.*] Good heavens, they've started again. That's Anne, I'm positive. She's been playing the British matron too and now she's having her fling.

ARTHUR: You girls, you never grow up.

HENRY: Are you ready for another turn, Violet?

ARTHUR: Don't dance any more, darling, you look worn out.

VIOLET: Supposing you danced with your mother, Henry. I can see her toes itching inside her black satin slippers.

CHRISTINA: Nonsense! I haven't danced for fifteen years.

HENRY: Come on, mother. Just to show them you know how.

[*He seizes her hand and drags her to her feet.*

CHRISTINA: I was just as good a dancer as anybody else in my day.

ARTHUR: When Christina says that she means she was a great deal better.

HENRY: Come on, mother, or it'll be over before we begin.

CHRISTINA: Don't be rough with me, Henry.

[*They go into the house.*

APPLEBY: We rather fancied ourselves too, Fanny, once upon a time. What d'you say to trying what we can do, my dear?

MRS. APPLEBY: You be quiet, George. Fancy me dancing with my figure!

APPLEBY: I don't deny you're plump, but I never did like a scrag. Perhaps it's the last chance we shall ever have.

MRS. APPLEBY: What would they say at home if they ever come to hear you and me had been dancing? Really, George, I'm surprised at you.

ARTHUR: [*Amused.*] I won't tell.

APPLEBY: You know you want to, Fanny. You're only afraid they'll laugh. Come on, or else I shall dance by myself.

MRS. APPLEBY. [*Getting up.*] I see you've quite made up your mind to make a fool of yourself.

[*They go out.* ARTHUR *watches them, smiling.*

ARTHUR: What good people! It's really a treat to see them together.

VIOLET: Mr. Appleby is very enthusiastic about you. He was telling me just now about his trip in Upper Egypt. He's tremendously impressed. He said I ought to be very proud of you.

ARTHUR: I can't imagine any remark more calculated to make you dislike me.

[*She gives him a long look and then glances away. When she speaks it is with embarrassment.*

VIOLET: Are you satisfied with me, Arthur?

ARTHUR: My dear, what do you mean?

VIOLET: Since that afternoon when I told you . . .

ARTHUR: Yes, I know.

VIOLET: We've never talked about it. [*Giving him her hand.*] I want to thank you for having been so good to me.

ARTHUR: I'm afraid you haven't got much to thank me for. It would have been easier if I'd been able to help you, but I didn't see anything I could do but just sit still and twiddle my thumbs.

VIOLET: I've felt your confidence in me and that has been a help. You've never given the slightest sign that anything was changed. You used sometimes to ask me what I'd been doing during the day. Of late you haven't even done that.

ARTHUR: I didn't want you to suspect for a moment that your actions were not perfectly free.

VIOLET: I know. No one could have been more considerate than you've been. Oh, I've been so unhappy, Arthur. I wouldn't go through the last six weeks for anything in the world.

ARTHUR: It's torn my heart to see you so pale and wan. And when, often, I saw you'd been crying I almost lost my head. I didn't know what to do.

VIOLET: I couldn't help it if I loved him, Arthur. That wasn't in my power. But all that was in my power I've done. Somehow I've managed not to be alone with him.

ARTHUR: Haven't you had any explanation with him?

VIOLET: There didn't seem to be anything to explain. D'you think I ought to have told him I didn't love him? I couldn't, Arthur. I couldn't.

ARTHUR: My dear! My dear!

VIOLET: Once or twice he wrote to me. I knew he would and I'd made up my mind not to read the letters. But when they came I couldn't help myself. I had to read them. I was so wretched and it meant so much to me that he loved me. [ARTHUR *makes an instinctive movement of pain.*] I didn't mean to say that. Please forgive me.

ARTHUR: I think I understand.

VIOLET: I didn't answer them.

ARTHUR: Did he only write once or twice?

VIOLET: That's all. You see, he can't make it out. He thinks I've treated him badly. Oh, I think that's the hardest thing of all. I've seen the misery in his eyes. And there was nothing I could do. I hadn't the courage to tell him. I'm weak. I'm so horribly weak. And when I'm with him alone I . . . Oh, it is cruel that I should make him suffer so when he loves me.

ARTHUR: I don't know what to say to you. It seems cold comfort to say that you must set your hope in the merciful effects of time. Time will ease your pain and his. Perhaps the worst is over already.

VIOLET: I hope with all my heart it is. I couldn't have borne any more, Arthur. I'm at the end of my strength.

ARTHUR: Dear heart, you're tired physically now. We'll send these people away and you must go to bed.

VIOLET: Yes. I'm exhausted. But I want to tell you, Arthur, I think you're right. The worst is over. I'm not suffering quite so much as I did. I find it a little easier not to think of him. When I meet him I can manage to be gay and flippant and indifferent. I'm so glad, Arthur.

ARTHUR: You've been very brave. I told you we were all strong enough to bear the burdens that are laid upon us.

VIOLET: You mustn't think too well of me. I couldn't have done what I have except for the consciousness of his great love for me. Is that awfully disloyal of me, Arthur?

ARTHUR: [Gravely.] No, darling.

VIOLET: You can understand, can't you? It means so much to me. It's helped me more than anything else in the world. It's the only thing that made these past weeks not intolerable. I'm satisfied to know he loves me. I want nothing more.

[MR. *and* MRS. APPLEBY *come in.* ARTHUR *immediately assumes a chaffing manner.*

ARTHUR: Why, what's this? You haven't given in already?

APPLEBY: The spirit is willing enough, but the flesh is weak.

MRS. APPLEBY: We wouldn't like it talked about at home, but the fact is we got a bit out of breath.

VIOLET: Well, sit down a moment and rest yourself.

MRS. APPLEBY: Just a moment if you don't mind, and then we'll be going.

[CHRISTINA *appears with* HENRY.

ARTHUR: Here is poor Christina in a state of complete mental and physical collapse.

CHRISTINA: Don't be ridiculous, Arthur.

ARTHUR: How did you get on?

HENRY: First-rate. Only mother won't let herself go. I kept on telling her there's only one thing to do in modern dancing—let all your bones go loose and leave the man to do the rest.

CHRISTINA: [*With a chuckle.*] I think modern dancing is an abandoned pastime. Nothing will induce me to let all my bones go loose.

HENRY: Mother's idea of dancing is to keep herself to herself.

CHRISTINA: [*Looking at him affectionately.*] You're an impudent boy.

MRS. APPLEBY: [*To* VIOLET.] I do wish I'd seen you dancing with Mr. Parry. He's a wonderful dancer.

VIOLET: He does dance well, doesn't he?

HENRY: Haven't you danced with him to-night, Violet?

VIOLET: No. He came rather late and my card was filled up. I promised him an extra, but some stuffy old diplomatist came and asked me for a dance, so I gave him Ronny's.

MRS. APPLEBY: It's too bad. It must be a rare sight to see you and Mr. Parry waltzing together.

VIOLET: How do you know he dances so well?

MRS. APPLEBY: There were two or three dances at our hotel last week and we saw him then.

VIOLET: Oh, I see.

APPLEBY: [*With a chuckle.*] I like that young man. When he gets hold of a good thing he freezes on to it.

VIOLET: Oh?

APPLEBY: There's a young American girl staying at the hotel. She's a Miss Pender. I wonder if you know her?

VIOLET: No, I don't think so. We get to know very few of the winter visitors.

MRS. APPLEBY: She's a perfect picture to look at. And a beautiful dancer.

APPLEBY: Everyone was looking at them last night. They made a wonderful pair.

VIOLET: Do you know this lady, Henry?

HENRY: Yes, I've met her two or three times. She's very pretty.

APPLEBY: I don't think anyone else had much of a look-in with her.

HENRY: Well, you needn't be disagreeable about it.

APPLEBY: As far as I could see she danced with Mr. Parry pretty well all the time.

MRS. APPLEBY: It was a treat to see them together.

VIOLET: [*A little uncertainly.*] If one gets hold of a partner who suits one I always think it's better to stick to him.

MRS. APPLEBY: Oh, I don't think it was only that. She's so much in love with him that she can't help showing it.

HENRY: I never saw such a fellow as Ronny. When there is a bit of luck going he always gets it.

VIOLET: And is he in love with her too?

APPLEBY: Oh, one can't tell that.

MRS. APPLEBY: If he isn't he very soon will be. She's too pretty for any man to resist long.

ARTHUR: [*Lightly.*] You know them, the brutes, don't you?

MRS. APPLEBY: Bless their hearts, I don't blame them. What are pretty girls for except to make nice men happy? I was a pretty girl myself once.

ARTHUR: And was Mr. Appleby a nice man?

APPLEBY: I think I must have been, for you've certainly made me happy, my dear.

MRS. APPLEBY: I wish you'd put that in writing, George. I'd like to have a little something like that by me when you've got a bit of a chill on your liver.

APPLEBY: H'm, I think bed's the place for you, Fanny. Say good night to her ladyship and let's be going.

MRS. APPLEBY: Good night, Lady Little, and thank you so much for asking us. We have enjoyed ourselves.

VIOLET: Good night.

APPLEBY: Good night.

ARTHUR: I hope you'll have a pleasant journey home. Lucky people, you'll see the spring in England. When you get back the hedgerows will be just bursting into leaf.

[*The* APPLEBYS *go out.*

VIOLET: How old is this American girl, Henry?

HENRY: Oh, I don't know, about nineteen or twenty.

VIOLET: Is she as pretty as they say?

HENRY: Rather.

VIOLET: Is she fair?

HENRY: Very. She's got wonderful hair.

VIOLET: You've never mentioned her. Do you think Ronny is in love with her?

HENRY: Oh, I don't know about that. She's great fun. And

you know, it's always flattering when a pretty girl makes a dead set at you.

> [*There is a momentary silence.* VIOLET *is extremely disturbed by the news that has just reached her.* ARTHUR *realises that a crisis has come.*

CHRISTINA: [*In a matter-of-fact way.*] Let us hope that something will come of it. There's no reason why Ronny shouldn't marry. I think men marry much too late nowadays.

> [ANNE *and* RONNY *appear.*

ANNE: I'm absolutely ashamed of myself. I half expected to find you'd all gone to bed.

VIOLET: [*Smiling.*] Have you been having a jolly dance?

ANNE: Think of having a good band and the whole floor to oneself. By the way, Violet, the band want to know if they can go away.

VIOLET: I'm sorry I had to cut your dance, Ronny.

RONNY: It was rotten luck. But I suppose on these occasions small fry like me have to put up with that sort of thing.

VIOLET: If you like we'll have a turn now before we send the band away.

RONNY: I'd love it.

> [ARTHUR *gives a little start and looks at* VIOLET *curiously.* ANNE *is surprised too.*

CHRISTINA: If you're going to start dancing again we'll go. Henry has to be at his office early in the morning.

VIOLET: Good night, then.

CHRISTINA: [*Kissing her.*] Your dance has been a great success.

VIOLET: It's nice of you to say so.

CHRISTINA: [*To* ARTHUR.] Good night, dear old thing. God bless and guard you always.

ARTHUR: My dear Christina, why this embarrassing emotion?

CHRISTINA: I don't know what we should do if anything happened to you.

ARTHUR: Don't be an idiot, my dear; nothing is going to happen to me.

CHRISTINA: [*With a smile.*] I can't get you out of thinking me a perfect fool.

ARTHUR: Be off with you, Christina. If you go on finding out things that are not your business I shall have you deported.

VIOLET: What has she found out now?

ARTHUR: A trifle that we thought it wouldn't hurt the public to know nothing about.

CHRISTINA: [*Shaking hands with* RONNY.] I don't grudge you your job any more. We're all under a debt of gratitude to you.

RONNY: I had a bit of luck, that's all. It's nothing to make a fuss about.

ARTHUR: Go and have your dance, darling. It's really getting very late.

VIOLET: [*To* RONNY.] Are you ready?

RONNY: What shall we make them play?

[*They go out.*

CHRISTINA: Good night, Anne.

ANNE: [*Kissing her.*] Good night, my dear. [HENRY *shakes hands with* ANNE *and* ARTHUR. *He and his mother go out.*] I suppose I mayn't ask what Christina was referring to?

ARTHUR: I can't prevent you from asking.

ANNE: But you have no intention of answering. What is the matter, Arthur? You look so deadly white.

ARTHUR: Nothing. I'm tired. I had a busy day and now the dance. [*The sound of a waltz is heard.*] Oh, damn that music!

ANNE: Sit down and rest yourself. Why don't you have a smoke? [*Putting her hand on his arm.*] My dear friend.

ARTHUR: For God's sake don't pity me.

ANNE: Won't you talk to me frankly? I may be able to help you. In the old days you used to bring your troubles to me, Arthur.

ARTHUR: I tell you I'm only tired. What is the use of talking about what can't be helped?

ANNE: You must know that I notice most things that concern your happiness. [*Looking away.*] Why did you imagine I took so much trouble to get Ronny moved to Paris?

ARTHUR: I suspected. Ought I to thank you? I'm too miserable and too humiliated.

ANNE: Have you heard about a Miss Pender? She's an American girl.

ARTHUR: Of course I have. It's my business to know everything that goes on in Cairo.

ANNE: Don't you think that may be the solution?

[HENRY *comes in.*

ARTHUR: [*Sharply.*] What d'you want?

HENRY: I beg your pardon. Mother left her fan here.

[*He takes it up from a chair.*

ARTHUR: I thought you'd gone five minutes ago.

HENRY: Oh, we just stood for a moment to look at Ronny and Violet dancing. Upon my soul it's a fair treat.

ARTHUR: They make a wonderful couple, don't they?

HENRY: I'm afraid Violet's awfully tired. She's not saying a word and she's as white as a sheet.

ARTHUR: I'll send her to bed as soon as they've finished.

HENRY: Good night.

ARTHUR: [*Smiling.*] Good night, my boy.

[*Exit* HENRY.

ANNE: Is anything the matter?

ARTHUR: Tell me about this American girl. She's in love with Ronny, isn't she?

ANNE: Yes, that's obvious.

ARTHUR: And he?

ANNE: He's been very unhappy, you know.

ARTHUR: [*Almost savagely.*] That is a calamity which I find myself able to bear with patience.

ANNE: And now he's surprised and pleased. I've met her. Poor dear, she did everything to make me like her, because Ronny was my brother. She's awfully pretty. He's not in love with her yet. But I think he may be. He's on the brink and if there were nothing else he'd fall over.

ARTHUR: That is what I suspected. You know, Anne, the longer I live the more inexplicable I find human beings. I always thought I was by way of being a fairly decent fellow. I never knew what mean beastliness there was inside me. It would be quite impossible for me to tell you how I hate your brother. I've had to be jolly and affable with him and, by George, I wanted to kill him.

ANNE: Why didn't you let him go? Are you sure it was necessary to give him that job?

ARTHUR: Already he's been invaluable.

ANNE: Then one can only hope for the best.

[*There is a moment's pause. When* ARTHUR *speaks it is at first rather to himself than to* ANNE.]

ARTHUR: No one knows what I've gone through during the last few months. I've been devoured with jealousy and I knew it would be fatal if I showed Violet the least trace of ill-temper. I kept on saying to myself that it wasn't her fault if she was in love with Ronny. [*Humorously.*] You can't think how devilish hard it is not to resent the fact that somebody doesn't care for you.

ANNE: [*With a chuckle.*] Oh yes, I can.

ARTHUR: I knew that almost everything depended on how I acted during these weeks, and the maddening thing was that I could do nothing but sit still and control myself. I saw her miserable and knew that she didn't want my comfort. I've yearned to take her in my arms and I've known she'd *let* me because it was her duty. Those dear good donkeys, the Applebys, told me just now they thought I must be the happiest man alive! Week after week, with an aching heart, I've forced myself to be gay and amusing. D'you think I'm amusing, Anne?

ANNE: Sometimes.

ARTHUR: The battle has been so unfair. All the dice are loaded against me. He has every advantage over me. But at last I thought I'd won. I thought Violet was getting more resigned. She told me herself just now that the worst was over. And those confounded people must go and upset the apple-cart. Damn their eyes!

ANNE: Why?

ARTHUR: The Applebys told her about Miss Pender. It was very natural. They knew no reason for not repeating the hotel gossip.

ANNE: Was that why she asked Ronny to dance with her?

ARTHUR: Yes. It's the crisis. She had the strength to keep him at arm's length when she knew he loved her. What will she do now?

ANNE: You heard what Henry said. They don't seem to be talking to one another.

ARTHUR: No.

ANNE: Why did you let them dance together? You might easily have said it was too late and the band must go.

ARTHUR: What good would that do? No. I've done nothing to prevent their meeting. I've left them absolute liberty.

ANNE: Do you think it's fair to Violet? You know, women act so much on impulse. The surroundings and the circumstances have so much influence on them. Think of the excitement of dancing, the magic of this wonderful night, and the solitude under these stars. You complain the dice are loaded against you, but now you're double-loading them against yourself.

ARTHUR: It tortures me, but I must give them the opportunity to fight the matter out for themselves.

ANNE: Poor child, she's so young.

ARTHUR: Too young.

ANNE: Don't say that; it sounds as though you regretted having married her.

ARTHUR: Don't you imagine that regret has been tormenting her ever since she found out what love really was? Even though I love her with all my heart I know now that I made a mistake. Do you think you can make anyone love you by constant tenderness, devotion, and kindness?

ANNE: Not a man perhaps. But a woman yes, yes, yes!

ARTHUR: Whoever loved that loved not at first sight? I want so tremendously to make her happy, and I've only made her utterly miserable. And there's no way out. It's a pity that a convenient attack of brain fever can't carry me off, but I'm as strong as a horse.

ANNE: You know, Arthur, there's one compensation about the pains of love. While one's suffering from them one feels one will never get over them, but one does, and when they're gone they don't even leave a scar. One looks back and remembers one's torment and marvels that it was possible to suffer like that.

ARTHUR: You talk as though you'd had experience.

ANNE: I have.

ARTHUR: I always look upon you as so calm and self-controlled.

ANNE: I was desperately in love for years with a man. I should have made him an excellent wife, although it's I as says it. But it never occurred to him for an instant that my feelings were more than friendly. And eventually he married somebody else.

ARTHUR: My dear friend, I hate to think of your being unhappy.

ANNE: I'm not. That's why I told you the tragic story. I've got over it so completely that now I have an equal affection both for him and his wife.

ARTHUR: D'you know, Anne, at one time I very nearly asked you to marry me?

ANNE: [*Gaily.*] Oh, what nonsense!

ARTHUR: I daresay it's as well I didn't. I should have lost the best friend I've ever had.

ANNE: On the other hand, I've lost the satisfaction of refusing the most distinguished man of our day. Why didn't you ask me?

ARTHUR: You were such an awfully good friend. I thought we were very well as we were.

ANNE: That isn't the reason, Arthur. You didn't ask me because you didn't love me. If you had you'd have let friendship go hang. [*Seeing that he is not paying any attention to her.*] What's the matter?

ARTHUR: The music has stopped.

ANNE: [*With a slight tightening of the lips.*] I'm afraid my concerns don't interest you very much. I was only talking about them to distract you.

ARTHUR: Forgive me, but I've got this anguish gnawing at my heart. Anne, when they come back here I want you to come with me for a stroll in the garden.

ANNE: Why? I'm frightfully tired. I think I shall go to bed.

ARTHUR: No, do this for me, Anne. I want to give them their chance. It may be the last chance for all of us.

ANNE: [*With a little sigh.*] Very well, I'll do even that for you.

ARTHUR: You are a good friend, and I'm a selfish beast.

ANNE: I wish you could have a child, Arthur. That might settle everything.

ARTHUR: That is what I look forward to with all my heart. I think she might love her baby's father.

ANNE: Then she'll realise that only you could have been so tolerant and so immensely patient. When she looks back she'll be filled with gratitude.

[RONNY *and* VIOLET *come in*.

VIOLET: I've told the band they can go.

ARTHUR: I don't suppose they wanted telling twice. Did you have a pleasant dance?

VIOLET: I was very tired.

RONNY: It was brutal of me to make you dance so long. I'll say good night before I'm turned out.

ARTHUR: Oh, won't you sit down and have a cigarette before you go? Anne and I were just going to stroll to the end of the garden to have a look at the Nile.

VIOLET: Oh.

ANNE: I'm too restless to go to bed just yet.

[ARTHUR *and* ANNE *go out*. VIOLET *and* RONNY *do not speak for a moment. At first the conversation is quite light*.

VIOLET: What was it that Christina was referring to just now? Had it anything to do with you?

RONNY: I don't think I'm justified in telling you about it. If Sir Arthur thinks you should know I daresay he'd rather tell you himself.

VIOLET: Of course you mustn't tell me if it's a secret.

RONNY: I'd almost forgotten what a beautiful dancer you were.

VIOLET: [*With a smile.*] So soon?

RONNY: You haven't given me much chance of dancing with you during the last few weeks.

VIOLET: I hear there's a girl at the Ghezireh Palace who dances very well. Miss Pender, isn't that her name?

RONNY: Yes, she's wonderful.

VIOLET: I'm told she's charming.

RONNY: Very.

VIOLET: I should like to meet her. I wonder whom I know that could bring us together.

RONNY: [*With a change of tone.*] Why do you speak of her?

VIOLET: Is there any reason why I shouldn't?

RONNY: Do you know that this is the first time I've been quite alone with you for six weeks?

VIOLET: [*Still quite lightly.*] It was inevitable that when you ceased being Arthur's private secretary we should see less of one another.

RONNY: I only welcomed my new job because I thought I shouldn't be utterly parted from you.

VIOLET: Don't you think it was better that we shouldn't see too much of one another?

RONNY: What have I done to you, Violet? Why have you been treating me like this?

VIOLET: I'm not conscious that I've treated you differently from what I used.

RONNY: Why didn't you answer my letters?

VIOLET: [*In a low voice.*] I hadn't anything to say.

RONNY: I wonder if you can imagine what I went through, the eagerness with which I looked forward to a letter from you, just a word or two would have satisfied me, how anxiously I expected each post, and my despair when day after day went by.

VIOLET: You ought not to have written to me.

RONNY: D'you think I could help myself? Have you forgotten that day when we thought we were never going to meet again? If you wanted me to be nothing more than a friend why did you tell me you loved me? Why did you let me kiss you and hold you in my arms?

VIOLET: You know quite well. I lost my head. I was foolish. You—you attached too much importance to the emotion of the moment.

RONNY: Oh, Violet, how can you say that? I know you loved me then. After all, the past can't be undone. I loved you. I know you loved me. We couldn't go back to the time when we were no more than friends.

VIOLET: You forget that Arthur is my husband and you owe him everything in the world. We both owe him everything in the world.

RONNY: No, I don't forget it for a moment. After all, we're straight, both of us, and we could have trusted ourselves. I wanted nothing but to be allowed to love you and to know that you loved me.

VIOLET: Do you remember what you said in the first letter you wrote me?

RONNY: Oh, you can't blame me for that. I'd loved you so long, so passionately. I'd never dared to hope that you cared for me. And when I knew! I never said a tenth part of what I wanted to. I went home and I just wrote all that had filled my heart to overflowing. I wanted you to know how humbly grateful I was for the wonderful happiness you'd given me. I wanted you to know that my soul to its most hidden corners was yours for ever.

VIOLET: How *could* I answer it?

RONNY: You needn't have been afraid of me, Violet. If it displeased you I would never even have told you that I loved you. I would have carried you in my heart like an image of the Blessed Virgin. When we met here or there, though there were a thousand people between us and we never exchanged a word, I should have known that we were the only people in the world, and that somehow, in some strange mystic fashion, I belonged to you and you belonged to me. Oh, Violet, I only wanted a little kindness. Was it so much to ask?

[VIOLET *is moved to the very depths of her heart. She can scarcely control herself; the pain she suffers seems unendurable; her throat is so dry that she can hardly speak.*

VIOLET: They saw that Miss Pender is in love with you. Is it true?

RONNY: A man's generally a conceited ass when he thinks girls are in love with him.

VIOLET: Never mind that. Is it true? Please be frank with me.

RONNY: Perhaps it is.

VIOLET: Would she marry you if you asked her?

RONNY: I think so.

VIOLET: She can't have fallen in love with you without some encouragement.

RONNY: She plays tennis a good deal and she's very fond of dancing. You know, I was rather wretched. Sometimes you looked at me as though you hated me. You seemed to try and avoid me. I wanted to forget. I didn't know what I'd done to make you treat me so cruelly. It was very pleasant to be with someone who seemed to want me. Everything I did pleased her. She's rather like you. When I was with her I was a little less unhappy. When I found she was in love with me I was touched and I was tremendously grateful.

VIOLET: Are you sure you're not in love with her?

RONNY: Yes, I'm quite sure.

VIOLET: But you like her very much, don't you?

RONNY: Yes, very much.

VIOLET: Don't you think if it weren't for me you would be in love with her?

RONNY: I don't know.

VIOLET: I'd like you to be frank with me.

RONNY: [*Unwillingly.*] You don't want my love. She's sweet and kind and tender.

VIOLET: I think she might make you very happy.

RONNY: Who knows?

> [*There is a pause.* VIOLET *forces herself to make the final renunciation. Her fingers move spasmodically in the effort she makes to speak calmly.*

VIOLET: It seems a pity that you should waste your life for nothing. I'm afraid you'll think me a heartless flirt. I'm not that. At the time I feel all I say. But . . . I don't quite understand myself. I take a violent fancy to someone, and I lose my head, but somehow it doesn't last. I . . . I suppose I'm not capable of any enduring passion. There are people like that, aren't there? It goes just as suddenly as it comes. And when it goes—well, it's gone for ever. I can't understand then what on earth I saw in the man who made my heart go pit-a-pat. I'm dreadfully sorry I caused you so much pain. You took it so much more seriously than I expected. And afterwards I didn't know what to do. You must—you must try to forgive me.

> [*There is a long pause.*

RONNY: Don't you love me at all now?

VIOLET: It's much better that I should tell you the truth, isn't it? even at the risk of hurting your feelings. I'm frightfully ashamed of myself. I'm afraid you'll think me awfully frivolous.

RONNY: Why don't you say it right out?

VIOLET: D'you want me to? [*She hesitates, but then takes courage.*] I'm very sorry, dear Ronny, I'm afraid I don't care for you in that way at all.

RONNY: I'm glad to know.

VIOLET: You're not angry with me?

RONNY: Oh, no, my dear, how can you help it? We're made as we're made. . . . D'you mind if I go now?

VIOLET: Won't you stop and say good night to Anne?

RONNY: No, if you don't mind, I'd like to go quickly.

VIOLET: Very well. And try to forgive me, Ronny.

RONNY: Good night.

> [*He takes her hand and they look into one another's eyes.*
VIOLET: Good night.

> [*He goes out.* VIOLET *clasps her hands to her heart as though to ease its aching.* ANNE *and* ARTHUR *return.*

ANNE: Where is Ronny?

VIOLET: He's gone. It was so late. He asked me to say good night to you.

ANNE: Thank you. It must be very late. I'll say good night too. [*She bends down and kisses* VIOLET.] Good night, Arthur.

ARTHUR: Good night. [*She goes out.* ARTHUR *sits down. A* SAIS *comes in and turns out some of the lights. In the distance is heard the wailing of an Arab song.* ARTHUR *motions to the* SAIS.] Leave these. I'll turn them out myself. [*The* SAIS *goes in and turns out all the lights in the lower rooms but one. The light remains now only just round* ARTHUR *and* VIOLET. *The Arab song is like a wail of pain*.] That sounds strangely after the waltzes and one-steps that we've heard this evening.

VIOLET: It seems to come from very far away.

ARTHUR: It seems to wail down the ages from an immeasurable past.

VIOLET: What does it say?

ARTHUR: I don't know. It must be some old lament.

VIOLET: It's heartrending.

ARTHUR: Now it stops.

VIOLET: The garden is so silent. It seems to be listening too.

ARTHUR: Are you awfully unhappy, Violet?

VIOLET: Awfully.

ARTHUR: It breaks my heart that I, who would do anything in the world for you, can do so little to console you.

VIOLET: Had you any idea that Ronny no longer cared for me?

ARTHUR: How should I know what his feelings were?

VIOLET: It never occurred to me that he could change. I felt so secure in his love. It never occurred to me that anyone could take him from me.

ARTHUR: Did he tell you he didn't care for you any more?

VIOLET: No.

ARTHUR: I don't think he's in love with Miss Pender.

VIOLET: I told him that he meant nothing to me any more. I told him that I took fancies and got over them. I made him think I was a silly flirt. And he believed me. If he loved me truly, truly, as he did before, whatever I'd said he'd have known it was incredible. Oh, I wouldn't have believed him if he'd made himself cheap in my eyes.

ARTHUR: My poor child.

VIOLET: He's not in love with her yet. I know that. He's only pleased and flattered. He's angry with me. If he's angry he *must* love me still. He asked so little. It only needed a word and he would have loved me as much as ever. What have I done? What harm would it have done you? I've sent him away now for good. It's all over and done with. And my heart aches. What shall I do, Arthur?

ARTHUR: My dear, have courage. I beseech you to have courage.

VIOLET: I suppose it's shameful that we should have loved one another at all. But how could we help it? We're masters of our actions, but how can we command our feelings? After all, our feelings are our own. I don't know what I'm going to do, Arthur. It wasn't so bad till to-night; I could control myself, I thought my pain was growing less. . . . I long for him with all my soul, and I must let him go. Oh, I hate him. I hate him. If he'd loved me he might have been faithful to me a few short weeks. He wouldn't cause me such cruel pain.

ARTHUR: Don't be unjust to him, Violet. I think he fell in love with you without knowing what was happening to him. And when he knew I think he struggled against it as honourably as you did. You know that very little escapes me. I've seen a sort of shyness in him when he was with me, as though he were a little ashamed in my presence. I even felt sorry for him because he felt he was behaving badly to me and he couldn't help himself. He's suffered just as much as you have. It's not very strange that when this girl fell in love with him it should seem to offer a new hope. He was unhappy and she comforted him. Anne says she's rather like you. If ever he loves her perhaps it will be you that he loves in her.

VIOLET: Why do you say all this to me?

ARTHUR: You've been so wretched. I don't want bitterness to come to you now. I can't bear that you should think your first love has been for someone not worthy of it. I think time will heal the wounds which now you think are incurable, but when it does I hope that you will look back on your love as a thing only of beauty.

VIOLET: I am a beast, Arthur. I don't deserve anyone to be so good to me as you are.

ARTHUR: And there's something else I must tell you. . . . It appears that various enterprising people have been laying plans to put me out of the way.

VIOLET: [*Startled.*] Arthur!

ARTHUR: I find that there was a plot to kill me this morning on my way to the review.

VIOLET: How awful!

ARTHUR: Oh, it's nothing to be alarmed about. We've settled everything without any fuss. Our old friend Osman Pasha is going to spend some time on his country estates for the good of his health, and half a dozen foolish young men are under lock and key. But it might have come off except for Ronny. It was Ronny who saved me.

VIOLET: Ronny? Oh, I'm so glad. It makes up a little for the rest.

ARTHUR: He did a fine thing. He showed determination and presence of mind.

VIOLET: Oh, my husband! My dear, dear Arthur!

ARTHUR: You're not sorry?

VIOLET: I'm glad I've done what I have, Arthur. I've sometimes felt I gave you so little in return for all you've given me. But at least now I've given you all I had to give.

ARTHUR: Don't think it will be profitless. To do one's duty sounds a rather cold and cheerless business, but somehow in the end it does give one a queer sort of satisfaction.

VIOLET: What should I do if I lost you? It makes me sick with fear.

ARTHUR: [*With a tender smile.*] I had an idea you'd be glad I escaped.

VIOLET: All I've suffered has been worth while. I've done something for you, haven't I? And even something for England. . . . I'm so tired.

ARTHUR: Why don't you go to bed, darling?

VIOLET: No, I don't want to go yet. I'm too tired. Let me stay here a little longer.

ARTHUR: Put your feet up.

VIOLET: Come and sit close to me, Arthur. I want to be

comforted. You're so good and kind to me, Arthur' I'm so glad I have you. You will never fail me.

ARTHUR: Never. [*She gives a little shudder*.] What's the matter?

VIOLET: I hope he'll marry her quickly. I want to be a good wife to you. I want your love. I want your love so badly.

ARTHUR: My dear one.

VIOLET: Put your arms round me. I'm so tired.

ARTHUR: You're half asleep. . . . Are you asleep?

> [*Her eyes are closed. He kisses her gently. In the distance there is heard again the melancholy wail of a Bedouin love-song.*

THE END

EAST OF SUEZ

A PLAY
in Seven Scenes

CHARACTERS

Daisy.
George Conway.
Henry Anderson.
Harold Knox.
Lee Tai Cheng.
Sylvia Knox.
Amah.
Wu.

———

The action of the play takes place in Pekin.

EAST OF SUEZ

SCENE I

SCENE: *A street in Peking. Several shops are shown. Their fronts are richly decorated with carved wood painted red and profusely gilt. The counters are elaborately carved. Outside are huge signboards. The shops are open to the street and you can see the various wares they sell. One is a coffin shop, where the coolies are at work on a coffin: other coffins, ready for sale, are displayed; some of them are of plain deal, others are rich with black and gold. The next shop is a money-changer's. Then there is a lantern shop in which all manner of coloured lanterns are hanging. After this comes a druggist's where there are queer things in bottles and dried herbs. A small stuffed crocodile is a prominent object. Next to this is a shop where crockery is sold, large coloured jars, plates, and all manner of strange animals. In all the shops two or three Chinamen are seated. Some read newspapers through great horn spectacles; some smoke water-pipes.*

The street is crowded. Here is an itinerant cook with his two chests, in one of which is burning charcoal: he serves out bowls of rice and condiments to the passers-by who want food. There is a barber with the utensils of his trade. A coolie, seated on a stool, is having his head shaved. Chinese walk to and fro. Some are coolies and wear blue cotton in various stages of raggedness; some in black gowns and caps and black shoes are merchants and clerks. There is a beggar, gaunt and thin, with an untidy mop of bristly hair, in tatters of indescribable filthiness. He stops at one of the shops and begins a long wail. For a time no one takes any notice of him, but presently on a word from the fat shop-keeper an assistant gives him a few cash and he wanders on. Coolies, half naked, hurry by, bearing great bales on their yokes.

They utter little sharp cries for people to get out of their way. Peking carts with their blue hoods rumble noisily along. Rickshaws pass rapidly in both directions, and the rickshaw boys shout for the crowd to make way. In the rickshaws are grave Chinese. Some are dressed in white ducks after the European fashion; in other rickshaws are Chinese women in long smocks and wide trousers, or Manchu ladies, with their faces painted like masks, in embroidered silks. Women of various sorts stroll about the street or enter the shops. You see them chaffering for various articles.

A water-carrier passes along with a creaking barrow, slopping the water as he goes; and an old blind woman, a masseuse, advances slowly, striking wooden clappers to proclaim her calling. A musician stands on the curb and plays a tuneless melody on a one-stringed fiddle. From the distance comes the muffled sound of gongs. There is a babel of sound caused by the talking of all these people, by the cries of coolies, the gong, the clappers, and the fiddle. From burning joss-sticks in the shops in front of the household god comes a savour of incense.

A couple of Mongols ride across on shaggy ponies; they wear high boots and Astrakhan caps. Then a string of camels sways slowly down the street. They carry great burdens of skins from the deserts of Mongolia. They are accompanied by wild-looking fellows. Two stout Chinese gentlemen are giving their pet birds an airing; the birds are attached by the leg with a string and sit on little wooden perches. The two Chinese gentlemen discuss their merits. Round about them small boys play. They run hither and thither pursuing one another amid the crowd.

END OF SCENE I

SCENE II

SCENE: *A small verandah on an upper storey of the British American Tobacco Company's premises, the upper part of which the staff lives in. At the back are heavy arches of whitewashed masonry and a low wall which serves as a parapet. Green blinds are drawn. There is a bamboo table on which are copies of illustrated papers, a couple of long bamboo chairs and two or three smaller arm-chairs. The floor is tiled.*

On one of the long chairs HAROLD KNOX *is lying asleep. He is a young man of pleasing appearance. He wears white ducks, but he has taken off his coat, which lies on a chair, and his collar and tie and pin. They are on the table by his side. He is troubled by a fly and, half waking but with his eyes still closed, tries to drive it away.*

KNOX: Curse it. [*He opens his eyes and yawns.*] Boy!

WU: [*Outside.*] Ye.

KNOX: What's the time?

    [WU *comes in; he is a Chinese servant in a long blue gown with a black cap on his head. He bears a tray on which is a bottle of whisky, a glass and a syphon.*

WU: My no sabe.

KNOX: Anyhow, it's time for a whisky and soda. [WU *puts the tray down on the table.* KNOX *smiles.*] Intelligent anticipation. Model servant and all that sort of thing. [WU *pours out the whisky.*] You don't care if I drink myself to death, Wu—do you? [WU *smiles, showing all his teeth.*] Fault of the climate. Give me the glass. [WU *does so.*] You're like a mother to me, Wu. [*He drinks and puts down the glass.*] By George, I feel another man. The bull-dog breed, Wu. Never say die. Rule, Britannia. Pull up the blinds, you lazy blighter. The sun's off and the place is like an oven.

> [WU *goes over and pulls up one blind after the other. An expanse of blue sky is seen.* HENRY ANDERSON *comes in. He is a man of thirty, fair, good-looking, with a pleasant, honest face. His obvious straightforwardness and sincerity make him attractive.*

HARRY: [*Breezily.*] Hulloa, Harold, you seem to be taking it easy.

KNOX: There was nothing to do in the office, and I thought I'd get in my beauty sleep while I had the chance.

HARRY: I thought you had your beauty sleep before midnight.

KNOX: I'm taking time by the forelock so as to be on the safe side.

HARRY: Are you going on the loose again to-night?

KNOX: Again, Henry?

HARRY: You were blind last night.

KNOX: [*With great satisfaction.*] Paralytic. . . . Hulloa, who's this?

> [*He catches sight of the* AMAH *who has just entered. She is a little, thin, wrinkled, elderly Chinawoman in a long smock and trousers. She has gold pins in her sleek black hair. When she sees she has been noticed she smiles obsequiously.*

KNOX: Well, fair charmer, what can we do for you?

HARRY: What does she want, Wu?

KNOX: Is this the face that launched a thousand ships?

AMAH: My Missy have pay my letter.

HARRY: [*With sudden eager interest.*] Are you Mrs. Rathbone's amah? Have you got a letter for me?

AMAH: My belong Missy Rathbone amah.

HARRY: Well, hurry up, don't be all night about it. Lend me a dollar, Harold. I want to give it to the old girl.

> [*The* AMAH *takes a note out of her sleeve and gives it to* HARRY. *He opens it and reads.*

KNOX: I haven't got a dollar. Give her a chit or ask Wu. He's the only man I know who's got any money.

HARRY: Let me have a dollar, Wu. Chop-chop.

WU: My go catchee.

> [*He goes out. The* AMAH *is standing near the table. While* KNOX *and* HARRY *go on talking she notices* KNOX's *pin. She smiles and smiles and makes little bows to the two men, but at the same time her hand cautiously reaches out for the pin and closes on it. Then she secretes it in her sleeve.*

HARRY: I thought you were going to play tennis this afternoon.

KNOX: So I am, later on.

HARRY: [*Smiling.*] Do it now, dear boy. That is a precept a business man should never forget.

KNOX: I should hate to think you wanted to be rid of me.

HARRY: I dote on your company, but I feel that I mustn't be selfish.

KNOX: [*Pulling his leg.*] To tell you the truth, I don't feel very fit to-day.

HARRY: A little bilious, I daresay. Half a dozen hard sets are just what you want.

> [*He hands* KNOX *his coat.*

KNOX: What is this?

HARRY: Your coat.

KNOX: You're making yourself almost distressingly plain.

> [WU *comes back and hands* HARRY *a dollar, then goes out.* HARRY *gives the dollar to the* AMAH.

HARRY: Here's a dollar for you, Amah. You go back to missy and tell her it's all right and will she come chop-chop. Sabe?

AMAH: My sabe. Goo'-bye.

KNOX: God bless you, dearie. It's done me good to see your winsome little face.

HARRY: [*With a smile.*] Shut up, Harold.

[*The* AMAH, *with nods, smiles, and bows, goes out.*

KNOX: Harry, my poor friend, is it possible that you have an assignation?

HARRY: What is possible is that if you don't get out quick I'll throw you out.

KNOX: Why didn't you say you were expecting a girl?

HARRY: I'm not; I'm expecting a lady.

KNOX: Are you sure you know how to behave? If you'd like me to stay and see you don't do the wrong thing I'll chuck my tennis. I'm always ready to sacrifice myself for a friend.

HARRY: Has it struck you that the distance from the verandah to the street is very considerable?

KNOX: And the pavement is hard. I flatter myself I can take a hint. I wonder where the devil my pin is. I left it on the table.

HARRY: I expect Wu put it away.

KNOX: It's much more likely that old woman pinched it.

HARRY: Oh, nonsense. She wouldn't dream of such a thing. I believe Mrs. Rathbone's had her for ages.

KNOX: Who is Mrs. Rathbone?

HARRY: [*Not wishing to be questioned.*] A friend of mine.

[GEORGE CONWAY *comes in. He is a tall dark man in the early thirties. He is a handsome well-built fellow, of a somewhat rugged appearance, but urbane and self-assured.*

GEORGE: May I come in?

HARRY: [*Eagerly, shaking him warmly by the hand.*] At last! By Jove, it's good to see you again. You know Knox, don't you?

GEORGE: I think so.

KNOX: I wash bottles in the B.A.T. I don't expect the Legation bloods to be aware of my existence.

GEORGE: [*With a twinkle in his eye.*] I don't know that an Assistant Chinese Secretary is such a blood as all that.

KNOX: You've just been down to Fuchow, haven't you?

GEORGE: Yes, I only got back this morning.

KNOX: Did you see Freddy Baker by any chance?

GEORGE: Yes, poor chap.

KNOX: Oh, I've got no pity for him. He's just a damned fool.

HARRY: Why?

KNOX: Haven't you heard? He's married a half-caste.

HARRY: What of it? I believe she's a very pretty girl.

KNOX: I daresay she is. But hang it all, he needn't have married her.

GEORGE: I don't think it was a very wise thing to do.

HARRY: I should have thought all those prejudices were out of date. Why shouldn't a man marry a half-caste if he wants to?

KNOX: It can't be very nice to have a wife whom even the missionary ladies turn up their noses at.

HARRY: [*With a shrug of the shoulders.*] You wait till Freddy's number one in Hankow and can entertain. I bet the white ladies will be glad enough to know his missus then.

GEORGE: Yes, but that's just it. He'll never get a good job with a Eurasian wife.

HARRY: He's in Jardine's, isn't he? Do you mean to say it's going to handicap a man in a shipping firm because he's married a woman who's partly Chinese?

GEORGE: Of course it is. Jardine's are about the most important firm in China, and the manager of one of their principal branches has definite social obligations. Freddy Baker will be sent to twopenny-halfpenny outports where his wife doesn't matter.

KNOX: I think he's damned lucky if he's not asked to resign.

HARRY: It's cruel. His wife may be a charming and cultivated woman.

KNOX: Have you ever known a half-caste that was?

HARRY: I have.

KNOX: Well, I've been in this country for seven years and I've never met one, male or female, that didn't give me the shivers.

HARRY: I've no patience with you. You're a perfect damned fool.

KNOX: [*A little surprised, but quite good-humoured.*] You're getting rather excited, aren't you?

HARRY: [*Hotly.*] I hate injustice.

GEORGE: Do you think it really is injustice? The English are not an unkindly race. If they've got a down on half-castes there are probably very good grounds for it.

HARRY: What are they?

KNOX: We don't much like their morals, but we can't stick their manners.

GEORGE: Somehow or other they seem to inherit all the bad qualities of the two races from which they spring and none of the good ones. I'm sure there are exceptions, but on the whole the Eurasian is vulgar and noisy. He can't tell the truth if he tries.

KNOX: To do him justice, he seldom tries.

GEORGE: He's as vain as a peacock. He'll cringe when he's afraid of you and he'll bully when he's not. You can never rely on him. He's crooked from the crown of his German hat to the toes of his American boots.

KNOX: Straight from the shoulder. Take the count, old man.

HARRY: [*Frigidly.*] Oughtn't you to be going?

KNOX: [*Smiling.*] No, but I will.

HARRY: I'm sorry if I was rude to you just now, old man.

KNOX: Silly ass, you've broken no bones; my self-esteem, thank God, is unimpaired.

[*He goes out.*

HARRY: I say, I'm awfully glad you're back, George. You can't think how I miss you when you're away.

GEORGE: As soon as the shooting starts we'll try and get two or three days together in the country.

HARRY: Yes, that would be jolly. [*Calling.*] Wu!

WU: [*Outside.*] Ye!

HARRY: Bring tea for three.

GEORGE: Who is the third?

HARRY: When you said you could come round I asked somebody I want you very much to meet.

GEORGE: Who is that?

HARRY: Mrs. Rathbone. . . . I'm going to be married to her and we want you to be our best man.

GEORGE: Harry!

HARRY: [*Boyishly.*] I thought you'd be surprised.

GEORGE: My dear old boy, I am so glad. I hope you'll be awfully happy.

HARRY: I'm awfully happy now.

GEORGE: Why have you kept it so dark?

HARRY: I didn't want to say anything till it was all settled. Besides, I've only known her six weeks. I met her when I was down in Shanghai. . . .

GEORGE: Is she a widow?

HARRY: Yes, she was married to an American in the F.M.S.

GEORGE: Is she American?

HARRY: Only by marriage. I'm afraid she didn't have a very happy married life.

GEORGE: Poor thing. I think I'd take a small bet that you won't beat her.

HARRY: I mean to try my best to make her happy.

GEORGE: You old fool, I've never known a man who was likely to make a better husband.

HARRY: I'm most awfully in love with her, George.

GEORGE: Isn't that ripping! How old is she?

HARRY: Only twenty-two. She's the loveliest thing you ever saw.

GEORGE: And is she in love with you?

HARRY: She says so.

GEORGE: She damned well ought to be.

HARRY: I do hope you'll like her, George.

GEORGE: Of course I shall. You're not the sort of chap to fall in love with a woman who isn't nice.

[HARRY *walks up and down for a moment restlessly.*

HARRY: Will you have a whisky and soda?

GEORGE: No, thanks. . . . I'll wait for tea.

HARRY: She ought to be here in a moment. [*Suddenly making up his mind.*] It's no good beating about the bush. I may as well tell you at once. Her—her mother was Chinese.

GEORGE: [*Unable to conceal his dismay.*] Oh, Harry. [*A pause.*] I wish I hadn't said all that I did just now.

HARRY: Of course you didn't know.

GEORGE: [*Gravely.*] I should have had to say something very like it, Harry. But I shouldn't have put it so bluntly.

HARRY: You said yourself there were exceptions.

GEORGE: I know. [*Distressed.*] Won't your people be rather upset?

HARRY: I don't see how it can matter to them. They're nine thousand miles away.

GEORGE: Who was her father?

HARRY: Oh, he was a merchant. He's dead. And her mother is too.

GEORGE: That's something. I don't think you'd much like having a Chinese mother-in-law about the place.

HARRY: George, you won't let it make any difference, will you? We've known one another all our lives.

GEORGE: My dear old chap, as far as I'm concerned I shouldn't care if you married the first cousin of the Ace of Spades. I don't want you to make a hash of things.

HARRY: Wait till you see her. She's the most fascinating thing you ever met.

GEORGE: Yes, they can be charming. I was awfully in love with a half——, with a Eurasian girl myself years ago. It was before you came out to the country. I wanted to marry her.

HARRY: Why didn't you?

GEORGE: It was up in Chung-King. I'd just been appointed vice-consul. I was only twenty-three. The Minister wired from Peking that I'd have to resign if I did. I hadn't a bob except my salary, and they transferred me to Canton to get me away.

HARRY: It's different for you. You're in the service and you may be Minister one of these days. I'm only a merchant.

GEORGE: Even for you there'll be difficulties, you know. Has it occurred to you that the white ladies won't be very nice?

HARRY: I can do without their society.

E*

GEORGE: You must know some people. It means you'll have to hobnob with Eurasian clerks and their wives. I'm afraid you'll find it pretty rotten.

HARRY: If you'll stick to me, I don't care.

GEORGE: I suppose you've absolutely made up your mind?

HARRY: Absolutely.

GEORGE: In that case I've got nothing more to say. You can't expect me not to be a little disappointed, but after all the chief thing is your happiness, and whatever I can do I will. You can put your shirt on that.

HARRY: You're a brick, George.

GEORGE: The little lady ought to be here, oughtn't she?

HARRY: I think I hear her on the stairs.

> [*He goes to the entrance and goes out.* WU *brings in the tea and sets it on the table.* GEORGE *walks over to the parapet and looks thoughtfully out. There is a sound of voices in the adjoining room.*

HARRY: [*Outside.*] Come in; he's on the verandah.

DAISY: [*Outside.*] One brief look in the glass and then I'm ready.

> [HARRY *enters.*

HARRY: She's just coming.

GEORGE: I bet she's powdering her nose.

DAISY: Here I am.

> [DAISY *enters. She is an extremely pretty woman, beautifully, perhaps a little showily, dressed. She has a pale, very clear, slightly sallow skin, and beautiful dark eyes. There is only the very faintest suspicion in them of the Chinese slant. Her hair is abundant and black.*

HARRY: This is George Conway, Daisy.

> [GEORGE *stares at her. At first he is not quite sure that he recognises her, then suddenly he does, but only the slightest movement of the eyes betrays him.*

DAISY: How do you do? I told Harry I had an idea I must have met you somewhere. I don't think I have after all.

HARRY: George flatters himself he's not easily forgotten.

DAISY: But I've heard so much about you from Harry that I feel as though we were old friends.

GEORGE: It's very kind of you to say so.

HARRY: Supposing you poured out the tea, Daisy.

GEORGE: I'm dying for a cup.

[*She sits down and proceeds to do so.*

DAISY: Harry is very anxious that you should like me.

HARRY: George and I have known one another since we were kids. His people and mine live quite close to one another at home.

DAISY: But I'm not blaming you. I'm only wondering how I shall ingratiate myself with him.

HARRY: He looks rather severe, but he isn't really. I think you've only got to be your natural charming self.

DAISY: Have you told him about the house?

HARRY: No. [*To* GEORGE.] You know the temple the Harrisons used to have. We've taken that.

GEORGE: Oh, it's a ripping place. But won't you find it rather a nuisance to have those old monks on the top of you all the time?

HARRY: Oh, I don't think so. Our part is quite separate, you know, and the Harrisons made it very comfortable.

[HAROLD KNOX *comes in. He has changed into tennis things.*

KNOX: I say, Harry. . . . [*He sees* DAISY.] Oh, I beg your pardon.

HARRY: Mr. Knox—Mrs. Rathbone.

[KNOX *gives her a curt nod, but she holds out her hand affably. He takes it.*

DAISY: How do you do?

KNOX: I'm sorry to disturb you, Harry, but old Ku Faung Min is downstairs and wants to see you.

HARRY: Tell him to go to blazes. The office is closed.

KNOX: He's going to Hankow to-night, and he says he must see you before he goes. He's got some big order to give.

HARRY: Oh, curse him. I know what he is. He'll keep me talking for half an hour. D'you mind if I leave you?

DAISY: Of course not. It'll give me a chance of making Mr. Conway's acquaintance.

HARRY: I'll get rid of him as quickly as I can.

[*He goes out accompanied by* KNOX.

KNOX: [*As he goes.*] Good-bye.

[GEORGE *looks at* DAISY *for a moment. She smiles at him. There is a silence.*

GEORGE: Why didn't you warn me that it was you I was going to meet?

DAISY: I didn't know what you'd say about me to Harry if you knew.

GEORGE: It was rather a risk, wasn't it? Supposing I'd blurted out the truth.

DAISY: I trusted to your diplomatic training. Besides, I'd prepared for it. I told him I thought I'd met you.

GEORGE: Harry and I have been pals all our lives. I brought him out to China and I got him his job. When he had cholera he would have died if I hadn't pulled him through.

DAISY: I know. And in return he worships the ground you tread on. I've never known one man think so much of another as he does of you.

GEORGE: All that's rot, of course. Sometimes I don't know how I'm going to live up to the good opinion Harry has of me. But when you've done so much for a pal as I have for him, it gives you an awful sense of responsibility towards him.

DAISY: What do you mean by that?

GEORGE: I'm not going to let you marry him.

DAISY: He's so much in love with me that he doesn't know what to do with himself.

GEORGE: I know he is. But if you were in love with him you wouldn't be so sure of it.

DAISY: [*With a sudden change of tone.*] Why not? I was sure of your love. And God knows I was in love with you.

> [GEORGE *makes a gesture of dismay. He is taken aback for a moment, but he quickly recovers.*

GEORGE: You don't know what sort of a man Harry is. He's not like the fellows you've been used to. He's never knocked around as most of us do. He's always been as straight as a die.

DAISY: I know.

GEORGE: Have mercy on him. Even if there were nothing else against you, he's not the sort of chap for you to marry. He's awfully English.

DAISY: If he doesn't mind marrying a Eurasian, I really don't see what business it is of yours.

GEORGE: But you know very well that that isn't the only thing against you.

DAISY: I haven't an idea what you mean.

GEORGE: Haven't you? You forget the war. When we heard there was a very pretty young woman, apparently with plenty of money, living at the Hong Kong Hotel on very familiar terms with a lot of naval fellows, it became our business to make inquiries. I think I know everything there is against you.

DAISY: Have you any right to make use of information you've acquired officially?

GEORGE: Don't be a fool, Daisy.

DAISY: [*Passionately.*] Tell him then. You'll break his heart. You'll make him utterly wretched. But he'll marry me all the same. When a man's as much in love as he is he'll forgive everything.

GEORGE: I think it's horrible. If you loved him you couldn't marry him. It's heartless.

DAISY: [*Violently.*] How dare you say that. You . . . you. You know what I am. Yes, it's all true. I don't know what you know, but it can't be worse than the truth. And whose fault is it? Yours. If I'm rotten, it's you who made me rotten.

GEORGE: I? No. You've got no right to say that. It's cruel. It's infamous.

DAISY: I've touched you at last, have I? Because you know it's true. Don't you remember when I first came to Chung-King? I was seventeen. My father had sent me to England to school when I was seven. I never saw him for ten years. And at last he wrote and said I was to come back to China. You came and met me on the boat and told me my father had had a stroke and was dead. You took me to the Presbyterian mission.

GEORGE: That was my job. I was awfully sorry for you.

DAISY: And then in a day or two you came and told me that my father hadn't left anything and what there was went to his relations in England.

GEORGE: Naturally he didn't expect to die.

DAISY: [*Passionately.*] If he was going to leave me like that, why didn't he let me stay with my Chinese mother? Why did he bring me up like a lady? Oh, it was cruel.

GEORGE: Yes. It was unpardonable.

DAISY: I was so lonely and so frightened. You seemed to be sorry for me. You were the only person who was really kind to me. You were practically the first man I'd known. I loved you. I thought you loved me. Oh, say that you loved me then, George.

GEORGE: You know I did.

DAISY: I was very innocent in those days. I thought that when two people loved one another they married. I wasn't a Eurasian then, George. I was like any other English girl. If you'd married me I shouldn't be what I am now. But they took you away from me. You never even said good-bye to me. You wrote and told me you'd been transferred to Canton.

GEORGE: I couldn't say good-bye to you, Daisy. They said that if I married you I'd have to leave the service. I was absolutely penniless. They dinned it into my ears that if a white man marries a Eurasian he's done for. I wouldn't listen to them, but in my heart I knew it was true.

DAISY: I don't blame you. You wanted to get on, and you have, haven't you? You're Assistant Chinese Secretary already, and Harry says you'll be Minister before you've done. It seems rather hard that I should have had to pay the price.

GEORGE: Daisy, you'll never know what anguish I suffered. I can't expect you to care. It's very natural if you hate me. I was ambitious. I didn't want to be a failure. I knew that it was madness to marry you. I had to kill my love. I couldn't. It was stronger than I was. At last I couldn't help myself. I made up my mind to chuck everything and take the consequences. I was just starting for Chung-King when I heard you were living in Shanghai with a rich Chinaman.

[DAISY *gives a little moan. There is a silence.*

DAISY: They hated me at the mission. They found fault with me from morning till night. They blamed me because you wanted to marry me, and they treated me as if I was a designing cat. When you went away they heaved a sigh of relief. Then they started to convert me. They thought I'd better become a school teacher. They hated me because I was seventeen. They hated me because I was pretty. Oh, the brutes. They killed all the religion I'd got. There was only one person who seemed to care if I was alive or dead. That was my mother. Oh, I was so ashamed the first time I saw her. At school in England I'd told them so often that she was a Chinese princess that I almost believed it myself. She looked like an amah. My mother was a dirty little ugly Chinawoman. I'd forgotten all my Chinese and I had to talk to her in English. She asked me if I'd like to go to Shanghai with her. I was ready to do anything in the world to get away from the mission, and I thought in Shanghai I shouldn't be so far away from you. They didn't want me to go, but they couldn't keep me against my will. When we got to Shanghai she sold me to Lee Tai Cheng for two thousand dollars.

GEORGE: How terrible!

DAISY: I've never had a chance. O George, isn't it possible for a woman to turn over a new leaf? You say that Harry's good and kind. Don't you see what that means to me? Because he'll think me good I shall be good. After all, he couldn't have fallen in love with me if I'd been entirely worthless. I hate the life I've led. I want to go straight. I swear I'll make him a good wife. O George, if you ever loved me have pity on me. If Harry doesn't marry me I'm done.

GEORGE: How can a marriage be happy that's founded on a tissue of lies?

DAISY: I've never told Harry a single lie.

GEORGE: You told him you hadn't been happily married.

DAISY: That wasn't a lie.

GEORGE: You haven't been married at all.

DAISY: [*With a roguish look.*] Well, then, I haven't been happily married, have I?

GEORGE: Who was this fellow Rathbone?

DAISY: He was an American in business at Singapore. I met him in Shanghai. I hated Lee. Rathbone asked me to go to Singapore with him, and I went. I lived with him for four years.

GEORGE: Then you went back to Lee Tai Cheng.

DAISY: Rathbone died. There was nothing else to do. My mother was always nagging me to go back to him. He's rich and she makes a good thing out of it.

GEORGE: I thought she was dead.

DAISY: No. I told Harry she was because I thought it would make it easier for him.

GEORGE: She isn't with you now, is she?

DAISY: No, she lives at Ichang. She doesn't bother me as long as I send her something every month.

GEORGE: Why did you tell Harry that you were twenty-two? It's ten years since you came to China, and you were seventeen then.

DAISY: [*With a twinkle in her eye.*] Any woman of my age will tell you that seventeen and ten are twenty-two.

[GEORGE *does not smile. With frowning brow he walks up and down.*

GEORGE: Oh, I wish to God I knew nothing about you. I can't bring myself to tell him, and yet how can I let him marry you in absolute ignorance? O Daisy, for your sake as well as for his I beseech you to tell him the whole truth and let him decide for himself.

DAISY: And break his heart? There's not a missionary who believes in God as he believes in me. If he loses his trust in me he loses everything. Tell him if you think you must, if you have no pity, if you have no regret for all the shame and misery you brought on me, you, you, you— but if you do, I swear, I swear to God that I shall kill myself. I won't go back to that hateful life.

[*He looks at her earnestly for a moment.*

GEORGE: I don't know if I'm doing right or wrong. I shall tell him nothing.

> [DAISY *gives a deep sigh of relief.* HARRY *comes in.*

HARRY: I say, I'm awfully sorry to have been so long. I couldn't get the old blighter to go.

DAISY: [*With complete self-control.*] If I say you've been an age, it'll look as though Mr. Conway had been boring me.

HARRY: I hope you've made friends.

DAISY: [*To* GEORGE.] Have we?

GEORGE: I hope so. But now I think I must bolt. I have a long Chinese document to translate. [*Holding out his hand to* DAISY.] I hope you'll both be very happy.

DAISY: I think I'm going to like you.

GEORGE: Good-bye, Harry, old man.

HARRY: I shall see you later on in the club, shan't I?

GEORGE: If I can get through my work.

> [*He goes out.*

HARRY: What have you and George been talking about?

DAISY: We discussed the house. It'll be great fun buying things for it.

HARRY: I could have killed that old Chink for keeping me so long. I grudge every minute that I spend away from you.

DAISY: It's nice to be loved.

HARRY: You do love me a little, don't you?

DAISY: A little more than a little, my lamb.

HARRY: I wish I were more worth your while. You've made me feel so dissatisfied with myself. I'm such a rotter.

DAISY: You're not going to disagree with me already.

HARRY: What about?

DAISY: About you. I think you're a perfect duck.

> [*The* AMAH *appears.*

HARRY: Hulloa, who's this?

DAISY: Oh, it's my amah.

HARRY: I didn't recognise her for a moment.

DAISY: She doesn't approve of my being alone with strange gentlemen. She looks after me as if I was a child of ten.

AMAH: Velly late, Missy Daisy. Time you come along.

HARRY: Oh, nonsense.

DAISY: She wants me to go and be fitted. She never lets me go out in Peking alone.

HARRY: She's quite right.

DAISY: Amah, come and be introduced to the gentleman. He's going to be your master now.

AMAH: [*Smiling, with little nods.*] Velly nice gentleman. You keepy Missy Daisy old amah—yes? Velly good amah—yes?

DAISY: She's been with me ever since I was a child.

HARRY: Of course we'll keep her. She was with you when you were in Singapore?

DAISY: [*With a little sigh.*] Yes, I don't know what I should have done without her sometimes.

HARRY: O Daisy, I do want to make you forget all the unhappiness you have suffered.

> [*He takes her in his arms and kisses her on the lips. The* AMAH *chuckles to herself silently.*

END OF SCENE II

SCENE III

SCENE: *The Temple of Fidelity and Virtuous Inclination. The courtyard is shown. At the back is the sanctuary in which is seen the altar table; on this are two large vases in each of which are seven lotus flowers, gilt but discoloured by incense, and in the middle there is a sand-box in which are burning joss-sticks; behind is the image of Buddha. The sanctuary can be closed by huge doors. These are now open. A flight of steps leads up to it.*

A service is finishing. The monks are seen on each side of the altar kneeling in two rows. They are clad in grey gowns and their heads are shaven. They sing the invocation to Buddha, repeating the same words over and over again in a monotonous chant. DAISY *stands outside the sanctuary door, on the steps, listlessly. The* AMAH *is squatting by her side. Now the service finishes; the monks form a procession and two by two, still singing, come down the steps and go out. A tiny acolyte blows out the oil lamps and with an effort shuts the temple doors.*

DAISY *comes down the steps and sits on one of the lower ones. She is dreadfully bored.*

AMAH: What is the matter with my pletty one?

DAISY: What should be the matter?

AMAH: [*With a snigger.*] Hi yah. Old Amah got velly good eyes in her head.

DAISY: [*As though talking to herself.*] I've got a husband who adores me and a nice house to live in. I've got a position and as much money as I want. I'm safe. I'm respectable. I ought to be happy.

AMAH: I say, Harry no good, what for you wanchee marry? You say, I wanchee marry, I wanchee marry. Well, you married. What you wanchee now?

DAISY: They say life is short. Good God, how long the days are.

AMAH: You wanchee pony—Harry give you pony. You wanchee jade ring—Harry give you jade ring. You wanchee sable coat—Harry give you sable coat. Why you not happy?

DAISY: I never said I wasn't happy.

AMAH: Hi yah.

DAISY: If you laugh like that I'll kill you.

AMAH: You no kill old Amah. You wanchee old Amah. I got something velly pletty for my little Daisy flower.

DAISY: Don't be an old fool. I'm not a child any more. [*Desperately.*] I'm growing older, older, older. And every day is just like every other day. I might as well be dead.

AMAH: Look this pletty present old Amah have got.

[*She takes a jade necklace out of her sleeve and puts it, smiling, into* DAISY'S *hand.*

DAISY: [*With sudden vivacity.*] Oh, what a lovely chain. It's beautiful jade. How much do they want for it?

AMAH: It's a present for my little Daisy.

DAISY: For me? It must have cost five hundred dollars. Who is it from?

AMAH: To-day is my little Daisy's wedding-day. She have married one year. Perhaps old Amah wanchee give her little flower present.

DAISY: You! Have you ever given me anything but a beating?

AMAH: Lee Tai Cheng pay me necklace and say you give to Daisy.

DAISY: You old hag.

[*She flings the necklace away violently,*

AMAH: You silly. Worth plenty money. You no wanchee, I sell rich Amelican.

> [*She is just going after the necklace, when* DAISY *catches her violently by the arm.*

DAISY: How dare you? How dare you? I told you that you were never to let Lee Tai speak to you again.

AMAH: You very angry, Daisy. You very angry before, but you go back to Lee Tai; he think maybe you go back again.

DAISY: Tell him that I loathe the sight of him. Tell him that if I were starving I wouldn't take a penny from him. Tell him that if he dares to come round here I'll have him beaten till he screams.

AMAH: Hi yah.

DAISY: And you leave me alone, will you? Harry hates you. I've only got to say a word and he'll kick you out in five minutes.

AMAH: What would my little Daisy do without old Amah, hi yah? What for you no talkee true? You think old Amah no got eyes? [*With a cunning, arch look.*] I got something make you velly glad.

> [*She takes a note out of her sleeve.*

DAISY: What's that?

AMAH: I got letter.

DAISY: [*Snatching it from her.*] Give it me. How dare you hide it?

AMAH: Have come when you with Harry. I think maybe you no wanchee read when Harry there. [DAISY *tears it open.*] What he say?

DAISY: [*Reading.*] "I'm awfully sorry I can't dine with you on Thursday, but I'm engaged. I've just remembered it's your wedding day and I'll look in for a minute. Ask Harry if he'd like to ride with me."

AMAH: Is that all?

DAISY: "Yours ever. George Conway."

AMAH: You love him very much, George Conway.

DAISY: [*Taking no notice of her, passionately.*] At last. I haven't seen him for ten days. Ten mortal days. Oh, I want him. I want him.

AMAH: Why you not talkee old Amah?

DAISY: [*Desperately.*] I can't help myself. Oh, I love him so. What shall I do? I can't live without him. If you don't want me to die make him love me.

AMAH: You see, you wanchee old Amah.

DAISY: Oh, I'm so unhappy. I think I shall go mad.

AMAH: Sh, sh! Maybe he love you too.

DAISY: Never. He hates me. Why does he avoid me? He never comes here. At first he was always looking in. He used to come out and dine two or three days a week. What have I done to him? He only comes now because he does not want to offend Harry. Harry, Harry, what do I care for Harry?

AMAH: Sh! Don't let him see. Give Amah the letter.

> [*She snatches it from* DAISY *and hides it in her dress just as* HARRY *comes in.* DAISY *pulls herself together.*]

HARRY: I say, Daisy, I've just had the ponies saddled. Put on your habit and let's go for a ride.

DAISY: I've got a headache.

HARRY: Oh, my poor child. Why don't you lie down?

DAISY: I thought I was better in the air. But there's no reason why you shouldn't ride.

HARRY: Oh no, I won't ride without you.

DAISY: Why on earth not? It'll do you good. You know when my head's bad I only want to be left alone. Your pony wants exercising.

HARRY: The boy can do that.

DAISY: [*Trying to conceal her growing exasperation.*] Please do as I ask. I'd rather you went.

HARRY: [*Laughing.*] Of course, if you're so anxious to get rid of me. . . .

DAISY: [*Smiling.*] I can't bear that you should be done out of your ride. If you won't go alone you'll just force me to come with you.

HARRY: I'll go. Give me a kiss before I do. [*She puts up her lips to his.*] I'm almost ashamed of myself, I'm just as madly in love with you as the day we were married.

DAISY: You are a dear. Have a nice ride, and when you come back I shall be all right.

HARRY: That's ripping. I shan't be very long.

> [*He goes out. The lightness, the smile with which she has spoken to* HARRY *disappear as he goes, and she looks worried and anxious.*

DAISY: Supposing they meet?

AMAH: No can. Harry go out back way.

DAISY: Yes, I suppose he will. I wish he'd be quick. [*Violently.*] I *must* see George.

AMAH: [*Picking up the necklace.*] Velly pletty necklace. You silly girl. Why you no take?

DAISY: Oh, damn, why can't you leave me alone? [*Listening.*] What on earth is Harry doing? I thought the pony was saddled.

AMAH: [*Looking at the necklace.*] What shall I do with this?

DAISY: Throw it in the dustbin.

AMAH: Lee Tai no likee that very much.

DAISY: [*Hearing the sound of the pony, with a sigh of relief.*] He's gone. Now I'm safe. Where's my bag? [*She takes a little mirror out of it and looks at herself.*] I look perfectly hideous.

AMAH: Don't be silly. You velly pletty girl.

DAISY: [*Her ears all alert.*] There's someone riding along.

AMAH: That not pony. That Peking cart.

DAISY: You old fool, I tell you it's a pony. At last. Oh, my heart's beating so. . . . It's stopping at the gate. It's George. Oh, I love him. I love him. [*To the* AMAH, *stamping her foot.*] What are you waiting for? I don't want you here now; and don't listen, d'you hear? Get out, get out!

AMAH: All light. My go away.

> [*The* AMAH *slinks away.* DAISY *stands waiting for* GEORGE, *holding her hands to her heart as though to stop the anguish of its beating. She makes a great effort at self-control as* GEORGE *enters. He is in riding kit. He has a bunch of orchids in his hand.*

GEORGE: Hulloa, what are you doing here?

DAISY: I was tired of sitting in the drawing-room.

GEORGE: I remembered it was your wedding-day. I've brought you a few flowers.

> [*She takes them with both hands.*

DAISY: Thank you. That *is* kind of you.

GEORGE: [*Gravely.*] I hope you'll always be very happy. I hope you'll allow me to say how grateful I am that you've given Harry so much happiness.

DAISY: You're very solemn. One would almost think you'd prepared that pretty speech beforehand.

GEORGE: [*Trying to take it lightly.*] I'm sorry if it didn't sound natural. I can promise you it was sincere.

DAISY: Shall we sit down?

GEORGE: I think we ought to go for our ride while the light lasts. I'll come in and have a drink on the way back.

DAISY: Harry's out.

GEORGE: Is he? I sent you a note this morning. I said I

couldn't dine on Thursday and I'd come and fetch Harry for a ride this afternoon.

DAISY: I didn't tell him.

GEORGE: No?

DAISY: I don't see you very often nowadays.

GEORGE: There's an awful lot of work to do just now. They lead me a dog's life at the Legation.

DAISY: Even at night? At first you used to come and dine with us two or three nights a week.

GEORGE: I can't always be sponging on you. It's positively indecent.

DAISY: We don't know many people. It's not always very lively here. I should have thought if you didn't care to come for my sake you'd have come for Harry's.

GEORGE: I come whenever you ask me.

DAISY: You haven't been here for a month.

GEORGE: It just happens that the last two or three times you've asked me to dine I've been engaged.

DAISY: [Her voice breaking.] You promised that we'd be friends. What have I done to turn you against me?

GEORGE: [His armour pierced by the emotion in her voice.] Oh, Daisy, don't speak like that.

DAISY: I've tried to do everything I could to please you. If there's anything I do that you don't like, won't you tell me? I promise you I won't do it.

GEORGE: Oh, my dear child, you make me feel such an awful beast.

DAISY: Is it the past that you can't forget?

GEORGE: Good heavens, no! What do I care about the past?

DAISY: I have so few friends. I'm so awfully fond of you, George.

GEORGE: I don't think I've given you much cause to be that.

DAISY: There must be some reason why you won't ever come near me. Why won't you tell me?

GEORGE: Oh, it's absurd, you're making a mountain out of a molehill.

DAISY: You used to be so jolly, and we used to laugh together. I looked forward so much to your coming here. What has changed you?

GEORGE: Nothing has changed me.

DAISY: [*With a passion of despair.*] Oh, I might as well batter my head against a brick wall. How can you be so unkind to me?

GEORGE: For God's sake. . . . [*He stops.*] Heaven knows, I don't want to be unkind to you.

DAISY: Then why do you treat me as an outcast? Oh, it's cruel, cruel.

> [GEORGE *is excessively distressed. He walks up and down, frowning. He cannot bear to look at* DAISY *and he speaks with hesitation.*

GEORGE: You'll think me an awful rotter, Daisy, but you can't think me more of a rotter than I think myself. I don't know how to say it. It seems such an awful thing to say. I'm so ashamed of myself. I don't suppose two men have ever been greater pals than Harry and I. He's married to you and he's awfully in love with you. And I think you're in love with him. I was only twenty-three when I—first knew you. It's an awful long time ago, isn't it? There are some wounds that never quite heal, you know. Oh, my God, don't you understand? [*His embarrassment, the distraction of his tone, and the way the halting words fall unwillingly from his lips have betrayed the truth to* DAISY. *She does not speak, she does not stir, she looks at him with great shining eyes. She hardly dares to breathe.*] If ever you wanted revenge on me you've got it now. You must see that it's better that I shouldn't come here too often. Forgive me—Good-bye.

> [*He hurries away with averted face.* DAISY *stands motionless, erect; she is almost transfigured. She draws a long breath.*

DAISY: O God! He loves me.

> [*She takes the orchids he has brought her and crushes them to her heart. The* AMAH *appears.*

AMAH: You wanchee buy Manchu dress, Daisy?

DAISY: Go away.

AMAH: Velly cheap. You look see. No likee, no buy.

DAISY: [*Impatiently.*] I'm sick of curio-dealers.

AMAH: Velly pletty Manchu dress.

> [*She draws aside a little and allows a man with a large bundle wrapped up in a blue cotton cloth to come in. He is a Chinese. He is dressed in a long black robe and a round black cap. It is* LEE TAI CHENG. *He is big and rather stout. From his smooth and yellow face his black eyes gleam craftily. He lays his bundle on the ground and unties it, showing a pile of gorgeous Manchu dresses.* DAISY *has taken no notice of him. Suddenly she sees that a man, with his back turned to her, is there.*

DAISY: [*To the* AMAH.] I told you I wouldn't see the man. Send him away at once.

LEE TAI: [*Turning round, with a sly smile.*] You look see. No likee, no buy.

DAISY: [*With a start of surprise and dismay.*] Lee!

LEE TAI: [*Coming forward coolly.*] Good afternoon, Daisy.

DAISY: [*Recovering herself.*] It's lucky for you I'm in a good temper or I'd have you thrown out by the boys. What have you brought this junk for?

LEE TAI: A curio-dealer can come and go and no one wonders.

AMAH: Lee Tai velly clever man.

DAISY: Give me that chain. [*The* AMAH *takes it out of her sleeve and gives it to her.* DAISY *flings it contemptuously at* LEE TAI's *feet.*] Take it. Pack up your things and go. If you ever dare to show your face here again I'll tell my husband.

LEE TAI: [*With a chuckle.*] What will you tell him? Don't you be a silly girl, Daisy.

DAISY: What do you want?

LEE TAI: [*Coolly.*] You.

DAISY: Don't you know that I loathe you? You disgust me.

LEE TAI: What do I care? Perhaps if you loved me I shouldn't want you. Your hatred is like a sharp and bitter sauce that tickles my appetite.

DAISY: You beast.

LEE TAI: I like the horror that makes your body tremble when I hold you in my arms. And sometimes the horror turns on a sudden into a wild tempest of passion.

DAISY: You liar.

LEE TAI: Leave this stupid white man. What is he to you?

DAISY: He is my husband.

LEE TAI: It is a year to-day since you were married. What has marriage done for you? You thought when you married a white man you'd become a white woman. Do you think they can look at you and forget? How many white women do you know? How many friends have you got? You're a prisoner. I'll take you to Singapore or Calcutta. Don't you want to amuse yourself? Do you want to go to Europe? I'll take you to Paris. I'll give you more money to spend in a week than your husband earns in a year.

DAISY: I'm very comfortable in Peking, thank you.

LEE TAI: [*Snapping his fingers.*] You don't care that for your husband. He loves you. You despise him. Don't you wish with all your heart that you hadn't married him?

AMAH: He velly silly white man. He no likee Daisy's old Amah. Maybe one day he b'long sick. Daisy cry velly much if he die?

DAISY: [*Impatiently.*] Don't be such a fool.

AMAH: Maybe one day he drink whisky soda. Oh, velly ill, velly ill. What's the matter with me? No sabe. No can stand. Doctor no sabe. Then die. Hi yah.

DAISY: You silly old woman. Harry's not a Chinaman and he wouldn't call in a Chinese doctor.

LEE TAI: [*With a smile.*] China is a very old and a highly civilised country, Daisy. When anyone is in your way it's not very difficult to get rid of him.

DAISY: [*Scornfully.*] And do you think I'd let poor Harry be murdered so that I might be free to listen to your generous proposals? You must think I'm a fool if you expect me to risk my neck for that.

LEE TAI: You don't take *any* risk, Daisy. You know nothing.

AMAH: Lee Tai velly clever man, Daisy.

DAISY: I thought so once. Lee Tai, you're a damned fool. Get out.

LEE TAI: Freedom is a very good thing, Daisy.

DAISY: What should I do with it?

LEE TAI: Wouldn't you like to be free now? [*She looks at him sharply. She wonders if it can possibly be that he suspects her passion for* GEORGE CONWAY. *He meets her glance steadily.*] One day Sen Shi Ming was sitting with his wife looking at a Tang bronze that he had just bought when he heard someone in the street crying for help. Sen Shi was a very brave man and he snatched up a revolver and ran out. Sen Shi forgot that he had cheated his brother out of a house in Hatamen Street or he would have been more prudent. Sen Shi was found by the watchman an hour later with a dagger in his heart. Who killed cock-robin?

AMAH: Hi yah. Sen Shi velly silly man.

LEE TAI: His brother knew that. They had grown up together. If I heard cries for help outside my house late in the night, I should ask myself who had a grudge against me and I should make sure the door was bolted. But white men are very brave. White men don't know the Chinese customs. Would you be very sorry if an accident happened to your charming husband?

DAISY: I wonder what you take me for?

LEE TAI: Why do you pretend to me, Daisy? Do you think I don't know you?

DAISY: The door is a little on the left of you, Lee Tai. Would you give yourself the trouble of walking through it.

LEE TAI: [*With a smile.*] I go, but I come back. Perhaps you'll change your mind.

[*He ties up his bundle and is about to go.* HARRY *enters.*

DAISY: O Harry, you're back very soon.

HARRY: Yes, the pony went lame. Fortunately I hadn't gone far before I noticed it. Who's this?

DAISY: It's a curio-dealer. He has nothing I want. I was just sending him away.

[LEE TAI *takes up his bundle and goes out.*

HARRY: [*Noticing the orchids.*] Someone been sending you flowers?

DAISY: George.

HARRY: Rather nice of him. [*To the* AMAH.] Run along, Amah, I want to talk to missy.

AMAH: All light.

HARRY: And don't let me catch you listening round the corner.

AMAH: My no listen. What for I listen?

HARRY: Run along—chop-chop.

AMAH: Can do.

[She goes out.

HARRY: [*With a laugh.*] I couldn't give you a greater proof of my affection than consenting to have that old woman around all the time.

DAISY: I don't know why you dislike her. She's devoted to me.

HARRY: That's the only reason I put up with her. She gives me the creeps. I have the impression that she watches every movement I make.

DAISY: Oh, what nonsense.

HARRY: And I've caught her eavesdropping.

DAISY: Was it Amah that you wanted to talk to me about?

HARRY: No, I've got something to tell you. How would you like to leave Peking?

DAISY: [*With a start, suddenly off her guard.*] Not at all.

HARRY: I'm afraid it's awfully dull for you here, darling.

DAISY: I don't find it so.

HARRY: You're so dear and sweet. Are you sure you don't say that on my account?

DAISY: I'm very fond of Peking.

HARRY: We've been married a year now. I don't want to hurt your feelings, darling, but it's no good beating about the bush, and I think it's better to be frank.

DAISY: Surely you can say anything you like to me without hesitation.

HARRY: Things have been a little awkward in a way. The women I used to know before we married left cards on you——

DAISY: Having taken the precaution to discover that I should be out.

HARRY: And you returned those cards and that was the end of it. I asked George what he thought about my taking

you to the club to play tennis, and he said he thought
we'd better not risk it. The result is that you don't
know a soul.

DAISY: Have I ever complained?

HARRY: You've been most awfully decent about it, but I
hate to think of your spending day after day entirely
by yourself. It can't be good for you to be so much
alone.

DAISY: I might have known Mrs. Chuan. She's a white
woman.

HARRY: Oh, my dear, she was—Heaven knows what she
was. She's married to a Chinaman. It's horrible. She's
outside the pale.

DAISY: And there's Bertha Raymond. She's very nice even
though she is a Eurasian.

HARRY: I'm sure she's very nice, but we couldn't very well
have the Raymonds here and refuse to go to them. Her
brother is one of the clerks in my office. I don't want to
seem an awful snob . . .

DAISY: You needn't hesitate to say anything about the
Eurasians. You can't hate and despise them more than
I do.

HARRY: I don't hate and despise them. I think that's odious.
But sometimes they're not very tactful. I don't know
that I much want one of my clerks to come and slap me
on the back in the office and call me "old chap."

DAISY: Of course not.

HARRY: The fact is we've been trying to do an impossible
thing. It's no good kicking against the pricks. What
with the Legations and one thing and another Peking's
hopeless. We'd far better clear out.

DAISY: But if I don't mind, why should you?

HARRY: Well, it's not very nice for me either. It's for my
sake just as much as for yours that I'd be glad to go

F

elsewhere. Of course everybody at the club knows I'm married. Some of them ignore it altogether. I don't mind that so much. Some of them ask after you with an exaggerated cordiality which is rather offensive. And every now and then some fool begins to slang the Eurasians and everybody kicks him under the table. Then he remembers about me and goes scarlet. By God, it's hell.

DAISY: [*Sulkily.*] I don't want to leave Peking. I'm very happy here.

HARRY: Well, darling, I've applied for a transfer.

DAISY: [*With sudden indignation.*] Without saying a word to me?

HARRY: I thought you'd be glad. I didn't want to say anything till it was settled.

DAISY: Do you think I am a child to have everything arranged for me without a word? [*Trying to control herself.*] After all, you'd never see George. Surely you don't want to lose sight of your only real friend.

HARRY: I've talked it over with George and he thinks it's the best thing to do.

DAISY: Did he advise you to go?

HARRY: Strongly.

DAISY: [*Violently.*] I won't do it. I won't leave Peking.

HARRY: Why should his advice make the difference?

DAISY: Why? [*She is confused for a moment, but quickly recovers herself.*] I won't let George Conway—or anybody else— decide where I'm to go.

HARRY: Don't be unreasonable, darling.

DAISY: I won't go. I tell you I won't go.

HARRY: Well, I'm afraid you must now. It's all settled. The transfer is decided.

DAISY: [*Bursting into tears.*] O Harry, don't take me away from here. I can't bear it. I want to stay here.

HARRY: O darling, how can you be so silly? You'll have a much better time at one of the outports. You see, there are so few white people there that they can't afford to put on frills. They'll be jolly glad to know us both. We shall lead a normal life and be like everybody else.

DAISY: [*Sulkily.*] Where do you want to go?

HARRY: I've been put in charge of our place at Chung-King.

DAISY: [*Starting up with a cry.*] Chung-King. Of course you'd choose Chung-King.

HARRY: Why, what's wrong with it? Do you know it?

DAISY: No—oh, what am I talking about? I'm all confused. Yes, I was there once when I was a girl. It's a hateful place.

HARRY: Oh, nonsense. The consul's got a charming wife, and there are an awfully nice lot of people there.

DAISY: [*Distracted.*] Oh, what shall I do? I'm so unhappy. If you cared for me at all you wouldn't treat me so cruelly. You're ashamed of me. You want to hide me. Why should I bury myself in a hole two thousand miles up the river? I won't go. I won't go. I won't go.

> [*She bursts into a storm of hysterical weeping.*

HARRY: [*Trying to take her in his arms.*] O Daisy, for God's sake don't cry. You know I'm not ashamed of you. I love you more than ever. I love you with all my heart.

DAISY: [*Drawing away from him.*] Don't touch me. Leave me alone. I hate you.

HARRY: Don't say that, Daisy. It hurts me frightfully.

DAISY: Oh, go away, go away.

HARRY: [*Seeking to reason with her.*] I can't leave you like this.

DAISY: Go, go, go, go, go! I don't want to see you. O God, what shall I do?

[*She flings herself down on the steps, weeping hysterically.* HARRY, *much distressed, looks at her in perplexity. The* AMAH *comes in.*

AMAH: You make missy cly. You velly bad man.

HARRY: What the devil do you want?

AMAH: [*Going up to* DAISY *and stroking her head.*] What thing he say to my poor little flower? Maskee. He belong velly bad man.

HARRY: Shut up, you old . . . I won't have you talk like that. I've put up with a good deal from you, but if you try to make mischief between Daisy and me, by God, I'll throw you out into the street with my own hands.

AMAH: What thing you do my Daisy? You no cly, Daisy.

HARRY: Darling, don't be unreasonable.

DAISY: Go away, don't come near me. I hate you.

HARRY: How *can* you say things so unkind?

DAISY: Send him away.

[*She begins to sob again more violently.*

AMAH: You go away. You no can see she no wanchee you. You come back bimeby. My sabe how talk to little flower.

[HARRY *hesitates for a moment. He is harassed by the scene. Then he makes up his mind the best thing is to leave* DAISY *with the* AMAH. *He goes out.* DAISY *raises her head cautiously.*

DAISY: Has he gone?

AMAH: Yes. He go drink whisky soda.

DAISY: Do you know what he wants?

AMAH: What for he tell me no listen? So fashion I sabe he say something I wanchee hear. He wanchee you leave Peking.

DAISY: I won't go.

AMAH: Harry velly silly man. He alla same pig. You pull thisa way, he pull thata way. If Harry say you go way from Peking—you go.

DAISY: Never, never, never!

AMAH: You go away from Peking you never see George any more.

DAISY: I should die. Oh, I want him. I want him to love me. I want him to hurt me. I want . . .

[*In her passion she has dug her hands hard into the* AMAH.

AMAH: [*Pushing away* DAISY's *hands.*] Oh!

DAISY: He loves me. That's the only thing that matters. All the rest . . .

AMAH: Harry wanchee you go Chung-King. Missionary ladies like see you again, Daisy. Maybe they ask you how you like living along Lee Tai Cheng. Maybe somebody tell Harry.

DAISY: The fool. Of all the places in China he must hit upon Chung-King.

AMAH: You know Harry. If he say go Chung-King, he go. You cly, he velly solly, he all same go.

DAISY: Oh, I know his obstinacy. When he's once made up his mind—[*Contemptuously.*]—he prides himself on his firmness. Oh, what shall I do?

AMAH: I think more better something happen to Harry.

DAISY: No, no, no.

AMAH: What you flightened for? You no do anything. I tell Lee Tai more better something happen to Harry. I say you not velly solly if Harry die.

DAISY: [*Putting her hands over her ears.*] Be quiet. I won't listen to you.

AMAH: [*Roughly tearing her hands away.*] Don't you be such a big fool, Daisy. You go to Chung-King and Harry know everything. Maybe he kill you.

DAISY: What do I care?

AMAH: You go to Chung-King, you never see George no more. George, he love my little Daisy. When Harry gone—George, he come say . . .

DAISY: Oh, don't tempt me, it's horrible.

AMAH: He put his arms round you and you feel such a little small thing, you hear his heart beat quick, quick against your heart. And he throw back your head and he kiss you. And you think you die, little flower.

DAISY: Oh, I love him, I love him.

AMAH: Hi yah.

DAISY: [*Thinking of the scene with* GEORGE.] He would hardly look at me and his hands were trembling. He was as white as a sheet.

AMAH: [*Persuasively.*] I tell you, Daisy. You no say yes, you no say no. I ask Buddha.

DAISY: [*Frightened.*] What for?

AMAH: If Buddha say yes, I talk with Lee Tai; if Buddha say no, I do nothing. Then you go to Chung-King and you never see George any more.

> [*The* AMAH *goes up the temple steps and flings open the great doors.* DAISY *watches her with an agony of horror, expectation, and dread. The* AMAH *lights some joss-sticks on the altar, and strikes a deeptoned gong.* HARRY *comes in, followed by* LEE TAI *with his bundle.*

HARRY: [*Anxious to make his peace.*] Daisy, I found this fellow hanging about in the courtyard. I thought I'd like to buy you a Manchu dress that he's got.

DAISY: [*After a moment's reflection, with a change of tone.*] That's very nice of you, Harry.

HARRY: It's a real beauty. You'll look stunning in it.

LEE TAI: [*Showing the dress, speaking in pidgin-English.*] Firs class dless. He belong Manchu plincess. Manchus no got money. No got money, no can chow. Manchus sell velly cheap. You take it, Missy.

> [DAISY *and* LEE TAI *exchange glances.* DAISY *is grave and tragic, whereas* LEE TAI *has an ironical glint in his eyes. Meanwhile the* AMAH *has been bowing before the altar. She goes down on her knees and knocks her head on the ground.*

HARRY: What in God's name is Amah doing?

DAISY: She's asking Buddha a question?

HARRY: What question?

DAISY: [*With the shadow of a smile.*] How should I know?

HARRY: What's the idea?

DAISY: Haven't you ever seen the Chinese do it? You see those pieces of wood she's holding in her hands. She's holding them out to the Buddha so that he may see them, and she's telling him that he must answer the question. [*Meanwhile the* AMAH, *muttering in a low tone, is seen doing what* DAISY *describes.*] The Buddha smells the incense of the burning joss-sticks, and he's pleased, and he listens to what she says.

HARRY: [*Smiling.*] Don't be so absurd, Daisy. One might almost think you believed all this nonsense. Why, you're quite pale.

DAISY: Then she gets up. The pieces of wood are flat on one side and round on the other. She'll lift them above her head and she'll drop them in front of the Buddha. If they fall with the round side uppermost it means yes. [*DAISY has been growing more and more excited as the ceremony proceeds. Now the* AMAH *steps back a little and she raises her arms.* DAISY *gives a shriek and starts to run forward.*] No, no. Stop!

HARRY: [*Instinctively seizing her arms.*] Daisy.

> [*At the same moment the* AMAH *has let the pieces of wood fall. She looks at them for an instant and then turns round.*

AMAH: Buddha say can do.

DAISY: [*To* HARRY.] Why did you stop me?

HARRY: Daisy, how can you be so superstitious? What is the result?

DAISY: Amah asked Buddha a question and the answer is yes. [*She puts her hand to her heart for an instant, then, looking at* HARRY, *she smiles.*] I'm sorry I was silly and unreasonable just now, Harry.

END OF SCENE III

SCENE IV

SCENE: *The sitting-room in the Andersons' apartments. At the back are two double doors. The lower part of them is solid, but above they are cut in an intricate trellis. The ceiling is raftered, painted red and decorated with dim gold dragons; the walls are whitewashed. On them hang Chinese pictures on rolls. Between the doors is a little image of the domestic god and under it a tiny oil lamp is burning. The furniture is partly Chinese and partly European. There is an English writing-table, but the occasional tables, richly carved, are Chinese. There is a Chinese pallet-bed, covered with bamboo matting, and there is an English Chesterfield. There are a couple of Philippine rattan chairs and one or two of Cantonese blackwood. On the floor is a Chinese carpet. A Ming tile here and there gives a vivid note of colour. It is a summer night and the doors are wide open. Through them you see one of the courtyards of the temple.*

The AMAH *is seated in one of the blackwood chairs by the side of a table. She has her water-pipe. She puts a pinch of tobacco in, and then going to the lamp under the image lights a taper. Crossing back, she seats herself again, and lights her pipe. She smokes quietly.*

DAISY *comes in. She wears an evening dress somewhat too splendid for dinner with only her husband and a friend.*

AMAH: B.A.T. fellow, when he go?

DAISY: You know his name. Why don't you call him by it? I think he's going almost at once.

AMAH: What for he go so soon?

DAISY: That's his business, isn't it? As a matter of fact his sister is arriving from England, and he has to go to meet her.

AMAH: More better he go soon.

DAISY: Why do you smoke your pipe here? You know Harry doesn't like it.

AMAH: Harry one big fool, I think. When you go to Chung-King?

DAISY: Harry hasn't said a word about it since.

AMAH: You got key that desk?

DAISY: No. Harry keeps all his private papers there.

> [*The* AMAH *goes to the desk and tries one of the drawers. It is locked and she cannot open it.*

AMAH: What Harry do now?

DAISY: He and Mr. Knox are drinking their port.

> [*The* AMAH *takes a skeleton key out of her sleeve and inserts it in the lock. She turns the key.*

AMAH: Velly bad lock. I think made in Germany. Hi yah. [*She opens the drawer and takes out a revolver. She hands it to* DAISY.] Lee Tai say, you take out cartridges.

DAISY: What do you mean? [*She suddenly realises the truth and gives a cry.*] Oh!

AMAH: [*Hurriedly putting her hand over* DAISY's *mouth.*] Sh! you no make noise. [*Holding out the revolver.*] Lee Tai say, more better you do it.

DAISY: Take it away. No, no, I won't, I won't.

AMAH: Sh, sh! I do it. I sabe.

> [*She takes the cartridges out of the revolver and hides them about her.* DAISY *looks at her with horror.*

DAISY: It's not for to-night?

AMAH: My no sabe.

DAISY: I won't have it. Do you hear? Oh, I shall go mad.

AMAH: Then Harry shut you up. Hi yah. All same Chung-King.

> [*She puts the revolver back into the drawer and shuts it*

just as HARRY *and* HAROLD KNOX *come in. They wear dinner jackets.*

KNOX: Hulloa, there's the little ray of sunshine. I missed your bonny face before dinner.

AMAH: You velly funny man.

KNOX: No wonder I dote upon you, dearie. You're the only attractive woman I've ever been able to persuade that I was a humorist.

HARRY: [*Catching sight of the* AMAH'S *water-pipe.*] I told you I wouldn't have your disgusting pipe in here, Amah.

AMAH: Belong velly nice pipe.

HARRY: I swore I'd throw the damned thing out myself if I found it lying about.

AMAH: [*Snatching it away.*] You no touch my pipe. You velly bad man. Velly bad temper. You no Christian.

HARRY: A fat lot you know about Christianity.

AMAH: I know plenty about Christianity. My father velly poor man. He say, you go and be Christian. I go Catholic mission and they baptize me. English Church missionary, he come along and say, Catholic mission no good, you go to hell, I baptize you. All right, I say, you baptize me. By and by Baptist missionary come along and say, English Church mission no good, you go to hell, I baptize you. All right, I say, you baptize me. By and by Presbyterian missionary come along and say, Baptist mission no good, you go to hell, I baptize you. All right, I say, you baptize me. [*To* KNOX.] You know Seventh Day Adventists?

KNOX: I've heard of them.

AMAH: By and by Seventh Day Adventist he come along and say, Presbyterian mission no good.

KNOX: You go to hell.

AMAH: How fashion you sabe what he said?

KNOX: I guessed it.

AMAH: You go to hell, he say. I baptize you. I been baptized one, two, three, four, five times. I velly Christian woman.

HARRY: [*Smiling.*] I apologise.

AMAH: They all say to poor Chinese, love one another. I no think missionaries love one another velly much. Hi yah.

KNOX: [*Taking out his watch.*] D'you mind if I look at the time? I don't want to get to the station late.

HARRY:' Of course not. I say, won't you have a cigar? [*He goes to his desk.*] I have to keep them locked up. I think the boys find them very much to their taste. [*He puts the key into the lock.*] Hulloa, the drawer's open. I could have sworn I locked it.

> [*He takes out a box of cigars and hands it to* KNOX.

KNOX: [*Helping himself.*] Thanks very much.

DAISY: You know, you mustn't let me keep you if you want to be off.

KNOX: I've got two or three minutes.

HARRY: O Daisy, before Harold goes I wish you'd show him that Manchu dress I bought you.

DAISY: I'll go and fetch it. [*To the* AMAH.] Is it hanging up in the cupboard?

AMAH: No, I have puttee in paper. I velly careful woman.

> [*They both go out.*

KNOX: I say, old man, I hope you don't think I'm an awful swine to rush off like this the moment I've swallowed my dinner.

HARRY: Rather not. As a matter of fact it's not exactly inconvenient, because I'm expecting George. I want him to have a heart-to-heart talk with Daisy.

KNOX: Oh!

HARRY: She's grousing rather about going to Chung-King

and I want him to tell her it's a very decent place. He was vice-consul up there once. He's dining at the Carmichaels', but he said he'd come along here as soon as he could get away.

KNOX: Then it's all for the best in the best of all possible worlds.

[DAISY *comes in with the dress.*

DAISY: Here it is.

KNOX: By George, isn't it stunning? I must try to get one for my sister. She'd simply go off her head if she saw that.

DAISY: Harry spoils me, doesn't he?

KNOX: Harry's a very lucky young fellow to have you to spoil.

DAISY: [*Smiling.*] Go away or you'll never arrive in time.

KNOX: I'm off. Good-bye, and thanks very much. Dinner was top-hole.

DAISY: Good-bye.

[*He goes out.* HARRY *accompanies him into the courtyard and for a moment is lost to view. The gaiety on* DAISY'S *face vanishes and a look of anxiety takes its place.*

DAISY: [*Calling hurriedly.*] Amah, Amah.

AMAH: [*Coming in.*] What thing?

DAISY: What have you done? Have you? . . .

[*She stops, unable to complete the agonised question.*

AMAH: What you talk about? I done nothing. I only have joke with you. Hi yah.

DAISY: Will you swear that's true?

AMAH: Never tell a lie. Velly good Christian.

[DAISY *looks at her searchingly. She does not know whether to believe or not.* HARRY *returns.*

HARRY: I say, Daisy, I wish you'd put on the dress. I'd love to see how you look in it.

DAISY: [*With a smile.*] Shall I?

HARRY: Amah will help you. It'll suit you right down to the ground.

DAISY: Wait a minute. Bring the dress along, Amah.

AMAH: All light.

> [DAISY *goes out, followed by the* AMAH *with the Manchu dress.* HARRY *goes to his desk and opens the drawer. He examines the lock and looks at the keyhole.*

HARRY: [*To himself.*] I wonder if that old devil's got a key.

> [*He shuts the drawer, but does not lock it. He strolls back to the middle of the room.*

DAISY: [*In the adjoining room.*] Are you getting impatient?

HARRY: Not a bit.

DAISY: I'm just ready.

HARRY: I'm holding my breath. [DAISY *comes in. She is in full Manchu dress. She is strangely changed. There is nothing European about her any more. She is mysterious and enigmatical.*] Daisy! [*She gives him a little smile but does not answer. She stands quite still for him to look at her.*] By George, how Chinese you look!

DAISY: Don't you like it?

HARRY: I don't know. You've just knocked me off my feet. Like it? You're wonderful. In my wildest dreams I never saw you like that. You've brought all the East into the room with you. My head reels as though I were drunk.

DAISY: It's strange that I feel as if these things were made for me. They make me feel so different.

HARRY: I thought that no one in the world was more normal than I. I'm ashamed of myself. You're almost a stranger to me, and by God, I feel as though the marrow of my bones were melting. I hear the East a-calling. I have

such a pain in my heart. Oh, my pretty, my precious,
I love you.

> [*He falls down on his knees before her and clasps both his arms round her.*

DAISY: [*In a low voice, hardly her own.*] Why, Harry, what are you talking about?

> [*She caresses his hair with her long, delicate Chinese hand.*

HARRY: I'm such a fool. My heart is full of wonderful thoughts and I can only say that—that I worship the very ground you walk on.

DAISY: Don't kneel, Harry, that isn't the way a woman wants to be loved.

> [*She raises him to his feet, and as he rises he takes her in his arms.*

HARRY: [*Passionately.*] I'd do anything in the world for you.

DAISY: You could make me so happy if you chose.

HARRY: I do choose.

DAISY: Won't you give up this idea of leaving Peking?

HARRY: But, my darling, it's for your happiness I'm doing it.

DAISY: Don't you think that everyone is the best judge of his own happiness?

HARRY: Not always.

DAISY: [*Disengaging herself from his arms.*] Ah, that's the English way. You want to make people happy in your way and not in theirs. You'll never be satisfied till the Chinese wear Norfolk suits and eat roast beef and plum pudding.

HARRY: Oh, my dear, don't let's argue now.

DAISY: You say you'll give me everything in the world, and you won't give me the one thing I want. What's the good of offering me the moon if I have a nail in my shoe and you won't take it out?

HARRY: Well, you can smile, so it's not very serious, is it?

DAISY: [*Putting her arms round his neck.*] O Harry, I'll love you so much if you'll only do what I ask. You don't know me yet. O Harry.

HARRY: My darling, I love you with all my heart and soul, but when I've once made up my mind nothing on earth is going to make me change it. We can only be happy and natural if we go. You must submit to my judgment.

DAISY: How *can* you be so obstinate?

HARRY: My dear, look at yourself in the glass now.

> [*She looks down at her Manchu dress. She understands what he means. She is a Chinese woman.*

DAISY: [*With a change of tone.*] Amah, bring me a tea-gown.

> [*She begins to undo the long Manchu coat. The AMAH comes in with a tea-gown.*

HARRY: [*Dryly.*] It's very convenient that you should always be within earshot when you're wanted, Amah.

AMAH: My velly good Amah. Velly Christian woman.

> [DAISY *slips off the Manchu clothes and is helped by the* AMAH *into the tea-gown. She wraps it round her. She is once more a white woman.*

DAISY: [*Pointing to the Manchu dress.*] Take those things away. [*To* HARRY.] Would you like to have a game of chess?

HARRY: Very much. I'll get the men.

> [DAISY *goes to the gramophone and turns on a Chinese tune. It is strange and exotic. Its monotony exacerbates the nerves.* HARRY *gets the chessboard and sets up the pieces. They sit down opposite one another. The* AMAH *has disappeared with the discarded dress.*

HARRY: Will you take white?

DAISY: If you like.

> [*She moves a piece.*

HARRY: I hate your queen opening. It always flummoxes me. I don't know where you learned to play so well. I never have a chance against you.

DAISY: I was taught by a Chinaman. It's a game they take to naturally.

[*They make two or three moves without a word. Suddenly, breaking across the silence, stridently, there is a shriek outside in the street.* DAISY *gives a little gasp.*

HARRY: Hulloa, what's that?

DAISY: Oh, it's nothing. It's only some Chinese quarrelling.

[*Two or three shouts are heard and then an agonised cry of* "Help, help!" HARRY *springs to his feet.*

HARRY: By God, that's English.

[*He is just going to rush out when* DAISY *seizes his arm.*

DAISY: What are you going to do? No, no, don't leave me, Harry.

[*She clings to him. He pushes her away violently.*

HARRY: Shut up. Don't be a fool.

[*He runs to the drawer of his desk. The cry is repeated:* "For God's sake, help, help, oh!"

HARRY: My God, they're killing someone. It can't be . . .

[*He remembers that* GEORGE *is coming that evening.*

DAISY: [*Throwing herself on him.*] No, Harry, don't go, don't go. I won't let you.

HARRY: Get out of my way.

[*He pushes her violently aside and runs out.* DAISY *sinks to the floor and buries her face in her hands.*

DAISY: Oh, my God!

[*The* AMAH *has been waiting just outside one of the doors, in the courtyard, and now she slips in.*

AMAH: Harry velly blave man. He hear white man being murdered. He run and help. Hi yah.

DAISY: Oh, I can't. Harry, Harry.

[*She springs to her feet and runs towards the courtyard, with some instinctive idea of going to her husband's help. The* AMAH *stops her.*

AMAH: What side you go?

DAISY: I can't stand here and let Harry be murdered.

AMAH: You stop here.

DAISY: Let me go. For God's sake let me go. Wu! Wu!

[*The* AMAH *puts her hand over* DAISY's *mouth.*

AMAH: You be quiet. You wanchee go prison?

DAISY: [*Snatching away her hand.*] I'll give you anything in the world if you'll only let me go.

AMAH: You silly little fool, Daisy.

[DAISY *struggles to release herself, but she is helpless in the* AMAH's *grasp.*

DAISY: [*In an agony.*] It'll be too late.

AMAH: Too late now. You no can help him.

[*She releases* DAISY. DAISY *staggers forward and covers her face with her hands.*

DAISY: Oh, what have I done?

AMAH: [*With a snigger.*] You no do nothing, you sabe nothing.

DAISY: [*Violently.*] Curse you. It's you, you, you!

AMAH: I velly wicked woman. Curse me. Do me no harm.

DAISY: I told you I wouldn't have anything done to Harry.

AMAH: You say no with your lips, but in your belly you say yes.

DAISY: No, no, no!

AMAH: You just big damned fool, Daisy. You no love Harry. Him not velly rich. Not velly big man. No good. You velly glad you finish with him.

DAISY: But not that way. He never did me any harm. He was always good to me and kind to me.

AMAH: That velly good way. Velly safe way.

DAISY: You devil. I hate the sight of you.

AMAH: What for you hate me? I do what you wanchee. Your father velly clever man. He say: no break eggs, no can eat omlette.

DAISY: I wish I'd never been born.

AMAH: [*Impatiently.*] What for you tell me lies? You want Harry dead. Well, I kill him for you. [*With a sudden gust of anger.*] You no curse me or I beat you. You velly bad girl.

DAISY: [*Giving way.*] Oh, I feel so awfully faint.

AMAH: [*Tenderly, as though* DAISY *were still a child.*] You sit down. You take smelly salts. [*She helps* DAISY *into a chair and holds smelling salts to her nostrils.*] You feel better in a minute. Amah love her little Daisy flower. Harry him die and Daisy velly sorry. She cry and cry and cry. George velly sorry for Daisy. By and by Daisy not cry any more. She say, more better Harry dead. Good old Amah, she do everything for little Daisy.

    [DAISY *has been looking at her with terrified eyes.*

DAISY: What a brute I am. I'd give anything in the world to have Harry back, and yet in the bottom of my heart there's a feeling—if I were free there'd be nothing to stand between George and me.

AMAH: I think George he marry you maybe.

DAISY: Oh, not now. It'll bring me bad joss.

AMAH: You no wanchee fear, my little flower. You sit still or you feel bad again.

DAISY: [*Jumping up.*] How can I sit still? The suspense is awful. Oh, my God, what's happened?

AMAH: [*With a cunning smile.*] I tell you what's happened. Harry run outside and he see two, three men makee fighting. They a little way off. One man cry, help! help!

Harry give shout and run. He fall down and him not get up again.

DAISY: He's as strong as a horse. With his bare hands he's a match for ten Chinamen.

AMAH: Lee Tai velly clever man. He no take risks. I think all finish now.

DAISY: Then for God's sake let me go.

AMAH: More better you stay here, Daisy. Maybe you get into trouble if you go out. They ask you why you go out. Why you think something happen to your husband?

DAISY: I can't let him lie there.

AMAH: He no lie velly long. By and by night watchman come here, and he say white man in the street—him dead. I think his throat cut.

DAISY: Oh, how horrible. Harry, Harry!

[*She buries her face in her hands.*

AMAH: I light joss-stick. Make everything come all light.

[*She goes over to the household image and lights a joss-stick in front of it. She bows before it, and going on her knees knocks her head on the ground.*

DAISY: How long is it going on? How long have I got to wait? Oh, what have I done? The silence is awful. [*There is a silence. Suddenly* DAISY *breaks out into a shriek.*] No, no, no! I won't have it. I can't bear it. Oh, God help me. [*In the distance of the next courtyard is heard the chanting of the monks at the evening service. The* AMAH, *having finished her devotions, stands at the doorway looking out steadily.* DAISY *stares straight in front of her. Suddenly there is a loud booming of a gong.* DAISY *starts up.*] What's that?

AMAH: Be quiet, Daisy. Be careful.

[*The door of the courtyard is flung open.* HARRY *comes in, through the courtyard, into the room, pushing*

*before him a coolie whom he holds by the wrists and
by the scruff of the neck.*

DAISY: Harry!

HARRY: I've got one of the blighters. [*Shouting.*] Here, bring
me a rope.

DAISY: What's happened?

HARRY: Wait a minute. Thank God, I got there when I
did. [WU *brings a rope and* HARRY *ties the man's wrists
behind his back.*] Keep quiet, you devil, or I'll break your
ruddy neck. [*He slips the rope through the great iron ring
of one of the doors and ties it so that the man cannot get away.*]
He'll be all right there for the present. I'll just go and
telephone to the police station. Wu, you stand outside
there. You watch him. Sabe?

WU: I sabe.

> [*As* HARRY *goes out a crowd of people surge through the
> great open doorway of the courtyard. They are monks
> of the temple, attracted to the street by the quick
> rumour of accident, coolies, and the night watchman
> with his rattle. Some of them bear Chinese lanterns
> and some, hurricane lamps. The crowd separate out
> as they approach the room, and then it is seen that
> three men are bearing what seems to be the body of
> a man.*

DAISY: What's that?

AMAH: I think belong foreign man. [*The men bring in the
body and lay it on the sofa. The head and part of the chest
are covered with a piece of blue cotton.* DAISY *and the* AMAH
*look at it with dismay. They dare not approach. The abbot
drives the crowd out of the room and shuts the doors, only
leaving that side of one open at which the prisoner is attached.
The* AMAH *turns on the god in the niche.*] You say can do.
What for you make mistake?

> [*She seizes a fan which is on the table under her hand,
> and with angry violence hits the image on the face two*

or three times. DAISY *has been staring at the body.*
She goes up to it softly and lifts the cloth; she gives
a start, and with a quick gesture snatches it away.
She sees GEORGE CONWAY.

DAISY: George!

> [*She opens her mouth to shriek.*

AMAH: Sh! take care. Harry hear.

DAISY: What have you done?

AMAH: I do nothing. Buddha, he maky mistake.

DAISY: You fiend!

AMAH: How do I know, Daisy? I no can tell George
coming here to-night. [*The words come gurgling out, for*
DAISY *has sprung upon her and seized her by the throat.*]
Oh, let me go.

DAISY: You fiend!

> [HARRY *comes in. He is astounded at what he sees.*

HARRY: Daisy, Daisy. What in God's name are you doing?

> [*Restrained by his voice,* DAISY *releases her hold of the*
> AMAH, *but violently, pushing her so that she falls*
> *to the ground. She lies there putting her hand to her*
> *throat.* DAISY *turns to* HARRY.

DAISY: It's George.

HARRY: [*Going up to the sofa and putting his hand on* GEORGE'S
heart.] Confound it, I know it's George.

DAISY: Is he dead?

HARRY: No, he's only had a bang on the head. He's stunned.
I've sent for the doctor. Luckily he was dining at the
Carmichaels' and I sent George's rickshaw to bring him
along as quick as he could come.

DAISY: Supposing he's gone?

HARRY: He won't have gone. They were going to play
poker. By God, what's this? [*He takes away his hand*
and sees blood upon it.] He's been wounded. He's bleeding.

[DAISY *goes up to the body and, kneeling down, feels the pulse.*

DAISY: Are you sure he's alive?

HARRY: Yes, his heart's beating all right. I wish the doctor would make haste. I don't know what one ought to do.

DAISY: How do you know he's at the Carmichaels'?

HARRY: George told me yesterday he was going to be there. George said he did not want to play poker, and he'd come along here after dinner.

DAISY: [*Springing to her feet.*] Did you know George was coming?

HARRY: Of course I did. When I heard someone shouting in English the first thing I thought of was George.

  [DAISY *bursts into a scream of hysterical laughter. The* AMAH *suddenly looks up and becomes attentive.*

HARRY: Daisy, what's the matter?

AMAH: [*Sliding to her feet and going up to* DAISY, *trying to stop her.*] Maskee. She only laughy laughy. You no trouble.

HARRY: Get some water or something.

AMAH: [*Frightened.*] Now, my pletty, my pletty.

DAISY: [*Recovering herself, violently.*] Let me be.

HARRY: By George, I believe he's coming to. Bring the water here.

  [DAISY *takes the glass and, leaning over the sofa, moistens* GEORGE'S *lips with it. He slowly opens his eyes.*

GEORGE: Has it been boiled and filtered?

HARRY: [*With a chuckle that is half a sob.*] Don't be a fool. O George, you have given me a nasty turn.

GEORGE: There's something the matter with the water.

DAISY: [*Looking at it quickly.*] What?

GEORGE: Damn it all, there's no brandy in it.

DAISY: If you make a joke I shall cry.

      [He *tries to move, but suddenly gives a groan.*

GEORGE: O Lord. I've got such a pain in my side.

HARRY: Keep quiet. The doctor will be here in a minute.

GEORGE: What is it?

HARRY: I don't know. There's a lot of blood.

GEORGE: I hope I haven't made a mess on your nice new sofa.

HARRY: Damn the sofa. It's lucky I heard you shout.

GEORGE: I never shouted.

HARRY: Oh, nonsense, I heard you. I thought it was you at once.

GEORGE: I heard a cry for help too. I was just coming along. I nipped out of my rickshaw and sprinted like hell. I saw some fellows struggling. I think someone hit me on the head. I don't remember much.

HARRY: Who did cry for help?

GEORGE: [After a pause.] Nobody.

HARRY: But I heard it. Daisy heard it too. It sounded like someone being murdered. [As GEORGE gives a little chuckle.] What's the joke?

GEORGE: Someone's got his knife into you, old man, and the silly ass stuck it into me instead.

[The AMAH pricks up her ears.

DAISY: I'm sure you oughtn't to talk so much.

GEORGE: It's a very old Chinese trick. They just got the wrong man, that's all.

HARRY: By George, that explains why I tripped.

GEORGE: Did you trip? A piece of string across the street.

HARRY: I wasn't expecting it. I went down like a ninepin. I was up again in a flash and just threw myself at the blighters. You should have seen 'em scatter. Luckily I got one of them.

GEORGE: Good. Where is he?

HARRY: He's here. I've tied him up pretty tight.

GEORGE: Well, we shall find out who's at the bottom of this. The methods of the Chinese police may be uncivilised, but they are . . . O Lord, I do feel rotten.

HARRY: O George.

[DAISY *gives* HARRY *the glass and he helps* GEORGE *to drink.*

GEORGE: That's better.

HARRY: We'd better get you to bed, old man.

GEORGE: All right.

HARRY: Wu and I will carry you. Wu, come along here.

[*The boy approaches. The* AMAH *realises that for a moment the prisoner is to be left unguarded. There is a table-knife on one of the occasional tables, with which* DAISY *has been cutting a book. The* AMAH's *hand closes over it.*

GEORGE: Oh no, that's all right. I can walk.

[*He gets up from the sofa.* HARRY *gives him an arm. He staggers.*

HARRY: Wu, you fool. [DAISY *springs forward.*] No, let me take him, Daisy. You're not strong enough.

GEORGE: [*Gasping.*] Sorry to make such an ass of myself.

[HARRY *and* WU, *holding him one on each side, help him out of the room.*

DAISY: Shall I come?

HARRY: Oh, I'll call you if you're wanted.

[DAISY *sinks into a chair, shuddering, and covers her face with her hands. The* AMAH *seizes her opportunity. She cuts the rope which binds the prisoner. As soon as he is free he slips out into the darkness. The* AMAH *watches for a moment and then cries out.*

AMAH: Help! help!

[DAISY *springs up and* HARRY *hurries in.*

HARRY: What's the matter?

AMAH: Coolie. Him run away.

HARRY: [*Looking at the place where he had been tied up.*] By God!

AMAH: Missy feel velly ill. No can stand blood. Feel faint. I run fetch smelly salts, and when I come back him gone. Him bad man.

[HARRY *goes to the door and looks at the rope.*

HARRY: This rope's been cut.

AMAH: Maybe he have knife. Why you no look see before you tie him?

HARRY: [*Looking at her sternly.*] How do you think he could get a knife with his hands tied behind his back?

AMAH: I no sabe. Maybe he have friend.

HARRY: Didn't you hear anything, Daisy?

DAISY: No. I wasn't thinking about him. O Harry, George isn't going to die, is he?

HARRY: I hope not. I don't know what sort of a wound he's got. [*The* AMAH, *thinking attention is withdrawn from her, is slipping away.*] No, you don't. You stop here.

AMAH: What thing you wanchee?

HARRY: You let that man go.

AMAH: You velly silly man. What for I wanchee let him go?

HARRY: [*Pointing.*] What's that knife doing there? That's one of our knives.

AMAH: Missy takey that knife cutty book.

HARRY: When I got into the street I wanted to fire my revolver to frighten them. There wasn't a cartridge in it. I always keep it loaded and locked up.

AMAH: Revolver! I don't know him. I never have see revolver. Never. Never.

[*She makes a movement as though to go away. He seizes her wrist.*

HARRY: Stop!

AMAH: My go chow. My belong velly hungly. You talkey by and by.

HARRY: If I hadn't come in just now Daisy would have strangled you.

AMAH: Daisy velly excited. She no sabe what she do. She never hurt old Amah.

HARRY: Why were you angry with her, Daisy?

DAISY: [*Frightened.*] I was beside myself. I don't know what I was doing.

HARRY: [*With sudden suspicion.*] Are you trying to shield her?

DAISY: Of course not. Why on earth should I do that?

HARRY: I suppose you look on it as a matter of no importance that she tried to kill me.

DAISY: O Harry, how can you say anything so cruel? Why should she try to kill you?

HARRY: I don't know. How do you expect me to guess what is at the back of a Chinese brain? She's hated me always.

AMAH: You no lovey me velly much.

HARRY: I've put up with her just because she was attached to you. I knew she was a liar and a thief. It was a trap, and I escaped by a miracle. Only, George has got to suffer for it.

DAISY: Harry, you're nervous and excited.

HARRY: What are you defending her for?

DAISY: I'm not defending her.

HARRY: One would almost think she had some hold on you. I've never seen any one let an amah behave as you let her behave.

DAISY: She's been with me since I was a child. She—she can't get it into her head that I'm grown up.

HARRY: Well, I've had about enough of her. [*To the*

AMAH.] The police will be here in ten minutes and I shall give you in charge instead of the man you allowed to escape.

AMAH: You give me policeman? I no have do wrong. What for you send me prison?

HARRY: I dare say you know what a Chinese prison is like better than I do. I don't think it'll be long before you find it worth while to tell the truth.

DAISY: [*With increasing nervousness*.] O Harry, I don't think you ought to do anything before you've had time to think. After all, there's absolutely no proof.

HARRY: [*Looking at her with perplexity*.] I don't understand. What is the mystery?

DAISY: There is no mystery. Only I can't bear the idea that my old Amah should go to prison. She's been almost a mother to me for so many years.

[*There is a pause.* HARRY *looks from* DAISY *to the* AMAH.

HARRY: [*To the* AMAH.] Then get out of here before the police come.

AMAH: You talkee so quick. No can understand.

HARRY: Yes, you can. Unless you're out of here in ten minutes I shall give you in charge. . . . Go while the going's good.

AMAH: I think I go smoke pipe.

HARRY: No, you don't, you get out quick or I'll throw you out myself.

AMAH: You no throw me out and I no go to prison.

HARRY: We'll soon see about that.

[*He seizes her roughly and is about to run her out into the courtyard.*

DAISY: No, don't, Harry.

HARRY: [*Wheeling round, still holding the* AMAH.] What's the matter with you?

DAISY: She's my mother.

HARRY: That!

> [*He is aghast. He releases the* AMAH. *He looks at her with horror.* DAISY *covers her face with her hands. The* AMAH *gives a little snigger.*

AMAH: Yes, Daisy my daughter. She no wanchee tell. I think she a little ashamed of her mother.

HARRY: My God!

AMAH: I velly pletty girl long time ago. Daisy's father, he call me his little lotus flower, he call me his little peach-blossom. By and by I not velly pletty girl any more and Daisy's father he call me, you old witch. Witch, that's what he call me. Witch. He call me, you old hag. You velly bad man, I say to him. You no Christian. You go to hell, he say. All light, I say, you baptize me.

> [HARRY *turns away, looking straight in front of him, with an expression of dismay and repulsion. The* AMAH *takes her pipe and lights it.*

END OF SCENE IV

SCENE V

SCENE: *The courtyard in the Andersons' part of the temple. At the back is the outer wall raised by two or three steps from the ground. From the top of the wall projects a shallow roof of yellow tiles supported by wooden pillars painted red, shabby and rather weather-worn, and this roof is raised in the middle of the wall where there is a huge wooden gateway. When this is opened the street is seen, and on the other side of it is a high, blank, white wall. The courtyard is paved with great flags. On each side of it are living-rooms.*

There is a long rattan chair, a round table, and a couple of arm-chairs. GEORGE is lying on the long chair, looking at an illustrated paper, and the AMAH is seated on the ground, smoking her water-pipe.

GEORGE: [*With a smile, putting down the paper.*] You're not as chatty as usual this afternoon, Amah.

AMAH: Suppose I got nothing to talk about I no talkee.

GEORGE: You are an example of your sex, Amah. Your price is above rubies.

AMAH: No likee rubies velly much. No can sell velly much money.

GEORGE: In point of fact, I wasn't thinking of giving you rubies, even reconstructed, but if I did I can't think you'd be so indelicate as to sell them.

AMAH: I no think you velly funny man.

GEORGE: I was afraid you didn't. Would you think it funny if I sat on my hat?

AMAH: Yes, I laugh then. Hi yah.

GEORGE: Who was it who said that East is East and West is West, and never the twain shall meet? The inscrutable

heart of China expands to the self-same joke that con-
vulses a duchess in London and a financier in New York.

AMAH: You more better read the paper.

GEORGE: Where's missy?

AMAH: I think she in her room. You wanchee?

GEORGE: No.

AMAH: I think she come by and by.

GEORGE: [*Looking at his watch.*] Mr. Anderson ought to be
back from the office soon. [*There is a loud knocking at the
door.*] Hulloa, who's that?

> [*A servant comes out of the house, and going to the gateway
> withdraws the bolt.*

AMAH: I think doctor come see you, maybe.

GEORGE: Oh no, he's not coming to-day. He said he'd look
in to-morrow before I started.

> [*The* AMAH *gets up and looks at the doorway, of which now
> the servant has opened one side.* HAROLD KNOX *and
> his sister* SYLVIA *are seen.*

KNOX: May we come in?

GEORGE: Good man. Of course.

> [*They come towards* GEORGE. SYLVIA *is a very pretty,
> simple, healthy, and attractive girl. She is dressed in a
> light summer frock. There is in her gait and manner
> something so springlike and fresh that it is a pleasure
> to look at her.*

KNOX: I've brought my young sister along with me.
[*As* GEORGE *rises to his feet.*] Don't get up. You
needn't put on any frills for a chit like that.

GEORGE: Nonsense. I'm perfectly well. [*Shaking hands with*
SYLVIA.] How d'you do? My name is Conway.

KNOX: I only omitted to inform her of that fact because she
already knew it.

SYLVIA: Strangely enough, that happens to be true. But I
wish you'd lie down again.

GEORGE: I'm sick of lying down. The doctor says I'm perfectly all right. I'm going home to-morrow.

KNOX: [*Catching sight of the* AMAH.] Hulloa, sweetheart, I didn't see you. Sylvia, I want you to know the only woman I've ever loved.

GEORGE: [*Smiling.*] This is Mrs. Anderson's Amah.

SYLVIA: [*With a little friendly nod.*] How do you do?

AMAH: [*All in a breath.*] Velly well, thank you. How do you do? Velly well, thank you. . . . You Mr. Knox sister?

SYLVIA: Yes.

AMAH: You missionary lady?

SYLVIA: No.

AMAH: What for you come China, then?

SYLVIA: I came to see my brother.

AMAH: How old are you?

KNOX: Be truthful, Sylvia.

SYLVIA: I'm twenty-two.

AMAH: How many children you got?

SYLVIA: I'm not married.

AMAH: What for you no marry if you belong twenty-two?

SYLVIA: It does need an explanation, doesn't it? The truth is that nobody's asked me.

KNOX: What a lie.

AMAH: You come China catchee husband?

SYLVIA: Certainly not.

AMAH: You Christian?

SYLVIA: Not a very good one, I'm afraid.

AMAH: Who baptized you?

SYLVIA: Well, you know, it's an awfully long time ago. I forget.

KNOX: She's like me, Amah, she's a Presbyterian.

AMAH: You go hell then. Only Seventh Day Adventists no go hell.

SYLVIA: It'll be rather crowded then, I'm afraid.

AMAH: You only baptized once?

SYLVIA: So far as I know.

AMAH: I baptized one, two, three, four, five times. I velly Christian woman.

KNOX: I say, old man, I don't want to dash your fond hopes, but in point of fact we didn't come here to see you.

GEORGE: Why not? Surely Miss Knox must want to see the principal sights of Peking.

KNOX: The man is not a raving lunatic, Sylvia. His only delusion is that he's a humorist. . . . Sylvia thought she'd like to call on Mrs. Harry.

GEORGE: I'm sure Daisy will be very glad. Amah, go and tell Missy that there's a lady.

AMAH: Can do.

[*Exit.*

KNOX: I say, have they caught any of those blighters who tried to kill you?

GEORGE: No, not a chance. They weren't after me, you know, they were after Harry.

KNOX: Is there any one who has a grudge against him?

GEORGE: I don't think so. He doesn't seem very keen on discussing the incident.

[DAISY *comes in.*

KNOX: Here she is. I've brought my sister to see you, Mrs. Harry.

DAISY: [*Shaking hands.*] How do you do?

SYLVIA: What a wonderful place you live in.

DAISY: It's rather attractive, isn't it? You must see the temple before you go.

SYLVIA: I'd love to.

G

DAISY: Do sit down. [*To* KNOX.] What do you think of my patient?

KNOX: I think he's a fraud. I never saw any one look so robust.

DAISY: [*Delighted.*] He's made a wonderful recovery.

GEORGE: Thanks to you, Daisy. You can't think how she nursed me.

KNOX: It was rather a narrow escape, wasn't it?

DAISY: For two days we thought he might die at any minute. It was—it was rather dreadful.

GEORGE: And do you know, all that time she never left me for a minute. [*To* DAISY.] I don't know how I can ever thank you.

DAISY: Oh, well, Harry had his work. I didn't think he ought to be robbed of his night's rest for a worthless creature like you, and I hated the idea of a paid nurse looking after you.

SYLVIA: You must have been worn out at the end of it.

DAISY: No, I'm as strong as a horse. And it was such a relief to me when the doctor said he was out of danger, I forgot I was tired.

KNOX: I don't know why you bothered about him. There are such a lot of fellows who want his job, and they all know they could do it much better than he can.

GEORGE: Every one's been so awfully good to me. I had no idea there was so much kindness in the world.

DAISY: [*To* SYLVIA, *very pleasantly.*] Will you come and look at the temple now while they're bringing tea?

SYLVIA: Yes, I'd like to very much.

DAISY: I think you'll enjoy your tea more if you feel you've done the sight.

SYLVIA: It's all so new to me. Everything interests me. I've fallen passionately in love with Peking.

[*They wander off talking gaily.*

GEORGE: Harold, you're a very nice boy.

KNOX: That's what the girls tell me. But I don't know why you should.

GEORGE: I think it was rather sporting of you to bring your sister to see Daisy.

KNOX: I don't deserve any credit for that. She insisted on coming.

GEORGE: Oh?

KNOX: She met Harry at the club and took rather a fancy to him. When I told her Daisy was a half-caste and people didn't bother much about her she got right up on her hind legs. I told her she'd only just come out to China and didn't know what she was talking about, and then she gave me what she called a bit of her mind. I was obliged to remark that if that was a bit I didn't much care about knowing the rest.

GEORGE: It sounds as though you'd had a little tiff.

KNOX: She said she had no patience with the airs people gave themselves in the East. A Eurasian was just as good as anybody else. And when I happened to say I was coming here to-day to see how you were she said she'd come too.

GEORGE: It's very kind of her. Daisy leads a dreadfully lonely life. It would mean so much to her if she knew one or two white women. If they take to one another you won't try to crab it, will you? I fancy Daisy wants a friend rather badly.

KNOX: I shouldn't like it very much, you know. Would you much care for your sister to be very pally with a half-caste?

GEORGE: Daisy is one in a thousand. You can't think what she's done for me during my illness. My mother couldn't have taken more care of me.

KNOX: They're often very good-hearted. But as a matter of fact nothing I can say will have the least effect on Sylvia.

Girls have changed a lot since the war. If she wants to do a thing and she thinks it right, she'll do it. And if I try to interfere she's quite capable of telling me to go to the devil.

GEORGE: She seems to be a young woman of some character.

KNOX: Perhaps because she's had rather a rough time. The fellow she was engaged to was killed in the war and she was awfully cut up. She drove an ambulance for the last two years and then she went up to Girton. After that my father thought she'd better come out here for a bit.

GEORGE: She ought to like it.

KNOX: If she doesn't put up people's backs too much. She can't stand anything like injustice or cruelty. If she thinks people are unkind to Daisy or sniffy about her she'll stick to her like a leech. However, I daresay she'll get married.

GEORGE: [*Smiling.*] That'll learn her.

KNOX: Why don't you marry her? It's about time you settled down.

GEORGE: [*With a chuckle.*] You fool.

KNOX: Why? You're by way of being rather eligible, aren't you?

GEORGE: I don't know why you want to get rid of her. She seems a very nice sister.

KNOX: Of course I love having her with me, but she does cramp my style a bit. And she ought to marry. She'd make you a first-rate wife.

GEORGE: Much too good for the likes of me.

KNOX: Of course she's a bit independent, but one has to put up with that in girls nowadays. And she's as good as gold.

GEORGE: One can see that at a mile, my son.

KNOX: I say, who was Rathbone, Daisy's first husband?

GEORGE: [*His face a blank.*] Harry told me he was an American. He said he was in business in the F.M.S.

KNOX: That's what Harry told me. I met a fellow the other day who lives in Singapore and he told me he'd never heard of Rathbone.

GEORGE: [*Chaffing him.*] Perhaps he didn't move in the exalted circles that a friend of yours would naturally move in.

KNOX: I suppose there was a Mr. Rathbone?

> [*During the last few speeches,* WU *has appeared with the tea. He sets it down on the table.* DAISY *and* SYLVIA *come out of the house.*

DAISY: Oh, here's tea.

SYLVIA: I don't think we'll stay, thank you very much. We have another call to make.

DAISY: How tiresome of you. Harry ought to be back in a few minutes. He'll be disappointed not to have seen you.

SYLVIA: I promised to go and see Mrs. Stopfort. Do you know her?

DAISY: I know whom you mean.

SYLVIA: I think people are being absolutely beastly to her. It simply makes my blood boil.

DAISY: Oh, how?

SYLVIA: Well, you know that her husband's a drunken brute who's treated her abominably for years. At last she fell in love with a man and now her husband is going to divorce her. It's monstrous that he should be able to.

DAISY: Are the ladies of Peking giving her the cold shoulder?

KNOX: The cold shoulder hardly describes it. The frozen silverside.

GEORGE: I think she's well rid of Reggie Stopfort at any price, but I'm sorry the other party is André Leroux.

SYLVIA: Why? She introduced me to him. I thought he was a very nice fellow.

GEORGE: Well, you see, if he'd been English or American he would have married her as a matter of course.

SYLVIA: So I should hope.

DAISY: Because she was divorced on his account, you mean?

GEORGE: Yes. But the French haven't our feeling on that matter. I'm not quite sure if André will be willing to marry her.

SYLVIA: Oh, that would be dreadful. Under those circumstances the man must marry the woman. He simply must.

GEORGE: Of course.

KNOX: Come along, Sylvia. We won't discuss women's rights now.

SYLVIA: [*Giving* DAISY *her hand very cordially.*] And if there's anything I hate it's people who say they're going and then don't go. Good-bye, Mrs. Anderson.

DAISY: It's been very nice to see you.

SYLVIA: I do hope you'll come and see me soon. I'm so very much alone, you'd be doing me a charity if you'd look me up. We might do the curio shops together.

DAISY: That would be great fun. Boy, open the gate.

SYLVIA: Good-bye, Mr. Conway. I'm glad to see you so well.

GEORGE: Thank you very much. Good-bye.

> [*On receiving* DAISY'S *order* WU *goes to the doorway and draws the bolt. He pulls back one heavy door. A beggar shows himself. He is excessively thin, and he has a bush of long bristly hair; he is clothed in patched rags, torn and patched; his legs and feet are bare. He puts out a long hand and breaks into a long, high-pitched whine.*

KNOX: O Lord, get out.

DAISY: Oh no, please, Harold, give him a copper or two.

GEORGE: Daisy never lets a beggar go away without something.

DAISY: It's not because I'm charitable. I'm afraid they'll bring me bad luck.

KNOX: [*Taking a coin from his pocket.*] Here you are, Clarence. Now buzz off.

> [*The beggar takes his dole and saunters away.*

SYLVIA: Good-bye.

DAISY: Good-bye.

> [KNOX *and* SYLVIA *go out.* DAISY *has walked with them towards the doorway and now returns to* GEORGE.

GEORGE: What a very nice girl, Daisy.

DAISY: She seems to make a speciality of speckled peaches. First me and then Mrs. Stopfort.

GEORGE: I was hoping you'd like her.

DAISY: It's hardly probable. She's everything that I'm not; She has everything that I haven't. No, I don't like her; But I'd give anything in the world to be her.

GEORGE: [*Smiling.*] I don't think you need envy her.

DAISY: Don't you think she's pretty?

GEORGE: Yes, very. But you're so much more than pretty. I expect you have more brains in your little finger than she has in her whole body.

DAISY: [*Gravely.*] She has something that I haven't got, George, and I'd give my soul to have.

GEORGE: [*Embarrassed.*] I don't know what you mean. [*Changing the conversation abruptly.*] Daisy, now that I'm going away. . . .

DAISY: [*Interrupting.*] Are you really going to-morrow?

GEORGE: [*Breezily.*] I'm quite well. I'm ashamed to have stayed so long.

DAISY: I don't look forward very much to the long, empty days when you're no longer here.

GEORGE: [*Seriously.*] I must go, Daisy. I really must.

DAISY: [*After a moment's pause.*] What were you going to say to me? Don't thank me for anything I may have done. It's given me a happiness I never knew before.

GEORGE: Except for you I should have died. And when I think of the past I am ashamed.

DAISY: What does the past matter? The past is dead and gone.

GEORGE: And I'm ashamed when I think how patient you were when I was irritable, how kind and thoughtful. I hardly knew I wanted a thing before you gave it to me. Sometimes when I felt I couldn't breathe, the tenderness of your hand on my forehead—oh, it was like a dip in a highland stream on a summer day. I think I never knew that there was in you the most precious thing that any one can have, goodness. O Daisy, it makes me feel so humble.

DAISY: Goodness? [*With the shadow of a laugh.*] O George.

GEORGE: It's because Harry is better and simpler than I am that he was able to see it in you. He felt it in you always, and he was right.

[*The* AMAH *comes in.*

DAISY: [*Sharply.*] What d'you want?

[*The* AMAH *crosses from one to the other and a thin smile crosses her eyes.*

AMAH: Master telephone, Daisy.

DAISY: Why didn't you take the message?

[*She is about to go into the house.*

AMAH: He have go now. He say very much hurry. I say no can findee you. I think you go out.

DAISY: Why did you say that?

AMAH: I think more better, maybe.

GEORGE: [*Smiling.*] That's right, Amah. Never tell the truth when a lie will do as well.

DAISY: Well, what was the message?

AMAH: Master say he must go Tientsin. Very important business. No come back to-night. Come back first train to-morrow.

DAISY: Very well. Tell the boy that we shall be only two to dinner.

AMAH: I go talkee he.

[*Exit.*

GEORGE: [*Urbanely.*] I say, I don't want to be an awful trouble to you. I think I'd better go back to my own place to-night.

DAISY: [*Looking at him.*] Why should you do that?

GEORGE: I was going to-morrow anyway.

DAISY: Do you think my reputation is such a sensitive flower?

GEORGE: [*Lightly.*] Of course not. But people aren't very charitable. It seems rather funny I should stay here when Harry's away.

DAISY: What do you suppose I care if people gossip?

GEORGE: I care for you.

DAISY: [*With a smile, almost archly.*] It's not very flattering to me that you should insist on going the moment Harry does. Do I bore you so much as all that?

GEORGE: [*With a chuckle.*] How can you talk such nonsense? I haven't wanted to get well too quickly. I've so enjoyed sitting quietly here while you read or sewed. I've got so much in the habit of seeing you about me that if I don't go at once I shall never be able to bring myself to go at all.

DAISY: Since that horrible accident I've been rather nervous at the thought of sleeping here by myself. I'm terrified at the thought of being left alone to-night.

GEORGE: Come in with me, then. The Knoxes will be delighted to put you up for the night.

G*

DAISY: [*With a sudden change of manner.*] I don't want you to go, George. I want you to stay.

GEORGE: [*As serious as she is.*] Daisy, don't be too hard on me. You don't know. You don't know. [*With an effort he regains his self-control and returns to his easy chaffing tone.*] Don't forget it's not only a wound in the lung that I've been suffering from. While you and the doctor between you have been patching that up, I've been busy sticking together the pieces of a broken heart. It's nicely set now, no one could tell that there'd ever been anything wrong with it, but I don't think it would be very wise to give it a sudden jolt or jerk.

DAISY: [*In a low quivering voice.*] Why do you say things like that? What is the good of making pretences?

GEORGE: [*Determined to keep the note of lightness.*] It was very silly of me to bother you with my little troubles. It was very hot. I was overworked and nervous at the time or I shouldn't have made so much of it. I'm sure that you'll be as pleased as I am to know that I'm making a very good recovery, thank you.

DAISY: [*As though asking a casual question.*] You don't care for me any more?

GEORGE: I have the greatest affection for you. I admire you and of course I'm grateful to you. But if I thought I was in love with you I was mistaken.

DAISY: Do you know why I wouldn't have a professional nurse, and when you were unconscious for two days refused to leave you for a minute? Do you know why, afterwards, at night when you grew delirious, I wouldn't let Harry watch you? I said it would interfere with his work. I dared not leave you for a single moment. And it was your secret and mine. I wouldn't let anybody in the world share it with me. Do you know what you said in your delirium?

GEORGE: [*Disturbed.*] I expect I talked an awful lot of rot People always do, I believe.

DAISY: [*Passionately.*] You used to call me, Daisy, Daisy, as though your heart was breaking. And when I leaned over you and said, I'm here, you would take my face in your hands so that I could hardly believe you weren't conscious. And you said, I love you.

GEORGE: O God.

DAISY: And sometimes I didn't know how to calm you. You were frantic because you thought they were taking me away from you. I can't bear it, you said, I shall die. I had to put my hands over your mouth so that no one should hear.

GEORGE: I didn't know what I was saying. I wasn't myself. It was just the madness of fever.

DAISY: And sometimes you were so exquisitely tender. Your voice was soft and caressing. And you called me by sweet names so that the tears ran down my cheeks. You thought you held me in your arms and you pressed me to your heart. You were happy then, you were so happy that I was afraid you'd die of it. I know what love is, and you love me.

GEORGE: For God's sake stop. Why do you torture me?

DAISY: And then you were madly jealous. You hated Harry. I think you could have killed him.

GEORGE: That's not true. That's infamous. Never! Never!

DAISY: You know as well as I do that he's no more than a puppet. You despise him.

GEORGE: Harry? Why, he's ten times better than I am. I'm fonder of him than of any one in the world. He's the straightest man I ever knew.

DAISY: Oh, you can say that with your lips. Sometimes you thought he put his arms round me and kissed me, and you sobbed aloud. Oh, it was so painful. I forgot that you were unconscious and I took your hands and said, He's not here. You and I are alone, alone. And sometimes I think you understood. You fell back, and a look of peace came on your face as if you were in heaven, and you said—do you know what you said? You said, Beloved, beloved, beloved.

[*Her voice breaks and the tears course down her cheeks.* GEORGE *is shattered by what she has told him.*

GEORGE: I'm vile. I suppose there are few of us that wouldn't turn away from ourselves in horror if the innermost thoughts of our heart, the thoughts we're only conscious of to hate, were laid bare. But that shameful thing that showed itself in me isn't me. I disown it. . . .

DAISY: I thought you had more courage. I thought you had more sense. Do you call that you, a few conventional prejudices? The real you is the love that consumes you more hotly than ever the fever did. The only you is the one that loves me. The rest is only frills. It's a domino that you put on at a masked ball.

GEORGE: You don't know what you say? Frills? It's honour, and duty, and decency. It's everything that makes it possible for me to cling to the shadow of my self-respect.

DAISY: Oh, all that means nothing. You fool. You might as well try with your bare hands to stop the flow of the Yangtse.

GEORGE: If I perish, I perish. Oh, of course I love you. All night I'm tortured with love and tortured with jealousy, but the day does come at last, and then I can get hold of myself again. My love is some horrible thing gnawing at my heart-strings. I hate it and despise it. But I can fight it, fight it all the time. Oh, I've been here too long. I ought to have got back to work long ago. Work is my only chance. Daisy, I beseech you to let me go.

DAISY: How can I let you go? I love you.

GEORGE: [*Thunderstruck.*] You? [*Impatiently, with a shrug of the shoulders.*] Oh, you're talking nonsense.

DAISY: Why do you suppose I've said all these things? Do you think a woman cares twopence for a man's love when she doesn't love him?

GEORGE: Oh, it's impossible. You don't know what you're saying. I know how good and kind you are. You've been touched by my love. You mistake pity for love.

DAISY: I'm not good and I'm not kind. There's no room in my soul for pity. In my soul there's only a raging hunger. If I know what you feel it's because I feel it too. I love you, I love you, I love you.

GEORGE: And Harry?

DAISY: What do I care about Harry? I hate him because he's stood between me and you. You said yourself that he was empty and trivial.

GEORGE: Never. I've never said a word against him. What I said in my delirium means nothing.

DAISY: It was the truth. It was your heart that spoke. He is nothing.

GEORGE: He's your husband. He's my friend.

DAISY: He doesn't exist. I've loved you always from the first day I saw you. The others were nothing to me, Lee Tai and Harry and the rest. I've loved you always. I've never loved any one but you. All these years I've kept the letters you wrote to me. I've read them till I know every word by heart. They're all blurred and smudged with the tears I've wept over them. They were all I had. Do you think I'm going to let you go now? All my pain, all my anguish, are nothing any more. I love you and you love me.

GEORGE: Oh, don't, don't.

DAISY: You can't leave me now. If you leave me I shall kill myself.

GEORGE: I must go away. I must never see you again. Whatever happens we must never meet.

DAISY: [*Exasperated and impatient.*] That's impossible. What will you say to Harry?

GEORGE: If need be I'll tell him the truth.

DAISY: What difference will that make? Will you love me any the less? Yes, tell him. Tell him that I love you and you only, and that I belong to you and to you only.

GEORGE: O Daisy, for God's sake try and control yourself. We must do our duty, we must, we must.

DAISY: I know no duty. I only know love. There's no room in my soul for anything else. You say that love is like a wild beast gnawing at your entrails. My love is a liberator. It's freed me from a hateful past. It's freed me from Harry. There's nothing in the world now but you and me and the love that joins us. I want you, I want you.

GEORGE: Don't, don't. Oh, this is madness. There's only one thing to be done. God, give me strength. Daisy, you know I love you. I love you with all my heart and soul. But it's good-bye. I'll never see you again. Never, never. So help me, God.

DAISY: How can you be so cruel? You're heartless. I've wanted you all these years. I've hungered for you. You don't know what my humiliation has been. Pity me because I loved you. If you leave me now I shall die. You open the doors of heaven to me and then you slam them in my face. Haven't you made me unhappy enough? You'd have done better to kill me ten years ago. You trampled me in the mud and then you left me. Oh, what shall I do?

> [*She sinks to the ground weeping as though her heart would break.* GEORGE *looks at her for a minute, his face distorted with agony; he clenches his hands in the violence of his effort to control himself. He takes his hat and walks slowly towards the gate. He withdraws the great bolt that holds it. When* DAISY *hears the*

sound of this she starts to her feet and staggers towards him.

DAISY: George. No, no. Not yet.

[*She staggers and with a cry falls headlong. She has fainted.*

GEORGE: [*Rushing towards her.*] Daisy, Daisy. [*He kneels down and takes her head in his hands. He is fearfully agitated.*] O my darling, what is it? O my God, Daisy. Speak to me. [*Calling.*] Amah! Amah! [DAISY *slowly opens her eyes.*] O my beloved, I thought you were dead.

DAISY: Lift me up.

GEORGE: You can't stand.

[*He raises her to her feet so that when she is erect she is in his arms. She puts her arms round his neck.*

DAISY: Don't leave me.

GEORGE: My precious. My beloved.

[*She turns her face to him, offering her lips, and he bends his head and kisses her. She closes her eyes in ecstasy.*

DAISY: Take me in. I feel so ill.

GEORGE: I'll carry you.

[*He lifts her up and carries her into the house. From the opposite side the* AMAH *appears. She goes to the gateway and slips the bolt forward into position. Then she comes to the tea-table, sits down, and takes a scone.*

AMAH: Hi yah.

[*She bites the scone and chews placidly. On her face is a smirk of irony.*

END OF SCENE V

SCENE VI

SCENE: *A small room in a Chinese house in Peking. The walls are whitewashed, but the whitewash is not a little stained. Three or four scrolls hang on them, written over in large characters with inscriptions. On the floor is matting. The only furniture consists of a table, with a couple of chairs, a wooden pallet covered with matting, with cushions at one end of it, and a Korean chest heavily ornamented with brass. At the back are a couple of windows, elaborately latticed and covered with rice paper, and a lightly-carved door.*

DAISY *is seated in one of the chairs. She has taken her pocket mirror out of her bag and is looking at herself. She is gay and happy. The* AMAH *comes in. She carries a long-necked vase in which are a couple of carnations.*

AMAH: I bring you flowers make room look pletty.

DAISY: O you nice old thing. Put them on the table.

AMAH: You look at yourself in looking-glass?

DAISY: I'm looking young. It suits me to be happy.

AMAH: You very pletty girl. I very pletty girl long time ago. You look alla same me some day.

DAISY: [*Amused.*] Heaven forbid.

AMAH: You velly good temper to-day, Daisy. You glad because George come.

DAISY: I didn't see him yesterday.

AMAH: He keep you waiting.

DAISY: The wretch. He always keeps me waiting. But what do I care as long as he comes? We shall have three hours. Perhaps he'll dine here. If he says he can, give him what he likes to eat. No one can make such delicious things as you can if you want to.

AMAH: You try flatter me.

DAISY: I don't. You know very well you're the best cook in China.

AMAH: [*Tickled.*] O Daisy. I know you more better than you think.

DAISY: You're a wicked old woman. [*She gives her a kiss on both cheeks.*] What are they making such a row about next door?

AMAH: Coolie, he got killed this morning. He have two small children. Their mother, she die long time ago.

DAISY: How dreadful. Poor little things.

AMAH: You like see them? They here.

> [*She goes to the door and beckons. A little, old, shabby Chinaman comes in with two tiny children, a boy and a girl, one holding on to each hand. They are very solemn and shy and silent.*

DAISY: Oh, what lambs.

AMAH: They no got money. This old man he say he take them and he bring them up. But he only coolie. He no got much money himself.

DAISY: Is he related to them?

AMAH: No, him just velly good man. He no can do velly much. He just do what he can. The neighbours, they help little.

DAISY: But I'll help too. Have you got any money on you?

AMAH: I got two, three dollars.

DAISY: What's the good of that? Let him have this.

> [*She has a chain of gold beads round her neck. She takes it off and puts it in the old man's hands.*

AMAH: That chain very ispensive, Daisy.

DAISY: What do I care? Let him sell it for what it'll fetch. It'll bring me luck. [*To the old man.*] You sabe?

> [*He nods, smiling.*

AMAH: I think he understand all right.

DAISY: [*Looking at the children.*] Aren't they sweet? And so solemn. [*To the* AMAH.] You go chop-chop to the toyshop opposite and buy them some toys.

AMAH: Can do.

> [*She goes out.* DAISY *takes the children and sets them up on the table.*

DAISY: [*Charmingly.*] Now you come and talk to me. Sit very still now or you'll fall off. [*To the little boy.*] I wonder how old you are. [*To the old man.*] Wu? Liu?

OLD MAN: Liu.

DAISY: [*To the little boy.*] Six years old. Good gracious, you're quite a man. If I had a little boy he'd be older than you now. If I had a little boy I'd dress him in such smart things. And I'd bath him myself. I wouldn't let any horrid old amah bath him. And I wouldn't stuff him up with sweets like the Chinese do; I'd give him one piece of chocolate when he was a good boy. Gracious me, I've got some chocolates here. Wait there. Sit quite still. [*She goes over to the shelf on which is a bag of chocolates.*] There's one for you and one for you and [*to the old man*] one for you. And here's one for me.

> [*The children and the Chinaman eat the chocolates solemnly. The* AMAH *returns with a doll and a child's Peking cart.*

AMAH: Have catchee toys.

DAISY: Look what kind old Amah has brought you. [*She lifts the children off the table and gives the doll to the little girl and the cart to the boy.*] Here's a beautiful doll for you and here's a real cart for you. [*She sits down on the floor.*] Look, the wheels go round and everything.

AMAH: Have got more presents.

> [*She takes out of her sleeve little bladders with mouthpiece attached so that they can be blown up.*

DAISY: What on earth is this? Oh, I love them. We must all have one. [*She distributes them and they all blow them up. There is the sound of scratching at the door.*] Who's that, I wonder?

AMAH: If you say come in, maybe you see.

DAISY: Open the door, you old silly. [*She begins to blow up the balloon again. The* AMAH *goes to the door and opens it.* LEE TAI *steps in.*] Send these away. [*The* AMAH *makes a sign to the old Chinaman; he gives each child a hand and with their presents they go out. The* AMAH *slips out after them.*] I thought you were dead.

LEE TAI: I'm very much alive, thank you.

DAISY: Ah, well, we'll hope for the best.

LEE TAI: I trust you're not displeased to see me.

DAISY: [*Gaily.*] If you'd come yesterday I should certainly have smacked your face, but to-day I'm in such a good humour that even the sight of you is tolerable.

LEE TAI: You weren't here yesterday.

　　　[*The* AMAH *comes in carrying on a little wooden tray two Chinese bowls and a teapot.*

DAISY: My dear mamma seems to think you've come to pay me a visit. You mustn't let me keep you too long.

LEE TAI: You are expecting some one? I know.

　　　　　　　　　　　　　　　　　[*The* AMAH *goes out.*

DAISY: [*Chaffing him.*] I always said you had a brain.

LEE TAI: No better a one than yours, Daisy. It was a clever trick when you got me to try to put your husband out of the way so that you should be free for George Conway.

DAISY: It was nothing to do with me. I told you I'd have nothing to do with it. You made a hash of it. One can forgive the good for being stupid, but when rascals are fools there's no excuse.

LEE TAI: The best laid schemes of mice and men, as my

favourite poet, Robert Burns, so elegantly puts it, gang aft agley.

DAISY: I don't care a damn about your favourite poet. What have you come here for to-day?

LEE TAI: As it turns out, I do not see that there is any cause for regret that George Conway got the knife thrust that was intended for your husband. I wish it had gone a little deeper.

DAISY: [*Coolly.*] As it turns out, you only did me a service. But still you haven't told me to what I owe the honour of your visit.

LEE TAI: Civility. I like to be on friendly terms with my tenants.

DAISY: [*Surprised.*] Your what?

LEE TAI: [*Urbanely.*] This happens to be my house. When I discovered that your honourable mother had taken the rooms in this courtyard so that you might have a place where George Conway and you could safely meet, I thought I would buy the whole house.

DAISY: I hope it was a good investment.

LEE TAI: Otherwise perhaps I should have hesitated. It was clever of you to find so convenient a place. With a curio shop in front into which any one can be seen going without remark, and an ill-lit passage leading to this court, it is perfect.

DAISY: What is the idea?

LEE TAI: [*With a twinkle in his eyes.*] Are you a little frightened?

DAISY: Not a bit. What can you do? You can tell Harry. Tell him.

LEE TAI: [*Affably.*] George Conway would be ruined.

DAISY: [*With a shrug.*] He'd lose his job. Perhaps you would give him another. You're mixed up in so many concerns you could surely find use for a white man who speaks Chinese as well as George does.

LEE TAI: I find even your shamelessness attractive.

DAISY: I'm profoundly grateful for the compliment.

LEE TAI: But do not fear. I shall do nothing. I bought this house because I like you to know that always, always you are in my hand. Where you go, I go. Where you are, I am. Sometimes you do not see me, but nevertheless I am close. I do nothing. I am content to wait.

DAISY: Your time is your own. I have no objection to your wasting it.

LEE TAI: One day, and I think that day is not very far distant, you will come to me. I was the first and I shall be the last. If you like I will marry you.

DAISY: [*With a smile.*] I thought you had two, if not three, wives already. I fancy that number four would have rather a thin time.

LEE TAI: My wife can be divorced. I am willing to marry you before the British Consul. We will go to Penang. I have a house there. You shall have motor-cars.

DAISY: It's astonishing how easy it is to resist temptations that don't tempt you.

LEE TAI: Sneer. What do I care? I wait. . . . What have you to do with white men? You are not a white woman. What power has this blood of your father's when it is mingled with the tumultuous stream which you have inherited through your mother from innumerable generations? Our race is very pure and very strong. Strange nations have overrun us, but in a little while we have absorbed them so that no trace of a foreign people is left in us. China is like the Yangtse, which is fed by five hundred streams and yet remains unchanged, the river of golden sand, majestic, turbulent, indifferent, and everlasting. What power have you to swim against that mighty current? You can wear European clothes and eat European food, but in your heart you are a China-woman. Are your passions the weak and vacillating

passions of the white man? There is in your heart a
simplicity which the white man can never fathom and a
deviousness which he can never understand. Your soul
is like a rice patch cleared in the middle of the jungle.
All around the jungle hovers, watchful and jealous, and
it is only by ceaseless labour that you can prevent its
inroads. One day your labour will be vain and the jungle
will take back its own. China is closing in on you.

DAISY: My poor Lee Tai, you're talking perfect nonsense.

LEE TAI: You're restless and unhappy and dissatisfied
because you're struggling against instincts which were
implanted in your breast when the white man was a
hungry, naked savage. One day you will surrender.
You will cast off the white woman like an outworn
garment. You will come back to China as a tired child
comes back to his mother. And in the immemorial
usages of our great race you will find peace.

> [*There is a moment's silence.* DAISY *passes her hand over
> her forehead. Against her will she is strangely
> impressed by what* LEE TAI *has said. She gives a little
> shudder and recovers herself.*

DAISY: George Conway loves me, and I——. Oh!

LEE TAI: The white man's love lasts no longer than a
summer day. It is a red, red rose. Now it flaunts its
scented beauty proudly in the sun, and to-morrow its
petals, wrinkled and stinking, lie scattered on the ground.

> [*There is a sound of a footstep in the courtyard outside.*

DAISY: Here he is. Go quickly.

> [GEORGE *opens the door and stops as he catches sight of*
> LEE TAI.

GEORGE: Hulloa, who's this?

> [LEE TAI *steps forward, smiling and obsequious.*

LEE TAI: I am the owner of this house. The Amah complained that the roof leaked, and I came to see for
myself.

GEORGE: [*Frowning.*] It's of no consequence. Please don't bother about it.

LEE TAI: I wish I needn't. The Amah has a virulent and an active tongue—I am afraid she will give me no peace till I have satisfied her outrageous demands.

GEORGE: You speak extraordinarily good English.

LEE TAI: I am a graduate of the University of Edinburgh.

DAISY: Robert Burns is his favourite poet.

LEE TAI: I spent a year at Oxford and another at Harvard. I can express myself in English not without fluency.

GEORGE: Let me compliment you on your good sense in retaining your national costume. I think it a pity that the returned students should insist on wearing ugly tweed suits and billycock hats.

LEE TAI: I spent eight years abroad. I brought back with me no more admiration for Western dress than for Western civilisation.

GEORGE: That is very interesting.

LEE TAI: You are pleased to be sarcastic.

GEORGE: And you, I think, are somewhat supercilious. Believe me, the time has passed when the mandarins of your country, in their impenetrable self-conceit, could put up a barrier against the advance of civilisation. If you have any love for China, you must see that her only chance to take her rightful place in the world is to accept honestly and sincerely the teaching of the West.

LEE TAI: And if in our hearts we despise and detest what you have to teach us? For what reason are you so confident that you are so superior to us that it behoves us to sit humbly at your feet? Have you excelled us in arts or letters? Have our thinkers been less profound than yours? Has our civilisation been less elaborate, less complicated, less refined than yours? Why, when you lived in caves and clothed yourselves with skins we were a cultured people. Do you know that we tried an experiment which is unique in the world?

GEORGE: [*Good-naturedly.*] What experiment is that?

LEE TAI: We sought to rule this great people not by force, but by wisdom. And for centuries we succeeded. Then why does the white man despise the yellow? Shall I tell you?

GEORGE: Do.

LEE TAI: [*With a smiling contempt.*] Because he has invented the machine-gun. That is your superiority. We are a defenceless horde and you can blow us into eternity. [*With a tinge of sadness.*] You have shattered the dream of our philosophers that the world could be governed by the power of law and order. . . . And now you are teaching our young men your secret. You have thrust your hideous inventions upon us. Fools. Do you not know that we have a genius for mechanics? Do you not know that there are in this country four hundred millions of the most practical and industrious people in the world? Do you think it will take us long to learn? And what will become of your superiority when the yellow man can make as good guns as the white and fire them as straight? You have appealed to the machine-gun and by the machine-gun shall you be judged.

> [*There is a pause. Suddenly* GEORGE *gives* LEE TAI *a scrutinising glance.*

GEORGE: What is your name?

LEE TAI: [*With a thin, amused smile.*] Lee Tai Cheng.

GEORGE: [*With a frigid politeness.*] I'm sure you are very busy, Mr. Lee. I won't detain you any longer.

LEE TAI: [*Still smiling.*] I wish you a good day.

> [*He bows slightly and shakes his own hands in the Chinese manner. He goes out. He leaves behind him an impression that is at once ironic and sinister.*

GEORGE: What the devil is he doing here?

DAISY: [*Amused.*] He came to make me an offer of marriage. I pointed out to him that I was married already.

GEORGE: [*Not without irritation.*] How did he know you were here?

DAISY: He made it his business to find out.

GEORGE: Does he know that . . . ?

DAISY: [*Coolly.*] You know China better than most Englishmen. You know that the white man can do nothing without the Chinese knowing it. But they won't tell other white men unless—unless it's to their advantage to do so.

GEORGE: You told me that this house belonged to the Amah.

DAISY: [*Smiling.*] That was a slight exaggeration.

GEORGE: You put it very mildly.

DAISY: You said you wouldn't come to the temple. It meant finding some place where we could meet or never seeing you at all.

GEORGE: [*Sombrely.*] We began with deceit and with deceit we've continued.

DAISY: [*Tenderly.*] There's no deceit in my love, George. After all, our love is the only thing that matters.

GEORGE: [*With a certain awkwardness.*] I'm afraid I've kept you waiting. André Leroux came to see me just as I was leaving the Legation.

DAISY: [*Remembering.*] I know. Mrs. Stopfort's young man.

GEORGE: He said he knew Mrs. Stopfort's friends were rather anxious about her future, and he wanted them to know that he was going to marry her as soon as she was free.

DAISY: Oh!

GEORGE: Of course it's the only decent thing to do, but I wasn't sure if he'd see it. He's a very good fellow.

[*With a smile.*] He spent at least half an hour telling me how he adored Mrs. Stopfort.

DAISY: [*Good-humouredly.*] Oh, you know I'm not the sort of woman to grouse because you're a little late. I can always occupy myself by thinking how wonderful it will be to see you. And if I get bored with that I read your letters again.

GEORGE: I shouldn't have thought they were worth that.

DAISY: I think I have every word you have ever written to me—those old letters of ten years ago and the little notes you write to me now. Even though they're only two or three lines saying you'll come here or can't come, they're precious to me.

GEORGE: But do you keep them here?

DAISY: Yes, they're safe there. They're locked up in that box. Only Amah has the key of this room. . . . George.

GEORGE: Yes.

DAISY: Will you do something for me?

GEORGE: If I can.

DAISY: Will you dine here to-night? Amah will get us a lovely little dinner.

GEORGE: Oh, my dear, I can't. I've got an official dinner that I can't possibly get out of.

DAISY: Oh, how rotten.

GEORGE: But I thought Harry was coming back this morning. He's been gone a week already.

DAISY: I had a letter saying he had to go on to Kalgan. But don't say anything about it. He told me I was to keep it a secret.

GEORGE: He must hate having to be away so much as he's been lately. The death of that man Gregson has upset things rather.

DAISY: [*Smiling.*] I wish I could thank Gregson for the good turn he did *us* by dying at the psychological moment.

GEORGE: [*Drily.*] I don't suppose that was his intention.

DAISY: Except for that Harry would have insisted on going to Chung-King. Now there's no possibility of that for at least a year.

GEORGE: I suppose not.

DAISY: We've got a year before us, George, a whole year. And in a year anything can happen.

GEORGE: [*Gravely.*] Do you never have any feeling that we've behaved rottenly to Harry?

DAISY: I? I've been happy for the first time in my life. At last I've known peace and rest. O George, I'm so grateful for all you've given me. In these three months you've changed the whole world for me. I thought I couldn't love you more than I did. I think every day my love grows more consuming.

GEORGE: [*With a sigh.*] I've never known a single moment's happiness.

DAISY: That's not true. When I've held you in my arms I've looked into your eyes and I've seen.

GEORGE: Oh, I know. There've been moments of madness in which I forgot everything but that I loved you. I'm a low rotten cad. No one could despise me more than I despise myself. I've loved you so that there was room for nothing else in my soul. Waking and sleeping you've obsessed me.

DAISY: That's how I want you to love me.

GEORGE: And I've hated myself for loving you. I've hated you for making me love you. I've struggled with all my might and a hundred times I thought I'd conquered myself, and then the touch of your hand, the softness of your lips—I was like a bird in a cage. I beat myself against the bars and all the time the door was open and I hadn't the will to fly out.

DAISY: [*Tenderly.*] O darling, why do you make yourself unhappy when happiness lies in the hollow of your hand?

GEORGE: Have you never regretted anything?

DAISY: Never.

GEORGE: You're stronger than I am. I'm as weak as dishwater. It's funny that it should have taken me all these years to find it out. I was weak from the beginning. But I was weakest of all that day. I was distracted, I thought you were dying, I forgot everything except that I loved you.

DAISY: [*With passion.*] O my sweetheart. Don't you remember how, late in the night, we went outside the temple and looked at the moonlight on the walls of the Forbidden City? You had no regrets then.

GEORGE: [*Going on with his own thoughts.*] And afterwards your tears, your happiness, the dread of giving you pain and the hot love that burnt me—I was in the toils then. I too knew a happiness that I had never known before. On one side was honesty and duty and everything that makes a man respect himself—and on the other was love. I thought you'd be going away in two or three weeks and that would be the end of it. Oh, it was no excuse—there are no excuses for me, I can never look Harry in the face again; but though my heart was breaking at the thought, I—I knew that in a few days I should see you for the last time.

DAISY: [*Scornfully.*] Do you think I'd have gone then?

GEORGE: And then came that sudden, unexpected, disastrous change in all Harry's plans. And this house and all the sordid horror of an intrigue. And then there was nothing to do but face the fact that I was a cur. I wouldn't wish my worst enemy the torture that I've undergone.

DAISY: [*Full of love and pity.*] O my darling, you know I'd do anything in the world to give you happiness.

GEORGE: [*Sombrely, looking away from her.*] Daisy, I think
you can never give me happiness, but you can help me,
not to make amends, because that's impossible, but
to. . . . [*Impulsively, looking at her now.*] O Daisy, do you
really love me?

DAISY: With all my heart. With all my soul.

GEORGE: Then help me. Let us finish.

DAISY: [*Quickly.*] What do you mean?

GEORGE: I don't want to seem a prig. I don't want to
preach. Heaven knows, I've never pretended to be a
saint. But what we've done is wrong. You must see that
as plainly as I do.

DAISY: Is it wrong to love? How can I help it?

GEORGE: Daisy, I want to—cease doing wrong.

DAISY: You make me impatient. How can you be so weak?

GEORGE: I want you to believe that I love you. But I can't
go on with this deceit. I'd sooner shoot myself.

DAISY: You couldn't say that if you loved me as I love you.

GEORGE: [*Brutally.*] I *don't* love you any more.

DAISY: [*With a scornful shrug.*] That's not true.

GEORGE: [*Clenching his teeth.*] I came here to-day to tell you
that—well, that it's finished and done with. O God, I
don't want to make you unhappy. But you must see we
can't go on. Everything that's decent in me revolts at the
thought. I beseech you to forget me.

DAISY: As if I could.

GEORGE: I'm going away for a bit.

DAISY: [*Startled.*] You? Why?

GEORGE: I didn't trust myself. You see, I've lost my nerve,
so I applied for short leave. I'm sailing for Vancouver on
the *Empress*. I leave here the day after to-morrow.

DAISY: [*Suddenly distraught.*] You don't mean that you're
going to leave me? I didn't pay any attention to what you

said. I thought it was just a mood. George, George, say that you don't mean that?

GEORGE: It's the only thing to do, for your sake and Harry's and mine. [*Taking his courage in both hands.*] This is good-bye, Daisy.

DAISY: [*Seizing him by the shoulders.*] Let me look at your eyes. George, you're crazy. You can't go.

GEORGE: [*Drawing away.*] For God's sake, don't touch me. I wanted to break it to you gently. I don't know what's happened. Everything has gone wrong. I'm going, Daisy, and nothing in the world can move me. I implore you to bear it bravely. [*She looks at him with suffering, anxious eyes. She is stunned.*] I'm afraid you're going to be awfully unhappy for a little while. But I beseech you to have courage. Soon the pain won't be so great, and then you'll see I've done the only possible thing.

DAISY: [*Sullenly.*] How long are you going for?

GEORGE: Three or four months. [*A pause.*] I knew you'd be brave, Daisy. Do you know, I was afraid you'd cry most awfully. It tears my heart to see you cry.

DAISY: Do you think I'm a child? Do you think I can cry now?

GEORGE: It's good-bye then, Daisy.

> [*She goes not answer. She hardly hears what he says. He hesitates an instant wretchedly, and then goes quickly out of the room. DAISY stands as if she were turned to stone. Her face is haggard. In a minute LEE TAI comes softly in. He stands at the door, looking at her, then gives a little cough. She turns round and sees him.*

DAISY: [*Fiercely.*] What do you want?

LEE TAI: I was waiting till you were disengaged.

DAISY: Have you been listening?

LEE TAI: I have heard.

DAISY: I wish I could have seen you with your ear to the keyhole. You must have looked dignified.

[*She begins to laugh, angrily, hysterically, beside herself.*

LEE TAI: Let me give you a cup of tea. It's quite warm still.

DAISY: I should have thought you were rather old and fat to stoop so much.

LEE TAI: Fortunately the windows are only covered with rice paper, so I was saved that inconvenience.

[*He hands her a cup of tea. She takes it and flings it at him. The tea is splashed over his black robe.*

DAISY: Get out of here or I'll kill you.

[*He wipes his dress with a large silk pocket handkerchief.*

LEE TAI: You forget sometimes the manners that were taught you at that elegant school for young ladies in England.

DAISY: I suppose you've come to crow over me. Well, crow.

LEE TAI: I told you that I thought I should not have to wait very long.

DAISY: [*Scornfully.*] You fool. Do you think it's finished?

LEE TAI: Did I not tell you that the white man's love was weak and vacillating?

DAISY: He's going away for four months. Do you think that frightens me? He's loved me for ten years. I've loved him for ten years. Do you think he can forget me in four months? He'll come back.

LEE TAI: Not to you.

DAISY: Yes, yes, yes. And when he comes it'll be for good. He'll hunger for me as he hungered before. He'll forget his scruples, his remorse, his stupid duties, because he'll only remember me.

LEE TAI: [*Very quietly.*] He's going to be married to Miss Sylvia Knox.

[DAISY *springs at him and seizes him by the throat.*

DAISY: That's a lie. That's a lie. Take it back. You pig.

> [*He takes her hands and drags them away from his throat. He holds her fast.*

LEE TAI: Ask your mother. She knows. The Chinese all know.

DAISY: [*Calling.*] Amah, Amah. It's a lie. How dare you?

LEE TAI: He told you he was going to an official dinner, but he didn't tell you that as soon as he could get away he was going to play bridge at the Knoxes'. Pity you don't play. They might have asked you too.

> [*The* AMAH *comes in.*

AMAH: You call me, Daisy?

DAISY: [*Snatching her hands away.*] Let me go, you fool. [*To the* AMAH.] He says George Conway is engaged to Harold Knox's sister. It's not true.

AMAH: I no sabe. George's boy say so. Knox the night before last at the club, he say to his friend, George Conway and my sister, they going to make a match of it.

> [*A horrible change comes over* DAISY'S *face as all its features become distorted with rage and jealousy.*

DAISY: The liar.

> [*She stares in front of her, hatred, anger, and mortification seething in her heart. Then she gives a cruel malicious chuckle. She goes quickly to the Korean chest and flings it open. She takes out a parcel of letters, and crossing back swiftly to* LEE TAI *thrusts them in his hands.*

LEE TAI: What is this?

DAISY: They're the letters he wrote me. Let them come into Harry's hands.

LEE TAI: Why?

DAISY: So that Harry may know everything.

LEE TAI: [*After a moment's thought.*] And what will you do for me if I do this for you?

DAISY: What you like. . . . Only the
    quickly. George goes away the da

LEE TAI: Where is your husband?

DAISY: Kalgan.

LEE TAI: The letters shall reach him t
    I'll send them by car.

DAISY: It'll be a pleasant surprise for his breakfast.

LEE TAI: Daisy.

DAISY: Go quickly—or I shall change my mind. There'll be
    plenty of time for everything else after to-morrow.

LEE TAI: I'll go.

       [LEE TAI *goes out*. DAISY *gives him a look of contempt.*

DAISY: Fool.

AMAH: What you mean, Daisy?

DAISY: Harry will divorce me. And then. . . .

           [DAISY *gives a little cry of triumph.*

END OF SCENE VI

H

SCENE VII

SCENE: *The sitting-room in the Andersons' apartments.*

The scene is the same as Scene IV. DAISY *and the* AMAH. DAISY *is walking restlessly backwards and forwards.*

DAISY: At what time does the train from Kalgan get in?

AMAH: Five o'clock, my think so.

DAISY: What time is it now?

　　　[*The* AMAH *takes a large gold watch out and looks at it.*

AMAH: My watch no walkee.

DAISY: Why don't you have it mended? What's the good of a watch that doesn't go?

AMAH: Gold watch. Eighteen carats. Cost velly much money. Give me plenty face.

DAISY: [*Impatiently.*] Go and ask Wu what time it is.

AMAH: I know time. I tell by the sun. More better than European watch. I think half-past four maybe.

DAISY: Why doesn't George come?

AMAH: Maybe he velly busy.

DAISY: You gave him the note yourself?

AMAH: Yes, I give him letter.

DAISY: What did he say?

AMAH: He no say nothing. He look: damn, damn.

DAISY: Did you tell him it was very important?

AMAH: I say, you come quick. Chop-chop.

DAISY: Yes.

AMAH: I tell you before. Why you want me tell you again? He say he come chop-chop when he get away from office.

DAISY: As if the office mattered now. I ought to have gone to him myself.

AMAH: You no make him come more quick because you walk about. Why you no sit still?

DAISY: The train's never punctual. It'll take Harry at least twenty minutes to get out here.

AMAH: Lee Tai. . . .

DAISY: [*Interrupting.*] Don't talk to me of Lee Tai. Why on earth should I bother about Lee Tai?

[Wu *comes in with a card. He gives it to* DAISY.

DAISY: Miss Knox. Say I'm not at home.

WU: Yes, Missy.

[*He is about to go out.*

DAISY: Stop. Is she alone?

WU: She ride up to gate with gentleman and lady. She say can she see you for two, three minutes.

DAISY: [*After a moment's consideration.*] Tell her to come in.

[Wu *goes out.*

AMAH: What for you want to see her, Daisy?

DAISY: Mind your own business.

AMAH: George come very soon now.

DAISY: I shall get rid of her as soon as he does. . . .
[*Almost to herself.*] I want to see for myself.

[SYLVIA *comes in. She wears a riding habit.* DAISY *greets
her cordially. Her manner, which was restless,
becomes on a sudden gay, gracious, and cordial.*

DAISY: O my dear, how sweet of you to come all this way.

[*The* AMAH *slips out.*

SYLVIA: I can only stop a second. I was riding with the Fergusons and we passed your temple. I thought I'd just run in and see how you were. I haven't seen you for an age.

DAISY: Are the Fergusons waiting outside?

SYLVIA: They rode on. They said they'd fetch me in five minutes.

DAISY: [*Smiling.*] How did your bridge party go off last night?

SYLVIA: How on earth did you hear about that? Did Mr. Conway tell you? I wish you played bridge. We really had rather a lark.

DAISY: George didn't come in till late, I suppose?

SYLVIA: Oh no, he got away in fairly decent time. Where there's a will there's a way, you know, even at official functions.

DAISY: [*With a little laugh.*] Oh, I know. I'm expecting him here in a minute. I hope you won't have to go before he comes.

SYLVIA: Well, I saw him yesterday. I can live one day without seeing him.

DAISY: I wonder if he can live one day without seeing you.

SYLVIA: I'm tolerably sure he can do that.

DAISY: [*As if she were merely teasing.*] A little bird has whispered to me that there's a very pretty blonde in Peking . . .

SYLVIA: [*Interrupting.*] Probably peroxide.

DAISY: Not in this case. Who is not entirely indifferent to the Assistant Chinese Secretary at the British Legation.

SYLVIA: Fancy.

DAISY: I suppose you haven't an idea whom I'm talking about.

SYLVIA: Not a ghost.

DAISY: Then why do you blush to the roots of your hair?

SYLVIA: I was outraged at your suggestion that my hair was dyed.

DAISY: It's too bad of me to tease you, isn't it?

SYLVIA: I'm a perfect owl. You know what a tactless idiot

my brother is. He will chaff me about George Conway, so it makes me self-conscious when anybody talks about him.

DAISY: Darling, it's nothing to be ashamed of. Why shouldn't you be in love with him.

SYLVIA: [*With a laugh.*] But I'm not in love with him.

DAISY: Why does your brother chaff you then?

SYLVIA: Because he's under the delusion that it's funny.

DAISY: But you do like him, don't you?

SYLVIA: Of course I like him. . . . I think he's a very good sort.

DAISY: Would you marry him if he asked you?

SYLVIA: My dear, what are you talking about? The thought never entered my head.

DAISY: Oh, what nonsense. When a man's as attentive to a girl as George has been to you she can't help asking herself if she'd like to marry him or not.

SYLVIA: [*Coldly, but still smiling.*] Can't she? I'm afraid I haven't a close acquaintance with that sort of girl.

DAISY: Am I being vulgar? You know, we half-castes are sometimes.

SYLVIA: [*With a trace of impatience.*] Of course you're not vulgar. But I don't know why you want to talk about something that's absolute Greek to me.

DAISY: The natural curiosity of the Eurasian. Everybody tells me that you're engaged to George.

SYLVIA: Look at my hand.

[*She stretches out her left hand so that* DAISY *should see there is no ring on the fourth finger.* DAISY *stares at it for a moment.*]

DAISY: You always used to wear an engagement ring.

SYLVIA: [*Gravely.*] It was put on my finger by a poor boy who was killed. I meant to wear it always.

DAISY: Why have you taken it off?

[*She looks at* SYLVIA. *She can no longer preserve her artificial gaiety and her voice is cold and hard. Before* SYLVIA *can answer* GEORGE CONWAY *comes in.*

DAISY: [*Regaining with an effort her earlier sprightliness.*] There you are at last.

GEORGE: I couldn't come sooner. I was with the Minister.

DAISY: We were wondering why you were so late.

SYLVIA: Daisy was wondering.

GEORGE: [*Shaking hands with* SYLVIA.] I thought that was your pony outside.

SYLVIA: Clever.

GEORGE: The Fergusons were just riding up as I came.

SYLVIA: Oh, they've come to fetch me. I must bolt.

GEORGE: I'm afraid we kept you up till all sorts of hours last night.

SYLVIA: Not a bit. Do I look jaded?

GEORGE: Of course not. You young things can stay up till three in the morning and be as fresh as paint. Wait till you're my age.

SYLVIA: You haven't passed your hundredth birthday yet, have you?

GEORGE: Not quite. But I'm old enough to be your father.

SYLVIA: I will not stay and listen to you talk rubbish. Good-bye, Daisy. Do come and see me one day this week.

DAISY: Good-bye.

GEORGE: I'll come and help you mount, shall I?

SYLVIA: Oh no, don't bother. Mr. Ferguson is there.

GEORGE: Oh, all right.

[*She goes out.*

DAISY: [*Her smiles vanishing, hostile and cold.*] You might shut the door.

GEORGE: [*Doing so.*] I will.

DAISY: Aren't you going to kiss me?

GEORGE: Daisy.

DAISY: [*Hastily.*] Oh no, it doesn't matter. Don't bother.

GEORGE: You said you wanted to see me very importantly.

DAISY: It's kind of you to have come.

GEORGE: [*With an effort at ease of manner.*] My dear child, what are you talking about? You must know that if there's anything in the world I can do for you, I'm only too anxious to do it.

DAISY: Is that girl in love with you?

GEORGE: Good heavens, no. What put that idea in your mind?

DAISY: The eyes in my head.

GEORGE: What perfect nonsense.

DAISY: Has it never occurred to you that she was in love with you?

GEORGE: Never.

DAISY: Why do you lie to me? I've been told that you were engaged to her.

GEORGE: That's ludicrous. It's absolutely untrue.

DAISY: Yes, I think it is. At the first moment I believed it. And then I thought it over and I knew it couldn't be true. I don't think you'd do anything underhand.

GEORGE: At all events, I shouldn't do that.

DAISY: In fairness to me or in fairness to her?

GEORGE: My dear Daisy, what do you mean?

DAISY: Did you break with me yesterday so that you might be free to propose to her?

GEORGE: No, I swear I didn't.

DAISY: Why are you so emphatic?

GEORGE: O Daisy, what's the good of tormenting yourself and tormenting me? You know I loved you just as much as you loved me. But I'm not like you. It was a torture. I knew it was wrong and hateful. I couldn't go on.

DAISY: Do you think it would have seemed wrong and hateful if it hadn't been for Sylvia?

GEORGE: Yes.

DAISY: You don't say that very convincingly.

GEORGE: I do think it is because she is so loyal and good and straight that I saw so clearly what a cad I was. I think I found courage to do the only possible thing in her frankness and honesty.

DAISY: I think you deceive yourself. Are you sure this admiration of yours for all her admirable qualities isn't—love?

GEORGE: My dear, I'm unfit to love her.

DAISY: She doesn't think so. If you asked her to marry you she'd accept.

GEORGE: [Impatiently.] What nonsense. What in Heaven's name made you think that?

DAISY: I made it my business to find out.

GEORGE: Well, you can set your mind at rest. I'm not going to ask her to marry me.

[The AMAH comes in.

AMAH: Five o'clock, Daisy.

DAISY: Leave me alone.

[The AMAH goes out.

GEORGE: When does Harry come back?

DAISY: [After a pause, in a strange, hoarse voice.] To-day.

GEORGE: [Surprised at her tone and manner.] Is anything the matter, Daisy?

DAISY: I'm afraid I have some very bad news for you.

GEORGE: [Startled.] Oh!

DAISY: You know those letters. I kept them locked in the box. Lee Tai was furious because I wouldn't have anything to do with him. Last night he broke open the box. He's sent the letters to Harry.

GEORGE: [*Overwhelmed.*] My God!

DAISY: I'm awfully sorry. It wasn't my fault. I couldn't dream that there was any risk.

GEORGE: Was that why you sent for me?

DAISY: Say you don't hate me.

GEORGE: Oh, poor Harry.

DAISY: Don't think of him now. Think of me.

GEORGE: What do we matter now, you and I? We're a pair of rotters. Harry is a white man through and through. He loved you, and he trusted me.

DAISY: What are we going to do?

GEORGE: Give me a minute. I'm all at sixes and sevens. It's such a knock-out blow.

DAISY: Harry will be here soon. His train's due at five.

GEORGE: We'll wait for him.

DAISY: What?

GEORGE: Did you think I was going to run away? I'll stay and face him.

DAISY: He'll kill you.

GEORGE: [*With anguish.*] I wish to God he would.

DAISY: O George, how can you be so cruel? Don't you love me any more? I love you. George, what is to become of me if you desert me?

GEORGE: Harry loves you so much and he loves me too. Heaven knows what sacrifices he's not capable of. Oh, I'm so ashamed.

DAISY: Why do you bother about him? He doesn't count. He'll get over it. After all, what can he do? He can only divorce me, and perhaps we can get him to let me divorce him.

GEORGE: Could you *allow* him to do that?

H*

DAISY: It means so little to a man. I don't care, I was thinking of you. It would make it so much easier for you.

> [*He gives her a quick look. He perceives the allusion to marriage.*

DAISY: George, George, you wouldn't leave—leave me in the cart?

GEORGE: Of course I'll marry you.

DAISY: [*Smiling now, loving and tender.*] O George, we shall be so happy. And you know, some day I'm sure you'll think it's better as it's turned out. I hate all this deceit just as much as you do. Oh, it'll make such a difference when our love can be open and above-board. When I'm your wife you'll forget all that has tormented you. O George, I know we shall be happy.

> [*All this time* GEORGE *has been thinking deeply.*

GEORGE: How do you know that Lee Tai sent those wretched letters to Harry?

DAISY: He sent me a message. He wasn't satisfied with doing a dirty trick. He wanted me to know that he'd done it.

GEORGE: How did he know you kept my letters there?

DAISY: I told you I was reading them while I waited for you. He came in and I put them away. I suppose he suspected. It was very easy for him to get into the room after Amah and I went away.

GEORGE: [*Sarcastically.*] Had you left the key of the box on the table?

DAISY: What do you mean, George? I'd locked it up. Of course I took the key with me. I suppose he broke it open. What does it matter? The harm's done.

GEORGE: How do you know Harry received the letters this morning?

DAISY: Lee Tai said he would.

GEORGE: In Kalgan?

DAISY: Yes.

GEORGE: How did he know Harry was in Kalgan?

DAISY: The Chinese know all one's movements.

GEORGE: They can't do miracles. Harry was going up there unexpectedly on a private mission. The fellows in that company know very well how to keep their own counsel when it's needful. . . . I imagine you were the only person in Peking who knew Harry was going to Kalgan.

DAISY: [*Casually.*] Well, it appears I wasn't.

GEORGE: How do you suppose Lee Tai found out something that Harry had particularly told you to keep quiet about?

DAISY: How can I tell? He may have found out from the Amah, for all I know.

GEORGE: Surely you hadn't told her?

DAISY: Of course not. She may have read the letter. She always does read my letters.

GEORGE: Can she read English?

DAISY: Enough to find out about other people's business.

GEORGE: Why should she have told Lee Tai?

DAISY: I suppose he bribed her. She'd do anything for a hundred dollars.

GEORGE: Not if it would do you harm.

DAISY: She's not so devoted to me as all that.

GEORGE: She's your mother, Daisy.

DAISY: [*Quickly.*] How d'you know?

GEORGE: Harry told me.

DAISY: I thought he was too ashamed of it to do that.

GEORGE: [*Persistently.*] How did Lee Tai know that Harry was in Kalgan?

DAISY: I tell you I don't know. Why do you cross-examine

me? Good God, I'm harassed enough without that. What do you mean?

[*He seizes her wrists and draws her violently to him.*

GEORGE: Daisy, did you send those letters to Harry yourself?

DAISY: Never. Do you think I'm crazy?

GEORGE: Did you give them to Lee Tai to send?

DAISY: No.

GEORGE: God damn you, speak the truth. I will have the truth for once in your life.

[*They stare at one another. He is stern and angry. She pulls herself together. She is fierce and defiant. She shakes herself free of him.*

DAISY: I gave them to Lee Tai.

GEORGE: [*Hiding his face with his hands.*] My God!

DAISY: He told me you were engaged to Sylvia. For a moment I believed it and gave him the letters. I hardly knew what I was doing. And now, even though I know it wasn't true, I'm glad. I wish I'd done it long before.

GEORGE: You fiend.

DAISY: [*Violently.*] Do you think I'm going to let you go so easily? Do you think I've done all I have, to let you marry that silly little English girl?

GEORGE: [*With anguish.*] O Daisy, how could you?

DAISY: Has it never struck you how you came to be wounded that night? It wasn't you they wanted. It was Harry.

GEORGE: I know. [*Suddenly understanding.*] Daisy.

DAISY: Yes, I could do that. I only wish it had succeeded.

GEORGE: I can't believe it.

DAISY: You're mine, mine, mine, and I'll never let you go.

GEORGE: [*With increasing violence.*] Do you think I can ever look at you again without horror? In my heart I've known always that you were evil. Ten years ago when I first loved you there was a deep instinct within that warned me. Even though my heart was breaking for love of you, I knew that you were truthless and cruel. I've loved you, yes, but all the time I've hated you. I've loved you, but with the baser part of me. All that was in me that was honest and decent and upright revolted against you. Always, always. This love has been a loathsome cancer in my heart. I couldn't rid me of it without killing myself, but I abhorred it. I felt that I was degraded by the love that burned me.

DAISY: What do I care so long as you love me? You can think anything you like of me. The fact remains that you love me.

GEORGE: If you had no pity for Harry who raised you from the gutter and gave you everything he had to give, oh, if you'd loved me you'd have had mercy on me. What do you think our life can be together? Don't you know what I shall be? Ruined and abject and hopeless. Do you think there's much happiness for you there?

DAISY: I shall have you. That's all the happiness I want. I'd rather be wretched with you—oh, a thousand times— than happy with anyone else.

GEORGE: [*Wrathfully, trying to wound her.*] You were tormenting me just now because you were jealous of Sylvia. Do you know what I felt for her? It wasn't love—at least not what you mean by love. I can never love anyone as I've loved you, and God knows I'm thankful. But I had such a respect for her. I've been so wretched, and she offered me peace. And I did think that some day when all this horror was over, if I could do something to make myself feel clean again, I should go to her and, all unworthy, ask her if she would take me. And now the bitterest pang of all is to think that she must know what an unspeakable cad I've always been.

[*He has flung himself into a chair. He is in despair.*

> Daisy *goes up to him, and falling on her knees beside him puts her arm round him. She is very tender.*

Daisy: O George, I can make you forget her so easily. You don't know what my love can do. I know I've been horrible, but it's only because I loved you. Ten years ago I was all that she is. I'm like clay in your hands and you can make me what you will. O George, say you forgive me.

> [*In the caressing gestures of her hands as she tries to move him one of them rests by chance on his coat pocket. She feels something hard. He moves slightly away.*

George: Take care.

Daisy: What's that in your pocket?

George: It's my revolver. Since my accident I've always carried it about with me. It's rather silly, but the Minister asked me to. He said he'd feel safer.

Daisy: O George, if you only knew the agony I suffered when you were brought in. The remorse, the fear. I thought I should go mad.

George: [*With a bitter chuckle.*] It must have been rather a sell for you.

Daisy: Oh, you can laugh. I knew you'd forgive me. My darling.

George: I'm sorry for all the rough things I said to you, Daisy. I don't blame you for anything. You only acted according to your lights. The only person I can blame is myself. It's only reasonable that I should suffer the punishment.

Daisy: My sweetheart.

George: I suppose you know that I shall be quite ruined.

Daisy: You'll have to leave the service. Does that really matter to you very much?

George: It was my whole life.

Daisy: You'll get a job in the post office. With **your**

knowledge of the language they'll simply jump at you. It's a Chinese service. It has nothing to do with Europeans.

GEORGE: Do you think the postmaster in a small Chinese city is a very lucrative position?

DAISY: What does money matter? If I'd wanted money I could have got all I wanted from Lee Tai. We can do with so little. You don't know what a clever house-keeper I am.

GEORGE: [*In a level, dead voice.*] I'm sure you're wonderful.

DAISY: We'll go to some city where there are no foreigners. And we shall be together always. We'll have a house high up on the bank and below us the river will flow, flow endlessly.

GEORGE: You seem to have got it all mapped out.

DAISY: If you only knew how often I've dreamed of it. O George, I want rest and peace too. I'm so tired. I want endless days to rest in. [*With a puzzled look at him.*] What is the matter? You look so strange.

GEORGE: [*With a weary sigh.*] I was thinking of all the things you've been saying to me.

DAISY: If you think it'll be easier for you if you don't marry me, you need not. I don't care anything about that. I'll be your mistress and I'll lie hidden in your house so that no one shall know I'm there. I'll live like a Chinese woman. I'll be your slave and your plaything. I want to get away from all these Europeans. After all, China is the land of my birth and the land of my mother. China is crowding in upon me; I'm sick of these foreign clothes. I have a strange hankering for the ease of the Chinese dress. You've never seen me in it?

GEORGE: Never.

DAISY: [*With a smile.*] You'd hardly know me. I'll be a little Chinese girl living in the foreigner's house. Have you ever smoked opium?

GEORGE: No. [*She takes the* AMAH's *long pipe in her hands.*] Whom does that belong to?

DAISY: It's Amah's. One day you shall try and I'll make your pipes for you. Lee Tai used to say that no one could make them better than I.

GEORGE: However low down the ladder you go, there's apparently always a rung lower.

DAISY: After you've smoked a pipe or two your mind grows extraordinarily clear. You have a strange facility of speech and yet no desire to speak. All the puzzles of this puzzling world grow plain to you. You are tranquil and free. Your soul is gently released from the bondage of your body, and it plays, happy and careless, like a child with flowers. Death cannot frighten you, and want and misery are like blue mountains far away. You feel a heavenly power possess you and you can venture all things because suffering cannot touch you. Your spirit has wings and you fly like a bird through the starry wastes of the night. You hold space and time in the hollow of your hand. Then you come upon the dawn, all pearly and grey and silent, and there in the distance like a dreamless sleep, is the sea.

GEORGE: You are showing me a side of you I never knew.

DAISY: Do you think you know me yet? I don't know myself. In my heart there are secrets that are strange even to me, and spells to bind you to me, and enchantments so that you will never weary.

[*A pause.*

GEORGE: [*Standing up.*] I'll go and get myself a drink. After all these alarums and excursions I really think I deserve it.

DAISY: Amah will bring it to you.

GEORGE: Oh, it doesn't matter. I can easily fetch it myself. The whisky's in the dining-room, isn't it?

DAISY: I expect so.

[*He goes out.* DAISY *goes over to a chest which stands*

in the room and throws it open. She takes out the Manchu dress which HARRY *once gave her and handles it smilingly. She holds up in both her hands the sumptuous headdress. There is the sound of a door being locked.* DAISY *puts down the headdress and looks at the door inquiringly.*

DAISY: [*With a little smile.*] What are you locking the door for, George? [*The words are hardly out of her mouth before there is a report of a pistol shot.* DAISY *gives a shriek and rushes towards the door*.] George! George! What have you done? [*She beats frantically on the door.*] Let me in. Let me in. George!

> [*The* AMAH *comes running from the courtyard.*

AMAH: What's the matter? I hear shot.

DAISY: Send the boys, quick. We must break down this door.

AMAH: I send the boys away. I no want them here when Harry come.

DAISY: George! George! Speak to me. [*She beats violently on the door.*] Oh, what shall I do?

AMAH: Daisy, what's the matter?

DAISY: He's killed himself sooner—sooner than . . .

AMAH: [*Aghast.*] Oh!

> [DAISY *staggers back into the room.*

DAISY: O my God!

> [*She sinks down on the floor. She beats the floor with her fist. The* AMAH *looks at her for a moment, then with quick determination seizes her shoulder.*

AMAH: Daisy, Harry come soon.

DAISY: [*With a violent gesture.*] Leave me alone. What do I care if Harry comes?

AMAH: You no can stay here. Come with me quick.

DAISY: Go away. Damn you.

AMAH: [*Stern and decided.*] Don't you talk foolish now. You come. Lee Tai waiting for you.

DAISY: [*With sudden suspicion.*] Did you know this was going to happen? George! George!

AMAH: Harry will kill you if he find you here. Come with me.

> [*There is a knocking at the outer gate.*

AMAH: There he is. Daisy! Daisy!

DAISY: Don't torture me.

AMAH: I bolt that door. He no get in that way. He must come round through temple. You come quick and I hide you. We slip out when he safe.

DAISY: [*With scornful rage.*] Do you think I'm frightened of Harry?

AMAH: He come velly soon now.

> [DAISY *raises herself to her feet. A strange look comes over her face.*

DAISY: The day has come. The jungle takes back its own. Bolt that door.

> [*The* AMAH *runs to it and slips the bolt.*

AMAH: What you do, Daisy?

> [DAISY *goes to the Manchu clothes and takes them up.*

DAISY: Help me to put these on.

AMAH: What you mean, Daisy?

DAISY: Curse you, do as I tell you.

AMAH: I think you crazy. [DAISY *slips into the long skirt and the* AMAH *helps her into the coat. In the middle of her dressing* DAISY *staggers.*] Daisy!

DAISY: [*Recovering herself.*] Don't be a fool. I'm all right.

AMAH: [*In a terrified whisper.*] There's Harry.

DAISY: Give me the headdress.

HARRY: [*Outside.*] Open the door.

DAISY: Be quick.

AMAH: I no understand. I think you crazy.

[*The knocking is repeated more violently.*

HARRY: [*Shouting.*] Daisy! Amah! Open the door. If you don't open I'll break it down.

[DAISY *is ready. She slips on to the pallet and sits in the Chinese fashion.*

DAISY: Go to the door. Open when I tell you.

[*There is by* DAISY'S *side a box in which are the paints and pencils the Chinese lady uses to make up her face.* DAISY *opens it. She takes out a hand mirror.*

HARRY: Who's there? Open, I tell you. Open.

[DAISY *puts rouge on her cheeks. She takes a black pencil and touches her eyebrows. She gives them a slight slant so that she looks on a sudden absolutely Chinese.*

DAISY: Open.

HARRY: Daisy. [*He comes forward impetuously and then on a sudden stops. He is taken aback. Something, he knows not what, comes over him and he feels helpless and strangely weak.*] Daisy, what does it mean? These letters. [*He takes them out of his pocket, and thrusts them towards her. She takes no notice of him.*] Daisy, speak to me. I don't understand. [*He staggers towards her with outstretched hands. He throws himself on his knees and buries his face in the skirt of her dress.*] O Daisy, for God's sake say it isn't true.

[*He bursts into a storm of sobs. Motionless she contemplates in the glass the Chinese woman of the reflection.*

THE END

THE SACRED FLAME

A PLAY
in Three Acts

CHARACTERS

MAURICE TABRET
DR. HARVESTER
MRS. TABRET
NURSE WAYLAND
ALICE
MAJOR LICONDA
STELLA TABRET
COLIN TABRET

———

The action takes place at Gatley House, Mrs. Tabret's residence, near London.

THE SACRED FLAME

THE FIRST ACT

SCENE: *The drawing-room at Gatley House. It is a large easy room furnished comfortably in rather an old-fashioned way, with spacious chairs covered in faded chintz, great bowls of flowers, English china, Victorian water colours and photographs in silver frames. It is the drawing-room of an elderly lady who has furnished it in the way she has since her childhood known a drawing-room furnished. An interior decorator has never been inside the door. No stranger entering it would cry, How lovely! but if he were sensitive to his surroundings he might think it a very good room to eat muffins in for tea and he would slip his hand behind the cushions on the sofa in the certainty that he would find fat little lavender bags in the corners.*

It is now the height of June, the weather is very fine, and the French windows that lead into the garden are wide open. Through them you see the starry radiant night.

When the curtain rises, it discovers MAURICE *and* MRS. TABRET, NURSE WAYLAND, *and* DR. HARVESTER. MRS. TABRET *is working at her tapestry. She is a slim, small, grey-haired lady, with a gentle manner, but her face is determined; it has a ravaged look as though fate had borne her many a blow, but also a serenity that suggests that she has found in herself the character and the courage to put up a good fight. She is dressed in semi-evening dress, in black.* NURSE WAYLAND *is reading a book. She is a girl of twenty-seven or so, handsome rather than pretty, with fine eyes, a little sullen, perhaps, and in her expression the hungry, somewhat pathetic look that some women have at her age. She is dressed not in uniform, but in a pretty, simple frock that sets off her fine figure.*

DR. HARVESTER *and* MAURICE *are playing chess.* DR. HAR-
VESTER *is the family doctor; he is a youngish man, fresh-
complexioned and of an open countenance, fair, clean and
amiable. He wears a dinner jacket.* MAURICE *is lying on
an invalid bed, in pyjamas and a bed-jacket. He is trim and
neat, with his hair close-cropped and his face fresh-shaven;
he has a handsome head and his manner is cheerful and even
hearty; but he is very thin, his cheeks are pale and hollow, and
his dark eyes look enormous. But they are constantly smiling.
He gives no sign of being sorry for himself.*
There is a pause while the doctor considers the situation.

MAURICE: [*With good-humoured sarcasm.*] Speed is the essence
of this game, old boy!

HARVESTER: Don't let the brute bully me, Mrs. Tabret.

MRS. TABRET: [*Smiling.*] I think you're quite capable of
taking care of yourself, Doctor.

MAURICE: If you moved your bishop you'd make things a
bit awkward for me.

HARVESTER: [*Imperturbably, considering the game.*] When I
want your advice, I'll ask for it.

MAURICE: Mother, is that the way respectable general prac-
titioners talked to their patients in the days of your
far-distant youth?

MRS. TABRET: How on earth do you expect poor Nurse
Wayland to read when you never for an instant hold
your tongue? I can't even hear myself tatting.

NURSE: [*Looking up for an instant, with a pleasant smile.*] I
don't mind, Mrs. Tabret, don't bother about me.

MAURICE: After listening to my sprightly conversation for
nearly five years Nurse Wayland pays no more attention
to me than if I were a deaf mute.

MRS. TABRET: [*Dryly.*] Who can blame her?

MAURICE: [*Cheerily.*] Even when pain and anguish wring
my brow and I swear like fifty thousand troopers I

never manage to bring the blush of shame to her maiden cheek.

NURSE: [*Smiling.*] I know it's exasperating.

MAURICE: It's worse than that, Nurse. It's inconsiderate. It would relieve me to see you blench with horror and smother a sob of mortification in an adhesive bandage. . . . Watch the Doctor, he's about to move. Be very careful, old boy, the position is fraught with danger.

HARVESTER: [*Moving a piece.*] I'm going to move my knight.

MAURICE: What would you say if I gave that pawn a little push and murmured check?

HARVESTER: I should say it was your right, but I should think it a trifle vulgar.

MAURICE: Do you know what I'd do now in your place?

HARVESTER: No, I don't.

MAURICE: I'd catch my foot in the leg of the table and kick it over accidentally. That's the only way you can save yourself from getting the worst hiding I've ever given you.

HARVESTER: [*Moving a piece.*] Go to the devil.

MAURICE: Oh, you do that, do you? All right.

[ALICE, *the maid, comes in.*

ALICE: If you please, ma'am, Major Liconda wants to know if it's too late for him to come in and have a drink.

MAURICE: Of course not. Where is he?

ALICE: He's at the door, sir.

MRS. TABRET: Ask him to come in.

ALICE: Very good, ma'am.

[*She goes out.*

MAURICE: You know him, don't you, old boy?

HARVESTER: No, I've never met him. He's the fellow who's just taken that furnished house on the golf links, isn't he?

MRS. TABRET: Yes. I knew him years ago in India. That's why he came here.

MAURICE: He was one of Mother's numerous admirers. I understand that she treated him very badly.

HARVESTER: I can well believe it. Does he still cherish a hopeless passion for you, Mrs. Tabret?

MRS. TABRET: [*Taking the chaff in good part.*] I don't know at all, Dr. Harvester. You'd better ask him.

HARVESTER: Is he a soldier?

MAURICE: No, he was a policeman. He's just retired. He's a very good chap, and I believe he's rather a good golfer. Colin has played with him two or three times.

MRS. TABRET: I'd asked him to dine to-night so that Maurice could get a game of bridge, but he couldn't come.

> [ALICE *comes in followed by* MAJOR LICONDA, *and, when she has announced him, goes out.*

ALICE: Major Liconda.

> [*He is a tallish, middle-aged man, with grey hair and a sunburnt face, spare of build, active and alert. He wears a dinner jacket.*

MRS. TABRET: [*Shaking hands with him.*] How d'you do? How very nice of you to look in.

LICONDA: I was on my way home and saw that your lights were on, so I thought I'd just ask if anyone would like to give me a doch-an-dorris.

MRS. TABRET: Help yourself. [*With a gesture of the head.*] The whisky's on the table.

LICONDA: [*Going over to it and pouring himself out a drink.*] Thank you. How are you, Nurse?

NURSE: How do you do?

LICONDA: And the patient?

MAURICE: [*Lightly.*] Bearing up pretty well considering all he has to put up with.

LICONDA: [*Smiling.*] You're in your usual high spirits.

MAURICE: I have much to be thankful for, as the lady said

when her husband was run over by a motor bus just as he was stepping out of the office after insuring his life.

HARVESTER: [*Laughing.*] You fool, Maurice.

MRS. TABRET: I don't think you know Dr. Harvester.

> [*The two men shake hands.*

HARVESTER: How d'you do?

LICONDA: Mrs. Tabret tells me you're a very good doctor.

HARVESTER: I take great pains to impress the fact on my patients.

MAURICE: His only serious fault is that he thinks he can play chess.

LICONDA: Don't let me disturb your game.

MAURICE: It's finished.

HARVESTER: Not at all. I have three possible moves. [*Making one.*] What do you say to that?

MAURICE: Mate, you poor fish.

HARVESTER: Damn.

MRS. TABRET: Have you beaten him?

MAURICE: Hollow.

NURSE: Shall I put the chess things away?

MAURICE: If you wouldn't mind.

> [*She takes the board and the chessmen and puts them away, while the conversation proceeds.*

LICONDA: I won't keep you up. I'll just swallow my drink and take myself off. I really only came to say I was sorry I couldn't come to dinner.

MAURICE: There's no hurry, you know. I'm not going to bed for hours.

MRS. TABRET: We're really waiting up for Stella and Colin. They've gone to the opera.

LICONDA: I'm a night owl. I never go to bed till I can help it.

MAURICE: You're the man for my money.

HARVESTER: I've got a day's work before me. I'll just have a drop of Scotch to assuage the pangs of defeat and then I must run.

MAURICE: Let's send the rest of them off to bed, Major, and have a good old gossip by ourselves.

LICONDA: I'm willing.

MRS. TABRET: If you really want to stay up, Maurice, let Nurse Wayland get you ready and then you'll only just have to slip into bed, and Colin can help you.

MAURICE: All right. What do you say to that, Nurse?

NURSE: Well, it's just as you like. I'm quite prepared to stay up until Mrs. Maurice comes in. I'll put you to bed after you've said good night to her.

MAURICE: No, come on. You're looking tired.

MRS. TABRET: You are looking a little peaked, Nurse. I think it's nearly time you had another holiday.

NURSE: Oh, I don't want a holiday for months.

MAURICE: Put your shoulder to the wheel, Nurse, and gently trundle the wounded hero to his bedchamber.

HARVESTER: Shall I come and help?

MAURICE: Not on your life. It's bad enough to be messed about by one person. I don't want a crowd, damn it.

HARVESTER: Sorry.

MAURICE: I shall only be ten minutes.

> [NURSE WAYLAND *wheels out the bed and closes the doors behind her.*

LICONDA: She seems a very nice woman, that nurse.

MRS. TABRET: Yes. She's extremely competent. And I must say she's very gentle and kind. Her patience is really wonderful.

LICONDA: You've had her ever since poor Maurice crashed, haven't you?

MRS. TABRET: Oh, no. We had three or four before she came. All more or less odious.

HARVESTER: She's a rattling good nurse. I think you're lucky to have got her.

MRS. TABRET: I'm sure we are. The only fault I have to find with her is that she's so very reserved. There's nothing come-hither about her. Except for her month's holiday every August she's been with us all day and every day for nearly five years, and I only just know that her name's Beatrice. She calls the boys Mr. Maurice and Mr. Colin, and Stella she calls Mrs. Maurice. She seems to be always a little on her guard. She certainly doesn't encourage familiarity.

HARVESTER: I can't imagine skylarking with her at a Sunday-school treat, I must admit.

MRS. TABRET: And of course she's a little tactless. It never seems to occur to her that Maurice wants to be alone with his wife. Poor lamb, he has so little. He likes to say good night to Stella the last thing and he likes to say it without anyone looking on. That's why he's staying up now.

LICONDA: Poor old boy.

MRS. TABRET: He can't bear the thought of going to sleep without kissing her. And Nurse Wayland always seems to find something to do just that last moment. He doesn't want to hurt her feelings by sending her out of the room, and he's terrified of being thought sentimental, so he uses every sort of trick and device to get her out of the way.

HARVESTER: But, good Lord, why don't you tell her? After all, there's no reason why a man shouldn't kiss his wife good night if he wants to.

MRS. TABRET: She's terribly sensitive. Haven't you noticed how often rather tactless people are? They'll stamp on your toes and then when you tuck them up out of harm's way they're so offended you feel quite miserable about it.

LICONDA: I suppose Maurice is absolutely dependent upon her?

MRS. TABRET: Absolutely. All sorts of rather unpleasant things have to be done for him, poor dear, and he can't bear that anyone should know about them. Especially Stella.

HARVESTER: Yes, I've discovered that. He doesn't want Stella to have anything to do with his illness.

LICONDA: [To HARVESTER.] Is there really no chance of his getting better?

HARVESTER: I'm afraid not.

MRS. TABRET: It's a miracle that he's alive at all.

HARVESTER: He was terribly smashed up, you know. The lower part of his spine was broken and the plane caught fire and he was badly burnt.

LICONDA: It was rotten bad luck.

MRS. TABRET: And when you think that he was flying all through the war and never even had a mishap. It seems so silly that this should happen just when he was trying a new machine. It was so unexpected.

LICONDA: It seems such a pity he didn't stop flying when he married.

MRS. TABRET: It's easy to say that now.

HARVESTER: He was a born flyer. Fellows have told me that he seemed to have a sort of instinct for it.

MRS. TABRET: It was the one thing he was interested in. He wouldn't have given it up for anything in the world. And he was so good at it, it never occurred to me that he could have an accident, he always felt so safe.

LICONDA: I've been told he was absolutely fearless.

HARVESTER: And you know, the strange thing is this, he's just as much interested in it all as he ever was. He follows all the important flights and the tests and so on. If anyone does a new stunt he's full of it.

LICONDA: His courage amazes me. He never seems low or depressed.

MRS. TABRET: Never. His spirits are wonderful. It's one of the most anguishing things I know to see him, when he's in pain and there are beads of sweat on his brow, force a joke from his lips.

HARVESTER: I'm sorry to think Colin is going away so soon, Mrs. Tabret. I think his being here has done Maurice a lot of good.

MRS. TABRET: When they were boys they were always great friends, and you know brothers aren't always.

LICONDA: They're not, indeed.

MRS. TABRET: And Colin has been away so long. He went to Central America just before Maurice crashed, you know.

LICONDA: Well, has he got to go back?

MRS. TABRET: He put all his share of his father's money in a coffee plantation and it's doing very well. He loves the life out there and it seems cruel to ask him to give it up to help us to look after his crippled brother.

HARVESTER: I think it would be very unfair. One has no right to ask anyone to give up his own chance of making the best he can of life.

MRS. TABRET: [*With a dry smile.*] At all events with the young one may ask, but the likelihood of their consenting is very slight.

HARVESTER: Not at all, Mrs. Tabret. The country is full of desiccated females who've given up their lives to taking care of an invalid mother.

LICONDA: When I was at Bath a little while ago I saw a good many couples like that, and to tell you the truth I sometimes wondered why the daughters didn't murder their mothers.

I

HARVESTER: They often do. Every doctor will tell you that he's had a case where he has a strong suspicion that some old woman who lived too long has been poisoned by her relatives. But he takes jolly good care not to say anything about it.

LICONDA: Why?

HARVESTER: Oh, it's rotten for a man's practice. Nothing can do you so much damage as to be mixed up in a murder case.

MRS. TABRET: I've often pondered over the problem of the woman like myself who is no longer young and suffers from indifferent health. I'm not sure if the best way of dealing with us wouldn't be to do as some African tribes do. At a certain age take us to the river's brim and push us gently but firmly in.

LICONDA: [*With a smile.*] What happens if they swim?

MRS. TABRET: The family is prepared for that. They stand on the banks with brickbats and take pot shots at their struggling but aged grandmother. It discourages her efforts to get out.

[NURSE WAYLAND *opens the door and the* DOCTOR, *getting up, helps her to wheel back the bed on which* MAURICE *is lying.*

MAURICE: Here we are again. I'm all fixed up and ready for any excitement. What about a tune on the gramophone?

HARVESTER: I must go.

MRS. TABRET: And Nurse Wayland should go to bed.

NURSE: I'll just gather my things together and say good night. Are you sure Mrs. Maurice and your brother won't go and have supper after the opera?

MAURICE: I'm sure they will. I particularly told Stella she was to have a real bust. It's not often she goes on the loose, poor dear.

NURSE: Then they won't be home till four.

MAURICE: Does that mean you disapprove of my staying up, you hard and brutal woman?

NURSE: Doesn't Dr. Harvester?

HARVESTER: Very much. But I'm aware that Maurice has no intention of going to sleep till he knows his wife is safely home again, and my theory is that it only does people good now and then to do what they shouldn't.

LICONDA: That is the kind of doctor for me.

HARVESTER: Hurry up and get a nice long lingering illness, will you, so that I can put down a hard court in my garden.

LICONDA: I'll see what I can do about it.

MAURICE: [*Pricking up his ears.*] What's that?

MRS. TABRET: What, Maurice?

MAURICE: I thought I heard a car. Yes, by jove. It's Stella. I'd know the sound of that car in a thousand.

[*Now the sound of a car driving up is almost distinct.*

LICONDA: Do you mean to say you can hear from this distance?

MAURICE: You bet your life I can. That's the family bus. Now just stay a minute and see Stella, Doctor. She's got her best bib and tucker on and she's a sight for sore eyes.

LICONDA: What were they giving at the opera to-night?

NURSE: *Tristan.*

MAURICE: That's why I insisted on Stella's going. It was after *Tristan* that we got engaged. D'you remember, Mother?

MRS. TABRET: Of course I do.

MAURICE: We'd all been to hear it and then we went on to supper. I drove Stella round Regent's Park in a little two-seater I had then and I swore I'd go on driving round and round till she promised to marry me. *Tristan* had given her such an appetite that by the time we were half-way around the second time, she said, oh, hell, if I must either marry you or die of starvation I'd sooner marry you.

HARVESTER: Is there a word of truth in this story, Mrs. Tabret?

MRS. TABRET: I don't know. They were both as mad as hatters in those days. All I know is that the rest of us had only just ordered our supper when they came in looking like a pair of cats who'd swallowed a canary and said they were engaged.

> [*The door is opened and* STELLA *comes in, followed by her brother-in-law,* COLIN TABRET. STELLA *is twenty-eight and beautiful. She is wearing an evening dress and an opera cloak.* COLIN, *a tall, dark, handsome fellow in the early thirties, is in full evening dress, long coat and white tie.*

MAURICE: Stella.

STELLA: Darling. Have you missed me?

> [*She goes over to him and lightly kisses him on the forehead.*

MAURICE: Why are you back already, you wretched girl? You promised me to go and have supper.

STELLA: I was so thrilled and excited by the opera. I felt I simply couldn't eat a thing.

MAURICE: Hang it all, you might have gone to Lucien's and had a dance or two and a bottle of bubbly! What's the good of my spending the eyes of my head on buying you a new dress when you won't let anyone see it. [*To* LICONDA.] She said it was too dressed up to go to the opera in, but I exercised my marital authority amd made her.

STELLA: Darling, I wanted to show it off in the intervals, but I hadn't the nerve and I kept my cloak on.

MAURICE: Well, take it off now and show the gentlemen. The only way I managed to get them to stay was by promising to let them have a look at your new dress when you came home.

STELLA: What nonsense. As if Major Liconda or Dr. Harvester knew one frock from another.

MAURICE: Don't be so damned contemptuous of the male sex, Stella. Take off your cloak and let's have a good look at you.

STELLA: You brute, Maurice, you've made me feel shy now.
[*She is sitting on the end of his bed and slips off her cloak.*

MAURICE: Stand up.

[*She hesitates a moment and then, still holding the cloak about her hips, stands up. She lets it fall to her feet.*

HARVESTER: It's lovely.

[*She staggers a little and smothers a cry.*

MAURICE: Halloa, what's the matter?

[COLIN *catches her and helps her to a chair.*

STELLA: It's nothing. I feel so frightfully faint.

MRS. TABRET: Oh, my dear.

MAURICE: Stella.

[*The* NURSE *and the* DOCTOR *go up to her.*

HARVESTER: It's all right, Maurice. Don't fuss. [*To* STELLA.] Put your head down between your legs.

[*He puts his hand on her neck to force her head down.* NURSE WAYLAND *puts her hands to her side as though to support her. But* STELLA *pushes her away.*

STELLA: No, don't. Don't come near me. I shall be all right again in a minute. It's silly of me.

MAURICE: I'm sorry, darling. It was my fault.

STELLA: It's nothing. I feel better already.

MRS. TABRET: My own belief is that she's just faint from lack of food. At what time did you dine?

COLIN: We didn't dine. We just had some caviar and half a bottle of pop before the opera.

MRS. TABRET: You are a ridiculous pair.

STELLA: I enjoy Wagner so much more on an empty stomach. I'm really quite all right now.

MRS. TABRET: Nurse, would you mind going to the kitchen and seeing if you can find anything for these silly young things to eat?

NURSE: Of course not. There ought to be some ham. I'll make them some sandwiches.

MRS. TABRET: Colin can get a bottle of champagne out of the cellar.

COLIN: All right, Mother. Is there any ice in the house? I've got a thirst I wouldn't sell for twenty pounds.

> [*He opens the door for* NURSE WAYLAND *and they both go out.*

LICONDA: Well, I'll say good-bye. [*To* STELLA.] I'm sorry you're feeling poorly.

STELLA: I shall be all right when I've had something to eat. I think Mrs. Tabret is quite right. What I want is a large ham sandwich with a lot of mustard on it.

MAURICE: You're looking better, you know. Just for a moment you were as white as a sheet.

LICONDA: Good-bye.

MRS. TABRET: Good-bye. It was so nice of you to look in.

> [*He goes out.*

HARVESTER: I'll just stay a moment or two longer if you don't mind. I don't trust these young women who don't feed themselves properly.

> [MRS. TABRET *gives* MAURICE *and* STELLA *a glance. She knows they want to have a moment to themselves.*

MRS. TABRET: [*To* DR. HARVESTER.] Let's take a turn in the garden, shall we? It's so warm and lovely.

HARVESTER: Come on. And I hope Nurse Wayland has the sense to cut a sandwich for me, too.

[*The* DOCTOR *and* MRS. TABRET *go out. As soon as they are alone* STELLA *goes over to her husband and gives him a long, loving kiss on the lips. He puts his arm round her neck.*

MAURICE: Darling.

[*She releases herself and sitting down on the bed holds one of his thin, sick hands.*

STELLA: I'm sorry I made such a fool of myself.

MAURICE: You scared the life out of me, you little beast. Why didn't you go on to some place and have a bite before you came home?

STELLA: I didn't want to. I wanted to get back.

MAURICE: Will you give me your word of honour that you didn't go on to dance because you thought I should be waiting up for you?

STELLA: Don't be an old silly. You know that I love to think you want me back so much. You don't imagine I care a hang about dancing.

MAURICE: You little liar. How can anyone dance as well as you without being crazy about it? You're the best dancer I ever danced with.

STELLA: Oh, but you know how one changes. All the dances are different now, and after all I'm not so young as I was either.

MAURICE: You're twenty-eight. You're only a girl. You ought to be having the time of your life. Oh, my dear, it is rotten for you.

STELLA: Oh, darling, don't. You mustn't think that. Don't imagine for a moment that I've given up a thing that meant anything to me.

MAURICE: You must allow me to have my own opinion.

Anyhow it's been a snip having old Colin here. It's damned well forced you to go out.

STELLA: Darling, you talk as though I was shut up like a nun. I'm always going out. I see all the plays.

MAURICE: Yes, at matinées with my mother. She's a dear old thing, but she's not precisely exhilarating. After all, when one's young one wants to be with young people. One wants to say and do all sorts of things that seem merely silly to the elderly. They smile indulgently because they have the tolerance of wise old people. Damn it all, one doesn't want their indulgence. One wants to play the fool because one's young. And it's wise for the young to be rather foolish.

STELLA: My dear, you mustn't be epigrammatic. They tell me it's so out of date.

MAURICE: I was hoping you'd dance till your feet were dropping off and then go for a spin in the moonlight. Do you remember, we did that once one night and we had breakfast at a pub on the river in our evening things. What a lark!

STELLA: We were a pair of lunatics in those days. I was much too tired to do anything like that. I only wanted to get home.

MAURICE: The honest fact is that you've lost the habit of going on a binge.

STELLA: I don't want to go on a binge if you can't come with me.

MAURICE: That is perfectly idiotic of you, my poor child. I wish that silly ass Colin weren't going away so soon.

STELLA: He only came home for six months and he's stayed nearly a year.

MAURICE: You promised you'd try to persuade him to stay on for a bit.

STELLA: He must get back to his work.

MAURICE: Why can't he sell his old plantation and settle down here?

STELLA: He'd be a fish out of water in England. When a man's got used to the sort of life he's lived out there it's frightfully difficult for him to settle down in an office or something like that.

MAURICE: I suppose it is really. I should have hated it, too. I wasn't really thinking of myself, and Mother must be used to having a pair of useless sons by now. I was thinking of you.

STELLA: I'm quite capable of thinking of myself, darling. I'm a very selfish woman.

MAURICE: My poor child, you mustn't think because I've got a broken back I'm a drivelling imbecile.

STELLA: How can I think anything else when I see you fussing like an old hen with an only chick because you imagine I may be having a rather thin time? I'm not having a thin time. You never try to prevent me from doing anything I want to. No one could be more considerate than you are. I'm busy all day long and the days just fly past. I don't know what it is to be bored. Why, I haven't time for half the things I want to do.

MAURICE: Yes, you're wonderful. . . . You've always been wonderful. You've made the best of a bad job, all right. I've had to. But why should you? Resignation. I've had to set my teeth and learn it. But what has a girl like you to do with resignation?

STELLA: Oh, darling, don't talk like that. You mustn't think such things. I married you because I loved you. What a foul brute I should be if I stopped loving you now that you want my love more than ever.

MAURICE: Oh, my dear, we can't love because we ought to. Love comes and goes and we can none of us help ourselves.

STELLA: [*With a sharp look at him.*] Maurice, what do you

mean? [*She looks away.*] Has there been anything in my behaviour to lead you to think that I wasn't the same as I'd always been?

MAURICE: [*With deep affection.*] No, darling. You've been angelic always, always. [*Taken aback.*] Why, what's the matter? You suddenly went quite white. You're not feeling faint again?

STELLA: No. I didn't know I went white.

MAURICE: You know, if I've seemed often to take for granted all you've done for me you mustn't think I'm not conscious all the time how much I owe you.

STELLA: That's very silly of you, my pet. I don't know that I've done anything for you at all except be moderately civil. You've never let me.

MAURICE: I've never let you nurse me. Not on your life. I couldn't have borne that you should have anything to do with the disgusting side of illness. [*With a grin.*] My precious, I don't want you to smell of antiseptics. I want you to smell of the dawn. I'm so grateful to you, Stella.

STELLA: God knows, you've got a cause to be.

MAURICE: [*Casually.*] You know that I'm never going to get well, Stella, don't you?

STELLA: I don't indeed. It's a long business, we know that, but I'm absolutely convinced you'll get at all events very much better.

MAURICE: They tell me that one of these days they'll try operating again to see if they can't possibly put me right. But I know they're lying. They pretend they can do something in order to give me hope, and I pretend to believe them because it's the easiest thing to do. I know I'm here for life, Stella.

[*There is a moment's pause. This is the first time that STELLA has realised that MAURICE knows his case is hopeless.*

STELLA: [*Very earnestly.*] Then let's take what comfort we can in the great joy we've had in one another in the days when you were well and strong. I shall always be grateful for the happiness you gave me and for your love, your great love.

MAURICE: Do you think that's changed? No. I love you as deeply, as devotedly as I ever did. I'm not often silly and sentimental, am I, Stella?

STELLA: [*With a little smile.*] Is it so silly to be sentimental? No, you're not often.

MAURICE: You're everything in the world to me, Stella. People have been most awfully kind to me, and it's not till you're crocked up as I am that you find out how kind people are. They've been simply topping. But there's not one of them that I wouldn't see in hell if it would save you from unhappiness or trouble.

STELLA: [*In a lighter tone, going back to her chaffing way with him.*] Well, I wouldn't tell them if I were you. I don't believe they'd awfully like it.

MAURICE: [*With a smile.*] I ought to be frightened because I'm so dependent on you, but I'm not because I know, not just with my mind or my heart, but with every nerve in me, with every little feeling and every pain, how good you are.

STELLA: [*Trying to take his speech lightly.*] Now, darling, you really are exaggerating. If you go on like this I shall send you to bed.

MAURICE: My precious. You can laugh at me, but I see the tears in your lovely eyes.

STELLA: [*With sudden emotion.*] Maurice, I'm a very weak, a very imperfect, and a very sinful woman.

MAURICE: [*Suddenly changing, but still with the greatest affection.*] Come down to earth, you silly little ass.

STELLA: [*Unable not to feel a trifle anxious.*] Why are you saying all this to me just to-night?

MAURICE: [*Smiling.*] One can't always jump through a hoop to make people laugh. It's hardly becoming in a gentleman approaching middle age who's chained to an invalid bed. You must forgive me if my flow of jokes sometimes runs dry.

STELLA: You're sure you're not worrying about anything?

MAURICE: You know, when you're shut up as I am you find out all sorts of interesting things. Being an invalid fortunately has its compensations. Of course, people are very sympathetic, but you mustn't abuse their sympathy. They ask you how you are, but they don't really care a damn. Why should they? Life is for the living and I'm dead.

STELLA: [*Strangely harassed.*] Maurice, oh, my darling.

MAURICE: You soon cotton on to it and you say you're as fit as a fiddle. You must take care not to bore the people who come to see you and you soon discover that it bores them if you talk about yourself. Let them talk about themselves. That always interests them and they say, what an intelligent fellow he is. Make jokes. Make all the jokes you can—good, bad, and indifferent; when you've made them laugh, they feel they needn't be sorry for you, and that's a relief to them. And when they go away they feel so kindly disposed towards you.

STELLA: Oh, my precious, you break my heart. It's so cruel to think that you should have had to learn such bitter truths.

MAURICE: My dear, they're not so bitter as all that. That's only human nature and I get a lot of fun out of observing it. I'm not so terribly to be pitied. I've learnt to take pleasure in all sorts of things, other people's affairs and books and so on, that I never cared a tinker's damn for before. I should never have mentioned it only I wanted to tell you that it's you who've given me the courage to carry on. I'm not unhappy. I don't know how many years I shall hang on, but if you'll help me, darling, I think I can make a pretty good job of it. I owe everything to you. Nothing matters to me very much when I know I shall see you to-morrow and the next day and the day after that and always. And when I've had a bit of pain I think to myself when you come in next you'll kiss me, and I feel the tenderness of your lips on my beating heart.

STELLA: [*Shattered by emotion.*] Maurice, I'm unworthy of such love. I'm so ashamed. I'm so selfish. I'm so thoughtless.

MAURICE: Never.

STELLA: Why did you make me go out to-night? Did you think it was any pleasure to me?

MAURICE: I didn't care. I was thinking of my pleasure. I wanted you to hear again the music we'd heard together that night we got engaged. I was crazy about you. Do you remember how you cried in the second act when Tristan and Isolde sing that duet of theirs and I held your hand in the dark? Why did you cry?

STELLA: I cried because I loved you and I was happy.

MAURICE: Did you cry to-night?

STELLA: I don't know.

MAURICE: You know that music is stunning, isn't it?

STELLA: [*Smiling through her tears.*] People seem to think it's above the average.

MAURICE: You seemed to carry it still in your eyes when you came in. They were bright and shining. They were like great deep pools of light. You've never looked so beautiful as you looked to-night. You made the Venus of Milo look like a lump of cheese.

STELLA: [*Recovered now and chaffing him again.*] Go on, darling, I can bear much more in the same strain.

MAURICE: I could go on for weeks.

STELLA: No, then I'd be afraid you were prejudiced. Go on till the sandwiches come in.

MAURICE: Give me your hands.

STELLA: No, I won't. Let's be sensible and talk about what's going to win the Grand National.

MAURICE: Of course the honest-to-God truth is that you're ever so much lovelier than when I married you. What is there that gives you this sudden new radiance? You look like a goddess who's just created a world and is about to step upon it for the first time.

STELLA: I don't know why I should look any different from usual.

MAURICE: I watch your face. I know every change in it from day to day. A year ago you had a strained, almost a hunted, look, but now lately you've had an air that is strangely peaceful. You've gained a sort of beautiful serenity.

STELLA: My poor lamb. I'm afraid that can only be due to advancing years. Soon you'll discover the first wrinkle on my forehead and then the first white hair.

MAURICE: No, no. You must never grow old. I couldn't bear it. Oh, how cruel that all that beauty, all that superb and shining youth of yours, . . .

STELLA: [*Interrupting him quickly.*] No, don't, Maurice, I beseech you.

MAURICE: It would have been better for both of us if I'd been killed when I crashed. I'm no use to you, I'm no use to anybody.

STELLA: Oh, Maurice, how *can* you say that? Don't you know how desperately afraid I was when they told me you were hurt and how relieved, how infinitely thankful, when they told me at last, after days and days of anguish, that you would live?

MAURICE: They should never have let me. Why didn't they put me out of my misery when I was all smashed up? It only wanted an injection a little stronger than usual.

That was the cruelty—to bring me back to life. Cruel to me and ten times more cruel to you.

STELLA: I won't let you say it. It's not true. It's not true.

MAURICE: I think I could have borne it if we'd had a child. Oh, Stella, if we'd only had a little kid and I could think to myself that it was you and me. And you would have something to console you. After all, it's a woman's destiny to have children. You wouldn't have felt that you had entirely wasted your life.

STELLA: But, Maurice, my dear, I *don't* feel I've wasted my life. You're not yourself to-night. You're ill and tired. Oh, what has come over you?

MAURICE: I love you, Stella. I want to take you in my arms as I used to. I want to press my lips to yours and see your eyes close and your head fall back and feel your dear soft body grow tense with desire. Stella, Stella. I can't bear it. [*He bursts into tears, clinging to her.*]

STELLA: Maurice, darling. Don't. Don't cry.

[*He sobs hysterically while she rocks him to and fro like a mother her child. Then he gets hold of himself.*

MAURICE: [*With a complete change of tone, in a matter-of-fact voice.*] Oh, my God, what a damned fool I am. Give me a handkerchief.

[*She gives him one from under the pillow and he blows his nose.*

STELLA: My dear, you did frighten me.

MAURICE: It's what they call a nerve storm. It's lucky it was only you there. It would have been a pretty kettle of fish if Nurse Wayland had seen me like that.

STELLA: [*Trying to laugh with him.*] It would have been a much prettier kettle of fish if I'd seen you clinging to her capacious bosom.

MAURICE: Now you mention it I must admit it is rather capacious.

STELLA: They're not worn now.

MAURICE: I say, you haven't got a glass, have you?

STELLA: My angel, how do you imagine I apply lipstick to my ruby lips? [*She takes a little glass out of her bag and hands it to him.*]

MAURICE: [*Laughing at himself.*] For an intrepid aviator I look rather tear-stained, if I may say so. [*He wipes his eyes with the handkerchief.*]

STELLA: Let me powder your nose. You can't think what a comfort it is after you've been upset.

MAURICE: Go on with you. You can give me a whisky and soda if you like.

STELLA: All right. But I'll powder mine.

MAURICE: I feel like a house on fire now.

STELLA: I wish someone would explain how it is that a dab of powder can in the twinkling of an eye reduce a woman's nose from an unwieldy lump to a dear little thing that no one can deny is her best feature.

MAURICE: These are the miracles of science that we read about.

STELLA: Now I'll get you your whisky and soda.

MAURICE: Here's Colin. I'll have a glass of bubbly instead.

[COLIN *comes in with a tray on which are glasses, ice, and a bottle of champagne.*

COLIN: I'm afraid I've been a devil of a time.

MAURICE: I knew you couldn't be trusted in the cellar by yourself. We were just going to send a search party after you.

COLIN: Well, first I couldn't find anything to break the ice with and then I couldn't find the nippers to cut the wire. And then I thought I might as well put the car away. I didn't want to leave it outside all night.

MAURICE: Meanwhile Stella is famishing.

COLIN: Nurse Wayland is just coming. She's making some sandwiches with bacon and they smell a fair treat.

[*The* NURSE *comes in with a covered entréc dish.*

STELLA: Here she is. That is kind of you, Nurse. If there's anything I adore it's bacon sandwiches.

NURSE: I haven't brought any knives and forks. I thought you could eat with your fingers.

STELLA: Heavenly.

COLIN: I'll just bolt up and change my coat. I might just as well be comfortable and I shan't be a minute.

STELLA: Well, I'm not going to wait for you.

COLIN: All right. Go right ahead. But leave me my fair share or else all is over between us.

[*He goes out.* STELLA *goes to the window.*

STELLA: Dr. Harvester, come and eat a sandwich before it gets cold.

MAURICE: I don't think I'll wait to see you people make pigs of yourselves. I think I'll turn in.

STELLA: Aren't you going to have a drink with us?

MAURICE: I don't think I will if you don't mind. I'm rather tired.

STELLA: Oh, I am sorry, Maurice. But there's nothing to stay up for if you're tired.

MAURICE: You might look in on your way up to bed, Stella.

STELLA: Yes, rather. But I shan't disturb you if you're asleep.

MAURICE: I shan't be asleep. I've got a bit of a head. I'll just lie still in the dark and it'll go away.

[*As* NURSE WAYLAND *starts to wheel him out.* MRS. TABRET *and* DR. HARVESTER *come in.*

HARVESTER: Did I hear you calling me?

STELLA: You did. Maurice is going to bed.

MRS. TABRET: Oh, I'm glad. It's fearfully late. Good night, old boy. Sleep well. [*She leans over and kisses him on the forehead.*]

MAURICE: Good night, Mother. Bless you.

HARVESTER: Let me give you a hand, Nurse.

NURSE: I can manage perfectly. I'm so used to wheeling the invalid bed and he weighs nothing.

MAURICE: I never weighed more than ten stone eight when I was well.

HARVESTER: Never mind. Let me push him in. I'd like to.

MAURICE: Let the man do something for his money, Nurse. [*Putting on a cockney accent.*] You bring me drops and me powder puff, dearie.

> [*The* NURSE *opens the door and* DR. HARVESTER *pushes the bed out.*

STELLA: Don't be long, Doctor, or the sandwiches will be stone cold.

> [*The door is closed.* STELLA *and* MRS. TABRET *are left alone.*

STELLA: Maurice is rather nervous to-night.

MRS. TABRET: Yes, I noticed it.

STELLA: I'm sorry I went to the opera.

MRS. TABRET: My dear, you go out so little.

STELLA: I haven't the inclination, really.

MRS. TABRET: I'm afraid you're awfully tired

STELLA: [*With a smile.*] Dead.

MRS. TABRET: Why don't you eat something?

STELLA: No, I'll wait till the others come.

MRS. TABRET: Whatever happens, darling, I want you to know that I'm deeply grateful for all you've done for Maurice.

STELLA: [*Startled.*] Why do you say that? You don't think he's any worse?

MRS. TABRET: No, I think he's just about the same as usual.

STELLA: He does get a little nervous and high-strung sometimes.

MRS. TABRET: Yes, I know.

STELLA: You startled me. I don't know why you should suddenly say a thing like that.

MRS. TABRET: [*Smiling.*] Is there any reason I shouldn't?

STELLA: It sounded strangely ominous.

MRS. TABRET: I feel I'd like you to know that I realise what a great sacrifice you've made for him for so many years. You mustn't think that I've taken it as a matter of course.

STELLA: Oh, my dear, don't. It would be inhuman if I didn't feel unspeakably sorry for Maurice. It's awful for him, poor darling. Naturally if there was anything I could do to make things a little easier for him I was anxious to do it.

MRS. TABRET: After all, you didn't marry him to be the helpmate of a hopeless cripple.

STELLA: One takes the rough with the smooth.

MRS. TABRET: I know it's very irksome to have an old woman like me always living with you. It's difficult to be a mother-in-law and welcome.

STELLA: [*Charmingly.*] My dear, you've been kindness itself to me. What should I have done without you?

MRS. TABRET: I will admit that I've tried not to be a pest. You'd have been within your rights if you'd refused to have me to live here. I must thank you for all you've done for me, too.

STELLA: Oh, my dear, you make me feel quite shy.

MRS. TABRET: You're a very young and a very beautiful woman. You have the right to live your life just as everyone else has. For six years now you've given up everything to be the sole comfort of a man who was your husband only because a legal ceremony had joined you together.

STELLA: No, no. Because love had joined us together.

MRS. TABRET: My poor child, I'm so desperately sorry for you. Whatever the future may have in store I shall never forget your courage, your self-sacrifice, and your patience.

STELLA: [*Puzzled and a little frightened.*] I don't understand what you mean.

MRS. TABRET: [*With a tolerant and ironic smile.*] Don't you? Well, let us suppose that this is the anniversary of my wedding-day and my thoughts have been much occupied with the ups and downs, the fortunes and misfortunes of married life.

[COLIN *comes in. He has taken off his long evening coat and wears a very shabby old golf coat.*

COLIN: Hulloa, where are the others?

STELLA: Maurice has gone to bed. Dr. Harvester is just coming.

MRS. TABRET: Now, come on, children. Sit down and have something to eat.

COLIN: I'll pour out some wine, shall I?

[*He pours out three glasses of champagne while* STELLA *helps herself to a sandwich.*

STELLA: Hm. Scrumptious.

MRS. TABRET: Nurse Wayland makes them well, doesn't she?

STELLA: Marvellously.

[DR. HARVESTER *comes in.*

STELLA: If you don't hurry up you'll be too late. They're simply divine.

HARVESTER: I'll just have one and swallow a glass of bubbly and bolt. It's any old time and I've got to be up bright and early in the morning.

COLIN: Is Maurice all right?

HARVESTER: Oh, fairly. He's a bit down to-night for some reason. I don't know why. He was in great spirits earlier in the evening.

MRS. TABRET: I expect he's just tired. He *would* sit up.

HARVESTER: Nurse Wayland says that something has happened to upset him. Is that true?

MRS. TABRET: Not that I know of.

HARVESTER: He says he's got a headache. I've left him a sleeping draught that he can take if he can't get off or wakes in the night and feels restless.

STELLA: I'll go in and see him before I go to bed. If he can only get a good rest I'm sure he'll be his usual self to-morrow.

MRS. TABRET: Sit with him a little, Stella.

STELLA: Of course I will.

HARVESTER: Well, I must be off. Good night, Mrs. Tabret. I've had a jolly evening.

MRS. TABRET: I'll come and see you to the door and then I shall go up to bed. Good night, children.

STELLA: Good night.

> [*They kiss one another and then* MRS. TABRET *kisses* COLIN.

MRS. TABRET: Good night, Colin dear. Don't stay up too late, either of you.

COLIN: And put out the lights and see that the windows are properly closed and the safety catches in place. I will, Mother.

MRS. TABRET: [*Pleased with his chaff, to* DR. HARVESTER.] You see how these boys treat me. They have no respect for their aged mother.

COLIN: A certain amount of restrained affection, however.

MRS. TABRET: Bless you, my dear, now and always.

HARVESTER: Good night.

STELLA: Good night. We shall see you in a day or two, I suppose.

HARVESTER: I expect so.

COLIN: Good night, old boy.

> [DR. HARVESTER *and* MRS. TABRET *go out.* COLIN *goes over to the windows and shuts them and draws the curtains. The moment the door closes on* MRS. TABRET, STELLA *puts down the sandwich she has been making a pretence of eating. She stands looking out into space. When* COLIN *has finished shutting up, he turns off most of the lights so that the room is shrouded in darkness and there is only light on* STELLA. *He turns to her.*

COLIN: Stella. . . . Stella.

> [*She gives a stifled sob and looks at him, misery in her eyes.*

STELLA: Oh, Colin. The anguish.

COLIN: [*Going towards her.*] My poor child.

STELLA: Don't touch me. Oh, what shall I do? Colin, what have we done?

COLIN: Darling.

STELLA: Maurice was so strange to-night. I couldn't make him out. I was almost afraid he suspected.

COLIN: Impossible.

STELLA: He must never know. Never! I'd do anything in the world to prevent it.

COLIN: I'm so terribly sorry.

STELLA: We're in a hopeless pass. Hopeless. Why did you ever love me? Why did I ever love you?

COLIN: Stella.

> [*He stretches out his arms, but she turns away.*

STELLA: Oh, I'm so ashamed. [*She hides her face with her hands.*]

END OF THE FIRST ACT

THE SECOND ACT

THE SCENE *is the same as in the preceding act.*
Next morning, and about midday.

COLIN *is seated at a writing-table writing letters.* MAJOR
LICONDA *is shown in by the* MAID. *He is in golfing things.*

ALICE: Major Liconda.

COLIN: [*Getting up.*] Oh, how do you do?

[*The* MAID *goes out.*

LICONDA: My dear boy, what an awful thing. I'm absolutely horrified. I've only just this minute heard.

COLIN: It's nice of you to have come. As you can imagine
we're all very much upset.

LICONDA: I've been playing golf. I went out early. I had a
match at nine. Someone told me at the clubhouse when
I got in. I could hardly believe it.

COLIN: I'm afraid it's true all the same.

LICONDA: But Maurice seemed comparatively well last
night.

COLIN: Anyhow no worse than usual.

LICONDA: I thought him in such good spirits. He was full of
fun. He was cracking jokes.

COLIN: Yes, I know.

LICONDA: Of course, I know nothing. You know Blake at
the club? I don't know if you've ever played with him.

COLIN: No. But I've met him.

LICONDA: Well, he came up when I was standing at the bar
having a drink and said to me: I say, have you heard
that poor Maurice Tabret died last night? By George, it
gave me a shock. You know, when one isn't as young as

255

one was, it always gives one a turn to hear of the death of someone you knew.

COLIN: I suppose it does.

LICONDA: Blake hadn't heard any of the details. Was he taken suddenly worse in the night?

COLIN: No, he said he was rather tired. Stella and I were going to have a snack before going to bed. He said he wouldn't wait. It was very natural; it was getting a bit late, you know. Harvester was here and he went along with him and Nurse Wayland and helped to put him to bed. He seemed all right then.

LICONDA: Did he just die in his sleep?

COLIN: I suppose so.

LICONDA: What a mercy. That's the best way, isn't it? We'd all give something to know for certain that when our time came we'd pass out like that.

COLIN: He can't have felt ill, or he'd have rung. He had a bell-push under his pillow and it rings in Nurse Wayland's room. She'd have been down like a flash if there'd been a sound.

LICONDA: She heard nothing?

COLIN: Nothing.

LICONDA: When did you find out then?

COLIN: Well, you see, sometimes, if he'd had a poorish night, you know, he slept rather late in the morning. And he was always allowed to sleep on. You know what nurses are. However rotten a night you've had they come bustling in at the crack of dawn and they don't care a damn if you're sleeping or not. You must be washed and have your hair brushed and your pillows shaken.

LICONDA: Don't I know it? I never know which I dread most, an attack of malaria or a really efficient nurse.

COLIN: Well, Stella stopped all that. She insisted that no one should go in to Maurice till he rang.

LICONDA: Poor devil, at all events when he was asleep he was happy.

COLIN: I believe it was the only matter on which there'd been any friction between Stella and Nurse Wayland. You know, Nurse Wayland is really a very good sort. She was never any trouble in the house and she was always good-tempered and that sort of thing.

LICONDA: Oh, I know. It struck me that she was a thoroughly nice girl.

COLIN: When she first came she wanted to get Maurice ready for the day as she called it, at eight o'clock every morning. Routine, you know. And she said if he was tired he could go to sleep again afterwards. But Stella put her foot down. She said she didn't want to interfere with anything else, but on that point she insisted. And Nurse Wayland could either knuckle under or go.

LICONDA: Quite right.

COLIN: We were just finishing breakfast, about half-past nine, I think, Stella and I and Mother, when Nurse Wayland came in. She never has breakfast. She just makes herself a cup of cocoa when she gets up at seven.

LICONDA: My God, these women, what a genius they have for doing the uncomfortable thing.

COLIN: I noticed she was very white. She said she'd just been in to Maurice. I never heard him ring, said Stella. You know what these jerry-built houses are. You hear every bell in the house.

LICONDA: Yes, mine's like that.

COLIN: He didn't ring, said Nurse Wayland. It was so late I thought I'd just peep in and see if he was all right. Then Stella got right up on her hind legs. I won't have it, she said. I've forbidden you to go in till he rings. How dare you disobey me. I've never seen Stella in such a passion. I saw that Nurse Wayland was trembling. She looked all funny. Scared, you know. But not of Stella. I had a sort of suspicion something was wrong. Hold hard, Stella, I said. I got up. Is anything the matter, Nurse? I asked. She gave a sort of cry and clenched her hands. I'm afraid he's dead, she said.

LICONDA: Good God! How awful.

COLIN: Stella gave a sort of gasp and then she went into a dead faint.

LICONDA: Your poor mother.

COLIN: Mother was wonderful. You know when half a dozen things happen at a time, you seem to see them all separately and yet together. I sprang forward to help Stella. She'd fallen on the floor with a thump. I don't know, for a moment I was afraid the shock had killed her. And I saw Mother sitting at the table with a piece of toast in her hand. And she just looked at Nurse Wayland, I don't know, as though she couldn't understand. She was awfully white and then she began to tremble. She never made a sound. She shrank back into her chair and seemed all of a sudden to become an old, old woman.

LICONDA: Why didn't the fool break it to you more gently?

COLIN: Then Mother stood up. She got hold of herself quicker than any of us. I never knew she had such nerve.

LICONDA: She's a woman in a thousand. I knew that.

COLIN: You'd better go for Dr. Harvester, she said to me. [*With a sudden falter.*] By God, I shall never get the sound of her voice out of my ears.

LICONDA: Hold on, old man. It's no good you going to pieces. Don't tell me any more if it upsets you.

COLIN: [*Pulling himself together.*] No, I'm all right. There's nothing more to tell. Mother said, Nurse and I'll see to Stella. Don't you bother. That seemed to pull Nurse Wayland up. She came forward and she and Mother began to try to get Stella round. I went into Maurice's room. I felt his pulse and I put my hand on his heart. He looked as if he was asleep. I knew he was dead. I got the car and went to Dr. Harvester's. He'd started on his rounds, but they knew where he'd gone more or less and I bolted after him. Luckily I caught him and I brought him back with me. He said he thought poor Maurice had been dead for a good two hours.

LICONDA: Did he say what had happened?

COLIN: He thinks it may have been an embolism. Or perhaps heart failure, you know.

LICONDA: How about Stella?

COLIN: She's all right, thank God. She came to after a bit. My God, she did give me a fright.

LICONDA: I don't wonder.

COLIN: Harvester wanted her to go to bed, but she wouldn't. She's in Maurice's room now.

LICONDA: What about your mother?

COLIN: Harvester's with her. He had to go and see some patients, but he said he'd come back, and he turned up just before you did. Here he is.

[*As he says these words,* DR. HARVESTER *comes in. He and* MAJOR LICONDA *shake hands.*

HARVESTER: Hulloa, Major.

LICONDA: This is a very sad errand that has brought you here, Doctor.

HARVESTER: It s naturally been a dreadful shock to Mrs. Tabret ar d Stella.

LICONDA: How is Mrs. Tabret?

HARVESTER: She's bearing up wonderfully. She's very much upset, but she's trying not to show it. She has a great deal of self-control.

LICONDA: I wonder if she'd like to see me.

HARVESTER: I'm sure she would.

COLIN: Shall I run up and see?

LICONDA: It would be very kind of you, Colin. Say that if she doesn't want to be bothered with me she has only to say so. I shall quite understand. I don't want to be a nuisance, but if it'll be any comfort to her to see me I shall be only too glad.

COLIN: All right.

[*He goes out.*

LICONDA: You know, I've known Mrs. Tabret for over thirty years. Her husband was in the Indian Civil.

HARVESTER: Yes, she told me.

LICONDA: They were almost the first people I got to know at all well when I went out to India. She's one of the best, you know. She always was. Everybody liked her.

HARVESTER: Of course, I've seen a good deal of her during the last five years. She's really been wonderful. So has Stella, for the matter of that.

LICONDA: One can't help being rather thankful it's all over.

HARVESTER: He never had a chance of getting better, poor devil.

LICONDA: Yes, you said that last night.

HARVESTER: Of course, he might have gone on for years like that. But what was the good? It was rotten for him and rotten for everyone connected with him.

LICONDA: You can't say that any of them grudged the sacrifices they had to make for his sake.

HARVESTER: No. Rather not. They were awfully good to him.

LICONDA: I could wish the end hadn't come quite so suddenly.

HARVESTER: Oh, why? It's much better that he should have passed out like that rather than get inflammation of the lungs or something of that sort that he just hadn't the strength to fight against.

LICONDA: So far as he was concerned, yes. I was thinking of his mother and Stella.

> [NURSE WAYLAND *comes in. She wears her nurse's uniform.*

HARVESTER: Hulloa, Nurse. I thought you were having a rest.

LICONDA: Good morning.

NURSE: Good morning, Major. I'm glad you came round. Mrs. Tabret will be glad to see you.

HARVESTER: I told you to go and lie down, Nurse.

NURSE: I couldn't. I was too restless.

HARVESTER: Then why don't you go for a walk? You can do no good by sitting about and moping.

LICONDA: I'm afraid it's been as great a shock to Nurse Wayland as to the rest of us. After all, she'd been looking after Maurice for a long time.

NURSE: Yes, it's been a great shock to me. He was a dear. One couldn't help admiring him. He bore his terrible misfortune with so much courage.

HARVESTER: He was topping. There's no doubt about that.

NURSE: I naturally grew attached to him. He was always so gay and so grateful for what one did for him.

LICONDA: I suppose you'll try to get a good long holiday before you take another job.

NURSE: I haven't made any plans yet.

HARVESTER: What about those friends of yours who live on the South Coast? Why don't you spend a few weeks with them? To tell you the truth, you're looking all in.

NURSE: [*Listlessly.*] Am I?

HARVESTER: You must try not to take it too hard.

NURSE: A nurse naturally doesn't like to lose a patient. Especially so unexpectedly.

HARVESTER: It was always on the cards that he'd go out suddenly.

NURSE: Like a candle that you blow out when you don't want it any more. Where does the flame go then?

[DR. HARVESTER *looks at her for a moment reflectively.*

HARVESTER: [*Kindly.*] My dear, I'm afraid you're taking poor Maurice's death a good deal more to heart than is quite wise.

NURSE: [*With bitterness.*] Did you think he was only a case to me? Even a nurse is human. Strange as it may seem, she has a heart like other people.

HARVESTER: Of course she has a heart. But it doesn't do her or her patients any good if she allows her emotions to get the better of her common sense.

NURSE: Does that mean you think I've been inefficient?

HARVESTER: No, of course not. Heaven knows, you never spared yourself. Perhaps you've been trying to do a little too much for your strength. You take my advice, my dear, and go for a holiday. What you want is a real rest.

NURSE: What is it, in your opinion, that Maurice Tabret actually died of?

HARVESTER: Heart failure.

NURSE: Everybody dies of heart failure.

HARVESTER: Of course. But that's as good a thing as any to put on the death certificate.

NURSE: Are you going to have a post-mortem?

HARVESTER: No, why should I? It's quite unnecessary.

NURSE: [*Looking him full in the face.*] I don't agree with you.

HARVESTER: [*Without a trace of asperity.*] I'm sorry. But it's my affair. If I'm prepared to sign the death certificate I don't know that anyone else has any right to say anything about it.

NURSE: You've told me half a dozen times that Maurice Tabret might have lived for years.

HARVESTER: So he might. I can tell you now that it's a blessing for everybody concerned with him that he didn't.

NURSE: [*Very deliberately.*] Dr. Harvester, Maurice Tabret was murdered.

HARVESTER: What *are* you talking about?

NURSE: Do you want me to repeat it? Maurice Tabret was murdered.

HARVESTER: Rubbish.

LICONDA: I daresay you're not quite yourself this morning, Nurse. It's very natural. But you must try to be reasonable. You oughtn't to say things that you can't possibly mean.

NURSE: I'm in complete possession of my senses, Major Liconda, and I know perfectly well what I'm saying.

LICONDA: Do you mean to say that you intended that statement to be taken literally?

NURSE: Quite.

LICONDA: [*Gravely.*] It's a very serious one, you know.

NURSE: I'm aware of that.

HARVESTER: It's grotesque.

NURSE: You've known me for five years, Dr. Harvester. Have I ever given you to imagine that I'm a neurotic or hysterical woman, given to talking in a wild and exaggerated way?

LICONDA: Let us listen to what Nurse Wayland has to say. Do you mean by any chance that you are dissatisfied with the way your patient was treated by Doctor Harvester?

HARVESTER: By George, that never occurred to me. Is that it, Nurse? Don't hesitate to say anything you want to. I shan't be in the least offended. I don't want to put on any frills, and if there's anything that's making you miserable it's much better that you should say it. I'll try to explain.

NURSE: So far as I could judge you did everything for Maurice Tabret that medical skill could do.

LICONDA: Besides, he was surely seen by several specialists.

HARVESTER: Half a dozen at the least.

LICONDA: Well, Nurse Wayland?

NURSE: I am a trained nurse, Major Liconda; you can't imagine that if Maurice Tabret had died as the result of an error in treatment on Dr. Harvester's part I should be so heartless as to distress the relatives by mentioning it.

HARVESTER: I don't want to seem flippant on such an occasion, but I am forced to say that your magnanimity overwhelms me, Nurse Wayland.

NURSE: You can be flippant or condescending or sarcastic, Dr. Harvester. It means nothing to me.

LICONDA: [*With a thin smile.*] I'm sure it will do no harm if we're all civil to one another, at least for a little while longer.

NURSE: I've made a definite charge and I stick to it.

HARVESTER: The charge being that some person or persons unknown murdered Maurice Tabret?

NURSE: Yes.

HARVESTER: But, my dear, why *should* anyone want to murder poor Maurice?

NURSE: That at present is no business of mine.

HARVESTER: Now, look here, Nurse, you know just as well as I do that everyone connected with him was devoted to Maurice. No one was ever more surrounded with love and affection than he was. It's incredible that anyone should even have *wished* him harm.

NURSE: Whatever I may think or may not think I am at liberty to keep to myself. I am not in the witness box.

HARVESTER: The witness box? [*Mockingly.*] Do you already see yourself giving sensational evidence at the Old Bailey?

NURSE: I can honestly say that I can imagine nothing more hateful than the notoriety that would be forced upon me if I were obliged to appear in court.

HARVESTER: There'd be notoriety all right. This is the sort of thing that would be jam for the papers. Come, now, be a sport, Nurse Wayland; you know just as well as I do that Maurice died of natural causes. What on earth is the use of making a fuss and getting everyone upset?

NURSE: If he died of natural causes a post-mortem will prove it and then I shall have nothing more to say.

HARVESTER: [*Irritably.*] I'm not going to have a post-mortem. You know how the relatives hate it.

NURSE: Are you afraid of what it will show?

HARVESTER: [*With decision.*] Not on your life.

NURSE: [*Defiantly.*] I warn you that if you sign the death certificate I shall go straight to the coroner and make a protest.

HARVESTER: I should have thought the Tabrets had had enough to put up with, without being obliged to go through the ordeal you want to force upon them.

NURSE: Major Liconda, you were in the Indian Police, weren't you? You ought to know about such things. Will you tell me what is the duty of a nurse who has reason to believe that her patient has come to his death by foul play?

LICONDA: That is a question I'd sooner you hadn't asked me. I suppose her duty is quite clear. But I think she should be very sure that her reasons are valid before she exposes to distress and publicity a family that has treated her with unvarying kindness.

HARVESTER: What are your reasons, anyway? You've made

a charge, but to the best of my recollection you haven't given us an inkling of what it's based on.

NURSE: If you'd been willing to have a post-mortem nothing need have been said till we knew the results of it. But you've put me with my back to the wall. Major Liconda is right. Everyone in this house has treated me with the greatest consideration. I do at least owe it to them to make no charges that may directly or indirectly concern them behind their backs.

HARVESTER: Does that mean you want them sent for?

NURSE: Please.

LICONDA: I think it's best. You've been so definite, Nurse Wayland, that neither Dr. Harvester nor I can keep the matter to ourselves. However distressing it may be I think Maurice's family should know what you have to say.

NURSE: I'm quite prepared to tell them. In point of fact, I think Mrs. Tabret is just coming.

LICONDA: Where is Stella?

HARVESTER: Do you want her, too?

LICONDA: I think it's better.

HARVESTER: I'll see if I can find her.

LICONDA: I believe she's in Maurice's room.

[HARVESTER *goes out*.

NURSE: Don't judge me till you've heard all I have to say, Major Liconda.

LICONDA: [*With a certain severity*.] Miss Wayland, I happen to be a very old friend of the Tabrets and deeply attached to Mrs. Tabret. I regret that you should think it your duty at this moment of all others to add to their great sorrow. I can only hope that you will be shown *not* to have been justified.

NURSE: In that case you will have good reason to throw me out of the house, bag and baggage.

LICONDA: It is not my house, Miss Wayland, and I doubt whether Colin Tabret would be willing to depute to me that pleasant task.

NURSE: I'm just as glad to know who are my friends and who are my enemies.

> [MRS. TABRET *comes in with* COLIN. *She goes up to* MAJOR LICONDA *with a little smile. She is calm and composed.*

MRS. TABRET: My dear old friend.

LICONDA: I felt that I must come and see you for a moment, my dear. I'm sure you know how deeply I sympathise with you, but I wanted to tell you that if in any way I can be of service to you. . . .

MRS. TABRET: [*Interrupting him with a little smile.*] It was very kind of you to come and just like you.

LICONDA: I'm relieved to see that you're bearing so bravely what must have been a bitter blow.

MRS. TABRET: I am trying to put my own feelings away out of sight and mind. I want only to think that my son has ended his long martyrdom. He had a brave, a carefree, and a happy nature. He was not meant to live on a bed of sickness.

LICONDA: I remember when he was a boy how amazing his vitality was.

MRS. TABRET: I will not weep because he is dead. I will rejoice because he is free.

> [STELLA *comes in from the garden, followed by* DR. HARVESTER. *She is all in white.*

STELLA: Dr. Harvester told me you were here and wanted to see me.

LICONDA: I wanted first of all to tell you how much I feel for you in your sad loss.

STELLA: You know, Maurice and I often talked of death. He was never afraid of it. He'd faced it often enough during the war. He didn't attach very much importance to it. He couldn't bear any of the trappings of woe. He told me that he didn't wish me to wear mourning for him. He said that if he died I was to carry on as usual. He wanted me to go about and do things exactly as if he were alive.

MRS. TABRET: He loved you so much, Stella. He put your happiness above everything.

STELLA: I know.

COLIN: Those lines of Stevenson's keep ringing in my ears: "Home is the sailor, home from the sea."

LICONDA: "And the hunter home from the hill." They're very moving to us who've spent our lives in distant places.

STELLA: You know, Maurice never quite believed that with this life everything ended for him. He didn't believe in a great many things that many people still more or less believe in. . . .

MRS. TABRET: [Interrupting.] I could never bring myself to teach my children what I couldn't myself believe. When they were little and I used to sit in the evenings in our house and look at the multitudinous stars sweeping across the blue sky of India and thought of what we are, so transitory and so insignificant, and yet with such a capacity for suffering, such a passion for beauty, I was overwhelmed by the mystery and the immensity of the universe. I could not conceive what was the cause of all those worlds I saw above me, nor what was the power that guided them, but my heart was filled with amazement and awe. What I vaguely divined was too stupendous to fit into the limits of any creed of men.

STELLA: You know how Maurice was always laughing and joking. Even when he was speaking seriously he kept a little twinkle in his eye, so that you weren't quite sure he wasn't making fun of himself. I think he'd never quite grown out of some of those beliefs that I suppose he'd acquired unconsciously in his childhood from nurses and servants.

MRS. TABRET: We always had native ayahs. Heaven knows what they taught the children.

STELLA: He didn't believe with his reason, but in some strange way with his nerves or his heart, that perhaps there was something in the Eastern notion of the transmigration of souls.

LICONDA: I wonder if one ever entirely ceases to believe in what one has been taught as a child.

STELLA: I think deep down in him was the faith that when his soul left his poor wounded body it would find another tenement. I think he had so much vitality that he felt it impossible that he should not live again on this earth.

MRS. TABRET: Ah, I've so often wished I had that comforting faith. Oh, to have a second chance and a third, to pass from life to life, purging yourself of imperfection and atoning for your sins, till at last you lose yourself in the infinite peace of the infinite soul of God.

STELLA: [*Turning to* NURSE WAYLAND.] I had something to say to you, Nurse. You'll be leaving us very soon now, I suppose?

NURSE: I suppose so.

STELLA: I want to thank you for everything you did for Maurice, and I want you to know how deeply grateful I am to you.

NURSE: I did no more than my duty.

STELLA: [*With a charming smile.*] Oh, no, you did much more than that. If it had been only your duty you could never have been so immensely thoughtful. You could never have anticipated Maurice's wants. You've been so awfully kind.

NURSE: [*A trifle sullenly.*] Your husband was a very easy patient. He was always anxious not to give trouble.

STELLA: I've got a little plan that I want to tell you about. I've talked it over with Mrs. Tabret and she very much approves of it. You've had a long and hard time here. And your month's holiday a year has been very little rest. You've often talked to me about your sister in Japan and I know how much you've wanted to travel. If you'll allow me I should like to make it possible for you to go out to the East and have a good time.

NURSE: [*Stonily on the defensive.*] I don't think I understand what you mean.

STELLA: [*A little shyly, but in a manner that is disarming.*] Well, my dear, a nurse's salary is never very large. I know that Maurice has left me everything he had and we've been living so economically, I shall be quite well off in a modest way. It would be dear of you if you'd let me make you a present of a few hundred pounds, a thousand, say, to make it a round sum, so that you could go for a nice long journey and need not think of earning your living for a while.

NURSE: [*Hoarsely, trembling in her effort to control herself.*] Do you think I would take money from you? Is that what you take me for?

STELLA: [*Surprised, but not taking her very seriously.*] But what on earth is the harm of it? Come, Nurse, don't be unreasonable. You know I don't want to offend you.

NURSE: What I've done I've been paid for. If I wasn't satisfied with the payment I received I only had to go.

STELLA: [*Taken aback, as though she had been suddenly slapped in the face.*] Nurse, what *is* the matter? What have I said? Why do you speak to me like that?

HARVESTER: You mustn't take what Nurse Wayland says too literally. She really isn't herself to-day.

LICONDA: No, Harvester, it's no good taking up that

attitude. The position is much too serious. Stella, I've got something very unpleasant to tell you. I would sooner not have added to your present trouble, but I'm afraid it can't be avoided.

STELLA: What is it?

LICONDA: Nurse Wayland is not satisfied that Maurice died from heart failure.

STELLA: But if Dr. Harvester says so? Surely he knows best.

HARVESTER: I am prepared to sign the death certificate. I have no doubt in my mind of the cause of death.

LICONDA: Nurse Wayland thinks there ought to be a post-mortem.

STELLA: [*With the utmost determination.*] Never. Never. Poor Maurice's body has suffered enough. I won't have him cut about to satisfy an idle curiosity. I absolutely refuse.

LICONDA: I understand that an autopsy cannot be held except with the consent of the next of kin.

NURSE: Or on the order of the coroner.

STELLA: What does she mean by that?

LICONDA: I'm afraid she means that if you persist in your refusal she will go to the proper authority and make the statement she has already made to Dr. Harvester and me.

STELLA: What is the statement?

LICONDA: Do you wish to repeat it, Nurse Wayland?

NURSE: [*Very coolly, almost with insolence.*] Not particularly. I have no objection to your doing so.

HARVESTER: Do you really insist on going through with this, Nurse? What you said to the Major and me was more or less confidential, wasn't it? Don't you think you'd better reflect a little more? If anything further is said the matter must necessarily go out of our control. I think you should consider the consequences of your attitude and the harm that may arise.

Nurse: I can't keep silent. I should never forgive myself.

Liconda: Nurse Wayland states that Maurice's death was not due to his illness, but to some other cause.

Stella: I'm dreadfully sorry, but I don't understand. What other cause could have brought about his death?

Liconda: She says he was murdered.

[Colin *and* Stella *start*. Mrs. Tabret *smothers a cry*.

Stella: Murdered? You must be mad, Nurse.

Liconda: Harvester and I have pointed out to her that he was regarded by everyone connected with him with the greatest affection.

Colin: It's preposterous.

Stella: After the first shock I'm almost inclined to laugh. Really, Nurse, you must be very nervous and over-wrought to have got such an idea in your head. Is that why you were so funny when I asked you to accept enough money to take a year's holiday?

Nurse: I had no wish that the matter should go so far now. If Dr. Harvester had agreed to my suggestion of having a post-mortem nothing need have been said till it was discovered if my suspicions were justified or not.

Harvester: Willing to wound and yet afraid to strike, Nurse Wayland.

Nurse: [*Turning on him.*] You have forced me into this position, Dr. Harvester. I only did my duty in telling you my very grave suspicions, and the moment I did, you took up a definitely hostile attitude towards me.

Harvester: Well, if you want to know, I thought you silly, nervous, and hysterical. Good heavens, I've been in practice long enough to know how wildly people talk. I should be kept pretty busy if I paid any attention, for instance, to what one woman says about another.

Nurse: Or is it that you're frightened to death of a scandal? You know that notoriety does a doctor no good, and you think it would hurt your practice if anything came of this that got into the papers. You don't want to have a post-mortem because if there is anything you don't want to know it. Deny it if you can.

HARVESTER: I admit I shouldn't welcome publicity. I put all the money I had into buying my practice and I don't suppose it would do it any good if I were mixed up in an unpleasant case.

MRS. TABRET: People want their doctor to be like their central heating: efficient, but not obtrusive.

HARVESTER: But I can honestly say that if it were my duty I wouldn't let my own interests stop me from doing it. In this case I don't think it is my duty. I am quite satisfied that there is no reason why I shouldn't sign the necessary documents.

COLIN: All that is neither here nor there. Nurse Wayland has presumably some grounds for her statement. Perhaps she'd better give them.

LICONDA: Yes, she has. I thought it better she should speak before all concerned.

NURSE: It was my wish to do so. I don't want to do anything underhand.

STELLA: Go on, Nurse Wayland.

NURSE: [To LICONDA.] I daresay you know that Mr. Maurice often had bouts of sleeplessness. Dr. Harvester had prescribed various sedatives. But he found that chloralin was the one he supported best. [To HARVESTER] Is that true?

HARVESTER: Quite. Chloralin is a new preparation in tabloid form. It's more convenient than the liquid chloral we've been in the habit of using. I explained to Maurice the danger of his growing dependent on drugs and begged him not to take a dose without my permission or Nurse Wayland's.

NURSE: I'm quite sure that he never did.

K*

HARVESTER: So am I. He was very sensible and he understood my point. He certainly wasn't lacking in self-
control.

NURSE: Will you tell Major Liconda what instructions you
gave me last night?

HARVESTER: He was excited and wrought up. I asked
Nurse Wayland to give him a tabloid and told him that if
he woke in the night he could take it. I thought he'd
probably drop off for half an hour or so and then wake
up and not be able to get to sleep again.

NURSE: I dissolved a tabloid in half a glass of water and put
it by his side. I noticed that there were only five tabloids
left in the bottle and I made up my mind to order some
more. This morning the bottle was empty.

STELLA: [*Puzzled.*] That's very strange.

NURSE: Very!

HARVESTER: How did you happen to notice?

NURSE: I was tidying up. I thought it better to put away all
the medicines and dressings and so on.

STELLA: [*To* HARVESTER.] Would five tabloids have a fatal
effect?

NURSE: Six. I left one dissolved in water by the side of his
bed.

HARVESTER: Yes, there's little doubt that the effect would be
fatal.

STELLA: It's all incredible. It's surely much more likely that
someone took them for his own use.

COLIN: Are you absolutely sure that last night the bottle
contained five tabloids?

NURSE: Absolutely. If anyone took them for his own use it
must have been after I went to bed.

STELLA: But no one went into Maurice's room last night
after that but me. I went in to say good night to him.

LICONDA: How do you know that no one else went into his room?

STELLA: Who could have? There was only Colin and Mother.

LICONDA: [*To* MRS. TABRET.] You went upstairs as I was letting myself out, Millie.

MRS. TABRET: I was very tired. [*With the shadow of a smile.*] I didn't see any reason to wait while Colin and Stella and the Doctor ate a bacon sandwich.

LICONDA: You didn't go into Maurice's room last night, Colin?

COLIN: No, why should I? I don't want a sleeping-draught to make me sleep.

STELLA: You're not under the impression that I took the tabloids, I suppose, Nurse Wayland?

HARVESTER: If you had you could presumably produce at least four of them. Believe me, if you'd taken twenty-five grains of chloralin at midnight you wouldn't be standing there now.

NURSE: The fact remains that five tabloids disappeared last night. Where are they?

HARVESTER: There's always the possibility that they were taken maliciously by someone who wanted to make trouble.

NURSE: Do you mean me, Dr. Harvester? What do you think I can get out of making trouble? Really I don't know how such a stupid idea can have crossed your mind. Why should I have asked you to have a post-mortem if I knew for certain—as I must if I'd taken the tabloids out of sheer malice—that it would discover nothing?

COLIN: Isn't it possible that they could have been taken by somebody this morning?

LICONDA: Who?

COLIN: The housemaid, for instance.

LICONDA: Chloralin is not a very common drug. I shouldn't have thought a housemaid would ever have heard of it. It's not as though it were aspirin or veronal.

HARVESTER: I don't know about that. There have been cases in the papers. It's not safe to take it for granted that a housemaid wouldn't have got into the habit of taking something when she couldn't sleep.

STELLA: Well, it's very easy to make sure. It's Alice who did Maurice's room. Let us send for her.

NURSE: That is unnecessary. She was frightened at the idea of going in. I told her she need not and said I would clean up the room and put everything to rights myself. I'm quite sure she has not been in this morning.

STELLA: What are we to do, Mother?

MRS. TABRET: You must do exactly what you think fit.

LICONDA: [*To the* DOCTOR.] Is it possible that Maurice can have died from chloral poisoning?

HARVESTER: I have told you that I am satisfied that death was due to natural causes.

LICONDA: I wasn't asking that.

HARVESTER: Yes, of course, it's possible. But I don't for an instant believe it.

NURSE: I know that this must add awfully to your grief, Mrs. Tabret. I can't tell you how sorry I am. It seems dreadful that I should have to repay all your kindness to me by increasing your troubles.

MRS. TABRET: My dear, I'm quite ready to believe that you will do nothing and say nothing but what you think is right.

STELLA: I'm all confused. It's come as such a dreadful shock. [*To the* NURSE.] Do you *really* think that Maurice died of an overdose of his sleeping-draught?

NURSE: [*Very deliberately, looking her straight in the eyes.*] I do.

STELLA: It's awful.

NURSE: [*Still looking at* STELLA.] I think I should tell you that when I found the tabloids were missing I looked in the glass in which I'd dissolved the one I'd prepared for him. There was still about a dessertspoonful of liquid in the bottom of it. I have put it aside and I suggest that it should be analysed.

MRS. TABRET: [*With faint mockery.*] You are wasted on your profession, Nurse Wayland. You have all the makings of a detective.

LICONDA: But wouldn't a draught in which half a dozen tabloids had been dissolved be very unpalatable?

HARVESTER: It would be rather bitter. I suppose if one swallowed it down at a gulp one would hardly notice till one had already drunk it.

STELLA: It all sounds very circumstantial. I'm afraid there's a dreadful probability in Nurse Wayland's story.

COLIN: But, my dear, it's absurd. Who on earth would have thought of murdering Maurice? It's out of the question.

STELLA: Oh, that, yes. I wasn't thinking of that. Nurse Wayland can't seriously think that anyone deliberately gave Maurice an overdose of his sleeping-draught. But I'm beginning to be desperately afraid that perhaps he took it himself.

HARVESTER: Suicide?

STELLA: [*With distress.*] He wasn't himself last night. He was very strange. I'd never seen him so nervous.

LICONDA: Was there any reason for that?

STELLA: [*After a moment's hesitation.*] I'm afraid so. You see I'd been to *Tristan*. And we'd seen it together the night we got engaged. It upset him to think of the past.

LICONDA: Did he speak of suicide?

STELLA: No.

LICONDA: Had he ever done so?

STELLA: Never. I don't believe it had entered his head.

LICONDA: What made you think he was upset last night?

STELLA: [*Much moved.*] He did a thing he'd never done before. It was dreadfully painful. He cried. He cried in my arms.

NURSE: Why, exactly?

STELLA: [*Desperately.*] Really, Miss Wayland, there are some things I can't tell you. What passed between my husband and myself was between ourselves. It concerned nobody but us.

NURSE: I beg your pardon. I should have thought it better for your own sake to be frank.

STELLA: What do you mean? Are you accusing me of holding anything back?

NURSE: I'm not accusing anybody.

LICONDA: My dear, I won't ask you anything that is painful for you to answer. But there's just this. If there's anything in what Miss Wayland says I suppose there'll have to be an inquest. The coroner will certainly ask you if your husband said anything at all that might indicate that suicide was in his mind.

STELLA: [*With a deep sigh.*] He said it would have been better if the accident had killed him outright. But he wasn't thinking of himself, he was thinking of me.

LICONDA: That's very important.

STELLA: Oh, Nurse, don't be hard on us. Don't be vindictive because I've been rather sharp with you. My nerves are all on edge to-day. After all, it's rather natural, isn't it? If poor Maurice did take an overdose of something, can't you square it with your conscience to say nothing about it? He had so little to live for. Can't you spare us the distress and horror of a post-mortem and an inquest?

LICONDA: The question is if Dr. Harvester is still willing to sign the death certificate.

HARVESTER: I think Nurse Wayland may very well have been mistaken about the tabloids. I can see no reason why I shouldn't.

NURSE: [*Deliberately.*] But you see, I am quite convinced that Maurice Tabret did not commit suicide.

LICONDA: For what reason?

NURSE: Well, here's one of them. There was a little liquid still in the glass from which he drank. About a dessert-spoonful. You remember I mentioned that, and I put the glass away so that the liquid could be examined.

LICONDA: Yes.

NURSE: Surely if a man were going to commit suicide he would drink the entire contents of the glass either in one gulp or two. He wouldn't risk making a bad job of what he was about by leaving something at the bottom. Least of all a man like Maurice Tabret.

COLIN: That seems very far-fetched to me.

LICONDA: I must say it seems rather a small point.

COLIN: Besides, the stuff hasn't been analysed yet.

LICONDA: Is your conviction based on nothing more than that, Nurse Wayland?

NURSE: No, it is not. Although Maurice Tabret was very good and I didn't believe he would ever take a tabloid without leave, one knows that it's very easy to get into the habit of drug-taking and then you can't be certain about anyone. Isn't that so, Dr. Harvester?

HARVESTER: Yes, I suppose it is.

NURSE: Sometimes he was terribly depressed. I didn't think it wise to let him have within reach the power of putting an end to himself.

STELLA: I never saw him depressed.

NURSE: [*Bitterly.*] I know you didn't. You never saw anything.

STELLA: Nurse Wayland, what have I done to you? Why do

you talk to me like that? Your face is all twisted with hate of me. I don't understand.

NURSE: Don't you?

[*The two women stare at one another for a moment, then* STELLA *gives a little shudder and turns her head away.*

STELLA: I'm beginning to be frightened of you. What sort of a woman are you that we've had in this house for five years?

MRS. TABRET: [*In a soothing tone.*] There's nothing to be frightened of, darling. Don't give way to your nerves.

NURSE: [*To* STELLA.] Because he joked and laughed when you were there, did it never occur to you that there were moments when he was overwhelmed with black misery?

STELLA: [*With deep sympathy.*] Poor lamb, why did he insist on hiding it from me?

NURSE: [*With a sort of restrained violence.*] His one aim was to make his suffering easy for *you* to bear. Whatever pain he had, he hid from you so that you shouldn't have the distress of being sorry for him.

STELLA: It's dreadful that you should say such things. You make me feel that I was so cruel to him.

NURSE: [*With increasing bitterness.*] Everything had to be hidden from you. When you were coming the medicine bottles and the dressings had to be put away, so that there should be nothing to remind you that there was anything the matter with him.

STELLA: I would willingly have done everything for him that you did. It was his most earnest wish that I shouldn't concern myself with the horrid part of his illness.

MRS. TABRET: That is true, Nurse. I'm sorry you don't think that Stella did all she could for Maurice. As his mother I'm perhaps no less competent to judge than you. I have only admiration for her unselfishness and consideration.

STELLA: Oh, Mother.

MRS. TABRET: I always think we do best by people when we help them in the way they want to be helped rather than in the way we may think they should be helped. I would sooner someone gave me a vanity bag that I hankered after than a shawl to wrap round my old bones that I didn't happen to want.

LICONDA: There's something in that, Nurse Wayland.

MRS. TABRET: I'm sure that Stella did Maurice most good by answering him back in the same strain when he chaffed her and when he laughed, laughing with him.

NURSE: I was nothing. I was only his paid nurse. He didn't try to hide from me the despair that filled his heart. He didn't have to pretend to me. He didn't have to be good-tempered or amusing with me. He could be morose and he knew I wouldn't mind. He could quarrel with me and then say he was sorry if he'd hurt me and know he couldn't hurt me. To make you laugh he plastered his face with flour and painted his nose red and jumped through a hoop. You only saw the white mask of the clown; I saw his naked, tortured, triumphant soul.

STELLA: [*The truth dawning on her, the truth that the* NURSE *had loved him.*] What are you telling us, Nurse Wayland?

NURSE: I'm telling the truth at last.

STELLA: I wonder if you know what strange truth it is.

LICONDA: But, Nurse, what you've been saying suggests that he did have at least moments of despair when he must have thought of suicide. We know that he was overwrought last night. If his death was not due to natural causes, surely it's extremely likely that he brought it about himself.

NURSE: It was just one of those moments that I was on my guard against. The chloralin was kept in the bathroom on an upper shelf that he could not possibly have got at. I had to stand on a chair myself to reach it.

LICONDA: If a man is determined to do a thing he can often surmount difficulties that others would have thought insuperable.

NURSE: Ask Dr. Harvester if it would have been possible for Maurice Tabret to cross the room and go into the bathroom and stand up on a chair.

HARVESTER: He had absolutely no power in the lower part of his body. His back was broken by the accident and the spinal cord terribly injured.

LICONDA: Couldn't he have crawled into the bathroom?

HARVESTER: With a great deal of difficulty. Yes, I think he might have done that.

NURSE: Could he have stood up on a chair?

HARVESTER: No, I'm bound to admit that is absolutely out of the question.

LICONDA: If he'd got into the bathroom, couldn't he have fished down the bottle with a stick or something?

HARVESTER: Perhaps.

NURSE: Why do you say that, Dr. Harvester? You know that he couldn't sit upright without help.

HARVESTER: I'm not so anxious to put the worst construction on everything as you seem to be, Nurse Wayland.

NURSE: And if he'd got the bottle down, how could he have put it up in its place again?

HARVESTER: [Irritably.] After all, we don't know yet that Maurice died of an overdose of chloralin.

LICONDA: The matter can't be left like this, Harvester. I'm afraid there'll have to be an inquest.

HARVESTER: Yes, obviously, I can't sign the death certificate now. I shall have to communicate with the coroner.

NURSE: I'm sorry, Dr. Harvester.

HARVESTER: I bet you are. I suppose you think it's very self-seeking of me not to want to be mixed up in a scandal. I suppose I ought to laugh through a horse collar at the prospect of smashing up a practice that I paid good money for and have spent seven years in building up.

LICONDA: Oh, come now, it's not going to be as bad as that. However distressing an inquiry may be to Maurice's family, I don't see how it can affect his doctor. For a hopeless invalid to take an overdose of his sleeping-draught is not so uncommon as to excite much comment.

HARVESTER: That, no.

LICONDA: Many of us can only admire a man who has a fatal illness and prefers to end his life painlessly rather than endure useless suffering. He is more merciful to himself and to those he loves.

NURSE: Dr. Harvester knows as well as I do that if Maurice Tabret died of an overdose of chloralin he couldn't have taken it himself. There's only one word for it and you all know it. It was murder.

HARVESTER: That's why I'm absolutely convinced that he died of natural causes. I can't offer an explanation of the disappearance of those damned tabloids, but there must be an explanation.

COLIN: The most likely one is that Nurse Wayland was mistaken. Surely it's only reasonable to suppose that if anyone had taken out half a dozen tabloids he would have put others in their place, aspirin or chlorate of potash or something, so that they wouldn't be missed.

NURSE: People don't think of everything. It's only because a murderer makes some mistake that he's caught.

HARVESTER: But, damn it all, no one commits a murder without a motive. No one had the smallest reason to wish Maurice dead.

NURSE: How do you know?

HARVESTER: Good God, how do I know that two and two are four? I know that everybody was devoted to him. And with reason, damn it. He was the best fellow in the world.

NURSE: Did you know that his wife was going to have a baby?

STELLA: [*With a gasp.*] You fiend!

COLIN: [*Aghast.*] Stella!

NURSE: I suspected it last night when she nearly fainted. This morning I knew for certain.

STELLA: What do you mean? Are you accusing me of having murdered my husband?

LICONDA: [*Very gravely.*] Is it true what she says, Stella?

> [*There is a pause.* STELLA *does not speak. There is anguish in her eyes.* ALICE, *the parlourmaid, comes briskly in, breaking the tension with the affairs of every day.*

ALICE: Shall I keep lunch back, madam?

MRS. TABRET: Is it one o'clock? No, you can serve up.

COLIN: We can't have lunch now, Mother.

MRS. TABRET: Why not? Lay for two extra. Major Liconda and Dr. Harvester will be lunching.

ALICE: Very good, madam.

> [*She goes out.*

COLIN: Mother, it's impossible. How can we all sit down together as though nothing had happened?

MRS. TABRET: I think it's just as well. We have a great deal more to say to one another. It will do none of us any harm to talk of other things for half an hour.

STELLA: I couldn't, I couldn't. Let me stay here.

MRS. TABRET: [*Firmly.*] I insist on your coming, my dear.

HARVESTER: I must bolt round to my house, Mrs. Tabret

I'll have a bite there and come back immediately afterwards.

MRS. TABRET: Very well.

LICONDA: My dear, I couldn't think of imposing myself on you.

MRS. TABRET: [*With a grim smile.*] You must eat. Will you come, Nurse Wayland?

NURSE: No.

MRS. TABRET: I'll have something sent up to your room.

NURSE: I want nothing.

MRS. TABRET: You may when it comes.

[ALICE *comes in again.*

ALICE: Lunch is served, madam.

MRS. TABRET: [*Giving* STELLA *her hand.*] Come, Stella.

END OF THE SECOND ACT

THE THIRD ACT

THE SCENE *is the same as in the preceding acts.*

Half an hour has passed.

STELLA *is standing at one of the windows looking into the garden.*
COLIN *comes in from the hall and she turns round.*

COLIN: Stella.

STELLA: Have you finished already?

COLIN: More or less. I told Mother I wanted to see if you
were all right.

STELLA: Yes, I'm all right.

COLIN: It was awful sitting there as though nothing had
happened. I don't know what induced Mother to make
us go through that farce.

STELLA: [*With a shrug.*] I daresay it was very sensible. With
the servants there it was obvious that we had to hold
our tongues. It gave us all a chance to collect ourselves.

COLIN: I'm afraid you didn't eat a thing.

STELLA: [*Smiling.*] You ate enough for both of us.

COLIN: Did you think it was rotten of me?

STELLA: No, I think it comforted me. To see you wolf
down great mouthfuls of lamb and green peas made me
realize that this nightmare isn't the whole of things. The
world is going on all around us. Whatever we may be
suffering the buses are going down Piccadilly and the
trains are running in and out of Paddington Station.

COLIN: Stella, is it true?

STELLA: Is what true?

COLIN: What that woman said.

STELLA: About the baby? I suppose so. Yes, it's true.

286

COLIN: Oh, Stella.

STELLA: I wasn't sure. I was afraid. I thought it might be a false alarm. It's only quite lately that I've been certain.

COLIN: Why didn't you tell me?

STELLA: I didn't want to.

COLIN: Not at all? Were you going to let me go away without knowing?

STELLA: It was only a month before you were going back to Guatemala. I didn't want to spoil those last weeks for you. Because I worried there didn't seem to be any reason why you should be worried, too.

COLIN: But what were you going to do?

STELLA: I don't know. I was looking for some way out. I thought it would be easier when you were gone. Whatever happened, I thought I'd like to keep you out of it.

COLIN: Why?

STELLA: I don't know, unless because I love you.

COLIN: Aren't I there to share your troubles with you?

STELLA: I suppose women are very silly, when they tell a man that they're going to have a child by him, it seems rather an important moment to them. I suppose they feel happy and a little frightened and awed. They want to be made a fuss of. I couldn't expect you to feel joy or pride, but only consternation.

COLIN: Oh, my sweetness, don't you know how devotedly I love you?

STELLA: No, don't. Don't say anything that's going to upset me. I don't want to get emotional. If we've got to talk it over we'd better try to talk it over as calmly as we can.

COLIN: What is that dreadful woman going to say now?

STELLA: I don't know. I don't care . . . I don't know why I say that. I'm frightened to death.

COLIN: You must keep a stiff upper lip.

STELLA: Oh, Colin, whatever happens you'll stand by me, won't you?

COLIN: Yes, I swear it.

[DR. HARVESTER *comes in from the garden.*

HARVESTER: Oh, have you finished your luncheon already?

STELLA: [*Forcing a smile to her lips.*] I'm afraid I couldn't make much of a pretence at eating. I wanted to be alone for a minute and came in here.

COLIN: I think Mother and Major Liconda will be here directly. They were just starting coffee when I left them.

HARVESTER: Where's Nurse Wayland? I came back rather soon because I thought I'd like to have a chat with her alone.

STELLA: Colin will go and fetch her. I suppose she lunched in her room.

COLIN: Right-ho.

[*He goes out.*

HARVESTER: I say, my dear, I hope this is going to come out all right.

STELLA: It doesn't look much like it, does it?

HARVESTER: My word, you're cool.

STELLA: When the earth is opening under your feet and the heavens are falling it doesn't seem much use to run about like a frightened hen.

HARVESTER: Do you mind my giving you a bit of advice?

STELLA: [*With a shade of irony.*] I'd welcome it, but I think it's very unlikely I shall take it.

HARVESTER: Well, it's just this, if I were you I'd take very great care not to say anything to put up Nurse Wayland's back.

STELLA: She can't very well make things much more disagreeable than she has already.

HARVESTER: I'm not so sure of that. That's why I wanted to see her alone. You know she's not a bad sort, really. Now that she's had half an hour to calm down, I don't see why she shouldn't be more reasonable.

STELLA: I wouldn't count on it in your place.

HARVESTER: I don't myself see what Nurse Wayland has to get out of making a fuss.

STELLA: She's a very conscientious woman and she mistakes her hatred of me for the call of duty.

HARVESTER: The good are difficult to get on with, aren't they?

STELLA: [*Smiling.*] Fortunately they're so few, it's not often they seriously inconvenience the rest of us.

HARVESTER: Nurse Wayland has got her knife into you all right.

STELLA: Dr. Harvester, will you tell me something?

HARVESTER: If I can.

STELLA: Do you think it possible that Maurice could have guessed—my condition?

HARVESTER: I shouldn't think so.

STELLA: I'm so thankful. I couldn't have borne the thought that he died rather than expose me to shame and disgrace. He was capable of it, you know.

HARVESTER: I'm afraid that if Maurice died of an overdose of chloral he can't have taken it himself.

STELLA: But who could have given it him?

HARVESTER: That is the question, isn't it?

STELLA: Wild and fantastic notions pass through my mind and one is more incredible than the other.

HARVESTER: I know.

STELLA: Why couldn't that wretched woman leave me for a

moment alone with my sorrow? My heart is burning with grief. I reproach myself so bitterly. I'm so ashamed of myself. You never knew Maurice in the old days. He was such a gallant figure. When I was in his room just now before all this horror burst upon us, I wept for myself as well as him. I wept for all the love I'd borne him in years gone by. Oh, how cruel death is.

HARVESTER: I know. However often your trade brings you in contact with it, you are overcome with the same dismay. It's so desperately final.

STELLA: I can't believe that it's final. It would be too unfair. Why shouldn't it be true what Maurice believed—that we are born again? Will you think me silly and childish if I tell you something? I have a strange, mystical feeling that that brave spirit has entered into the child that I shall bear, and that in him Maurice, forgiving me the wrong I did him, will live out the life that was his due.

HARVESTER: There are some who think that if you only believe enough that a thing is true, it becomes true. Who am I to decide such matters?

[*The door is opened and* COLIN *comes in immediately followed by the* NURSE.

COLIN: Here is Nurse Wayland.

STELLA: Oh, Nurse, Dr. Harvester wishes to speak to you by himself. Colin and I will go into the garden.

NURSE: It's very kind of you. But I have nothing private to say to Dr. Harvester and I do not wish to listen to anything Dr. Harvester has to say that anyone else may not hear. I want to do nothing underhand.

HARVESTER: I'm not going to ask you to do anything underhand.

NURSE: I know exactly what you want to say to me. You're going to point out that everyone here has been very kind to me and very generous. And they're prepared to be still kinder and still more generous. And if I make

a scandal I shall be exposed to every sort of unpleasantness and very likely have great difficulty in getting
another job. On the other hand, if I hold my tongue
I can go to Japan and have a good time. Well, I won't.

STELLA: [*Coolly.*] That seems very definite.

HARVESTER: All the same, I don't see how it can hurt you
to listen to me for five minutes.

STELLA: Now I put my foot down. I'm not prepared to
allow an appeal on my behalf to be made to Nurse
Wayland.

COLIN: I think I hear my mother and the major.

HARVESTER: Then it's too late.

[COLIN *goes over to the door and opens it for them.*
MRS. TABRET *and* MAJOR LICONDA *enter.*

MRS. TABRET: Have we kept you waiting? I hope you had
everything you wanted in your room, Nurse.

NURSE: Everything, thank you, Mrs. Tabret.

MRS. TABRET: Won't you sit down? There's no use in your
tiring yourself.

NURSE: [*Sitting down.*] Thank you.

MRS. TABRET: Have you been talking things over?

HARVESTER: I've only just come, Mrs. Tabret.

MRS. TABRET: I suppose we are in Nurse Wayland's hands.
What have you decided to do, Nurse Wayland?

NURSE: I must do what I think is my duty, Mrs. Tabret.

MRS. TABRET: Of course. We should all do our duty, and
how difficult it would be if at the same time we did not
often make ourselves a trifle disagreeable to others.

NURSE: Mrs. Tabret, Major Liconda asked your daughter-in-
law a question just before luncheon. She didn't answer it.

LICONDA: [*To* STELLA.] I am afraid you must have thought
me very impertinent. Nurse Wayland said that you were
going to have a baby, and I asked you if it was true.

STELLA: It's quite true.

LICONDA: [*Struggling with his embarrassment.*] I'm in a very false position. I am conscious that I am interfering in matters that are no affair of mine.

STELLA: My dear Major, I know that you are kindness itself. You've known Mrs. Tabret for ages and Maurice and Colin when they were small boys.

LICONDA: All the same you must see how difficult it is for me to ask the question that inevitably rises in one's mind.

STELLA: I'll answer without your asking. Of course it's quite impossible that Maurice should have been the father of the child I'm going to have. Since his accident he has been my husband only in name.

COLIN: [*Going up to her and putting his hand round her shoulders.*] I am the father, Major Liconda.

NURSE: [*Astounded.*] You?

MRS. TABRET: [*Ironically.*] Do you mean to say that it escaped your sharp eyes, Nurse, that Colin and Stella were in love with one another?

STELLA: [*With a little frightened gasp.*] Did *you* know?

MRS. TABRET: I think nowadays the young are apt to think their elders even more stupid than advancing years generally make them.

STELLA: Oh, Mother, what must you think of me?

MRS. TABRET: [*Dryly.*] Do you very much care?

STELLA: I suppose I ought to be terribly ashamed of myself. I must be sincere. I don't want to make a pretence of remorse that I don't feel. I can no more help loving Colin than I can help the rain falling or the trees bursting into leaf. I'm proud of the child he's given me.

NURSE: You're shameless.

STELLA: [*To* MRS. TABRET.] But *you* have every right to think that I treated Maurice abominably. He's beyond the reach of pain, but I bitterly regret the pain I've caused you. I have no excuses to make for myself.

MRS. TABRET: My dear, don't you remember what I said to you last night? I thanked you for all you had done for Maurice. Did you think I was talking at random? I knew then that you were going to have a baby and that Colin was its father.

COLIN: Mother, I blame myself so awfully.

STELLA: You mustn't do that, darling. [*To* MRS. TABRET.] If a woman doesn't want a man to make love to her she can very easily prevent it. Living side by side, in the same house for so many months, there's no reason why he should ever have looked upon me as anything but his sister. I was shameless. I didn't prevent him from making love to me because I wanted him to make love to me. I made him love me.

COLIN: Oh, Stella, how could I help loving you? I don't blame myself for that. I blame myself because when I knew I loved you I didn't bolt.

MRS. TABRET: Am I right in thinking that then it was too late?

COLIN: Do you remember, when we were kids in India they used to tell us of children who could recollect their past lives. They'd know who was who in the village and recognize the things that had belonged to them before and go straight to places that otherwise they couldn't have found. That's how I felt when I fell in love with Stella. I felt that I'd loved her always and that her love was home to me.

STELLA: Whatever you may think of me, Mother, and however badly you think I've behaved, I ask you to believe that I didn't give myself to Colin to gratify any passing whim. I loved him with all my heart.

MRS. TABRET: My dear, I know. You say you made him love you. Why do you say that except that you love him so much? You can't persuade yourself that this miracle should have happened that he loves you, too, unless you had done it. Love is always diffident. One can never be certain of love, one can only be certain of affection.

STELLA: You mustn't think I didn't struggle against the madness that possessed me. I said to myself that the only return I could make Maurice for all the devotion he gave me was by remaining faithful to him and loyal.

MRS. TABRET: I'm sure you did.

STELLA: I told myself that Maurice was a cripple, bedridden, sick, the victim of an unforeseen misfortune, and that it would be foul of me to betray him. I tried to drive Colin away. I was beastly to him, rude and sarcastic, and then the dumb misery in his eyes broke my heart. I did everything except ask him to go. I couldn't do that. I couldn't. I pretended to myself that it was on your account and on Maurice's. You hadn't seen him for so long. Maurice was so pleased to have him here.

MRS. TABRET: It's quite true that I hadn't seen Colin for a long time, and Maurice was tremendously pleased to have him here.   '

NURSE: [With exasperation.] I don't understand you, Mrs. Tabret. You seem to be going out of your way to find excuses for your daughter-in-law. If you knew what was going on, why didn't you stop it?

MRS. TABRET: I'm afraid I shall shock you, Miss Wayland; I want to put it as delicately as I can, but it's a matter that we English have made indelicate by prudishness and hypocrisy. Stella is young, healthy and normal. Why should I imagine she has not got the instincts that I had at her age? The sexual instinct is as normal as hunger and as pressing as the desire to sleep. Why should she be deprived of its satisfaction?

NURSE: [With a little shiver of disgust.] It seems to me that the modern world is obsessed by sex. Is there nothing else in it? After all, the answer is that you can't go without food and you can't go without sleep. But you can go without the satisfaction of your sexual appetites.

HARVESTER: But at what price of nervous disorders, crabbedness, and unhealthy emotions.

MRS. TABRET: When Maurice's accident made it impossible for him and Stella ever to live again as man and wife I asked myself if she would be able to support so false a relationship. They had loved one another as two healthy young things love. Their love was deep and passionate, but it was rooted in sex. It might have come about with time that it would have acquired a more spiritual character, it might have been that the inevitable trials of life endured together would have given birth to an affection and a confidence in one another that might have given a new glow to the fading fires of passion. They did not have the time.

NURSE: [*To* STELLA, *with irony*.] May I ask how long you'd been married?

STELLA: I was married to Maurice about a year before he crashed.

NURSE: A year. A whole year.

MRS. TABRET: Out of his suffering a new love did spring up in Maurice's heart, a hungry, clinging, dependent love. I didn't know how long Stella would be content with that.

NURSE: [*Bitterly*.] No one could say that you had much trust in human nature.

MRS. TABRET: I have a great deal. As much, in fact, as experience has taught me is justified. I knew that Stella's pity was infinite.

STELLA: Oh, infinite. Poor lamb.

Mrs. Tabret: I knew it was so great that she mistook it for love, and I prayed that she would never find out her mistake. She meant everything in the world to Maurice. Everything. At first it was easier when we were struggling for his life, but when he settled down to being a chronic invalid and we knew that he would never be anything else I was seized with a great fear. I feared that the time would come when she felt she couldn't stand any longer the miserable life that was all he had to offer her. If she wanted to go I felt we hadn't the right to prevent her, and I knew that if she went Maurice would die.

Stella: I would never have left him. It never entered my head that it was possible.

Mrs. Tabret: I saw the strain that it began to be on her nerves. She was as kind as ever, and as gentle, but it was an effort, and what is the good you do worth unless you do it naturally as the flowers give their scent?

Nurse: I have never been given to understand that good is only good if it's easy to do.

Mrs. Tabret: I don't suppose it is, but if it's difficult then I think it benefits the person who does it rather than the person it's done to. That is why it is more blessed to give than to receive.

Nurse: I don't understand you. I think what you say is odious and cynical.

Mrs. Tabret: Then I'm afraid you'll think what I'm going to say now even more cynical and odious. I found myself half wishing that Stella should take a lover.

Nurse: [*With horror.*] Mrs. Tabret!

Mrs. Tabret: I was willing to shut my eyes to anything so long as she stayed with Maurice. I wanted her to be kind and thoughtful and affectionate to him, and I didn't care for the rest.

Nurse: [*Brokenly.*] I had such a deep respect for you, Mrs.

Tabret. I admired you so much. I used to think that when I was your age I'd like to be a woman like you.

MRS. TABRET: When Colin came back and after a while I realized that he and Stella were in love with one another, I did nothing to prevent the almost inevitable consequences. I didn't deliberately say it to myself in so many words, that would have shocked me, but in my heart was a feeling that this would make it all right for Maurice. She wouldn't go now. She was bound to this house by a stronger tie than pity or kindness.

LICONDA: Didn't it strike you what great dangers you were exposing them to?

MRS. TABRET: I didn't care. I only thought of Maurice. When they were children I think I loved them equally. But since his accident I haven't had room in my heart for anyone but Maurice. He was everything to me. For him I was prepared to sacrifice Colin and Stella. [*With a little gesture of appeal to* STELLA.] I hope they'll forgive me.

STELLA: Oh, my dear, as though there was anything for me to forgive.

NURSE: You'll only laugh at me if I say I'm shocked. I can't help it. I'm shocked to the very depths of my soul.

MRS. TABRET: I was afraid you would be.

NURSE: I would have gone to the stake for my belief that no unclean thought had ever entered your head. Didn't it revolt you to think that your son's wife was having an affair with a man under your own roof?

MRS. TABRET: I suppose I'm not very easily revolted. I've lived too long abroad to think that my own standard of right and wrong is the only one possible. We all know nowadays that morality isn't one and the same in all countries and at all times. There are many things, for

L

instance, that we think right here and they think wrong in India . . .

LICONDA: And contrariwise.

MRS. TABRET: But I wonder why people don't see that morality isn't the same for everyone at the same time in the same country. I'm not sure that I'd go as far as to say that there's a morality for the rich and a morality for the poor, though I'm doubtful, but I do think there's a morality for the young and a morality for the old. Perhaps we should all look upon these matters very differently if our moral rules hadn't been made by persons who had forgotten the passion and the high spirits of youth. Do you think it so very wicked if two young things surrender to the instincts that nature has planted in them?

NURSE: Did the probable result never occur to you?

MRS. TABRET: A baby? It persuades me of Stella's essential innocence. If she'd been a loose or abandoned woman she would have known how to avoid such an accident.

NURSE: [Sardonically.] You must admit at all events that Maurice's death has come in the very nick of time to get her out of a very awkward predicament.

STELLA: Nurse, what a cruel—what a heartless thing to say.

LICONDA: [Sternly.] You must be very careful, Nurse. That sounds extremely like an accusation.

NURSE: I wanted to accuse nobody. Do me the justice to admit that I started by saying that I was not satisfied with the circumstances and thought there should be a post-mortem. That was my right and my duty. Isn't that so, Dr. Harvester?

HARVESTER: I suppose it is.

NURSE: You've forced me to this. You asked me who could have a motive for murdering Maurice Tabret. In self-defence I was obliged to tell you that his wife was going to have a child of which he couldn't be the father.

STELLA: You talk of your duty, Miss Wayland. Are you sure that your motive for all this is anything more than your bitter hatred of me?

NURSE: [*Scornfully.*] Why should I hate you? Believe me, I only despise you.

STELLA: You hate me because you were in love with Maurice.

NURSE: [*Violently.*] I? What do you mean? You're insulting me. How dare you say that?

STELLA: [*Coolly.*] You gave it away. It had often seemed to me that you were fonder of Maurice than a nurse generally is of her patient and I used to chaff him about it. It never struck me that it was serious till this morning. Then you betrayed yourself in every word you said. You were madly in love with Maurice.

NURSE: [*Defiantly.*] And if I was, what of it?

STELLA: Nothing, except that it's my turn to be shocked. I think it was rather horrible and disgusting.

NURSE: [*With increasing emotion.*] Yes, I loved him. My love grew as I saw yours fade. I loved him because he was so helpless and so dependent on me. I loved him because he was like a child in my arms. I never showed him my love, I would sooner have died, and I was ashamed because sometimes I thought, notwithstanding everything, he saw it. But if he saw it he understood and was sorry for me. He knew how bitter it is to long for the love of someone who has no love to give you. My love meant nothing to him, he had no room in his heart for any love but the love of you, and you had no use for it. He asked for bread and you gave him a stone. You think you were so kind and considerate. If you'd loved him as I loved him you'd have seen how less than nothing was all you did for him. I could think of a hundred ways to give him happiness, they would have meant nothing to him, and you hadn't the love to think of them.

STELLA: Miss Wayland, I'm sorry for what I said just now. It was stupid of me and rather horrid. I suppose there is something beautiful in love, of whatever kind it is. Will you let me thank you for the love you gave my husband?

NURSE: [*Violently.*] No, it's an impertinence to offer me your thanks.

STELLA: I'm sorry you should think that . . . It's quite true that I didn't love Maurice, at least not with the love of a woman for a man. I'm deeply conscious of the fact, and often I reproached myself because I couldn't feel— when at one moment I hadn't been able to help feeling. It seemed so ungrateful and so unkind. He was no more to me than a very dear friend for whom I was desperately sorry.

NURSE: Do you think he wanted your pity?

STELLA: I know he didn't. But pity was all I had to give him. Who was it that said that pity was akin to love? There's all the world between them.

NURSE: [*With angry vehemence.*] Yes, all the hideousness of sex.

STELLA: And do you believe there was nothing of sex in your love for Maurice? It was because I felt that there was in it an abnormal aborted sexuality that at the first moment it gave me a little shiver of repulsion.

NURSE: [*With a passionate emotion.*] No. No. My love for that poor boy was as pure and as spiritual as my love for God. There was never a shadow of self in it. My love was compassion and Christian charity. I never asked anything but to be allowed to serve and tend him. It was a sufficient reward for me to be able to wash and dry his poor wasted limbs and to hold the mirror in front of him while he shaved. I never touched his lips till they were cold in death. And now I've lost everything that made life lovely to me. What was he to you? What was he to his mother? To me he was my child, my friend, my lover, my god. And you killed him.

STELLA: That's a lie!

LICONDA: Come, Nurse Wayland, you have no right to say that.

NURSE: [*Beside herself.*] It's true and you know it!

LICONDA: [*Impatiently.*] I know nothing of the kind. I only know that you've worked yourself into a state in which you are saying all sorts of things for which you have no justification.

STELLA: [*With a tolerant shrug of the shoulders.*] My dear, I could no more have killed Maurice than I could walk a tight rope. Doesn't it occur to you that there was nothing to prevent my leaving him? Who could have blamed me?

NURSE: How would you have lived? You haven't a penny of your own. I've heard you tell Maurice a hundred times that you had to mind your p's and q's because he was your only means of livelihood.

STELLA: I certainly shouldn't have repeated a feeble little joke so often. I suppose I could have worked.

NURSE: [*Scornfully.*] You!

STELLA: I've often noticed that the average woman who works for a living looks upon it as a little miracle and can never believe that any other can be clever enough to do the same thing. I needn't have become a nurse, you know. I might have made hats or invented a face cream.

NURSE: Do you think this is the time to make cheap jokes?

STELLA: I shouldn't have thought so. But you surely began when you accused me of poisoning my husband.

NURSE: Do you know what it means to work for one's living? Do you think one doesn't often feel tired and ill but goes on because it's one's job? Do you think one doesn't want to go and have fun like other girls? All your life you've been petted and spoiled and pampered. And you were going to have a child. How could you have worked?

COLIN: You're really going too far, Miss Wayland. We can't stand here and let you insult Stella. The situation is preposterous.

STELLA: There was Colin, you know, Miss Wayland. I don't think he would have left me in the lurch.

COLIN: He certainly wouldn't.

NURSE: And what would you have had to go through before he could marry you? Not only exposure to your husband. But the divorce court. It wouldn't have been a very pretty case.

STELLA: It would have been horrible.

NURSE: [*With a gesture towards* COLIN.] Do you think his love would have stood that test? Are you sure he wouldn't have hated you for the disgrace you had thrust upon him? Men are sensitive, you know, more sensitive than women, and they're afraid of scandal.

STELLA: I may not be typical of my sex. I don't think I should like it either.

NURSE: [*With all the scorn of which she is capable.*] You don't have to tell me that. Why are you letting me stand here and talk as I'm talking, but that you think you can persuade me or bribe me into holding my tongue? Why haven't these men, who are your friends and who hate me, thrown me out? Because they're afraid of me. They're afraid of scandal. They're afraid of publicity. Is that true?

STELLA: Very probably.

NURSE: And you're not only afraid of scandal, you're afraid of your neck.

STELLA: No, that's not true.

NURSE: You were in a hopeless situation. There was only one way out of your difficulties. You know as well as I do that your treachery, your monstrous cruelty would have broken your husband's heart. You couldn't face that. You preferred to kill him.

STELLA: You've known me for five years, Nurse Wayland. I don't know how you can think me capable of such wickedness.

NURSE: Your husband trusted and loved you. He was bed-ridden. He was defenceless. I know that if you'd had a spark of decent feeling you couldn't have treated him as you did. If you were capable of being unfaithful to him you were capable of killing him.

MRS. TABRET: [*With her thin smile.*] Are you not falling into a rather vulgar error, my dear? I know that when people talk of a good woman they mean a chaste one, but isn't that a very narrow view of goodness? Chastity is a very excellent thing, but it isn't the whole of virtue. There's kindness and courage and consideration for others. I'm not sure if there isn't also humour and common sense.

NURSE: Are you defending her for having been untrue to your son?

MRS. TABRET: I'm excusing her, Nurse Wayland. I know she gave Maurice all she could. The rest was not in her power.

NURSE: Oh, I know how you look upon these things. Nothing matters very much. There's no guilt in sin and no merit in virtue.

MRS. TABRET: May I tell you a little story about myself? When I was still a young woman, with a husband and two children, I fell madly in love with a young officer who had charge of the police in my husband's district and he fell madly in love with me.

LICONDA: Millie!

Mrs. Tabret: I'm an old woman now and he's an elderly retired major. But in those days we were all the world to one another. I didn't yield to my love on account of my boys. It nearly broke my heart. Now, you know, I'm very glad I didn't. One recovers from the pain of love. When I look at that funny old-fashioned major now I wonder why he ever excited in me such turbulent emotions. I could have told Colin and Stella that in thirty years it wouldn't matter much if they'd resisted their love. But people don't learn from the experience of others.

Nurse: You resisted, you can always say that you clung to the right.

Mrs. Tabret: I think it was easier then, you know, for in that far-distant time we attached more importance to chastity than we do now. Yes, I resisted, but because I know the anguish it was, I feel I have the right to forgive those who were less virtuous, or perhaps only more courageous, than I.

Nurse: It is only by overcoming temptation that we strengthen our souls.

Mrs. Tabret: Perhaps. But I've sometimes noticed that our most spectacular victories are over temptations that don't really tempt us very much. When I consider human nature and temptation I can't help thinking of a river and its banks. So long as too much water doesn't flow down between them the banks do their work very well, but let a flood come and they're useless. The river overflows and havoc follows.

Stella: Oh, my dear, you're so kind and so wise.

Mrs. Tabret: No, darling, I'm only so old.

Liconda: [Kindly, but quite firmly.] Stella, Miss Wayland's accusation is very definite and must be met.

Stella: Her accusation is absurd.

LICONDA: If Maurice died of an overdose of chloral, it was administered by somebody.

STELLA: I suppose so.

LICONDA: Can you suggest anyone who had the slightest motive for wishing he was dead?

STELLA: No.

LICONDA: I'm sure you want to help us to get at the truth. You must forgive me if I ask you some embarrassing questions.

STELLA: Of course.

LICONDA: What did you propose to do when you discovered you were going to have a baby?

STELLA: I was frightened. At first I couldn't believe it. I didn't know what to do.

LICONDA: You were aware that it couldn't be concealed very long?

STELLA: Naturally. I thought something would happen. I was distracted.

LICONDA: Did you tell anyone?

STELLA: No, I was trying to screw up courage to ask Dr. Harvester what I had better do. I didn't mind for myself. It was Maurice I was thinking of.

LICONDA: You must have had some plan.

STELLA: Oh, a hundred. I thought of nothing else day and night. I tried to find out if there wasn't some place I could go to. I thought if the worst came to the worst I could get Dr. Harvester to say I was ill and run down and wanted a change and I could go away till the baby was born.

LICONDA: I suppose you never thought of making a clean breast of it to Maurice?

STELLA: No, never. It would have broken his heart. He would have forgiven me. He loved me so much. But I couldn't bear that he should lose that immense belief

L*

he had in me. It meant everything to him.

LICONDA: You appear to have been the last person who saw him alive?

STELLA: Yes, I went in to say good night to him just before I went up to bed.

LICONDA: What did you say to him then?

STELLA: Nothing particular.

LICONDA: Didn't you say that he'd been very much upset? He'd cried.

STELLA: Yes. Earlier in the evening, before he went to bed.

LICONDA: Why was he upset?

STELLA: Need I tell you? It was so very private.

LICONDA: No, of course not. I have no right to ask you anything. Only there is something very strange about the whole thing and for your own sake I think it would be better if you told us everything.

STELLA: He broke down because he couldn't love me as he wanted to love me. He would have so liked to have a baby.

LICONDA: And when you said good night to him did he make no further reference to that?

STELLA: No, none. He'd quite recovered. He was in perfectly good spirits again.

LICONDA: What did he say?

STELLA: He just asked me if we'd enjoyed our snack and then he said, you'd better get off to bed. I said, I'm simply dropping, and I kissed him and said, Good night, old thing.

LICONDA: How long were you in his room?

STELLA: Five minutes.

LICONDA: Did he say that he felt sleepy?

STELLA: No.

LICONDA: I suppose you knew where the chloralin was kept.

STELLA: Vaguely. I knew that all his bottles and things were in the bathroom. He hated his bedroom to be littered about.

LICONDA: Did he ask you for anything before you went?

STELLA: No, there was nothing he wanted. Nurse Wayland had fixed him up quite comfortably.

NURSE: [*To* STELLA *freezingly.*] You don't understand. Major Liconda is giving you an opportunity of saying that your husband asked you for the chloralin and you, thinking no harm, gave it to him. You saw him take out five or six tabloids and then you replaced the bottle on the shelf.

STELLA: [*With irony.*] I never thought of that. That would have been quite a good way out if I'd poisoned my husband. No, Major, Maurice never asked me for the chloralin and I never gave it to him.

NURSE: May I ask a question now?

STELLA: Certainly.

NURSE: Why were you so upset when I came in this morning and told you I'd been into your husband's room?

STELLA: Do you mean when you said he was dead? Did you expect me to go on eating an egg as though you'd said it was a fine day?

NURSE: No, you didn't know he was dead then. You couldn't have known unless you'd had second sight.

STELLA: Oh, I see what you mean now. I was angry with you for going into his room before he was called. Sleep is such a precious and lovely thing. I think one should never wake anyone without reason.

NURSE: Are you sure you weren't afraid I'd gone into his room too soon? Supposing he'd been still alive and it had been possible to save him?

STELLA: You've quite made up your mind that I murdered Maurice, haven't you?

NURSE: I'm not the only one.

STELLA: What makes you think that?

NURSE: Why do you suppose the Major gave you that loophole by suggesting that your husband asked you to give him the tabloids?

LICONDA: [*With some acerbity.*] You have done what you thought your duty, Miss Wayland. Well and good. If now you have other things to do, I don't think we need take up any more of your time.

NURSE: I'll go. There's nothing more for me to do here. I know you all hate me and you think I've done what I've done from unworthy motives. I started packing my things while you were having lunch. I shall be ready in ten minutes.

MRS. TABRET: You must take your time, Nurse.

NURSE: Believe me, I'm just as anxious to leave this house as you are to get rid of me. I shall be grateful if I can have a taxi rung up.

MRS. TABRET: Colin will get on to the rank. Perhaps you'd better get on at once, darling.

COLIN: All right, Mother.

> [*He opens the door for the* NURSE *and follows her out. The others watch her go in silence. The door is closed.*

MRS. TABRET: Poor Miss Wayland. She has right on her side, you know, and she feels like a criminal. One can't help feeling sorry for a girl who has so much virtue and so little charm.

LICONDA: Might I speak to Stella alone for a minute?

MRS. TABRET: If you wish to. Come with me, Dr. Harvester.

HARVESTER: With pleasure.

MRS. TABRET: It's too bad that you should have to waste so much time on what is no business of yours.

HARVESTER: Believe me, I'd give a farm to be quite certain of that.

> [*They go out.*

LICONDA: Stella, what are you going to do?

STELLA: I don't know. What can I do? I feel like a rat in a trap.

LICONDA: It's obvious that the matter can't rest here. It can't be hushed up now.

STELLA: What is going to happen, then?

LICONDA: I suppose Dr. Harvester must communicate with the coroner. There'll be a post-mortem. If, as I'm afraid seems almost certain, Maurice is found to have died of an overdose of chloral there'll be an inquest and we shall have to await the verdict of the jury.

STELLA: And then?

LICONDA: If they find that poison was administered by a person unknown I imagine that the police will step in. I am afraid you must be prepared for a very terrible ordeal.

STELLA: Do you mean that I should be tried for murder?

LICONDA: It might be that the Director of Public Prosecutions would think that there was insufficient evidence to justify him in instituting proceedings.

STELLA: Whatever else I've done you must know that it's incredible that I can be guilty of such a monstrous crime.

LICONDA: Let us get the facts quite straight. I'm afraid it's no good blinking them. You were going to have a child of which Maurice was not the father. You were desperately anxious that he shouldn't know of your condition.

STELLA: Desperately.

LICONDA: Something had happened between you that had greatly distressed him. You were the last person that saw him. He was allowed to sleep on in the morning as long as he could. You were very angry when you found the nurse had gone into his room. He was dead. Five tabloids of chloralin are missing from the bottle and he couldn't possibly have got them himself. Who gave them to him?

STELLA: How can I tell?

LICONDA: My dear, you know that I desire to help you. I am your friend. It's no good beating about the bush. You're in a frightful situation.

STELLA: Do *you* think I'm guilty?

LICONDA: Do you want the truth?

STELLA: Yes.

LICONDA: I don't know.

STELLA: [*As though she were thinking it over.*] I see.

LICONDA: Of course, it's only circumstantial, but it all hangs together pretty well. You can hardly be surprised if suspicion falls on you.

STELLA: [*With a touch of humour.*] It hangs together beautifully. If I didn't know I hadn't poisoned Maurice I should say I must be guilty. There's only one thing I can say on the other side. I should have thought anyone who knew me at all would know I couldn't have poisoned Maurice.

LICONDA: In the course of my career I've had to do with a lot of crime. To me one of the shattering things about it has been to notice that the most law-abiding and decent person may be driven to commit one. There are very few of us who can say that we shall certainly never do so. Sometimes crime seems to come to a man as accidentally as a chimney pot may fall on his head when he's walking down the street.

STELLA: [*With a shudder.*] It's rather terrible.

LICONDA: It's not my business to judge you. I can only feel the deepest sympathy for the dreadful position you are in. You know what we English are and how uncharitably we regard sexual delinquencies. A jury would be greatly prejudiced against you when they were told that you had committed adultery with your brother-in-law.

STELLA: Poor Colin. He'll have to put up with a good deal, won't he?

LICONDA: Do you love him very much?

STELLA: I love him as I never loved Maurice. My love for Maurice was open and sunny. It seemed as natural as the air I breathe. I thought it would last for ever. But in my love for Colin there is all my pain and my remorse and the bitterness of knowing that it's possible for love to die.

LICONDA: Yes, that is bitter, isn't it? It makes life look such a sell.

STELLA: Wouldn't it be possible in any way to keep Colin out of it?

LICONDA: Oh, I'm afraid not. Anyhow that is a question we can discuss with the lawyers. We must find out who are the best people to go to. There's one thing I should like to impress upon you at once. Don't try to hide anything from your lawyers. The only chance an accused person has is to tell his advisers the absolute truth.

STELLA: I have told the truth from the beginning.

LICONDA: I hope to God you have.

[COLIN *comes in. She sweeps up to him in a sudden storm of agitation.*

STELLA: Oh, Colin, you believe in me, don't you? You know I couldn't have done what they accuse me of.

COLIN: [*Taking her in his arms.*] Darling. Darling.

STELLA: Oh, Colin, I'm so frightened.

COLIN: There's nothing to be frightened of. You're innocent. They can't touch you.

STELLA: Whatever happens it means that we're finished. All our love is going to be told to everyone and they'll make us appear beastly and vicious. They'll say horrible things about me. They'll never know how hard I tried to resist. People blame you because you fall, they give you no credit for the effort you made to save yourself. The past counts for nothing.

COLIN: It's so cruel that I who'd give my life for you should have brought all this misery on you.

STELLA: How can I expect you to stay loving me when we've gone through what we've got to go through? Oh, the shame of it. Where should we go to hide our heads?

COLIN: I shall love you always. You're all the world to me You're all the world I want.

STELLA: Men used to try to flirt with me. It meant so little, I only laughed at them. Until you came the thought never entered my head that I could be unfaithful to Maurice. I wasn't troubled. I just put all that side of life on one side and never thought of it. I never knew I loved you till it was too late.

COLIN: The only thing I ask you is never to regret that you loved me, whatever happens.

STELLA: No, I shall never do that. I can't.

COLIN: [*With all his tenderness.*] Oh, my love. My sweetness.

STELLA: But what a rotten trick fate has played on me. I look as though I were a bad, beastly woman, and when I look into my heart I can't see any wickedness. What a punishment because I couldn't resist the love that swept me up, as a gust of wind in March sweeps up last year's dead leaf.

COLIN: Whatever the punishment is we can bear it together. Let's take our medicine, Stella; whatever happens, they can't take us away from one another.

STELLA: [*Desperately.*] Major Liconda, what are we to do? Can't you say something to help us?

LICONDA: [*Very gravely, in a low voice.*] How can I advise you? I can only tell you what I should do in your place.

STELLA: What is that?

LICONDA: If I were innocent I should stick it out. I should say to myself, I may have sinned, I don't know, the world says so and the world is my judge. Whatever I did, I did because I couldn't help it and I'm willing to put up with what is coming to me. But if I were guilty, if in a moment of terror or madness I had committed an act for which the punishment of the law is death, I wouldn't wait to let justice take its course. I would take the surest, quickest way to put myself beyond the reach of the law.

STELLA: I am innocent.

LICONDA: If you hadn't been I should have told you that in the drawer of my writing-desk is a loaded revolver and that no one would prevent your going the few steps to my house and letting yourself in through the study window.

> [STELLA *looks at him in horror, fear making her heart beat furiously; he drops his eyes and turns his head away. There is a terrible silence. Then* NURSE WAYLAND *comes in. She wears now a coat and skirt and carries a hat in her hand.* STELLA *pulls herself together. She addresses the* NURSE *with relief. She is cool and urbane.*

STELLA: You've been very quick, Nurse.

NURSE: I found I had practically nothing left to pack. I've asked Alice to have my trunk taken downstairs.

STELLA: The gardener's here to-day. He can give her a hand.

NURSE: Might I say good-bye to Mrs. Tabret before I go?

STELLA: I'm sure she'd like you to. She's in the garden.

NURSE: I'll go to her.

STELLA: Oh, don't bother. Colin will call her. She only went out because Major Liconda had something he wished to say to me in private.

[COLIN *goes to the window and calls.*

COLIN: Mother.

MRS. TABRET: [*From the garden.*] Are you calling me, Colin?

COLIN: Nurse Wayland is just going. She would like to say good-bye to you.

MRS. TABRET: I'll come.

> [*The four persons in the room stand in silence. To all of them the moment is fateful.* MRS. TABRET *comes in, followed by* DR. HARVESTER.

MRS. TABRET: [*With a little smile as though nothing very serious had happened.*] Is your taxi here, dear?

NURSE: Yes, I saw it drive up from my window. Mrs. Tabret, I couldn't go without thanking you for all your kindness to me during the five years I've lived here.

MRS. TABRET: My dear, you were never any trouble. It was never difficult to be kind to you.

NURSE: I'm dreadfully sorry to have to repay all you've done for me by bringing this confusion and unhappiness upon you. I know you must hate me. It seems frightful, but I do ask you to believe that I can't help myself.

MRS. TABRET: Before we part, my dear, I should like if I could to release your spirit from the bitterness that is making you so unhappy. We're none of us all of a piece, you know. We haven't one self but half a dozen. That's why you're wrong to have been jealous of Stella. You gave Maurice everything that one self of him craved and that self of his was yours. It may be that we can be all things to all men, but can any of us be all things to one man, can any man be all things to any one of us? I knew a self of Maurice that none of you knew, I gave him something that no one else could give. I did not interfere with anyone. How ungenerous it would have been of me to resent the passion that bound him to Stella and the tender, comradely habit that bound him to you. God bless you for the kindness you showed my poor Maurice and for the unselfish love you bore him.

[*She takes* NURSE WAYLAND'S *hands and kisses her on both cheeks.*

NURSE: [*With a sob.*] I'm so desperately unhappy.

MRS. TABRET: Oh, my dear, you mustn't lose your admirable self-control. No one can make an omelette without breaking eggs. And such is the depravity of human nature, I suppose even the most respectable citizen feels a slight twinge of discomfort when he delivers the criminal to justice.

LICONDA: I suppose you will leave an address, Miss Wayland. Dr. Harvester will communicate with the proper authorities and I have no doubt they will want to get into touch with you.

HARVESTER: I shall go and see the coroner and put the facts before him. Would you like to come with me, Nurse?

NURSE: No.

HARVESTER: If Mrs. Tabret doesn't mind I'll ring up his place from here and find out if he's in.

MRS. TABRET: Of course, I don't mind, but before you do that may I say a few words?

HARVESTER: As many as you like.

MRS. TABRET: I'll try to be brief. Nurse Wayland is mistaken in thinking that Stella was the last person who saw Maurice alive. I saw him and spoke to him later.

NURSE: [*With utter amazement.*] You!

HARVESTER: But was he wide awake? If he'd taken thirty grains of chloralin he'd have been certainly very drowsy, if not comatose.

MRS. TABRET: Wait a minute, Dr. Harvester. Let me tell you my story in my own way.

HARVESTER: I beg your pardon.

MRS. TABRET: You know that Maurice's room was just

under mine. His windows were always wide open and when he couldn't sleep, and put on his light, I could see the reflection from my room. Then I used to slip down and sit by him and we'd put out the light and talk. Sometimes we talked about his childhood in India and I used to tell him of my own youth. But sometimes we'd talk about things that few men care to speak of in the broad light of day. He'd tell me of his great love for Stella and how anxious he was for her welfare and happiness. We'd talk of the mystery that surrounds the life of man. And often he would fall asleep and I stole softly away. We never mentioned these long conversations we had. [*With a little ironical smile.*] The position of a woman living in the same house with her son and her daughter-in-law is a trifle delicate and I didn't want Stella to think that I was in any way taking her place.

STELLA: My dear, I wouldn't have grudged you anything.

MRS. TABRET: There was no need to. But one shouldn't put human nature to too great a strain. The self that Maurice gave me during those long watches of the night was a self that only I, his mother, could respond to. . . . I couldn't sleep last night. There was no light in Maurice's room, but I felt strangely that he was lying awake, too. I went downstairs and into the garden and looked in at his window. He saw my shadow and said, Is that you, mother? I thought you might come in.

HARVESTER: What time was that?

MRS. TABRET: I don't know. Perhaps an hour after you'd left. He told me that he'd taken his sleeping-draught but it didn't seem to be having any effect. He said he felt awfully wide awake. And then he said, Mother, be a sport and give me another, it can't hurt just for once, and I do want to have a decent sleep.

HARVESTER: Somehow or other he was very nervous last night. I suppose his usual dose wasn't any good.

MRS. TABRET: [*Very quietly.*] Very early after his accident I had promised Maurice that if life became intolerable to him I would give him the means of putting an end to it.

STELLA: Oh, God!

MRS. TABRET: I said that if his sufferings were so great that he couldn't bear them any more and he solemnly asked me to help him, I wouldn't shirk the responsibility of giving him whatever drug was necessary to put to a painless end an existence he was no longer willing to endure. And sometimes he'd say to me, Does the promise still hold? And I answered, Yes, dear, it holds.

STELLA: [*With the greatest agitation.*] Did he ask you last night?

MRS. TABRET: No.

LICONDA: What happened then?

MRS. TABRET: I knew that Stella's love meant everything to Maurice and I knew that she had none to give him because she had given all her love to Colin. What do we any of us live for but our illusions and what can we ask of others but that they should allow us to keep them? It was an illusion that sustained poor Maurice in his sufferings, and if he lost it he lost everything. Stella had done as much for him as even I, his mother, could ask of her. I was not so selfish as to demand from her the sacrifice of all that makes a woman's life worth while.

STELLA: Why didn't you give me the chance?

MRS. TABRET: Years ago, when for my sons' sake I put aside the great love I bore to that funny old major standing there, I thought that no greater sacrifice could ever be asked of me. I know now it was nothing. For I loved Maurice. I adored him. I am so lonely now he is dead. It was a lovely dream that he dreamed, and I loved him too much to let him ever awake from it. I gave him life and I took life away from him.

NURSE: [*Horror-struck.*] Mrs. Tabret! It's impossible! How dreadful!

LICONDA: Millie! Millie! What are you going to tell us?

MRS. TABRET: I went into the bathroom and climbed on the chair and got the bottle of chloralin. I took five tabloids, as you know, Nurse Wayland, and I dissolved them in a glass of water. I took it in to Maurice and he drank it at a gulp. But it was bitter; he mentioned it, and I suppose that's why he left a little at the bottom of the glass. I sat by the side of his bed holding his hand till he fell asleep, and when I withdrew my hand I knew it was a sleep from which he would never awake. He dreamed his dream to the end.

STELLA: [*Taking her in her arms.*] Oh, Mother, Mother. What have you done? And what will be the end of this? Oh, I'm so terrified.

MRS. TABRET: [*Gently releasing herself.*] My dear, don't bother about me. What I did I did deliberately and I am quite ready to put up with the consequences. I do not seek to shirk them.

STELLA: It's my fault. It's my weakness. How can I ever forgive myself? What have I done?

MRS. TABRET: You mustn't be silly and sentimental. You love Colin and Colin loves you. You mustn't think about me nor distress yourselves at what happens to me. You must go away and in America you can marry and have your child and you must forget the past and the dead. For you are young and the young have a right to life and the future belongs to them.

COLIN: Mother, darling. Oh, Mother, you make me so ashamed.

MRS. TABRET: My son, I love you, too. I have your happiness very much at heart.

LICONDA: Millie. My dear, dear Millie.

MRS. TABRET: [*With a slightly grim smile.*] Well, Nurse Wayland, you see you were quite right. Of course, I ought to have replaced the tabloids by others, aspirin or chlorate of potash, but as you said just now murderers often make mistakes and I'm not an habitual criminal.

> [*There is a moment's pause.*

NURSE: Dr. Harvester, are you still willing to sign the death certificate?

HARVESTER: Yes.

NURSE: Then sign it. If there were ever any question I am prepared to swear that I left the tabloids on Maurice's table by his bed.

STELLA: Nurse Wayland!

MRS. TABRET: [*To* HARVESTER.] Isn't it a dreadful risk you're taking?

HARVESTER: Damn it, I don't care.

LICONDA: Oh, Nurse, we're so grateful to you, so infinitely grateful.

> [NURSE WAYLAND *throws herself down on her knees and clasps* MRS. TABRET *in her arms.*

NURSE: Oh, Mrs. Tabret, I've been so horrible. I've been petty and revengeful. I never knew how mean I was.

MRS. TABRET: Come, come, my dear, don't let any of us get emotional. We are both of us lonely women now. Let us cleave to one another. So long as you and I can keep our love for Maurice alive in our hearts he is not entirely dead.

THE END

THE UNKNOWN

A PLAY
in Three Acts

CHARACTERS

Colonel Wharton
Major Wharton (John)
Mrs. Wharton
Mrs. Littlewood
Rev. Norman Poole
Mrs. Poole
Sylvia Bullough
Dr. Macfarlane
Kate
Cook

The action of the play takes place at the Manor House, Stour, in the County of Kent.

THE UNKNOWN

THE FIRST ACT

The drawing-room at the Manor House, COLONEL WHARTON'S *residence. It is a simple room, somewhat heavily furnished in an old-fashioned style; there is nothing in it which is in the least artistic; but the furniture is comfortable, and neither new nor shabby. On the papered walls are the Academy pictures of forty years ago. There are a great many framed photographs of men in uniform, and here and there a bunch of simple flowers in a vase. The only things in the room which are at all exotic are silver ornaments from Indian bazaars and flimsy Indian fabrics, used as cloths on the occasional tables and as drapery on the piano.*

At the back are French windows leading into the garden; and this, with its lawn and trees, is seen through them. It is summer, and the windows are open. Morning.

MRS. WHARTON *is sitting in the corner of the sofa, knitting a khaki comforter. She is a slight, tall woman of five-and-fifty; she has deliberate features, with kind eyes and a gentle look; her dark hair is getting very grey; it is simply done; and her dress, too, is simple; it is not at all new and was never fashionable.*

KATE, *a middle-aged maid-servant, in a print dress, a cap and apron, comes in.*

KATE: If you please, ma'am, the butcher's called.

MRS. WHARTON: Oh! I arranged with Cook that we should have cold roast beef again for luncheon to-day, Kate. Tell the butcher to bring two and a half pounds of the best end of the neck for to-night, and tell him to pick me out a really nice piece, Kate. It's so long since the Major has had any good English meat.

5

KATE: Very good, ma'am.

MRS. WHARTON: And he might send in a couple of kidneys. The Colonel and Major Wharton enjoyed the kidneys that they had for breakfast yesterday so much.

KATE: Very good, ma'am. If you please, ma'am, the gardener hasn't sent in a very big basket of peas. Cook says it won't look much for three.

MRS. WHARTON: Oh, well, it doesn't matter as long as there are enough for the gentlemen. I'll just pretend to take some.

KATE: Very good, ma'am.

> [*As she is going,* COLONEL WHARTON *enters from the garden with a basket of cherries. He is a thin old man, much older than his wife, with white hair; but though very frail he still carries himself erectly. His face is bronzed by long exposure to tropical suns, but even so it is the face of a sick man. He wears a light tweed suit which hangs about him loosely, as though he had shrunk since it was made for him. He has a round tweed hat of the same material.*

COLONEL WHARTON: Has the paper come yet, Kate?

KATE: Yes, sir. I'll bring it.

> [*Exit* KATE.

COLONEL WHARTON: I've brought you in some cherries, Evelyn. They're the only ripe ones I could find.

MRS. WHARTON: Oh, that is nice. I hope you're not tired.

COLONEL WHARTON: Great Scott, I'm not such a crock that it can tire me to pick a few cherries. If I'd been able to find a ladder I'd have got you double the number.

MRS. WHARTON: Oh, my dear, you'd better let the gardener get them. I don't approve of your skipping up and down ladders.

COLONEL WHARTON: The gardener's just as old as I am and not nearly so active. Hasn't John come in yet? He said he was only going to the post.

MRS. WHARTON: Perhaps he went in to see Sylvia on the way back.

COLONEL WHARTON: I shouldn't have thought she wanted to be bothered with him in the morning.

MRS. WHARTON: George!

COLONEL WHARTON: Yes, dear.

MRS. WHARTON: It seems so extraordinary to hear you say: "Hasn't John come in yet? He said he was only going to the post." It makes me rather want to cry.

COLONEL WHARTON: It's been a long time, Evelyn. It's been a bad time for both of us, my dear. But worse for you.

MRS. WHARTON: I tried not to be troublesome, George.

COLONEL WHARTON: Dear child, aren't I there to share your troubles with you?

MRS. WHARTON: It seems so natural that he should come in any minute, it seems as though he'd never been away—and yet somehow I can't quite believe it. It seems incredible that he should really be back.

COLONEL WHARTON: [Patting her hand.] My dear Evelyn!

[KATE brings in the paper and gives it to the COLONEL. She goes out.

COLONEL WHARTON: Thank you. [While he puts on his spectacles.] It's a blessing to be able to read the births, deaths, and marriages like a gentleman instead of turning before anything else to the casualties.

MRS. WHARTON: I hope before long that we shall be composing a little announcement for that column.

COLONEL WHARTON: Have they settled a day yet, those young people?

MRS. WHARTON: I don't know. John hasn't said anything, and I didn't see Sylvia yesterday except for a moment after church.

COLONEL WHARTON: Evelyn dear, the gardener tells me he

hasn't got much in the way of peas ready for to-night, so I've told him to send in a few carrots for me; I think they're probably better for my digestion.

MRS. WHARTON: Nonsense, George. You know how much you like peas, and I'm not very fond of them. I was hoping there'd only be enough for two so that I shouldn't have to eat any.

COLONEL WHARTON: Evelyn, where do you expect to go when you die if you tell such stories?

MRS. WHARTON: Now, George, don't be obstinate. You might give in to me sometimes. They're the first peas out of the garden and I should like you to eat them.

COLONEL WHARTON: No, my dear, I'd like to see you eat them. I'm an invalid, and I must have my own way.

MRS. WHARTON: You tyrant! You haven't seen Dr. Macfarlane this morning? I'm so anxious.

COLONEL WHARTON: You old fusser! No sooner have you stopped worrying over your boy than you start worrying over me.

MRS. WHARTON: Even though you won't let me call my soul my own, I don't want to lose you just yet.

COLONEL WHARTON: Don't be alarmed. I shall live to plague you for another twenty years.

[KATE *comes in.*

KATE: If you please, ma'am, Mrs. Poole has called.

MRS. WHARTON: Why haven't you shown her in?

KATE: She wouldn't come in, ma'am. She said she was passing and she just stopped to enquire how you were.

COLONEL WHARTON: Tell her to come in, Kate. What's she making all this fuss about?

KATE: Very well, sir.

[*Exit.*

MRS. WHARTON: I expect she wants to hear all about John.

COLONEL WHARTON: If she'll wait a minute she'll have the chance of seeing the young fellow himself.

[KATE *comes in, followed by* MRS. POOLE. *The visitor is a thin, rather dour person of middle age, brisk in her movements, competent and firm. She is a woman who knows her own mind and has no hesitation in speaking it. She is not unsympathetic. She wears a serviceable black coat and skirt and a black straw hat.*

KATE: Mrs. Poole.

[*Exit.*

COLONEL WHARTON: What do you mean by trying to get away without showing yourself? Is this how you do your district visiting?

MRS. POOLE: [*Shaking hands with* MRS. WHARTON *and with the* COLONEL.] I wanted to come in, but I thought you mightn't wish to see me to-day, so I put it like that to make it easier for you to send me about my business.

MRS. WHARTON: We always wish to see you, my dear.

MRS. POOLE: If I had a son that I hadn't seen for four years and he'd been dangerously wounded, I think I'd want to keep him to myself for the first few days after he got home.

COLONEL WHARTON: Then you're not as unselfish a woman as Evelyn.

MRS. WHARTON: Or perhaps not nearly so vain.

MRS. POOLE: Did you go down to the station to meet him on Saturday?

MRS. WHARTON: The Colonel went. He wouldn't let me go because he said I'd make a fool of myself on the platform.

COLONEL WHARTON: I took Sylvia. I thought that was enough. I knew I could trust her to control herself.

MRS. POOLE: And when are they going to be married?

MRS. WHARTON: Oh, I hope very soon. It's been a long and anxious time for her.

M

MRS. POOLE: Can you bear to give him up when he's only just come back to you?

MRS. WHARTON: Oh, but it's not giving him up when he's marrying Sylvia. She's been like a daughter to us. D'you know, they've been engaged for seven years.

MRS. POOLE: I hope they'll be very happy. Sylvia certainly deserves to be.

COLONEL WHARTON: She's done cheerfully the most difficult thing anyone can do. All through the war when she was pining to be off and do her bit she stayed at home with a bed-ridden mother.

MRS. WHARTON: Poor Mrs. Bullough.

COLONEL WHARTON: Yes, but poor Sylvia too. It's easy enough to do your duty when duty is dangerous and exciting, but when you can do nothing—no one knows better than I what it is to sit still and look on when others are doing the things that are worth while. This war came ten years too late for me.

MRS. POOLE: That's what the Vicar has been saying ever since the war began. But after all your son has taken your place, and I think you can be proud of him.

COLONEL WHARTON: [*With intense satisfaction.*] The rascal with his Military Cross and his D.S.O.

MRS. POOLE: I'm so glad that his first day here was a Sunday.

MRS. WHARTON: You don't know what I felt when we knelt down side by side in church. I was very grateful.

MRS. POOLE: I know. I could see it in your face and the Colonel's.

COLONEL WHARTON: God has vouchsafed us a great mercy.

MRS. POOLE: The Vicar was dreadfully disappointed that he didn't stay for Holy Communion. You know that he looks upon that as the essential part of the service.

MRS. WHARTON: I think we were a little disappointed, too. We were so surprised when John walked out.

MRS. POOLE: Did he say why he had?

MRS. WHARTON: No. I talked it over with the Colonel. We didn't quite know what to do. I don't know whether to mention it or not.

MRS. POOLE: I do hope he'll stay next Sunday.

MRS. WHARTON: He was always a very regular communicant.

COLONEL WHARTON: I don't see why you shouldn't say something to him about it, Evelyn.

MRS. WHARTON: I will if you like.

       [There is the sound of a laugh in the garden.

Why, here he is. And Sylvia.

    [SYLVIA BULLOUGH and JOHN WHARTON come in. She is no longer quite young. She has a pleasant, friendly look rather than beauty, and she suggests the homely virtues of a girl very well brought up in a nice English family; she gives the impression of a practical, competent, and sensible woman. She will make a good wife and an excellent mother. She is very simply dressed in light summery things, and she wears a straw hat. She is carrying a string bag, in which are a number of household purchases. JOHN WHARTON is in mufti. He is a man of thirty.

SYLVIA: Good morning, everybody!

MRS. WHARTON: My dear, how nice of you to come in.

JOHN: She didn't want to, but I made her.

    [SYLVIA kisses MRS. WHARTON and shakes hands with MRS. POOLE, then she kisses the COLONEL.

SYLVIA: [*Gaily.*] That's a deliberate lie, John.

MRS. WHARTON: This is my son, Mrs. Poole.

JOHN: [*Shaking hands with her.*] I daresay you suspected it.

MRS. POOLE: I had a good look at you in church, you know.

JOHN: Is that how vicars' wives behave themselves?

MRS. POOLE: They allow themselves a little licence when young people come home on leave.

COLONEL WHARTON: Did you meet in the village?

JOHN: Not exactly. I saw Sylvia darting into Mrs. Gann's shop, evidently to avoid me. . . .

SYLVIA: [*Interrupting.*] I don't know how you imagined I could see you out of the back of my head.

JOHN: So I ran like a hare, and caught her in the very act of buying two pounds of vermicelli.

SYLVIA: To say nothing of a tin of sardines and a packet of mustard.

JOHN: Now take off your hat, Sylvia. You mustn't hide the best feature you've got.

SYLVIA: [*Taking it off.*] I hope you don't think I shall go on doing exactly what you tell me a minute after the war's over.

JOHN: I haven't noticed any startling alacrity to do what I tell you as it is.

SYLVIA: You ungrateful fellow! When have I hesitated to carry out your slightest wish?

MRS. WHARTON: He's only been back forty-eight hours, poor dear.

JOHN: Didn't I go down to you on my bended knees in the middle of the road and ask you to come for a walk with me?

SYLVIA: Oh, well, I wanted to see your father. I was anxious to hear what the specialist had said.

JOHN: [*Surprised.*] Have you been seeing a specialist, father? Aren't you well?

COLONEL WHARTON: Perfectly. It was only to satisfy your poor mother.

JOHN: But why didn't you tell me? Is anything the matter with him, mother?

MRS. WHARTON: My dear, your father wouldn't let me tell you anything about it when you came. He didn't want you to be worried. And I thought myself it might just as well keep till to-day.

COLONEL WHARTON: The fact is I haven't been quite up to the mark lately, and Dr. Macfarlane thought I'd better see a specialist. So I went into Canterbury on Saturday and saw Dr. Keller.

MRS. POOLE: Yes, I heard you'd been to see him. They say he's very clever.

JOHN: What did he say?

COLONEL WHARTON: Well, you know what these doctor fellows are. He wouldn't say much to me. He said he'd write to Macfarlane.

JOHN: Well?

COLONEL WHARTON: I suppose Macfarlane got the letter this morning. He'll probably be round presently.

MRS. POOLE: I saw him going along the Bleane Road in his dog-cart about an hour ago. You might ask him who it was he was going to see.

JOHN: Are you feeling ill, father?

COLONEL WHARTON: No. I shouldn't have dreamed of going to a specialist, only your mother was worrying.

SYLVIA: Don't put all the blame on her. I was, too.

JOHN: [*Going over to him and putting his arm in his.*] Poor old father, you mustn't be ill.

COLONEL WHARTON: Oh, I'm not going to die just yet, you know.

JOHN: I should jolly well think not. Wait till you're a hundred and two, and then we'll begin talking about it.

[*The Vicar of Stour, the* REV. NORMAN POOLE, *appears at the window. He is a tall, thin man, bald, dressed in a short black coat, with a black straw hat. He is energetic, breezy, and cheerful. He likes to show that, although a clergyman, he is a man; and he affects a rather professional joviality.* MR. *and* MRS. POOLE *have that physical resemblance which you sometimes see in married people. You wonder if they married because they were so much alike, or if it is marriage which has created the similarity.*

VICAR: Hulloa, hulloa, hulloa! May I come in?

MRS. WHARTON: [*Smiling.*] Of course. How do you do?

COLONEL WHARTON: My dear Vicar!

VICAR: [*Entering.*] I suppose I ought to have gone round to the front door, and rung the bell like a gentleman. My dear Dorothy, when will you teach me how to behave?

MRS. POOLE: I've long given up the attempt.

VICAR: I thought I'd look in and say how-do-you-do to the wounded hero.

MRS. WHARTON: My son. The Vicar.

VICAR: Welcome! I passed you in the village just now. I had half a mind to come up and wring your hand, but I thought you'd say, who the deuce is this clerical gent?

JOHN: How do you do?

VICAR: An authentic hero. And he speaks just like you and me. The world's a strange place, my masters. Well, what d'you think of Blighty?

JOHN: I'm very glad to be home again. I thought I never should get back.

VICAR: You've not been home since the beginning of the war, have you?

JOHN: No, you see I was in India when it broke out. What with Gallipoli and one thing and another, I was done out of my leave every time.

VICAR: Well, it's a long lane that has no turning. But I understand that you've picked up some bits and pieces here and there. The Military Cross and the D.S.O., isn't it?

MRS. POOLE: You must be a very proud man.

VICAR: How did you win them?

JOHN: Oh, I don't know. Playing about generally.

MRS. WHARTON: I don't think you'll get very much more than that out of John.

VICAR: [*To* JOHN.] You lucky beggar! You've had your chance and you were able to take it. That's where I should have been, where my heart was, with the brave lads at the front. And my confounded chest has kept me chained to this little tin-pot parish.

MRS. POOLE: My husband suffers from his lungs.

JOHN: I'm sorry to hear that.

VICAR: Yes, the Great White Peril. They say its ravages are terrible. That's why I came here, you know; I was in charge of the parish of St. Jude's, Stoke Newington, when I crocked up. I tried to get them to let me go when the war broke out, but they wouldn't hear of it.

MRS. WHARTON: They also serve who only stand and wait.

VICAR: I know, I know. It's this confounded energy of mine. I'm a crock, and I've just had to make the best of it. I'm on the shelf. The future is in the hands of you brave lads who've been through the fire. I suppose you went to sleep during my sermon yesterday.

JOHN: Not at all. I listened to it very attentively.

VICAR: I shouldn't blame you if you had. That's about all I've been able to do during the war, to preach. And, upon my word, I sometimes wonder what good I've done.

MRS. WHARTON: You've been a great help to us all.

VICAR: For my part I don't deplore the war. Our Lord said: "Think not that I come to send peace on earth: I came not to send peace, but a sword." The Christian Church has lived by her sword. Every advance which this world of ours has known in liberty, in justice, in enlightenment, has been won for it by the sword of Jesus Christ.

COLONEL WHARTON: I wish all parsons were as broad-minded. I know what war is. I was in Egypt and in South Africa. I've been through half a dozen wars in India. I have no use for slop and sentimentality. My own belief is that war is necessary to a nation. It brings out all a man's best qualities.

VICAR: There I heartily agree with you. It is the great school of character. Amid the clash of arms the great Christian virtues shine forth with an immortal lustre. Courage, self-sacrifice, charity, self-reliance. No one knew before the war what a pinnacle of heroism was within the power of our brave lads at the front.

MRS. POOLE: What do you think about it, Major Wharton?

JOHN: [*Smiling.*] I? I think it's a lovely day. I have three weeks' leave, and the war is a long way off.

VICAR: [*With a chuckle.*] A very good answer. I've been saying the obvious, I know that just as well as you do, but you know, sometimes the obvious has to be said, and when it has, I think a man should have the courage to say it. Now, my dear, let's be off.

MRS. POOLE: I don't know what Mrs. Wharton will think of us for inflicting ourselves on her like this.

VICAR: We're all friends here, I hope and trust. If we weren't welcome, Mrs. Wharton only had to say so. To my mind the afternoon call is a convention more honoured in the breach than the observance.

MRS. WHARTON: It's been very good of you to come.

[*There is a general shaking of hands.*

VICAR: [*To* JOHN.] Well, good-bye, young fellow. I've tried to show you that I'm by way of being rather broad-minded as parsons go. It wouldn't shock me in the least to hear you say "damn" or "blast." I'm often inclined to use a bit of strong language myself. I asked you just now if you'd gone to sleep during my sermon. I wouldn't have turned a hair if you had.

JOHN: It's very kind of you to say so. I may avail myself of your suggestion on some future occasion.

VICAR: On a future occasion, perhaps—shall we say next Sunday?—I hope you won't leave the House of God without partaking in the greatest of all the Sacraments of our Church. Don't forget that the Almighty has in His mercy brought you in safety through great and terrible peril. That's all I wanted to say to you. Good-bye, God bless you.

JOHN: Good-bye.

VICAR: [*Shaking hands with* MRS. WHARTON.] Good-bye. These parsons, what a nuisance they make of themselves, don't they?

MRS. WHARTON: I wanted to ask you if you'd seen poor Mrs. Littlewood since her return.

VICAR: No, she didn't come to church yesterday. And of course, Sunday's my busy day—I'm the only man in the parish who works seven days a week—so I haven't had a chance to see her yet, poor soul.

SYLVIA: She came down by the 6.35 on Saturday. She was in the same train as John, but I wasn't bothering much about anyone else just then, and I didn't speak to her.

COLONEL WHARTON: I wish we could do something for her.

MRS. WHARTON: [*Explaining to* JOHN.] She was telegraphed for last week to go to Ned at Boulogne. He died on Tuesday.

JOHN: [*With astonishment.*] Ned! But he was only a kid.

MRS. WHARTON: Oh, he'd grown up since you were home. He was nearly nineteen.

MRS. POOLE: Both her sons are gone now. She's quite alone.

MRS. WHARTON: We must all be very kind to her. It will be

M*

terrible for her in that big house all by herself. I wish you'd spoken to her on Saturday, George.

COLONEL WHARTON: I felt rather shy about it. After all, we've had rather an anxious time over that young scamp there. If anything had happened to him—well, I should have had Evelyn, but she, poor soul, has nobody.

SYLVIA: I ought to have gone to see her yesterday.

MRS. WHARTON: She must be absolutely prostrated with grief.

VICAR: I wonder if she'd like to come and stay at the Vicarage. I can't bear to think of her all alone.

MRS. POOLE: That's a splendid idea, Norman, and just like you. I'll ask her at once. I'll be glad to do what I can for her.

SYLVIA: Of course one ought to try and find something to occupy her mind.

VICAR: Happily she has always been a deeply religious woman. When all's said and done, in grief like that there's only one unfailing refuge.

> [KATE *enters, followed by* MRS. LITTLEWOOD. *She is a little elderly woman. She is not dressed in mourning, but in the clothes she may be expected to have been wearing before her bereavement.*

KATE: Mrs. Littlewood.

> [*Exit* KATE.

MRS. WHARTON: [*Rising and going to meet her.*] My dear friend, how very glad I am to see you.

MRS. LITTLEWOOD: How do you do? [*She smiles brightly at the assembled company.*] Oh, John, have you come back? [*To* MRS. WHARTON.] I came to ask if you and the Colonel would come and play bridge this afternoon.

MRS. WHARTON: Bridge!

> [*They all look at her with surprise, but no one says anything.*

MRS. LITTLEWOOD: I was going to ask Dr. Macfarlane to make a fourth, but perhaps John will come.

MRS. WHARTON: [*With embarrassment.*] It's very kind of you, but the Colonel hasn't been very well lately. I don't think he feels like going out, and I shouldn't like to leave him.

MRS. LITTLEWOOD: Oh, I'm sorry.

MRS. WHARTON: Won't you sit down?

MRS. LITTLEWOOD: Thank you very much. I won't stay. I'll go round to the Wilkinsons and see if they'll play.

VICAR: I hope you weren't very tired by your journey.

MRS. LITTLEWOOD: I wasn't tired at all.

MRS. POOLE: We thought you were, because we didn't see you in church.

MRS. LITTLEWOOD: No, I didn't come. I thought it would bore me.

[*There is a moment's silence.*

MRS. WHARTON: Did you—did you come straight through from France?

MRS. LITTLEWOOD: No. I stayed a couple of nights in London.

MRS. WHARTON: [*With pity in her voice.*] All alone?

MRS. LITTLEWOOD: No. I picked up a very nice woman in the hotel, and we went out together. We went to the Gaiety one night and the next we went to the Empire. Do you know that I'd never seen George Robey before?

MRS. POOLE: Who is George Robey?

VICAR: I believe he's a comedian.

MRS. LITTLEWOOD: [*Very pleasantly.*] How long are you here for, John?

JOHN: I have three weeks' leave.

MRS. LITTLEWOOD: We must all make much of you. I'll give a tennis party for you, shall I?

SYLVIA: Oh, Mrs. Littlewood, I'm sure you don't want to give parties just now.

MRS. LITTLEWOOD: I'd love to. It's so seldom one gets an excuse for one in a place like this.

MRS. WHARTON: [*Taking her hand.*] My dear, I want you to know how deeply we all sympathise with you in you great loss.

MRS. LITTLEWOOD: [*Patting* MRS. WHARTON'S *hand, and then releasing her own.*] That's very kind of you. [*To* SYLVIA *and* JOHN.] Would Wednesday suit you young people? I'll have both courts marked out.

SYLVIA: [*Desperately.*] I couldn't come, Mrs. Littlewood, I couldn't come.

MRS. LITTLEWOOD: Why on earth not?

SYLVIA: [*Controlling herself to civility.*] I'm engaged that day.

COLONEL WHARTON: John has so short a time at home. I think he and Sylvia have a feeling that they don't want to go to parties.

VICAR: [*Deliberately.*] I hope you got over to France in time to find your son alive.

> [MRS. LITTLEWOOD *gives him a rapid glance, stops a moment as though to collect herself, then answers almost indifferently.*

MRS. LITTLEWOOD: No, he was dead, poor child. [*To* MRS. WHARTON.] Good-bye, my dear, I'm sorry you can't come and play bridge this afternoon. I suppose I shall have to send you a wedding-present. John.

JOHN: I suppose you will.

MRS. LITTLEWOOD: [*With a smile at the rest of the company.*] Good-bye.

> [*She goes out. They are left in amazement.*

MRS. POOLE: Is she absolutely heartless?

COLONEL WHARTON: I always thought she was devoted to her sons.

SYLVIA: And Ned was her favourite.

MRS. POOLE: She wasn't wearing mourning.

SYLVIA: Isn't she going to, do you suppose?

MRS. WHARTON: I can't understand it. She adored those boys.

MRS. POOLE: I didn't ask her to come and stay at the Vicarage, Norman.

VICAR: I don't think we'd better till the situation's a little clearer. She gives one the impression of not caring two straws for Ned's death. She must be as hard as nails.

MRS. WHARTON: No, she isn't that. I've known her for thirty-five years. D'you think she's mad?

COLONEL WHARTON: We'd better say a word to Macfarlane when he comes, Evelyn.

VICAR: I was never so taken aback in my life as when she said she didn't come to church because she thought she'd be bored.

MRS. POOLE: Norman, I must go. I've got a lot of things to do at home.

VICAR: Come along then. We'll just walk out through the garden.

> [*There are farewells, rather distracted by the queer incident that has just occurred, and the* VICAR *and* MRS. POOLE *go out. The* COLONEL *accompanies them to the door.*

SYLVIA: You're very silent, John.

JOHN: I was thinking about Mrs. Littlewood. She doesn't give me the impression of being either callous or mad.

SYLVIA: What does she mean, then?

JOHN: [*Reflectively.*] I don't know. [*With a shrug of the shoulders, throwing off his mood.*] And at the moment I don't very much care. Come and sit down and be a comfort to a wounded hero.

SYLVIA: Idiot!

MRS. WHARTON: Will you stay to luncheon, Sylvia dear?

SYLVIA: No, I think I ought to get back to mother.

JOHN: Before you go let's tell them what we've been talking about.

COLONEL WHARTON: I don't think it's very hard to guess.

JOHN: I want Sylvia to marry me as soon as ever it's possible

MRS. WHARTON: Of course.

JOHN: If we look nippy we can get a special licence and be married on Thursday. We don't want to go far for our honeymoon, because I have such a short time. And my suggestion is London.

SYLVIA: What do you think, Mrs. Wharton?

MRS. WHARTON: Well, my dear, I think that whatever you and John decide will be quite right.

SYLVIA: He's only just come back to you. I can't bear to take him away immediately. Wouldn't you prefer us to wait a little longer?

MRS. WHARTON: My dear, we've always decided that you should be married the moment he came back. We've been quite prepared to lose him. And perhaps after a few days, if the Colonel's well enough, you wouldn't mind if we came up to London, too. We'd try not to be in your way.

SYLVIA: [*Going down on her knees beside* MRS. WHARTON *and kissing her.*] Oh, my dear, you're so kind to me. I don't know how I can ever thank you for all your kindness.

MRS. WHARTON: It's been a weary, anxious time for all of us. I know how unhappy you've been sometimes. I want you to have him now. He's a good boy, and I think he'll make you happy.

SYLVIA: [*Getting up and giving* JOHN *her hand.*] I'm sure he will. I'll try to make you a good wife, John.

JOHN: I expect you'll be quite good enough for the likes of me. Then it's to be Thursday next.

SYLVIA: [*With a smile.*] It is.

> [*He draws her to him and kisses her. She very nearly breaks down.*

SYLVIA: I've wanted you for so long, John, so dreadfully long.

JOHN: For goodness' sake don't cry.

SYLVIA: [*Breaking away from him, with a chuckle.*] You brute, John! I hate you.

MRS. WHARTON: Did you like the Vicar, John?

JOHN: He seemed all right.

COLONEL WHARTON: He's a first-rate fellow. He had a very good living in London at one time, and he resigned and took one in the East End instead.

JOHN: Really?

COLONEL WHARTON: He said he wasn't ordained to drink China tea with elderly women of means. [*With a chuckle.*] He says very good things sometimes.

MRS. WHARTON: They were perfectly wonderful in the East End. They wanted to live in exactly the same way as their parishioners, so they did without a servant, and did all their housework, even their washing, themselves.

JOHN: It sounds hateful, but of course it really was heroic.

MRS. WHARTON: D'you remember what he said to you about Holy Communion? Your father and I were a little disappointed that you didn't stay for it yesterday.

JOHN: I'm sorry for that, mother dear.

MRS. WHARTON: It would have been such a great pleasure to both of us if we could all three have received it together.

JOHN: Dear mother. . . . If you're really going home to luncheon, Sylvia, I'll walk back with you.

MRS. WHARTON: The Vicar has a Communion service on Wednesday morning. Would you come then? It'll be the last opportunity before your marriage.

JOHN: Oh, my dear, you're not going to ask me to get up in the middle of the night? After all, one of the pleasures of coming home is to lie in bed in the morning. I don't know how I ever tear myself out of those lavender-scented sheets.

MRS. WHARTON: Dear John, won't you come to please us?

JOHN: [*Still trying to pass it off lightly.*] Oh, my dear mother, d'you think it's really necessary?

MRS. WHARTON: I should like it so much, my dear. You know, it means a great deal to us.

JOHN: [*More gravely.*] Don't you think one should go to a ceremony like that in a certain frame of mind?

COLONEL WHARTON: [*Good-humouredly.*] Come, my boy, you're not going to refuse the first request your mother has made you since you came back?

JOHN: I'm awfully sorry, mother. I beg you not to insist.

MRS. WHARTON: I don't quite know what you mean. It's not like you to be obstinate. . . . Won't you come, John?

JOHN: No, mother.

COLONEL WHARTON: Why not?

JOHN: I've been away a long time. There are some things one can't help, you know. I've been through very terrible experiences.

MRS. WHARTON: [*Aghast.*] Do you mean to say you've lost your—faith?

JOHN: I'm awfully sorry to give you pain, dear.

SYLVIA: [*Her eyes fixed on him.*] You've not answered your mother's question, John.

JOHN: If you want a direct answer, I'm afraid it must be—yes.

MRS. WHARTON: [*Overcome.*] Oh, John!

SYLVIA: But you came to church yesterday.

JOHN: That was just a formal ceremony. I assisted passively, as a Jew might assist at the wedding of one of his Christian friends.

SYLVIA: You stood when we stood, and knelt down, and seemed to pray.

JOHN: I would do that if I were in a Roman Catholic church. That seemed to me only good manners. [*With a smile.*] Do you think it was very deceitful?

SYLVIA: I don't quite see why you should strain at a gnat.

JOHN: I don't. It's the camel I can't swallow. I knew it would distress you if I refused to come to church. I didn't want to seem a prig. But the other seems to me different. When I'm asked to take an active part in a ceremony that means nothing to me it's quite another matter. I'd rather not tell a deliberate lie. And surely from your point of view it would be blasphemous.

MRS. WHARTON: [*Occupied with her own thoughts.*] How dreadful!

JOHN: [*Going up to her and putting his arm round her.*] Don't be unhappy, mother. I can't help feeling as I do. After all, these are matters that only concern oneself.

SYLVIA: [*Reflecting.*] Are they?

JOHN: Surely. [*To his mother.*] I would rather not have told you. I knew how much you'd take it to heart. But I was obliged to. And perhaps it's better as it is. I hated the thought of deceiving you and father. Now let's put it out of our minds.

COLONEL WHARTON: John, have you forgotten that in three weeks you'll be going back to the Front? Sooner or later you'll find yourself once more in the fighting line. Have you asked yourself what it will be like to face death without the help of Almighty God?

JOHN: It's always difficult to face death.

COLONEL WHARTON: You wouldn't be the first who found

it easy to stand alone when all was going well and found it a very different thing in danger or illness.

JOHN: [*With a smile.*] When the devil was sick, the devil a monk would be.

SYLVIA: Archie, Mrs. Littlewood's elder boy, was badly wounded on the Somme. His battalion had to retreat and somehow or other he wasn't picked up. He lay in the corner of a wood for three days and kept himself alive on a beet that he pulled out of the field. Heaven knows, I don't want anything like that to happen to you, but are you sure your courage wouldn't fail you then? Are you sure you wouldn't call on God instinctively to help you?

JOHN: And if I did, what of it? That wouldn't be me, that mangled, bleeding, starved, delirious thing. It's me now that speaks, now that I'm well and conscious and strong. It's the real me now. I disclaim and disown anything I may feel or say when I'm tortured with pain and sickness. It would give my real self just as little as a prisoner on the rack gives the truth.

SYLVIA: [*Looking at him fixedly.*] You're afraid of something like that happening, aren't you?

JOHN: Yes, I shouldn't like my body to play me a dirty trick when I hadn't the presence of mind to look after it.

COLONEL WHARTON: Have you ever been in real danger since you—since you began to think like this?

JOHN: Yes. Once I was in a trench the Germans had enfiladed. They'd got the line exactly. The shells fell one after another, first at the end of the trench, and then they came slowly down. One could calculate almost mathematically when the shell must come that would blow one to smithereens.

MRS. WHARTON: [*With a little gasp of terror.*] Oh, John, don't!

JOHN: [*Smiling.*] Well, something went wrong, or else I certainly shouldn't be here now.

COLONEL WHARTON: Do you mean to say you weren't frightened?

JOHN: Frightened isn't the word for it. Talk of getting the wind up: it was a perfect hurricane. I felt as though I were shrinking up so that my clothes suddenly hung about me like sacks. And against my will a prayer came to my lips. From long habit, I suppose, they tried to form themselves into an appeal to God to turn the shell away. I had to fight with myself. I had to keep saying to myself: "Don't be a fool. Don't be a damned fool."

MRS. WHARTON: And you resisted? It was the voice of God speaking to you. The prayer was said in your heart, and He in His mercy heard it. Doesn't that prove to you that you're wrong? At that moment you believed, even though you struggled not to. Your whole soul cried out its belief in God.

JOHN: No, not my soul: my fear of death.

COLONEL WHARTON: I've been in battle, too. In South Africa and in the Soudan we were in some pretty tight places now and then. When I went into action I commended my soul to God, and now that I'm an old man I can say that I never knew fear.

JOHN: I don't think I'm particularly brave. Before an attack I've often had to light a cigarette to hide the trembling of my lips.

COLONEL WHARTON: The Christian doesn't fear death. His whole life is but a preparation for that awful moment. To him it is the shining gateway to life everlasting.

JOHN: I should be sorry to think that life was nothing but a preparation for death. To my mind death is very unimportant. I think a man does best to put it out of his thoughts. He should live as though life were endless. Life is the thing that matters.

SYLVIA: Doesn't that suggest a very base materialism?

JOHN: No, because you can't make the most of life unless you're willing to risk it, and it's the risk that makes the difference. It's the most precious thing a man has, but it's valueless unless he's prepared to stake it.

SYLVIA: What do you think it can be worth while to risk life for?

JOHN: Almost anything. Honour or love. A song, a thought. [*After a moment's reflection, with a smile.*] A five-barred gate.

SYLVIA: Isn't that rather illogical?

JOHN: Perhaps. I don't put it very well. I think what I mean is that life in itself has no value. It's what you put in it that gives it worth.

COLONEL WHARTON: Why do you think you've come safely through the perils and dangers of the war? John, do you know that every day your mother and Sylvia and I prayed that God might see fit to spare you?

JOHN: [*With sudden energy.*] Were you the only ones? Why didn't He see fit to spare the others?

SYLVIA: Who are we to question the inscrutable designs of the Omnipotent?

COLONEL WHARTON: [*Answering his son.*] I don't know what you mean by that. In war somebody's got to be killed. When a commander gives battle he knows pretty accurately what his losses are going to be before he starts.

[JOHN *gives a slight shrug of the shoulders. He recovers his equanimity.*

JOHN: If you don't mind my saying so, I think we'd much better not start arguing. Arguments never bring one much forrader, do they?

MRS. WHARTON: [*Gently.*] But we want to understand, John. You were always such a pious boy.

JOHN: [*Smiling.*] Oh, mother, that's rather a terrible thing to say to anybody.

MRS. WHARTON: [*With an answering smile.*] Oh, I didn't mean it like that. On the contrary, you were rather troublesome. Sometimes you were very headstrong and obstinate.

JOHN: That's better.

MRS. WHARTON: We tried to bring you up to fear God. It used to make me happy sometimes to see how simple and touching your faith was. You used to pray to God for all sorts of absurd things, to make a lot of runs in a cricket match or to pass an exam. that you hadn't worked for.

JOHN: Yes, I remember.

MRS. WHARTON: If you've lost your faith, we know it can't be as so many lose it, on purpose, because they've given themselves over to sensuality, and dare not believe in a God whom every action of their lives insults. If you'll only tell us everything, perhaps we can help you.

JOHN: My dear, you'd much better let the matter rest. I should only have to say things that would hurt you all.

MRS. WHARTON: We're willing to take the risk of that. We know you wouldn't hurt us intentionally. Perhaps they're only difficulties that we might be able to explain. And if we're not clever enough perhaps the Vicar can.

[JOHN *shakes his head without speaking.*

SYLVIA: Don't you want to believe in God, John?

JOHN: No.

[*There is a moment's pause.* KATE *comes in to announce* DR. MACFARLANE. *This is a rather eccentric old man, with long white hair, small, with rosy cheeks. He is an old-fashioned country doctor, and wears rather shabby black clothes and carries a rusty silk hat in his hand. There is in him something of the gentleman farmer and something of the apothecary of a former day.*

KATE: Dr. Macfarlane.

[*Exit.*

MRS. WHARTON: Oh! I'd forgotten for the moment. [*With a smile of welcome.*] We've been expecting you.

DR. MACFARLANE: [*Shaking hands with the two ladies.*] I've been busy this morning. [*To* JOHN.] And how are you, John?

JOHN: Sitting up and taking nourishment, thank you.

DR. MACFARLANE: You look none the worse for all your adventures. A little older, perhaps.

MRS. WHARTON: Oh, of course, you've not seen John before.

DR. MACFARLANE: No. My wife saw him yesterday in church, but unfortunately I couldn't go. I had to see a patient.

JOHN: The same patient?

DR. MACFARLANE: I beg your pardon.

JOHN: You've had to see a patient at about eleven every Sunday morning for the last twenty-five years. I was wondering if it was the same one.

DR. MACFARLANE: If it is, I certainly deserve praise for keeping the undertakers at bay so long. [*Going up to the* COLONEL.] And how are you feeling to-day, Colonel?

COLONEL WHARTON: Oh, I'm feeling pretty well, thank you. Have you had a letter from that fellow in Canterbury?

DR. MACFARLANE: Yes.

COLONEL WHARTON: Well, what does he say?

DR. MACFARLANE: You military gentlemen, you want to go so fast.

MRS. WHARTON: Have you brought the letter with you?

DR. MACFARLANE: It's very technical. Saving your presence, I don't think any of you would make head or tail of it. Now, Mrs. Wharton, my dear, shall you and I go for a little stroll in your beautiful garden, and we'll have a talk about this old tyrant.

COLONEL WHARTON: What's the object of that? Evelyn will only tell me everything you've said the moment you're gone. She's never been able to keep anything from me in her life.

DR. MACFARLANE: You must have patience with me. I'm an old man, and I like to do things in my own way.

COLONEL WHARTON: Well, *I'm* no chicken, and I'm not going to stand any of your nonsense. Tell us straight out what the doctor says and be damned to you. I beg your pardon, my dear, but I have to talk to the old fool in the only way he understands.

DR. MACFARLANE: Very rough, isn't he?

JOHN: The gentlest pirate who ever cut a throat.

COLONEL WHARTON: You know, you're a transparent old fraud, Doctor. The moment you came in I saw you had some bad news for me. You were expecting to find Evelyn alone.

DR. MACFARLANE: This is the hour at which all self-respecting retired colonels are reading *The Times* in their study.

MRS. WHARTON: What does Dr. Keller say?

COLONEL WHARTON: I suppose he wants an operation. It's a nuisance but, with God's help, I can go through with it.

DR. MACFARLANE: Well, I suppose you'd have to know sooner or later. Let these young people clear out and we'll talk it all over quietly.

COLONEL WHARTON: Nonsense. John is my son and Sylvia is almost my daughter. What concerns me concerns them, I fancy. Why, you couldn't make more fuss if I'd only got a month to live.

DR. MACFARLANE: [*Hesitating.*] Do you want me to tell you the whole thing now—just like this?

COLONEL WHARTON: Yes. You don't think I'm afraid to hear the worst. Whatever it is, I hope I have the pluck to bear it like a Christian and a gentleman.

[*There is a pause.*

DR. MACFARLANE: You're quite right. I have bad news for you. Dr. Keller confirms my diagnosis. I was pretty sure of it, but I didn't want to believe it. I thought I might be mistaken . . . I'm afraid you're very ill indeed. You must be extremely careful.

MRS. WHARTON: George!

COLONEL WHARTON: Come, come, my dear, don't get in a state. And does he recommend an operation?

DR. MACFARLANE: No.

COLONEL WHARTON: [*Startled.*] Do you mean to say that . . . But I don't feel so bad as all that. Now and then I have attacks of pain, but then . . . you don't mean to say you think I'm going to die? For God's sake tell me the truth.

DR. MACFARLANE: My dear old friend!

COLONEL WHARTON: You mean I've got a fatal disease. Can—can nothing be done?

DR. MACFARLANE: I don't know about that. There's always something that can be done.

COLONEL WHARTON: But a cure, I mean. Can't I be cured?

DR. MACFARLANE: If you want the truth really, then I'm afraid I can hold out no hope of that.

COLONEL WHARTON: How long d'you give me? [*Trying to laugh.*] I suppose you're not going to grudge me a year or two?

DR. MACFARLANE: [*Pretending to take it lightly.*] Oh, you can be quite sure we'll keep you alive as long as we can.

JOHN: You've got a wonderful physique, father. My own impression is that you'll make fools of the doctors and live for another twenty years.

DR. MACFARLANE: Medicine isn't an exact science like surgery. It's a doctor's duty to tell a patient the truth when he asks for it, but if I were a patient I would always take it with a grain of salt.

[*The* COLONEL *looks at him suspiciously.*]

COLONEL WHARTON: You're keeping something from me. If it was only that, why did you want to see Evelyn alone?

DR. MACFARLANE: Well, some people are very nervous about themselves. I wasn't quite sure if you'd better know or not. I thought I'd talk it over with her.

COLONEL WHARTON: Am I in immediate danger of death? For God's sake tell me. It would be cruel to leave me in ignorance.

MRS. WHARTON: Please answer quite frankly, doctor.

DR. MACFARLANE: [*After a pause.*] I think if you have any arrangements to make, it would be wise if you made them soon.

COLONEL WHARTON: Then it's not a question of a year or two even? Is it months or weeks?

DR. MACFARLANE: I don't know. No one can tell.

COLONEL WHARTON: You're treating me like a child. [*With sudden rage.*] Confound you, sir, I order you to tell me.

DR. MACFARLANE: It may be at any time.

COLONEL WHARTON: [*With a sudden cry of terror.*] Evelyn! Evelyn!

MRS. WHARTON: Oh, my dear! My dear husband!
[*She takes him in her arms as though to protect him.*]

DR. MACFARLANE: Why did you force me to tell you?

COLONEL WHARTON: [*In a terrified whisper.*] Oh, Evelyn! Evelyn!

MRS. WHARTON: [*To the others.*] Please go.

JOHN: [*To* SYLVIA.] Come. They want to be alone. Dr. Macfarlane, will you come into the garden for a few minutes?

DR. MACFARLANE: Of course I will. Of course.

> [*They go out.* COLONEL *and* MRS. WHARTON *are left alone. For a moment they are silent.*

MRS. WHARTON: Perhaps it isn't true, my dear.

COLONEL WHARTON: It's true. I know it's true now.

MRS. WHARTON: Oh, it's so hard. I wish it were I instead. I'd be so glad to take your place, darling.

COLONEL WHARTON: We've been so happy together, Evelyn.

MRS. WHARTON: We have very much to be grateful for.

COLONEL WHARTON: Oh, Evelyn, what shall I do?

MRS. WHARTON: Oh, my dear, I'm so sorry for you. I'm so dreadfully sorry . . . I think you're very brave. If I'd been told like that I—I should have broken down.

COLONEL WHARTON: It was so unexpected.

MRS. WHARTON: [*Trying to comfort him.*] I'm thankful that your faith has always been so bright and clear. What a comfort that is now, darling, what an immense consolation! [*She draws him more closely to her.*] You're throwing aside these poor rags of mortality to put on a heavenly raiment. It is what we've always kept in our minds, isn't it? that this brief life is only a place of passage to the mansions of our dear Father. [*She feels the dismay in his heart and she strives to give him courage.*] You've never hesitated at the call of an earthly leader. You're a good soldier; it's a Heavenly Leader that's calling you now. Christ is holding out His loving arms to you.

COLONEL WHARTON: Evelyn—I don't want to die.

END OF THE FIRST ACT

THE SECOND ACT

The Scene is the same as in the preceding Act.
Two days have passed. It is Wednesday afternoon.

MRS. WHARTON *is sitting by a little table, looking reflectively*
in front of her. On the table is a work-basket, and by the
side of this a baby's shirt that she is making. A fire is alight
in the grate. After a minute, JOHN *comes in. She looks up*
at him with a pleasant smile. He goes to her and puts his
hand on her shoulder. She gently pats his hand.

JOHN: Are you idling, mother? It's not often I catch you
giving the devil an opportunity.

MRS. WHARTON: Isn't it wicked of me?

JOHN: What is this you're up to? What in Heaven's name
are you making a baby's shirt for? Hang it all, I'm
not married yet.

MRS. WHARTON: [*Pretending to be a little shocked.*] Don't be
naughty, John. It's for poor Annie Black's baby.

JOHN: Who's she?

MRS. WHARTON: She was engaged to Edward Driffield, the
carpenter's second man, and they were going to be
married next time he came home on leave. He's been
killed, and she's expecting a baby.

JOHN: Poor thing.

MRS. WHARTON: The Pooles are looking after her. You see,
she had nowhere to go, and they didn't want her to
have to go to the Workhouse, so Mrs. Poole has taken
her in at the Vicarage. And I said I'd make all the
baby's things.

JOHN: [*Affectionately.*] You're a nice old mother.

MRS. WHARTON: Don't you think it was good of the
Pooles?

JOHN: Yes, charming.

MRS. WHARTON: They're coming here this afternoon, John. I wanted the Vicar to see your father. . . . I haven't told your father they're coming.

JOHN: Haven't you?

MRS. WHARTON: He's rather sensitive just now. It's quite natural, isn't it? And I didn't know exactly how he'd take it. I thought if Mrs. Poole came too it would look as though it were just a friendly visit. And perhaps the Vicar will have an opportunity to say a few words to your father.

JOHN: [*Smiling.*] I take it that you want me to help you to leave them alone together.

MRS. WHARTON: I hate doing anything underhand, John, but I think it would help your father so much if he could have a little private talk with the Vicar.

JOHN: Why didn't you suggest it to him?

MRS. WHARTON: I didn't like to. I was afraid he'd be vexed. I thought he'd suggest it himself.

JOHN: [*Very tenderly.*] Don't distress yourself, mother.

MRS. WHARTON: I'm trying not to think of it, John. My only hope is that the end may come without suffering.

JOHN: I wasn't thinking of that.

MRS. WHARTON: [*After a moment's pause.*] I don't know what you mean, John.

JOHN: Yes, you do. You only have to look in father's face.

MRS. WHARTON: I really don't understand. [*Almost vehemently.*] You're wrong, John. He suffers much more pain than you think. That's what gives him that look.

JOHN: [*Gravely.*] It's fear that's in his face, mother, the fear of death. You know it just as well as I do.

MRS. WHARTON: [*With dismay.*] I was so hoping that no one would know but me. It tears my heart. And I can do nothing. And he's so strange. Sometimes he looks at me almost as though I were his enemy.

JOHN: He doesn't want to die, does he? At the bottom of his heart is envy because you can go on living.

MRS. WHARTON: Have you noticed that? I tried not to see it.

JOHN: Don't be angry with him or disappointed. You know, it's a hard thing to die for all of us. Generally one's vitality is lowered so that life seems rather a burden, and it's not very hard then to make a seemly end. But poor father's got something much more difficult to face.

MRS. WHARTON: He's been supported all his life by his confidence in the great truths of our religion. Oh, John, it's so dreadful that just at this moment, when he must put them all to the test, he should falter. It's almost a betrayal of the God who loves him.

JOHN: My dear, you can't imagine that God won't understand? What do these last weeks matter beside a life that has been cheerful and innocent, devout, unselfish, and dutiful? We were talking about it the other day, don't you remember? And I claimed that a man should be judged by what he believed and did in the heyday of his strength, and not by what was wrung from him in a moment of anguish. Pray that God may give my father courage and resignation.

MRS. WHARTON: How can you ask me to pray, John, when you don't believe in God?

JOHN: Pray all the same, my dear, and for me too.

MRS. WHARTON: I don't suppose I shall survive your father very long, dear. Husbands and wives who've been so much to one another as we have don't often make a very good job of separation. I'm so glad to think that you'll have Sylvia.

JOHN: Sylvia's a good girl, isn't she?

MRS. WHARTON: When you were away I was dreadfully

anxious on my own account, of course, but I was anxious on hers too. She's had a very hard time with her mother, and there's been dreadfully little money, only their pensions; if anything had happened to you, when her mother died she would have had practically nothing. You've been engaged so long and she's not very young any more. It's not likely that anyone else would have wanted to marry her.

JOHN: Mother darling, you're being terribly sentimental now.

MRS. WHARTON: [*With comic indignation.*] I'm not, John. You don't know what it is for a penniless woman to be quite alone in the world when she's lost her youth.

JOHN: Yes, I do. But the tears needn't come into your eyes, because Sylvia and I are going to be married and her future is quite adequately provided for.

MRS. WHARTON: She's the only girl I've ever known that I could bear to think of your marrying.

JOHN: Well, as she's the only girl I ever knew that I could bear to marry, we're both quite satisfied.

[KATE *enters, followed by* MRS. LITTLEWOOD.

KATE: Mrs. Littlewood.

[*Exit* KATE.

MRS. LITTLEWOOD: [*Kissing* MRS. WHARTON.] How do you do?

MRS. WHARTON: How are you, my dear?

MRS. LITTLEWOOD: [*To* JOHN.] I brought you a wedding present, John.

[*She hands him a small case in which is a pearl pin.*

JOHN: Oh, I say, that is splendid of you. Just look, mother. Isn't it a ripper?

MRS. LITTLEWOOD: It was Archie's, you know. He always used to be so proud of it.

JOHN: It's awfully good of you to give me something that belonged to him.

MRS. WHARTON: That is nice of you, Charlotte.

MRS. LITTLEWOOD: Nonsense. It wasn't any use to me any more. I thought it much better that John should have it than that it should lie in a safe. They tell me pearls go yellow if they're not worn.

MRS. WHARTON: John, dear, go and smoke a cigarette in the garden. I want to have a chat with Mrs. Littlewood.

JOHN: All right, mother.

[*He goes out.*

MRS. LITTLEWOOD: Do you know that I'm thinking of letting my house? I only kept it so that the boys should have a home to come to when they had a holiday, and now that they're both dead, I think I shall find it more amusing to live in London. I shall join a bridge club.

MRS. WHARTON: Charlotte, what does it mean? Why do you talk like that?

MRS. LITTLEWOOD: My dear, why shouldn't I join a bridge club? [*With a smile.*] At my age it's surely quite respectable.

MRS. WHARTON: I'm bewildered. Don't you want me to talk of your boys?

MRS. LITTLEWOOD: [*Dryly.*] If you feel you really must pour out your sympathy, you may, but I don't know that I particularly want it.

MRS. WHARTON: No one can understand you. You've behaved so strangely since you came back from France . . . I think it was dreadful of you to go to the theatre when the poor lad was hardly cold in his grave. You seem to think of nothing but bridge.

MRS. LITTLEWOOD: I suppose different people take things in different ways.

MRS. WHARTON: I wonder if you're quite in your right mind.

MRS. LITTLEWOOD: [*Somewhat amused.*] Yes, I saw you wondered that.

MRS. WHARTON: If you only knew how eager I am to help you. But you won't let me come near you. We've known one another for more than thirty years, Charlotte. Why do you put up a stone wall between us?

MRS. LITTLEWOOD: [*Gently, as though she were talking to a child.*] My dear, don't worry your kind heart. If I wanted your help I would come to you at once. But I don't. I really don't.

[MRS. WHARTON *hears her husband's step on the stairs.*

MRS. WHARTON: Here is George. [*Going to the window.*] You can come in when you want to, John.

[*The* COLONEL *comes into the room. His face is a little whiter than it was two days ago, and there is in his eyes every now and then a haunted look.*

MRS. WHARTON: Charlotte Littlewood is here, George.

COLONEL WHARTON: So I see. How do you do?

MRS. LITTLEWOOD: You're not looking quite up to the mark to-day, Colonel.

COLONEL WHARTON: That's a cheering thing to say to a man. I'm feeling pretty well.

MRS. WHARTON: I was thinking he was looking much better the last day or two.

COLONEL WHARTON: I presume it's not on my account that you've lit the fire on a day like this.

MRS. WHARTON: No, I feel a little chilly. You always forget that I'm not as young as I was, George.

[*The* COLONEL *sits down in an armchair and* MRS. WHARTON *takes a couple of cushions.*

MRS. WHARTON: Let me put them behind you, darling.

COLONEL WHARTON: For goodness' sake don't fuss me, Evelyn. If I want cushions I'm perfectly capable of getting them for myself.

[JOHN *enters with* SYLVIA *and hears the last two speeches.*

JOHN: Come, come, father, you mustn't spoil mother. She's waited on us both for thirty years. Don't let her get into bad habits at her time of life.

MRS. WHARTON: Oh, Sylvia, we didn't expect to see you to-day. You said you'd be too busy.

SYLVIA: I felt I must just look in and see how you all were.
[*The* COLONEL *gives her a suspicious look. She kisses* MRS. WHARTON *and* MRS. LITTLEWOOD *and the* COLONEL.

JOHN: [*Showing* SYLVIA *the pearl pin.*] Look what Mrs. Littlewood has given me. Makes it worth while being married, doesn't it?

SYLVIA: Oh, how lovely!

MRS. LITTLEWOOD: You'll find a little present waiting for you when you get home.

SYLVIA: How exciting! I shall run all the way back.

MRS. WHARTON: Now you're here you'd better stay to tea, darling.

SYLVIA: I really can't. I've got so much to do at home.

JOHN: Nonsense. You've got nothing to do at all. We're not going to dream of letting you go.

SYLVIA: Remember that you'll have me always from to-morrow on. Don't you think you could well spare me to-day?

JOHN: No.

SYLVIA: Tiresome creature. Though I must say it's rather pleasing.

COLONEL WHARTON: I never saw two young people who were so thoroughly satisfied with one another as you are.

JOHN: [*Putting his arm round* SYLVIA'S *waist.*] But I'm not in the least satisfied with Sylvia. I should like her to have jet-black hair and eyes like sloes.

SYLVIA: What are sloes, idiot?

N

JOHN: I don't know, but I've read about them from my youth up.

SYLVIA: Oh, Colonel, d'you know that on my way here through the fields, I actually saw a rabbit?

JOHN: I hear there's absolutely nothing on the place now, father.

COLONEL WHARTON: No, the vermin's been allowed to increase so. There are one or two cock pheasants round the house and that's about all. I don't know what next season—but after all, I needn't worry myself about next season. That'll be your trouble, John.

JOHN: I wish I had as much chance of getting a shot at those cock pheasants as you have.

COLONEL WHARTON: By George, I wish I were twenty years younger. I'd take my chance of being shot by a German. It's a bit better than dying like a rat in a trap.

[KATE *enters to announce the* VICAR *and* MRS. POOLE.

KATE: Mr. and Mrs. Poole.

[*Exit.*

MRS. WHARTON: How do you do?

[*There are general greetings. The* COLONEL *looks at them and from them to his wife, suspiciously. The* POOLES *are rather cold with* MRS. LITTLEWOOD.

COLONEL WHARTON: How do you do? It's good of you to have come. Sit down.

MRS. POOLE: Well, Sylvia, are you all ready for to-morrow?

SYLVIA: More or less.

MRS. POOLE: We thought you might intend to postpone the wedding for a few days.

COLONEL WHARTON: They've waited long enough. Why should they wish to do that?

SYLVIA: [*Hastily.*] I told Mrs. Poole yesterday that I didn't think I could possibly get everything arranged by to-morrow.

COLONEL WHARTON: I see that my wife has told you that I'm not very well.

MRS. POOLE: Oh, aren't you, Colonel? I'm so sorry to hear that.

VICAR: She told me this morning after Communion that you weren't quite up to the mark these days.

COLONEL WHARTON: I remember in Egypt, when a horse or a mule sickened, the vultures used to gather round out of an empty sky. Most remarkable.

MRS. WHARTON: George, what are you saying?

COLONEL WHARTON: [*With a bitter chuckle.*] Did Evelyn ask you to come and minister to me?

VICAR: It's not very unnatural that when I hear you're ill I should like to come and see you. And, of course, it does happen to be one of the duties of my office.

COLONEL WHARTON: I don't know why Evelyn should think I want to be molly-coddled out of the world like an old woman. I've faced death before. I don't suppose anyone wants to die before he must, but when my time comes I hope to face it like a gentleman and a soldier.

JOHN: Oh, that I should live to hear my own father talking through his hat. Don't you believe a word those rotten old doctors say. You'll live to bully your devoted family for another twenty years.

COLONEL WHARTON: Don't talk nonsense to me, John. You all treat me like a child. No one must cross me. I must be petted and spoilt and amused and humoured. God damn it, you never let me forget it for a minute.

MRS. WHARTON: Shall we go for a little turn in the garden? The sun is out now.

COLONEL WHARTON: If you like. I shall stay here. I'm chilly.

MRS. WHARTON: A stroll would do you good, George. The Vicar was asking how the new Buff Orpingtons were getting on.

COLONEL WHARTON: [*With a chuckle.*] You're very transparent, my poor Evelyn. When I want to have a chat with the Vicar I'll let him know.

MRS. LITTLEWOOD: [*Who has been watching the scene with some amusement.*] Why don't you have a game of piquet with me, Colonel?

COLONEL WHARTON: I haven't played piquet for years. I will with pleasure. Where are the cards, Evelyn?

MRS. WHARTON: I'll get them for you.

> [*She gets cards from a drawer, and puts them on the card table. The* COLONEL *sits down at the table and sorts the piquet cards out of the pack.*

VICAR: I called on you on Monday, Mrs. Littlewood.

MRS. LITTLEWOOD: So I heard.

VICAR: I was told you were not at home. As I walked away it was impossible for me not to see that you were in your garden.

MRS. LITTLEWOOD: It's inadequately protected from the road.

VICAR: I was rather hurt. I'm not aware that there's been anything in my behaviour since I came here to justify you in treating me with discourtesy. Our relations have always been more than cordial.

MRS. LITTLEWOOD: I didn't wish to see you.

VICAR: So much as that I had the intelligence to infer. But I felt it my duty not to allow pique to interfere with the due discharge of my office. I had various things to say to you which I thought you should hear, so yesterday I called again, and again was told you were out.

MRS. LITTLEWOOD: [*Coolly.*] I didn't wish to see you.

VICAR: May I ask why?

MRS. LITTLEWOOD: Well, I suppose you wanted to talk about my boy. I didn't think your conversation could give him back to me.

VICAR: Don't you think I could have helped you to bear your loss? I think I could have found in my heart words to persuade you to resignation. I might at least have offered you my sympathy.

MRS. LITTLEWOOD: I'm sorry to seem ungracious, but I don't want your sympathy.

VICAR: Your attitude amazes me.

MRS. POOLE: If we didn't all know how devoted you were to your sons, one might really think you were indifferent to their loss.

MRS. LITTLEWOOD: [*Reflectively.*] No, I'm not exactly indifferent.

VICAR: Since you won't see me alone, I must say things to you here and now which I should rather have kept for your private ear. I have a right to remonstrate with you because your behaviour is a scandal to my parish.

MRS. LITTLEWOOD: [*With a smile.*] Oh, I beg your pardon. I thought it was my welfare you were concerned with. If it's that of the parish, pray say anything you like.

VICAR: [*Flushing, but not to be put off.*] I think it was horrible to go to a music-hall on the very day you had returned from your son's grave in France. But that was in London, and you outraged nobody but yourself. What you do here is different. This is a very small place, and it's shameful that you should give parties and go about from house to house playing cards.

MRS. POOLE: It seems so heartless not to wear mourning.

JOHN: [*Rather flippantly, to prevent the conversation from growing too awkward.*] Why? I certainly should hate anyone to wear mourning for me.

VICAR: You give all and sundry the impression that you're perfectly callous. What influence do you think such a thing may have on these young fellows in the village who have to risk their lives with all the other brave lads at the Front? You take from them the comfort that we at home love them and if they fall will hold their memories gratefully in our hearts for ever.

MRS. LITTLEWOOD: I shouldn't have thought the eccentricity of one old woman could matter very much to anyone.

[*She pauses and looks out into the open for a moment, and then makes up her mind to speak. She speaks quite quietly, almost to herself.*

When they sent for me and I went over to France I wasn't very anxious, because I knew that God, who had taken my eldest son, would leave my second. You see, he was the only one I had left. And when I got there and found he was dead—I suddenly felt that it didn't matter.

MRS. WHARTON: My dear, what do you mean? How can you say such a thing?

JOHN: Don't, mother. Let her go on.

MRS. LITTLEWOOD: I didn't feel that anything very much mattered. It's difficult to explain exactly what I mean. I feel that I have nothing more to do with the world and the world has nothing more to do with me. So far as I'm concerned it's a failure. You know I wasn't very happy in my married life, but I loved my two sons, and they made everything worth while, and now they're gone. Let others take up the—the adventure. I step aside.

MRS. WHARTON: You've suffered too much, my dear.

MRS. LITTLEWOOD: No, the strange thing is that I haven't suffered very much. Don't you know how sometimes one has a horrid dream and knows one's only dreaming all the time? [*To the* VICAR, *with the same good temper, almost amused.*] You're surprised that I should go to the theatre. Why? To me, it's no more unreal a spectacle than life. Life does seem to me just like a play now. I can't take it very seriously. I feel strangely detached. I have no ill-feeling for my fellow-creatures, but you don't seem very real to me or very important. Why shouldn't I play bridge with you?

VICAR: Oh, but, my dear, my dear, there's one reality that you can never escape from. There's God.

[*A flash passes behind the old woman's eyes. She rises and puts out her hand as though to ward off a blow.*

MRS. LITTLEWOOD: I don't think we'll talk about God if you please. I prefer to play piquet.

[*She sits down at the table at which the* COLONEL *has already taken his seat.*

COLONEL WHARTON: Do you play four hands or six to the game?

MRS. LITTLEWOOD: Four—and double the first and last. It makes it more exciting.

COLONEL WHARTON: Shall we cut for deal?

MRS. LITTLEWOOD: [*Cutting.*] You're not likely to beat that.

COLONEL WHARTON: I suppose in the Vicar's presence we daren't play for money?

MRS. LITTLEWOOD: We'll pretend he's not here. Will a shilling a hundred suit you?

COLONEL WHARTON: I don't think that'll break either of us.

[KATE *enters, followed by* DR. MACFARLANE.

KATE: Dr. Macfarlane.

[*Exit.*

DR. MACFARLANE: How d'you do?

MRS. WHARTON: [*Shaking hands with him.*] So nice of you to come in.

DR. MACFARLANE: How is the Colonel to-day?

COLONEL WHARTON: Playing piquet.

JOHN: You're coming to-morrow, aren't you, Doctor?

DR. MACFARLANE: Of course I am. I brought you both

into the world. I have almost a personal interest in seeing you made one flesh.

VICAR: [*Jovially.*] It's many a long day since you've been inside a church, Doctor.

DR. MACFARLANE: Since you clerical gentlemen left off threatening me with eternal flames I feel justified in following my own inclinations in the matter.

VICAR: [*Chaffing him.*] But we still believe in annihilation.

DR. MACFARLANE: I'm willing to take my chance of that. It has no terrors for a man who's not had a holiday for twenty years.

VICAR: You're not an irreligious man. I don't know why you don't come to church.

DR. MACFARLANE: Shall I tell you? Because after repeated experiment I've reached the conclusion that I'm not a whit the better for it.

JOHN: You'll have to give him up, Vicar. He's a stubborn old thing. He takes advantage of the fact that he's the only doctor within ten miles who won't kill you so long as he can make seven and sixpence a visit by keeping you alive.

COLONEL WHARTON: Do you mean to say that our Church doesn't believe any longer in eternal punishment?

JOHN: Oh, father, hell has always left me perfectly cold. You and I are quite safe. You see, mother would never be happy in Heaven without us, and God couldn't refuse her anything she asked.

MRS. WHARTON: [*Affectionately.*] John, what nonsense you talk.

MRS. POOLE: I sometimes think the modern Church has been very rash in surrendering a belief which has the authority of Our Lord himself. How many sinners have been brought to repentance by the fear of everlasting punishment!

JOHN: That rather suggests calling down fire from Heaven to light a cigar.

MRS. POOLE: That may be funny, but I don't see the point of it.

JOHN: [*Good-humouredly.*] Well, I should have thought it hardly required anything so tremendous as eternity to deal with human wickedness. I suppose sin is due to a man's character, which he can't help, or to his ignorance, for which he isn't to blame.

VICAR: In fact, to your mind sin is all moonshine.

JOHN: I think it a pity that Christianity has laid so much stress on it. We assert in church that we're miserable sinners, but I don't think we mean it, and what's more, I don't think we are.

MRS. POOLE: We are conceived in sin, and sin is part of our inheritance. Why did Christ die if not to atone for the sin of men?

JOHN: In war one gets to know very intimately all sorts of queer people. I don't suppose I shall ever know any men so well as I knew the men in my company. They were honest and brave and cheerful, unselfish, good fellows; perhaps they swore a good deal, and they got drunk if they had the chance, and they had the glad eye for a pretty girl. But do you think they were sinners for that? I don't.

VICAR: Look in your own heart and say if you are not conscious of grievous, terrible sin.

JOHN: Frankly, I'm not.

VICAR: Do you mean to say that you have nothing to reproach yourself with?

JOHN: I've done a certain number of things which I think were rather foolish, but I can't think of anything that I'm particularly ashamed of.

VICAR: Do you mean to tell me that you've always been perfectly chaste?

N*

JOHN: I'm normal and healthy. I've been no more chaste than any other man of my age.

VICAR: And isn't that sin?

JOHN: I don't think so. I think it's human nature.

VICAR: We're arguing at cross-purposes. If when you say "white" you mean what the rest of the world calls "black," all words are futile.

JOHN: [*With a smile.*] The singular thing is that if I'd answered your question with a "yes," you would probably have thought me a liar or a fool.

VICAR: This terrible condition of humanity, which seems to cry out against the very idea either of man's dignity, or of God's justice, has but one explanation, and that is sin.

JOHN: You're referring to the war? It needs some explaining, doesn't it?

VICAR: Every Christian must have asked himself why God allows the infamous horror of war. I'm told the padres are constantly being asked by the brave lads at the Front why the Almighty allows it to continue. I can't blame anyone for being puzzled. I've wrestled with the question long and anxiously . . . I can't believe that God would leave His children to suffer without a clue to His intention.

MRS. POOLE: The ways of God are inscrutable. How can we tell what are the aims of the eternal? We only know that they are good.

JOHN: Meanwhile men are being killed like flies, their wives and mothers are left desolate, and their children fatherless.

VICAR: You mustn't forget exactly what is meant by "Almighty." It means not so much able to do all things as powerful over all things.

JOHN: Ah, the padre of my regiment told me that. I may be very stupid, but I think the distinction rather fine.

For the plain man the difficulty remains. Either God can't stop the war even if He wants to, or He can stop it and won't.

MRS. POOLE: In my opinion there can be no hesitation. It is written: "Not a sparrow shall fall on the ground without your Father."

VICAR: Remember that we have free will and God makes use of our free will to punish us and to teach us and to make us more worthy of His grace and mercy. Man, born in sin, justly brought this long-drawn disaster on himself as surely as Adam brought on himself the divine punishment which we all inherit.

JOHN: If I saw two small boys fighting I'd separate them, even though one was a lazy little beggar and the other had stolen Farmer Giles' apples. I wouldn't sit by and let them seriously hurt one another so that they should be better boys in future.

MRS. POOLE: But you speak as though all this suffering must be useless. We all know how suffering can purify and elevate. I've seen it myself over and over again.

DR. MACFARLANE: People say that. They're generally thinking of elderly ladies in comfortable circumstances who with the aid of a very good doctor show a becoming resignation in a chronic disease.

JOHN: I should like some of those people who talk about the purifying influence of suffering to have a mouthful of gas and see how they liked it.

VICAR: The war is terrible. Its cruelty is terrible. The suffering it has caused is terrible. There is only one explanation for it; and that is the loving kindness and the infinite mercy of our heavenly Father.

JOHN: Can you bring yourself to believe that?

VICAR: We were given over to drunkenness and lust, to selfishness and flippancy and pride. It needed this tremendous trial to purify us. It will be a nobler England that comes out of the furnace. Oh, I pray to God that all this blood may wash our souls clean so that we may once more be found worthy in His sight.

MRS. POOLE: Amen.

JOHN: You must evidently know much more about it than I do. When the men in my company did things I thought were wrong I used to jolly them a bit. I fancy I got better results than if I'd bashed them on the head with a sledge-hammer.

VICAR: Sin began with the beginning of the human story and has continued through all its course. The motive of the divine redemption lies in the fact that men, though created for so lofty a purpose, have plunged so deep into sin and have so deeply defaced in themselves the image of God, that only the self-sacrificing act of God in redeeming them can raise them from ruin.

JOHN: I wish you'd been a company-commander and had seen how gaily a man can give his life for his friend.

VICAR: But I know, my dear boy, I know. And do you think God will be unmindful of their sacrifice? I pray and believe that they will find mercy in His sight. I am sure He is more ready to pardon than to punish. After all, our Lord came to call sinners to repentance, and who should know better than the Ministers of God that to err is human, to forgive, divine?

> [*The piquet players have played their game with a certain distraction, and during the last few speeches have made no more pretence of playing at all.* MRS. LITTLEWOOD *has listened attentively. Now she puts down her cards, gets up, and walks up to the* VICAR.

MRS. LITTLEWOOD: And who is going to forgive God?

MRS. WHARTON: [*With horror.*] Charlotte!

VICAR: [*With grave disapproval.*] Don't you think that is rather blasphemous?

MRS. LITTLEWOOD: [*Quietly and deliberately at first, but with ever-increasing excitement.*] Ever since I was a child I've served God with all my might, and with all my heart, and with all my soul. I've tried always to lead my life in accordance with His will. I never forgot that I was as nothing in His sight. I've been weak and sinful, but I've tried to do my duty.

MRS. WHARTON: Yes, dear, you've been an example to us all.

MRS. LITTLEWOOD: [*Taking no notice.*] Honestly, I've done everything I could that I thought was pleasing in His sight. I've praised Him and magnified His name. You've heard that my husband deserted me when I'd borne him two children, and I was left alone. I brought them up to be honest, upright and God-fearing men. When God took my eldest son I wept, but I turned to the Lord and said: "Thy will be done." He was a soldier, and he took his chance, and he died in a good cause.

VICAR: A great and a good cause.

MRS. LITTLEWOOD: But why did God take my second? He was the only one I had left, the only comfort of my old age, my only joy, the only thing I had to prevent me from seeing that my life had been wasted and it would have been better if I had never been born. I haven't deserved that. When a horse has served me long and faithfully till he's too old to work, I have the right to send him to the knacker's yard, but I don't, I put him out to grass. I wouldn't treat a dog as my Father has treated me. I've been cheated. You say that God will forgive us our sins, but who is going to forgive God? Not I. Never. Never!

[*In a height of frenzy she rushes out into the garden. There is silence in the room.*

MRS. WHARTON: Don't be angry with her, Vicar. She's beside herself with grief.

VICAR: She'll come back. She's like a petulant child that has been thwarted for its good. It cries and stamps, but in a little while it throws itself into its mother's arms, and begs, all tears, for forgiveness.

MRS. POOLE: [*With a little sigh of relief.*] I knew you'd take it like that, Norman. You're so tolerant and broadminded.

VICAR: I think I see my way to help her, poor soul.

JOHN: I wonder how. Your only explanation of evil is sin. I daresay you can get people to acknowledge that they've deserved their own suffering. But you'll never prevent them from being revolted at the suffering of others. Why is evil permitted in the world by an all-good God?

VICAR: I can hardly hope that any answer of mine will satisfy you. By God's grace I am a Christian. You are an atheist.

[*There is a moment's embarrassment.* JOHN *realises that his mother or* SYLVIA *has repeated what he has said.*

JOHN: That suggests a very dogmatic attitude. I don't see how anyone can positively assert that there is no God. It would be as reasonable as to assert that there's nothing on the other side of a wall that you can't look over.

VICAR: Do you believe in God?

JOHN: I don't think it's quite your business to ask me. [*With a smile.*] Wasn't it St. Paul who said: "Be not zealous overmuch."

VICAR: You can't be unaware that by certain statements of yours the other day you gave the greatest pain to those nearest and dearest to you.

SYLVIA: What you said made me very unhappy, John. I didn't know what to do. I went to the Vicar and asked his advice.

JOHN: Don't you think that a man's belief is his own affair? I don't want to interfere with other people's. Why can't they leave me quietly to mine?

SYLVIA: It can't be entirely your affair, John. You and I propose to be married to-morrow. It's only reasonable that I should know exactly how you stand in a matter that concerns me so closely.

JOHN: I hadn't thought of that. I daresay there's something in what you say. I'm willing to do my best to explain to you and to father and mother. But I really think we needn't drag strangers in.

MRS. WHARTON: I think it would be much better if you would talk with the Vicar, John. We don't pretend to be very clever, and it wouldn't mean much if you asked us questions that we couldn't answer.

VICAR: When you're ill you send for a doctor, he prescribes for you, and you get well.

JOHN: [*With a smile.*] What do you think of that, doctor?

DR. MACFARLANE: It is an idea that we do our little best to spread about the world.

VICAR: Anyhow, you take a doctor's advice and you don't argue with him. Why? Because he's an expert, and you presume that he knows his business. Why should the science of the immortal soul be a less complicated affair than the science of the perishable body?

MRS. WHARTON: Look upon us as very silly, old-fashioned people, and be kind to us. If various doubts are troubling you, put them frankly before the Vicar. Perhaps he can help you.

VICAR: [*Sincerely.*] Believe me, I'll do everything in my power.

MRS. WHARTON: And if he can convince you that you were wrong, I know you too well to dream that pride would stop you from confessing it. It would give us such heartfelt joy, my dear, if you could believe again as you did when you were a little child and used to say your prayers kneeling on my lap.

VICAR: I really think I can help you. Won't you forget that I'm a stranger and let me try?

DR. MACFARLANE: Perhaps you'd like me to leave you. I was only waiting till the Colonel had finished his game so that I might take him upstairs and have a look at him. But I can come back later.

JOHN: I don't mind your staying at all. [*To the* VICAR.] What is it you wish to ask me?

VICAR: Do you believe in the God in whose name you were baptized into the Church?

JOHN: No!

VICAR: That at all events is frank and honest. But aren't you a little out of date? One of the most gratifying occurrences of recent years has been the revival of belief among thoughtful men.

JOHN: I should have thought it was a revival of rhetoric rather than of religion. I'm not enormously impressed by the cultured journalist who uses God to balance a sentence or adorn a phrase.

VICAR: But it hasn't only been among educated men. Not the least remarkable thing about the war has been the return of our brave lads at the Front to the faith which so many of us thought they had forgotten. What is your explanation of that?

JOHN: Fear with the most part. Perplexity with the rest.

VICAR: Don't you think it very rash to reject a belief that all the ablest men in the world have held since the dawn of history?

JOHN: When you're dealing with a belief, neither the number nor the ability of those who hold it makes it a certainty. Only proof can do that.

MRS. POOLE: Are you quite sure that at the bottom of your heart it's not conceit that makes you think differently from the rest of us?

VICAR: No, my dear, let us not ascribe unworthy motives to our antagonist.

JOHN: [*Smiling.*] At all events, not yet.

VICAR: What makes you think that the existence of God can't be proved?

JOHN: I suppose at this time of day people wouldn't still be proving it if proof were possible.

VICAR: My dear fellow, the fact that there is no people on the face of the earth, however barbarous and degraded, without some belief in God, is the most conclusive proof you can want.

JOHN: What of? It's conclusive proof that the desire for His existence is universal. It's not proof that the desire is fulfilled.

VICAR: I see you have the usual Rationalistic arguments at your fingers' ends. Believe me, they're old friends, and if I've answered them once I've answered them a thousand times.

JOHN: And have you ever convinced anyone who wasn't convinced before?

VICAR: I can't make the blind to see, you know.

JOHN: I wonder that hasn't suggested to you a very obvious conclusion.

VICAR: What?

JOHN: Why, that arguments are futile. Think for a minute. You don't believe in God for any of the reasons that are given for His existence. You believe in Him because with all your heart you *feel* that He exists. No argument can ever touch that feeling. The heart is independent of logic and its rules.

VICAR: I daresay there's something in what you say.

JOHN: Well, it's the same with me. If you ask me why I don't believe in the existence of God I suppose I can give you a certain number of reasons, but the real one, the one that gives all the others their force, is that I feel it in my heart.

VICAR: What is the cause of your feeling?

JOHN: I'm sure you'll think it very insufficient. I had a friend and he was killed.

VICAR: I'm afraid one must be prepared to lose one's friends in a war like this.

JOHN: I daresay it's very silly and sentimental of me. One gets used to one's pals dying. Someone says to you: "So-and-So's knocked out." And you answer: "Is he really? Poor chap." And you don't think very much more about it. Robbie Harrison wasn't quite an ordinary man.

MRS. WHARTON: I was afraid you'd feel his death very much. You never mentioned it in your letters. I felt it was because you couldn't bear to speak of it.

JOHN: He was one of those lucky beggars who do everything a little better than anybody else. He was clever and awfully nice-looking and amusing. I never knew anyone who loved life so much as he did.

MRS. WHARTON: Yes, I remember his saying to me once: "Isn't it ripping to be alive?"

JOHN: But there was something more in him than that. He had one quality which was rather out of the ordinary. It's difficult to explain what it was like. It seemed to shine about him like a mellow light. It was like the jolly feeling of the country in May. And do you know what it was? Goodness. Just goodness. He was the sort of man that I should like to be.

MRS. WHARTON: He was a dear.

JOHN: I was awfully excited when war was declared. I was in India at the time. I moved heaven and earth to get out to the Front. I thought war the noblest sport in the world. I found it a dreary, muddy, dirty, stinking, bloody business. And I suppose Robbie's death was the last straw. It seemed so unjust. I don't know that it was grief so much that I felt as indignation. I was revolted by all the horror and pain and suffering.

MRS. POOLE: You must have seen some dreadful things.

JOHN: Perhaps it's Christianity that has shown us the possibility of a higher morality than Christianity teaches. I daresay I'm quite wrong. I can only tell you that all that's moral in my soul revolts at the thought of a God who can permit the monstrous iniquity of war. I can't believe that there is a God in heaven.

VICAR: But do you realise that if there isn't, the world is meaningless?

JOHN: That may be. But if there is it's infamous.

VICAR: What have you got to put in the place of religion? What answer can you give to the riddle of the universe?

JOHN: I may think your answer wrong and yet have no better one to put in its place.

VICAR: Have you nothing to tell us at all when we ask you why man is here and what is his destiny? You are like a rudderless ship in a stormy sea.

JOHN: I suppose the human race has arisen under the influence of conditions which are part of the earth's history, and under the influence of other conditions it will come to an end. I don't see that there is any more meaning in life than in the statement that two and two are four.

SYLVIA: [*With suppressed passion.*] Then you think that all our efforts and struggles, our pain and sorrow, our aims, are senseless?

JOHN: Do you remember our going to the Russian ballet before the war? I've never forgotten a certain gesture of one of the dancers. It was an attitude she held for an instant, in the air; it was the most lovely thing I ever saw in my life; you felt it could only have been achieved by infinite labour, and the fact that it was so fleeting, like the shadow of a bird flying over a river, made it all the more wonderful. I've often thought of it since, and it has seemed to me a very good symbol of life.

SYLVIA: John, you can't be serious.

JOHN: I'll tell you what I mean. Life seems to me like a huge jig-saw puzzle that doesn't make any picture, but if we like we can make little patterns, as it were, out of the pieces.

SYLVIA: What is the use of that?

JOHN: There's no use, and no need. It's merely something we can do for our own satisfaction. Pain and sorrow are some of the pieces that we have to deal with. By making the most of all our faculties, by using all our opportunities, out of the manifold events of life, our deeds, our feelings, our thoughts, we can make a design which is intricate, dignified, and beautiful. And death at one stroke completes and destroys it.

[*There is a moment's silence.*

MRS. POOLE: I wonder why you're coming to church to-morrow to be married?

JOHN: [*With a smile.*] I think Sylvia would be outraged at the thought of being married in a registry office.

MRS. POOLE: It's lucky for you the Vicar is broad-minded. A stricter man might think it his duty to refuse the blessing of the Church to an unbeliever.

MRS. WHARTON: [*Anxiously.*] Vicar, you're not thinking of doing anything like that?

VICAR: I confess the question has crossed my mind. [*Kindly.*] I don't think I can bring myself to expose such good Christians as you and Sylvia to such a humiliation.

SYLVIA: You need not harass yourself, Vicar. I've decided not to marry John.

JOHN: [*Aghast.*] Sylvia! Sylvia, you can't mean that!

SYLVIA: I was dreadfully troubled the other day when you

told us you'd lost your faith, but I hadn't the courage to say anything then. It came as such an awful shock.

JOHN: But you never made the least sign.

SYLVIA: I hadn't time to think it out, but I've been thinking hard ever since, day and night, and I've listened very carefully to what you've said to-day. I can't keep up the pretence any more. I've quite made up my mind. I won't marry you.

JOHN: But in God's name, why?

SYLVIA: You are not the John I loved and promised myself to. It's a different man that has come back from abroad. I have nothing in common with that man.

JOHN: Sylvia, you don't mean to say that you don't care for me any more because on certain matters I don't hold the same views as you?

SYLVIA: But those matters are the most important in the world. You talk as though it were a difference of opinion over the colour of our drawing-room curtains. You don't even understand me any more.

JOHN: How can I understand something that seems absolutely unreasonable to me?

SYLVIA: Do you think religion is something I take up with my Prayer-book when I go to church, and put away on a shelf when I get home again? John, God is a living presence that is always with me. I never at any moment lose the consciousness of that divine love which with infinite mercy tends and protects me.

JOHN: But, dear heart, you know me well enough. You know I would never hinder you in the exercise of your religion. I would always treat it with the utmost respect.

SYLVIA: How could we possibly be happy when all that to me is the reason and the beauty of life, to you is nothing but a lie?

JOHN: With tolerance on both sides, and, I hope, respect,

there's no reason why two people shouldn't live peace-
ably together no matter how different their views
are.

SYLVIA: How can I be tolerant when I see you deep in error?
Oh, it's more than error, it's sin. You've had your
choice between light and darkness, and you've deliberately chosen darkness. You are a deserter. If words
mean anything at all you are condemned.

JOHN: But, my dear, a man believes what he can. You don't
seriously think that a merciful God is going to punish
him because he's unable to believe something that he
finds incredible?

SYLVIA: No one doubts that Our Lord will have mercy on
those who have never had the chance of receiving His
teaching. You've had the chance, and you've refused
to take it. Do you forget the Parable of the Ten Talents?
It is a terrible warning.

JOHN: After all, if I'm wrong I hurt nobody but myself.

SYLVIA: You forget what marriage is. It makes us one flesh.
I am bidden to cleave to you and to follow you. How
can I, when our souls must ever be separated by an
unsurpassable abyss?

MRS. WHARTON: Sylvia, this is a dreadfully grave decision
you're making. Be careful that you're acting rightly.

JOHN: Sylvia, you can't throw me over like this after we've
been engaged for seven years. It's too heartless.

SYLVIA: I don't trust you. I have no hold over you. What
have you to aim at beside the satisfaction of your own
vulgar appetite? Sin means nothing to you.

JOHN: My dear, you don't suppose it's religion that makes a
man decent? If he's kind and honest and truthful it's
because it's his nature, not because he believes in God or
fears hell.

SYLVIA: We're neither of us very young any more, there's
no reason why we should make a mystery of natural

things. If we married my greatest hope was that we should have children.

JOHN: It was mine too.

SYLVIA: Have you asked yourself how this would affect them? Which are they to be, Christians or Agnostics?

JOHN: My dear, I promise you I will not interfere with your teaching of them.

SYLVIA: Do you mean to say you will stand by while they are taught a pack of worthless lies?

JOHN: Your faith has been the faith of our people for hundreds of years. In the case of a difference of opinion I could not take it on myself to refuse children instruction in it. When they reach years of discretion they can judge for themselves.

SYLVIA: And supposing they ask you about things? The story of Our Saviour appeals to children, you know. It's very natural that they should put you questions. What will you answer?

JOHN: I don't think you could ask me to say what I thought untrue.

MRS. WHARTON: He could always refer them to you, Sylvia dear.

SYLVIA: You naturally wouldn't come to church. What sort of an example would you set your children in a matter of which I was impressing on them the enormous importance?

JOHN: [With a smile.] My dear, surely you're letting a lack of humour cloud a lively intelligence. Vast numbers of excellent churchmen don't go to church, and I'm not aware that their children are corrupted by it.

SYLVIA: [Passionately.] You don't understand. You'll never understand. It's a joke to you. It's all over and done with, John. Let me go. I beseech you to let me go.

COLONEL WHARTON: [Half rising from his chair.] I feel most awfully ill.

MRS. WHARTON: [*In alarm.*] George!

JOHN: [*Simultaneously.*] Father!

> [MRS. WHARTON, JOHN, *and the* DOCTOR *hurry towards him.*

DR. MACFARLANE: What's the matter?

MRS. WHARTON: George, are you in pain?

COLONEL WHARTON: Awful!

DR. MACFARLANE: You'd better lie down on the sofa.

COLONEL WHARTON: No, I'd rather go upstairs.

DR. MACFARLANE: Don't crowd round him.

COLONEL WHARTON: I feel as if I were going to die.

DR. MACFARLANE: Do you think you can manage to walk?

COLONEL WHARTON: Yes. Help me, Evelyn.

JOHN: Put your arm round my neck, father.

COLONEL WHARTON: No, it's all right. I can manage.

DR. MACFARLANE: We'll get you upstairs and put you to bed.

MRS. WHARTON: Come, darling, put all your weight on me.

DR. MACFARLANE: That's right. You needn't come, John. You'll only be in the way.

> [MRS. WHARTON *and the* DOCTOR *help the* COLONEL *out of the room.*

MRS. POOLE: We'd better go, Norman. [*To* JOHN.] I hope it's nothing very serious.

JOHN: I'm sure I hope not.

MRS. POOLE: Please don't bear us a grudge for any of the things Norman or I have said to you to-day. You know, I saw the letter your Colonel wrote to Mrs. Wharton when you were wounded, and I know how splendid you've been.

JOHN: Oh, nonsense!

VICAR: I'm afraid you may have to go through a good deal of distress in the near future. If you should change your mind in some of the things that we've talked about this afternoon no one would be more happy than myself.

JOHN: It's very good of you to say so, but I don't think it likely.

VICAR: One never knows by what paths the Most High will call His creatures to Himself.   He is more cunning to save His children than they are to lose themselves. If you listen to the call, come to the Communion Table. I will ask no questions. It will be a joyful day for me if I am privileged to offer you the Blessed Sacrament of Our Lord and Saviour.

> [*He stretches out his hand and* JOHN *takes it.*

JOHN: Good-bye.

> [*The* VICAR *and* MRS. POOLE *go into the garden.* JOHN *turns to* SYLVIA.

JOHN: Is it the question that the Vicar put me when we were talking about sin that has upset you, Sylvia?

SYLVIA: No, I don't think it was very nice of him to put it. I never thought about the matter. I don't see why I should expect you to be better than other men.

JOHN: Did you really mean all you said just now?

SYLVIA: Every word.

> [*She takes off her engagement ring and hands it to him. He does not take it.*

JOHN: [*With deep emotion.*] Sylvia, I couldn't say it before all those people, it seemed too intimate and private a matter. Doesn't it mean anything to you that I love you? It's been so much to me in all I've gone through to think of you. You've been everything in the world to me. When I was cold and wet and hungry and miserable, I've thought of you, and it all grew bearable.

SYLVIA: I'm very sorry. I can't marry you.

JOHN: How can you be so cold and heartless? Sylvia, my dear, I love you! Won't you give it a chance?

[*She looks at him steadily for a moment. She braces herself for the final effort.*

SYLVIA: But I don't love you any more, John.
   [*She hands him the ring again and he takes it silently.*

JOHN: It's not a very swagger one, is it? I was none too flush in those days and I didn't want to ask father to help me. I wanted to buy it out of my own money.

SYLVIA: I've worn it for seven years, John.

   [*He turns away from* SYLVIA *and walks over to the fireplace. When* SYLVIA *sees what he is going to do she makes a gesture as though to prevent him, but immediately controls herself. He stands looking at the fire for a moment, then throws the ring in; he watches what will happen to it.* SYLVIA *clutches her heart. She can hardly prevent the sobs which seem to tear her breast.*

SYLVIA: I think I'll be getting home. John—if your father or mother want me you can send, can't you?

JOHN: [*Looking over his shoulder.*] Of course. I'll let you know at once.

SYLVIA: [*In a natural voice.*] Good-bye, John.

JOHN: Good-bye, Sylvia.

   [*He turns back to look at the fire, and she walks slowly out of the room.*

END OF THE SECOND ACT

THE THIRD ACT

The Scene is the same as in the preceding Acts. It is early morning on the following Wednesday. The dead ashes of yesterday's fire are still in the grate. Not far away is heard the ringing of a church bell to call the faithful to the first service.

MRS. WHARTON *is standing by a table on which is a large basket of white flowers which she had just brought in from the garden. She picks up a rose, and with a faint smile gives it a little caress.* SYLVIA *comes in from the garden.*

SYLVIA: [*With surprise.*] Mrs. Wharton!

MRS. WHARTON: Oh, Sylvia, is it you?

SYLVIA: It startled me to see you there. I came in this way because I saw the door was open and your front-door bell's so noisy. I thought if the Colonel was asleep it might wake him.

MRS. WHARTON: It's early, isn't it?

SYLVIA: Yes, I'm on my way to the early service. I thought I'd look in just to ask how the Colonel was. But I didn't expect to see you. I thought Kate or Hannah might be about.

MRS. WHARTON: George is dead, Sylvia.

SYLVIA: [*In amazement.*] Mrs. Wharton!

MRS. WHARTON: He died quite peacefully about an hour ago. I've just been to gather some flowers to put in his room.

SYLVIA: Oh, Mrs. Wharton, I'm so sorry. I'm so dreadfully sorry for you.

MRS. WHARTON: [*Patting her hand.*] Thank you, my dear; you've been very kind to us during these days.

SYLVIA: Where is John?

MRS. WHARTON: I think he must have gone out for a walk. I went to his room a little while ago and he wasn't there. He wanted to sit up with me last night, but I wouldn't let him.

SYLVIA: But . . . but doesn't John know his father is dead?

MRS. WHARTON: No, not yet.

SYLVIA: Didn't you call him?

MRS. WHARTON: I had no idea the end was so near. George wanted to be alone with me, Sylvia. We'd been married for thirty-five years, you see. He was conscious almost to the last. He died quite suddenly, like a child going to sleep.

SYLVIA: It's such a terrible loss. You poor dear, you must be quite heart-broken.

MRS. WHARTON: It's a very great loss, but I'm not heart-broken. George is happy and at rest. We should be very poor Christians if the death of those we love made us unhappy. George has entered into eternal life.

SYLVIA: Oh, Mrs. Wharton, what a blessed thing it is to have a faith like yours.

MRS. WHARTON: My dear, a very wonderful thing happened last night. I can't feel grief for dear George's death because of the recollection of that. I feel so strange. I feel as though I were walking in an enchanted garden.

SYLVIA: I don't know what you mean.

MRS. WHARTON: Since that day when George refused to talk with the Vicar I never dared mention the subject. He was not himself. It made me so unhappy. And then last night, soon after Dr. Macfarlane went away, he asked of his own accord for Mr. Poole. The Vicar's a dear, kind man. He'd said to me that if ever George asked for him he'd come at once, at any hour of the day or night. So I sent for him. He gave George the Holy Sacrament. And Sylvia, a miracle happened.

SYLVIA: A miracle?

MRS. WHARTON: No sooner had the bread and the wine touched his lips than he was transfigured. All his—his anxiety left him, and he was once more his dear, good, brave self. He was quite happy to die. It was as though an unseen hand had pulled back a dark curtain of clouds and he saw before him, not night and a black coldness, but a path of golden sunshine that led straight to the arms of God.

SYLVIA: I'm so glad. I'm happy too now.

MRS. WHARTON: The Vicar read the prayers for the dying and then he left us. We talked of the past and of our reunion in a little while. And then he died.

SYLVIA: It's wonderful. Yes, it was a miracle.

MRS. WHARTON: All through my life I've been conscious of the hand of God shaping the destinies of man. I've never seen His loving mercy more plainly manifest.

[KATE *opens the door and stands on the threshold, but does not come into the room.*

KATE: The woman's come, ma'am.

MRS. WHARTON: Very well. I'm just coming.

[KATE *goes out and shuts the door behind her.* MRS. WHARTON *takes up her basket of flowers.*

MRS. WHARTON: John will be in immediately, Sylvia. He promised to come and relieve me at half-past eight, so that I might get something to eat. Will you see him?

SYLVIA: Yes, Mrs. Wharton, if you wish me to.

MRS. WHARTON: Will you tell him that his father is dead? I know you'll do it very gently.

SYLVIA: Oh, Mrs. Wharton, wouldn't you prefer to tell him yourself?

MRS. WHARTON: No.

SYLVIA: Very well.

MRS. WHARTON: You know he loves you, Sylvia. It would make me so happy if you two could arrive at some understanding. It seems such a pity that the happiness of both of you should be ruined.

SYLVIA: I would do anything in the world for John, but I can't sacrifice what is and must be dearer to me even than he.

MRS. WHARTON: Can't you teach him to believe?

SYLVIA: Oh, I wish I could. I pray for him night and day.

MRS. WHARTON: I wished afterwards that I'd asked him to be present when his father and I received the Communion. I think at that last solemn moment he might have been moved to receive it with us.

SYLVIA: D'you think. . . . Perhaps a miracle would have taken place in him, too. Perhaps he would have believed.

MRS. WHARTON: I must go upstairs.

> [*An idea seizes* SYLVIA, *and she gives a strange little gasp. As* MRS. WHARTON *is about to leave the room she stops her with a sudden question.*

SYLVIA: Mrs. Wharton. . . . Mrs. Wharton, do you think the end can ever justify the means?

MRS. WHARTON: My dear, what an extraordinary question! It can never be right to do evil that good may come.

SYLVIA: Are you quite sure that that's so always? After all, no one would hesitate to tell a lie to save another's life.

MRS. WHARTON: Perhaps not. [*With a faint smile.*] We must thank God that we're not likely to be put in such a position. Why did you ask me that?

SYLVIA: I was wondering what one should do if one could only rescue somebody from terrible danger by committing a great sin. Do you think one ought to do it or not?

MRS. WHARTON: My dear, you haven't the right to offend God for the sake of anyone in the world.

SYLVIA: Not even for the sake of anyone you loved?

MRS. WHARTON: Surely not, my dear. And no one who

loved you would wish you for a moment to do a wicked thing for his sake.

SYLVIA: But take your own case, Mrs. Wharton; if you saw the Colonel or John in deadly peril wouldn't you risk your life to save them?

MRS. WHARTON: [*With a smile.*] Of course I should. I should be happy and thankful to have the opportunity. But that's not the same. I should only be risking my life, not my soul.

SYLVIA: [*Almost beside herself.*] But if their souls were in peril, wouldn't you risk your soul?

MRS. WHARTON: My dear, what do you mean? You seem so excited.

SYLVIA: [*Controlling herself with a great effort.*] I? You mustn't pay any attention to me. I haven't been sleeping very well the last three or four nights. I daresay I'm a little hysterical.

MRS. WHARTON: Wouldn't you prefer to go home, darling?

SYLVIA: No, I'd like to stay here if you don't mind. I'd like to see John.

MRS. WHARTON: Very well. I shan't be very long.

[*She goes out. The church bell gives a hurried tinkle and then stops. SYLVIA walks up and down the room and stands still in front of a photograph of JOHN in his uniform. She takes it up and looks at it. Then putting it down she clasps her hands and raises her eyes. She is seen to be praying. She hears a sound in the garden, inclines her head to listen, and goes to the window. She hesitates a moment and then braces herself to a decision. She calls.*

SYLVIA: John!

[*He comes, stops for a moment on the threshold, and then walks forward casually.*

JOHN: Good morning! You're very early.

SYLVIA: I looked in to ask how your father was.

JOHN: When I left him last night he was fairly comfortable. I'll go and find out from mother how he is.

SYLVIA: No, don't—don't disturb him.

JOHN: I'm going to take mother's place in a few minutes. I awoke early, so I went for a walk. . . . You've been very good and kind to all of us during these wretched days, Sylvia. I don't know what we should have done without you.

SYLVIA: I've been so dreadfully sorry. And you all had so much to bear. It wasn't only the thought that the poor dear couldn't—can't recover, but . . . it was so much worse than that.

JOHN: [*With a quick glance at her.*] I suppose it was inevitable that you should see it too. Somehow I hoped that only I and mother knew.

SYLVIA: Oh, John, you can't mind about me. I've loved your father as though he were my own. Nothing he did could make me love him less.

JOHN: He's afraid to die. It's dreadful to see his terror and to be able to do nothing to help him.

SYLVIA: Would you do anything to help him if you could?

JOHN: Of course.

SYLVIA: It's unfortunate that you found it necessary to say what you did about religion. He's always been a very simple man. He always accepted without question the faith in which he was brought up. Perhaps he's not quite so sure now.

JOHN: Nonsense, Sylvia. Father's faith is very much too steady for it to be unsettled by any opinions of mine.

SYLVIA: Ordinarily, I dare say. But he's ill, he's in terrible pain, he's not himself. I think perhaps it's a pity you didn't hold your tongue. It's so easy to create doubts and so hard to allay them.

JOHN: [*Much disturbed.*] That's an awful thought to have put into my head, Sylvia. I should never forgive myself if. . . .

SYLVIA: If you'd believed as we believe, he would have been supported, as it were, by all our faith. It would have made that terrible passage from this life to the life to come a little less terrible. You've failed him just when he needed you.

JOHN: [*Indignantly.*] Oh, Sylvia, how can you say anything so heartless?

SYLVIA: [*Coldly.*] It's true.

JOHN: Heaven knows, I know that death isn't easy. You can't think I'd be so inhuman as to do anything to make it more difficult?

SYLVIA: Except mortify your pride.

JOHN: [*Impatiently.*] What has pride got to do with it?

SYLVIA: There was pride in every word you said. Are you sure it's not pride of intellect that's responsible for your change of heart?

JOHN: [*Icily.*] Perhaps. How do you suggest I should mortify it?

SYLVIA: Well, you see, you can confess your error.

JOHN: I don't think it's an error.

SYLVIA: At least you can undo some of the harm you've done. Do you know what is chiefly tormenting your father? Your refusal to receive the Holy Communion. He keeps talking about it to your mother. He keeps harping on it. He's dreadfully distressed about it. If you received the Communion, John, it would give your father peace.

JOHN: Sylvia, how can I?

SYLVIA: All your life your father has done everything in the world for you. Nothing's been too good for you. You owe him all your happiness, everything you are and hope to be. Can't you do this one little thing for him?

o

JOHN: No, it's out of the question. I really can't. I'm awfully sorry.

SYLVIA: How can you be so hard? It's the last wish he'll ever have in the world. It's your last chance of showing your love for him. Oh, John, show a little mercy to his weakness!

JOHN: But, Sylvia, it would be blasphemous.

SYLVIA: What are you talking about? You don't believe. To you it's merely an idle ceremony. What can it matter to you if you go through a meaningless form?

JOHN: I've been a Christian too long. I have a hundred generations of Christianity behind me.

SYLVIA: You never hesitated at coming to church when we were going to be married.

JOHN: That was different.

SYLVIA: How? That was a sacrament, too. Are you afraid of a little bread and wine that a priest has said a few words over?

JOHN: Sylvia, don't torment me. I tell you I can't.

SYLVIA: [*Scornfully.*] I never imagined you would be superstitious. You're frightened. You feel just like people about sitting thirteen at table. Of course it's all nonsense, but there may be something in it.

JOHN: I don't know what I feel. I only know that I, an unbeliever, can't take part in a ceremony that was sacred to me when I believed.

SYLVIA: [*Bitterly.*] It's very natural. It only means that you love yourself better than anyone else. Why should one expect you to have pity for your father, or gratitude?

JOHN: Oh, Sylvia, where did you learn to say such cruel things? I can't, I tell you, I can't. If father were in his normal mind, neither he nor mother would wish me to do such a thing.

SYLVIA: But your mother does wish it. Oh, John, don't be

stubborn. For God's sake give yourself the opportunity. Your father's dying, John; you have no time
to lose. . . . John, the Communion Service has only
just begun. If you get on your bicycle you'll be there in
time. The other day the Vicar said if you presented
yourself at the Communion table he would not hesitate
to administer it.

[JOHN *looks steadily in front of him for a moment, then
makes up his mind; he stands up suddenly and without a
word goes out of the room.*

SYLVIA: [*In a whisper.*] O God, forgive me, forgive me,
forgive me!

[*The Curtain is lowered for one minute to denote the lapse of
half an hour. When it rises* SYLVIA *is standing at the
window, looking out into the garden.* MRS. LITTLE-
WOOD *enters.*

MRS. LITTLEWOOD: May I come in?

SYLVIA: Oh, Mrs. Littlewood, do!

MRS. LITTLEWOOD: I met Dr. Macfarlane just outside my
house, and he told me the Colonel was dead. I came with
him to see if I could be of any use.

SYLVIA: It's very kind of you. Is Dr. Macfarlane here?

MRS. LITTLEWOOD: Yes. He went upstairs. Where is
John?

SYLVIA: He'll be here directly.

[MRS. WHARTON *comes in, followed by* DR. MACFAR-
LANE. MRS. LITTLEWOOD *goes up to her and the two
old ladies kiss one another. For a moment they stand
clasped in one another's arms.*

MRS. LITTLEWOOD: My dear old friend!

MRS. WHARTON: It was dear of you to come, Charlotte. I
knew you'd feel for me.

DR. MACFARLANE: Now sit down, my dear Mrs. Wharton,
sit down and rest yourself.

[*He puts her into a chair and places a cushion behind her.*

MRS. WHARTON: Hasn't John come in yet?

SYLVIA: I'm sure he won't be long now. He should be here almost at once.

DR. MACFARLANE: Sylvia, my dear child, won't you go and get Mrs. Wharton a cup of tea? I think it would do her good.

SYLVIA: Certainly.

MRS. WHARTON: Oh, my dear, don't trouble.

SYLVIA: But it's no trouble. You know I love doing things for you.

[*She goes out*.

MRS. WHARTON: Everybody's so very kind in this world. It makes one feel humble. . . . George and I have been married for five-and-thirty years. He never said a cross word to me. He was always gentle and considerate. I daresay I was very troublesome now and then, but he was never impatient with me.

MRS. LITTLEWOOD: Is it true that John and Sylvia are not going to be married after all?

MRS. WHARTON: I'm afraid so.

MRS. LITTLEWOOD: Isn't it strange how people in this world seem to go out of their way to make themselves unhappy!

MRS. WHARTON: I've talked it over with Sylvia. Religion means so much to her. She wouldn't have minded if John had come back blind and crippled, she'd have devoted her life to him without a murmur.

DR. MACFARLANE: People always think they could put up with the faults we haven't got. Somehow or other it's always those we have that stick in their throats.

MRS. WHARTON: Oh, Doctor, don't say sarcastic things. You don't know how deeply Sylvia is suffering. But it's a matter of conscience. And I do see that one can't ask anyone to compromise with his soul.

DR. MACFARLANE: I have an idea our souls are like our manners, all the better when we don't think too much about them.

MRS. WHARTON: Sylvia's giving up a great deal. I don't know what's to become of her if she doesn't marry John. When her mother dies she'll only have thirty pounds a year.

[SYLVIA *comes back with a cup of tea on a small tray and puts it on a table by* MRS. WHARTON'S *side.*

SYLVIA: Here is the tea, Mrs. Wharton.

MRS. WHARTON: Oh, thank you, my dear, so much. You do spoil me. . . . I can't imagine why John is so long. He's generally so very punctual.

SYLVIA: [*In a low voice.*] John came in, Mrs. Wharton.

MRS. WHARTON: Oh, then, you saw him?

SYLVIA: Yes.

MRS. WHARTON: Did you speak to him?

SYLVIA: Yes.

MRS. WHARTON: Why did he go out again? Where has he gone?

SYLVIA: He'll be back immediately.

DR. MACFARLANE: Drink your tea, dear lady, drink your tea.

[SYLVIA *takes her place again at the window and looks into the garden. She takes no notice of the people in the room.*

MRS. WHARTON: I'm glad to have you two old friends with me now. The only thing that really seems to belong to me any more is the past, and you were both so much part of it.

DR. MACFARLANE: You came here immediately after your honeymoon. Is that really thirty-five years ago?

MRS. LITTLEWOOD: My mother and I were the first people

who called on you. I remember how stylish we thought you in your green velvet, Evelyn.

MRS. WHARTON: I remember it well. I had it dyed black its third year. I think the fashions were very much more ladylike in those days. A bustle did set off a woman's figure, there's no denying that.

DR. MACFARLANE: What waists you had and how tight you used to lace!

MRS. WHARTON: I often wonder if the young people ever enjoy themselves as much as we used to. Do you remember the picnics we used to have?

MRS. LITTLEWOOD: And now it's all as if it had never been, all our love and pain and joy and sorrow. We're just two funny old women, and it really wouldn't have mattered a row of pins if we'd never been born.

DR. MACFARLANE: I wonder, I wonder.

MRS. WHARTON: You've had the privilege of giving two sons to a noble cause. Wasn't it worth while to be born for that?

MRS. LITTLEWOOD: Sometimes I've asked myself if this world in which we're living now isn't hell. Perhaps all the unhappiness my husband caused me and the death of those two boys of mine is a punishment for sins that I committed in some other life in some other part of the universe.

MRS. WHARTON: Charlotte, sometimes you say things that frighten me. I'm haunted by the fear that you may destroy yourself.

MRS. LITTLEWOOD: I? No, why should I? I don't feel that life is important enough for me to give it a deliberate end. I don't trouble to kill the fly that walks over my ceiling.

DR. MACFARLANE: I've been curing or killing people for hard on fifty years, and it seems to me that I've seen innumerable generations enter upon the shifting scene, act their little part, and pass away. Alas, who can deny that in this world virtue is very often unrewarded and vice unpunished? Happiness too rarely comes to the good, and the prizes of this life go too frequently to the undeserving. The rain falls on the just and on the unjust alike, but the unjust generally have a stout umbrella. It looks as though there were little justice in the world, and chance seems to rule man and all his circumstances.

MRS. WHARTON: But we know that all that is mere idle seeming.

DR. MACFARLANE: Seeming perhaps, but why idle? Seeming is all we know. The other day when you were talking I held my tongue, because I thought you'd say I was a silly old fool if I put my word in, but I've puzzled over suffering and pain too. You see, in my trade we see so much of them. It made me unhappy, and for long I doubted the goodness of God, as you doubt it, dear friend.

MRS. LITTLEWOOD: [*With a smile.*] I think you're preaching at me, Doctor.

DR. MACFARLANE: Then it's the first time in my life.

MRS. LITTLEWOOD: Go on.

DR. MACFARLANE: I want to tell you how *I* found peace. My explanation is as old as the hills, and I believe many perfectly virtuous persons have been frizzled alive for accepting it. Our good Vicar would say I was a heretic. I can't help it. I can't see any other way of reconciling the goodness of God with the existence of evil.

MRS. LITTLEWOOD: Well, what is it?

DR. MACFARLANE: I don't believe that God is all-powerful and all-knowing. But I think He struggles against evil as we do. I don't believe He means to chasten us by suffering or to purify us by pain. I believe pain and suffering are evil, and that He hates them, and would crush them if He could. And I believe that in this age-long struggle between God and evil we can help, all of us, even the meanest; for in some way, I don't know how, I believe that all our goodness adds to the strength of God, and perhaps—who can tell?—will give Him such power that at last He will be able utterly to destroy evil—utterly, with its pain and suffering. [*With a smile.*] When we're good, we're buying silver bullets for the King of Heaven, and when we're bad, well, we're trading with the enemy.

SYLVIA: [*Without looking round.*] John has just ridden back on his bicycle.

DR. MACFARLANE: Come, Mrs. Littlewood, they don't want us here just now.

MRS. LITTLEWOOD: [*Getting up.*] No, I'm sure you will prefer to be alone with John.

MRS. WHARTON: It was very good of you to come. Good-bye, my dear, and God bless you.

MRS. LITTLEWOOD: Good-bye.

[*They kiss one another and* MRS. LITTLEWOOD *goes out.*

DR. MACFARLANE: [*Shaking hands with* MRS. WHARTON.] I may look in later in the day to see how you are.

MRS. WHARTON: Oh, my dear doctor, I'm not in the least ill, you know.

DR. MACFARLANE: Still, don't try to do too much. You're not quite a young woman, you know. Good-bye, Sylvia.

[SYLVIA *does not answer.* DR. MACFARLANE *goes out.* SYLVIA *advances into the room and then turns and looks again at the door through which* JOHN *must come. She does all she can to control her great nervousness.*

MRS. WHARTON: Sylvia, is anything the matter?

SYLVIA: No. Why?

MRS. WHARTON: You seem so strange.

SYLVIA: [*Paying no attention to the remark.*] John is just coming.

MRS. WHARTON: You know, my dear, it seems to me that in this life most difficulties can be arranged if both parties are willing to give way a little.

SYLVIA: Sometimes it's impossible to give way, and then the only hope is—a miracle.

> [*She says the last word with a little smile to conceal the fact that she attaches the greatest importance to it.* JOHN *comes in. He is pale and looks extremely tired. He stops for a moment in surprise on seeing his mother. He goes over and kisses her.*

JOHN: Oh, mother, I thought you were upstairs. I'm afraid I'm very late.

MRS. WHARTON: It doesn't matter, my dear. How dreadfully white you look.

JOHN: I went for a walk this morning. I've had nothing to eat. I'm rather tired.

MRS. WHARTON: My dear, you frighten me, your face is all drawn and pinched.

JOHN: Oh, mother, don't worry about me. I shall be all right after breakfast. After all, it's quite enough to have one invalid on your hands.

> [MRS. WHARTON *looks at him in surprise.* SYLVIA *gives a nervous start, but immediately controls herself.*

SYLVIA: Have you been—where you said you were going?

JOHN: Yes.

> [SYLVIA *opens her mouth to speak, but stops; she gives* JOHN *a long, searching look; she realises that what she had hoped for has not taken place, and with a little gasp of misery turns away her head and sinks, dejected and exhausted, into a chair.* JOHN *has held her look with his and now turns to his mother.*

JOHN: Is father asleep?

MRS. WHARTON: [*With a little shiver.*] John!

o*

JOHN: What's the matter?

MRS. WHARTON: I thought you knew. My dearest, your father's dead.

JOHN: Mother!

MRS. WHARTON: I asked Sylvia to break it to you. I thought. . . .

SYLVIA: [*In a dull voice.*] I didn't tell him when you asked me to, Mrs. Wharton.

JOHN: I don't understand. It seems impossible. He was well enough last night. When did he die?

MRS. WHARTON: At about seven this morning.

JOHN: But, mother dear, why didn't you call me?

MRS. WHARTON: I didn't expect it. We'd been talking and he said he was tired and he thought he could sleep a little. He dozed off quietly, and in a little while I saw he was dead.

JOHN: Oh, my poor mother, how will you bear your grief?

MRS. WHARTON: You know, it's so strange, I'm not in the least unhappy. I don't feel that he's left me. I feel him just as near to me as before. I don't know how to explain it to you. I think he's never been so much alive as now. Oh, John, I know that the soul is immortal.

JOHN: Darling, I'm so glad you're not unhappy. Your dear eyes are positively radiant.

MRS. WHARTON: If you only knew what I seem to see with them!

JOHN: Won't you take me up and let me see him?

MRS. WHARTON: I think the women are not done yet, John. I'll go up and see. I'll call you as soon as everything is ready.

JOHN: I'm sorry I've caused you so much pain since I came back, mother. I wish I could have avoided it.

MRS. WHARTON: [*She puts her arms round his neck, and he kisses her.*] My dear son!

> [*She goes out.* JOHN *goes towards the window and looks out into the garden. For a moment* SYLVIA *does not dare to speak to him. At last she makes an effort.*

SYLVIA: [*Desperately.*] John, whatever you have to say to me, say it.

JOHN: [*With frigid politeness.*] I don't think I have anything in particular to say to you.

SYLVIA: I suppose you think I'm just a wicked liar.

JOHN: I ask you no questions. I make you no reproaches. What is the matter?

SYLVIA: Oh, John, after all we've been to one another it's brutal to talk to me like that. If you think I did wrong, say so.

JOHN: Why?

SYLVIA: You're cruel and hard. [*She goes up to him.*] John, you must listen to me.

JOHN: Well?

SYLVIA: Your mother asked me to tell you of your father's death. I concealed it from you. I told you a whole tissue of lies. I traded deliberately on your tenderness for your father. I was horrified at myself. It was my only chance of getting you to take the Communion.

JOHN: If you'd had any affection for me, you couldn't have done such an abominable thing. If you'd had any respect for me, you couldn't have done it.

SYLVIA: Let me speak, John.

JOHN: Be quiet! You've insisted on talking about it, and now, by God, you're going to listen to me. Do you know what I felt? Shame. When I took the bread and the wine, I thought they'd choke me. Because once I believed so devoutly it seemed to me that I was doing an awful thing. Deliberately, with full knowledge of what I was doing, I told a dirty lie. And I feel dirty to the depths of my soul.

SYLVIA: I thought perhaps it wouldn't be a lie. I had to do it, John. It was my only chance.

JOHN: Why did you do it?

SYLVIA: Don't look at me so sternly. I can't bear it. You frighten me. I can't collect my thoughts.

JOHN: Why did you do it? Shall I tell you? Because at the back of all your Christian humility there's the desire to dominate. It isn't so much that I didn't believe as that I didn't believe what you wanted me to believe. You wanted to grind my face in the dust.

SYLVIA: [*Passionately.*] John, if you only knew! I only thought of you. I only thought of you all the time.

JOHN: Don't be such a hypocrite.

SYLVIA: [*Brokenly.*] I expected a miracle.

JOHN: At this time of day?

SYLVIA: For God's sake have mercy on me! It was your mother who put the idea in my head. Your father received the Communion last night.

JOHN: You have no charity for human weakness. You were all so terrified that he shouldn't make an edifying end. As if it mattered if the poor dear's nerve failed him at the last.

SYLVIA: [*Eagerly.*] But it didn't. That's just it. You noticed your mother's face yourself. Notwithstanding all her grief she's happy. Do you know why?

JOHN: Why?

SYLVIA: [*As though suddenly inspired.*] Because when he'd received the Blessed Sacrament the fear of death left him. He was once more a brave and gallant gentleman. He had no dread any longer of the perilous journey before him. He was happy to die.

JOHN: [*More gently.*] Is that true? Dear father, I'm very glad.

SYLVIA: It was a miracle. It was a miracle.

JOHN: I still don't follow.

SYLVIA: I thought that when you knelt at the chancel steps, and received the Communion as you used to receive it when you were a boy, all the feelings of your boyhood would rush back on you. I had to make you take it.

JOHN: In my frame of mind? Surely I had no right to.

SYLVIA: I know. That's what makes my sin the greater. Perhaps I was mad. To God all things are possible. I felt certain you'd believe.

JOHN: [*Very gravely.*] Perhaps you have worked a miracle, but not the one you expected.

SYLVIA: What do you mean?

JOHN: When you said you wouldn't marry me I was—I was knocked endways—I felt like a man who's been shipwrecked. All my plans for the future had been bound up with you. I couldn't imagine it without you. I felt utterly forlorn.

SYLVIA: But don't you know what it cost me?

JOHN: At first I couldn't think you meant it. When you said you didn't love me, I couldn't believe it. It seemed too preposterous. I was awfully miserable, Sylvia.

SYLVIA: John, I didn't want you to be unhappy.

JOHN: And then, when I received the Communion something quite strange took place in me. I can't tell you what I felt. I felt as though mother had heard me saying something obscene. I forced myself to go through with it, because I really did think it might give poor father some peace of mind. But it was you who made me do it. The thought of you filled me with horror.

SYLVIA: [*With dismay.*] John!

JOHN: You've cured me, Sylvia. I ought to be grateful to you for that. My love for you has fallen from me as a cloak might fall from one's shoulders. I see the truth now. You were quite right. In these long years we've

become different people and we have nothing to say to
one another any more.

SYLVIA: [*Passionately.*] But I love you, John! How can
you be so blind? Don't you see that I only did it because
I loved you? Oh, John, you can't leave me now! I've
waited for you all these years. I've longed for you to
come back. Forgive me if I did wrong. I can't lose you
now. I love you, John, you won't leave me?

JOHN: [*After a moment's pause.*] Of course I won't leave you.
I thought you didn't want to marry me.

SYLVIA: [*Hardly knowing what she is saying.*] I'm not young
any more. I've lost my freshness. I've got nobody
but you now. Oh, John, don't forsake me! I couldn't
bear it.

JOHN: [*As though he were talking to a child.*] My dear, don't
distress yourself. I'm not thinking of forsaking you.
We'll be married as soon as ever we can.

SYLVIA: Yes, we'll be married, won't we? I love you so
much, John, I'll make you love me. I couldn't lose you
now. I've waited too long.

JOHN: Come, darling, you mustn't be unhappy. It's all
settled now. Dry your eyes. You don't want to look a
fright, do you?

SYLVIA: [*Clinging to him.*] I'm so miserable.

JOHN: Nonsense, give me a nice kiss, and we'll forget all
about our troubles. I'll try to make you a good husband,
Sylvia. I'll do all I can to make you happy. Give me a
kiss.

> [*When he seeks to raise her face in order to kiss her, she
> tears herself violently from him.*

SYLVIA: No, don't! Don't touch me! God give me strength!
I'm so pitifully weak.

JOHN: Sylvia!

SYLVIA: Don't come near me! For God's sake! [*She puts
her hands before her face, trying to control and to collect*

herself, and there is a moment's pause.] It never occurred to me that you didn't care for me any more, and when you told me, for a moment I lost my head. Forgive me for that, dear, and forget it. I'm not going to marry you.

JOHN: Now, Sylvia, don't be idiotic. It would be so unseemly if I had to drag you to the altar by the hair of your head.

SYLVIA: You're very kind, John. I suppose it wouldn't be very good form to back out of it now. I'm poor, and I've wasted my best years waiting for you. You needn't worry about what is going to happen to me. I can earn my living as well as other women.

JOHN: Oh, Sylvia, you're torturing yourself and me. Can't you forget what I said in a moment of exasperation? You must know how deep my affection is for you.

SYLVIA: I don't want to forget. It is the will of God. I lied. I did an abominable and evil thing. I don't think you can imagine how terrible my sin has been. I risked my soul to save you, John, and God has inflicted on me a punishment infinitely less than I deserved. He has taken out of your heart the love you bore me.

JOHN: But you love me, Sylvia.

SYLVIA: Better than anyone in the world. I've loved you ever since I was a child of ten. That's only the weakness of my flesh. My soul exults in the great mercy that God has shown me.

JOHN: Oh, my dear, you're going to be so unhappy.

SYLVIA: No, don't be sorry for me. You've given me a great opportunity.

JOHN: I?

SYLVIA: I've been mortified because I was able to do so little in the war. I knew it was my duty to stay here and look after mother. But I wanted to go out to France and do my bit like all my friends.

JOHN: That was very natural.

SYLVIA: Now at last I have the chance to do something. No sacrifice is worthless in the eyes of God. A broken and a contrite heart, O God, thou wilt not despise. I sacrifice now all that was precious to me in the world, my love and my hope of happiness in this life, and I sacrifice it with a cheerful heart, and I pray that God may accept it. So shall I do my part to atone for the sins which have brought on this horrible war.

JOHN: It would have been better if I'd never come back. I've caused misery and suffering to all of you.

SYLVIA: John, you took away the ring you gave me when we became engaged. You threw it in the fire.

JOHN: I'm afraid that was very silly of me. I did it in a moment of bitterness.

SYLVIA: You went into Canterbury to buy a wedding ring. What have you done with it?

JOHN: I have it here. Why?

SYLVIA: Can I have it?

JOHN: Of course.
> [*He takes it out of his waistcoat pocket, and, wondering, gives it to her.*

SYLVIA: [*Slipping the ring on her finger.*] I will put the love of man out of my life. I will turn from what is poor and transitory to what is everlasting. I will be the bride of One whose love is never denied to them that seek it. The love of God is steadfast and enduring. I can put all my trust in that and I shall never find it wanting. . . . Good-bye, John, God bless you now and always.

JOHN: Good-bye, dear child.
> [*She goes out quickly. In a minute* KATE *comes in. She is carrying a square wooden box in which are papers, firewood a hearth-brush, and a large soiled glove.*

KATE: Please, sir, Mrs. Wharton says, will you go upstairs now?

JOHN: Yes.

> [*He goes out.* KATE *goes to the fireplace, kneels down, puts on the glove and begins to rake out the ashes. The* COOK *enters. She is a stout homely body of forty-five.*

COOK: The butcher's come, Kate. I don't exactly like to go up to Mrs. Wharton just now. I've got the cold beef for lunch, but they'll be wanting something for dinner.

KATE: Oh, well, they always like best end. You can't go far wrong if you have that.

COOK: I've got a fine lot of pease.

KATE: Well, they'll do nicely.

COOK: I was thinking I'd make a fruit tart. I think p'raps I'd better order two and a half pounds of best end.

> [*She goes out.* KATE *continues to lay the fire.*

THE END

FOR SERVICES RENDERED

A PLAY
in Three Acts

CHARACTERS

LEONARD ARDSLEY
CHARLOTTE ARDSLEY, his wife
SYDNEY, his son
EVA ⎫
LOIS ⎭ his unmarried daughters
ETHEL BARTLETT, his married daughter
HOWARD BARTLETT, her husband
COLLIE STRATTON, Commander, R.N.
WILFRED CEDAR
GWEN, his wife
DR. PRENTICE, Mrs. Ardsley's brother
GERTRUDE, the Ardsleys' parlourmaid

The action takes place in the Ardsleys' house at Rambleston, a small country town in Kent near the cathedral city of Stanbury.

FOR SERVICES RENDERED

ACT I

*The scene is a terrace at the back of the Ardsleys' house. French
windows lead out on it from the house, and beyond is the
garden.*

LEONARD ARDSLEY *is the only solicitor in Rambleston and his
house faces the village street. Part of it is used as his office.*

Tea is laid. It is five o'clock on a warm afternoon in September.

MRS. ARDSLEY *is sitting in a chair, hemming a napkin. She is
a thin, grey-haired woman of more than sixty, with a severe
face but kind eyes. She is very quietly dressed.*

The MAID *brings in the tea.*

MRS. ARDSLEY: Is it tea-time?

GERTRUDE: The church clock's striking now, ma'am.

MRS. ARDSLEY: [*Getting up and putting her sewing aside.*] Go
down to the tennis court and tell them that tea is ready.

GERTRUDE: Very good, ma'am.

MRS. ARDSLEY: Have you told Mr. Sydney?

GERTRUDE: Yes, ma'am.

> [*She goes out into the garden.* MRS. ARDSLEY *brings
> two or three light chairs up to the table.* SYDNEY
> comes in from the house. He is a heavy man of hard
> on forty, with a big, fat face. He is blind and walks
> with a stick, but he knows his way about and moves
> with little hesitation.*

MRS. ARDSLEY: Where would you like to sit, dear?

SYDNEY: Anywhere.

> [*He lets himself down into a chair by the table and puts
> down his stick.*

MRS. ARDSLEY: What have you been doing all the afternoon?

SYDNEY: Nothing very much. Knitting a bit.

MRS. ARDSLEY: Ethel's here. Howard's coming to fetch her on his way home from Stanbury. He's gone to the cattle-market.

SYDNEY: I suppose he'll be as tight as a drum.

MRS. ARDSLEY: Sydney!

SYDNEY: [*With a little chuckle.*] What rot it all is. Does Ethel really think we don't know he drinks?

MRS. ARDSLEY: She's proud. She doesn't want to admit that she made a mistake.

SYDNEY: I shall never stop asking myself what on earth she saw in him.

MRS. ARDSLEY: Everything was so different then. He looked very nice in uniform. He was an officer.

SYDNEY: You and father ought to have put your foot down.

MRS. ARDSLEY: They were madly in love with one another. When all that slaughter was going on it seemed so snobbish to object to a man because he was just a small tenant farmer.

SYDNEY: Did you think the war was going on for ever?

MRS. ARDSLEY: No, but it looked as though the world would be a changed place when it stopped.

SYDNEY: It's funny when you think of it. Everything goes on in the same old way, except that we're all broke to the wide and a few hundred thousand fellows like me have had our chance of making a good job of life snatched away from us.

> [MRS. ARDSLEY *gives a sigh and makes an unhappy gesture.* SYDNEY *utters a little sardonic chuckle.*]

Cheer up, mother. You must console yourself by thinking that you've got a hero for a son. M.C. and mentioned in despatches. No one can say I didn't do my bit.

MRS. ARDSLEY: They're just coming.

> [GWEN CEDAR *and* ETHEL BARTLETT *come in from the garden.* ETHEL BARTLETT, MRS. ARDSLEY'S *second daughter, is a handsome woman of thirty-five, with regular features and fine eyes.* GWEN CEDAR *is fifty, a good deal painted, with dyed hair; she is too smartly dressed in a manner hardly becoming to her age. She has the mechanical brightness of a woman who is desperately hanging on to the remains of her youth.*

ETHEL: The others are coming as soon as they've finished the set. Hulloa, Sydney.

SYDNEY: Hulloa.

GWEN: [*Shaking hands with him.*] How are you to-day, Sydney? You're looking very well.

SYDNEY: Oh, I'm all right, thanks.

GWEN: Busy as a bee as usual, I suppose. You're simply amazing.

MRS. ARDSLEY: [*Trying to head her off.*] Let me give you some tea.

GWEN: I do admire you. I mean, you must have great strength of character.

SYDNEY: [*With a grin.*] A will of iron.

GWEN: I remember when I was ill last spring and they kept me in a darkened room for nearly a week, it was quite intolerable. But I kept on saying to myself, well, it's nothing compared to what poor Sydney has to put up with.

SYDNEY: And you were right.

MRS. ARDSLEY: One lump of sugar?

GWEN: Oh, no, I never take sugar. It's Lent all the year round for me. [*Brightly attacking* SYDNEY *again.*] It's a marvel to me how you pass the time.

SYDNEY: Charming women like you are very sweet to me, and my sisters are good enough to play chess with me. I improve my mind by reading.

GWEN: Oh, yes, Braille. I love reading. I always read at least one novel a day. Of course I've got a head like a sieve. D'you know, it's often happened to me to read a novel right through and never remember till the end that I'd read it before. It always makes me so angry. I mean, it's such a waste of time.

SYDNEY: How's the farm, Ethel?

ETHEL: We're making the most of the fine weather.

GWEN: It must be so interesting, living on a farm. Making butter and all that sort of thing.

ETHEL: One's at it from morning till night. It keeps one from thinking.

GWEN: But of course you have people to do all the rough work for you.

ETHEL: What makes you think that?

GWEN: You don't mean to say you do it yourself. How on earth d'you keep your hands?

ETHEL: [*With a glance at them, smiling.*] I don't.

> [*There is a sound of voices from the garden.*

MRS. ARDSLEY: Here are the others.

> [*Her two daughters come in with the two men they have been playing with. These are* WILFRED CEDAR *and* COLLIE STRATTON. WILFRED CEDAR *is a stout, elderly man, but well preserved, with a red face and grey, crisply curling hair. He is stout, jovial, breezy and sensual. He is out to enjoy all the good things of life.* COLLIE STRATTON *is between thirty-five and forty. He has been in the Royal Navy and has the rather school-boyish manner of those men who have never quite grown up. He has a pleasant, frank look.* EVA *is* MRS. ARDSLEY'S *eldest daughter. She is*

thin and of a somewhat haggard appearance. She is very gentle, a trifle subdued, but she does not give you the impression of being at peace with herself. Behind the placidity is a strange restlessness. She is thirty-nine. LOIS ARDSLEY *is the youngest of the family. She is twenty-six, but the peaceful, monotonous life she has led has preserved her youth and she looks little more than twenty. She is gay and natural. She is a very pretty young woman, but what is even more attractive in her than her blue eyes and straight nose is the air she has of immense healthiness.*

LOIS: Tea. Tea. Tea.

WILFRED: By George, they made us run about. Hulloa, Sydney.

MRS. ARDSLEY: How were you playing?

WILFRED: Lois and me against Eva and Collie.

EVA: Of course Wilfred's in a different class from us.

COLLIE: That forehand drive of yours is devilish.

WILFRED: I've had a lot of practice, you know, playing in tournaments on the Riviera and so on.

GWEN: Of course he was too old for singles, but a few years ago he was one of the best doubles players in Cannes.

WILFRED: [*Not too pleased.*] I don't know that I play any worse than I played a few years ago.

GWEN: Well, you can't expect to get across the court as you used to when you were young. I mean, that's silly.

WILFRED: Gwen always talks as if I was a hundred. What I say is, a woman's as old as she looks and a man as old as he feels.

SYDNEY: It has been said before.

MRS. ARDSLEY: [*To* WILFRED.] How do you like your tea?

LOIS: Oh, mother, I'm sure they want a drink.

WILFRED: Clever girl.

MRS. ARDSLEY: What would you like?

WILFRED: Well, a glass of beer sounds good to me. What about you, Collie?

COLLIE: Suits me.

EVA: I'll tell Gertrude.

MRS. ARDSLEY: [*As* EVA *is going.*] Tell your father that if he wants any tea he'd better come now.

EVA: Very well.

[*She goes into the house.*

WILFRED: Damned convenient for your husband having his office in the house.

LOIS: He's got a private door so that he can slip away without the clients seeing him.

GWEN: Evie's looking a little tired, I think.

MRS. ARDSLEY: She's been rather nervy lately. I've wanted her uncle to have a look at her, but she won't let him.

GWEN: So sad the man she was engaged to being killed in the war.

MRS. ARDSLEY: They were very much in love with one another.

ETHEL: She's never really got over it, poor dear.

GWEN: Pity she never found anyone else she liked.

MRS. ARDSLEY: In a place like this she could hardly hope to. By the end of the war there were very few young men left. And girls were growing up all the time.

GWEN: I heard there *was* someone.

MRS. ARDSLEY: Not very desirable. I believe he did ask her but she refused him.

GWEN: I'm told he wasn't quite, quite. It's always a mistake to marry out of one's own class. It's never a success.

[GWEN *has dropped a brick.* ETHEL *has married beneath her.*

LOIS: Oh, what nonsense. As if that sort of thing mattered any more. It depends on the people, not on their class.

[GWEN *suddenly realises what she has said, gives* ETHEL *a hurried look and tries to make everything right.*

GWEN: Oh, of course. I didn't mean that. All sorts of people keep shops nowadays and go in for poultry farming and things like that. I don't mind what a man is as long as he's a gentleman.

COLLIE: It's a relief to hear you say that, as I run a garage.

GWEN: That's just what I mean. It doesn't matter your running a garage. After all you were in the Navy and you commanded a destroyer.

SYDNEY: To say nothing of having the D.S.O. and the Legion of Honour.

WILFRED: In point of fact what made you go into the motor business when you were axed, Collie?

COLLIE: I had to do something. I was a pretty good mechanic. I got a bonus, you know, and I thought I might just as well put it into that as anything else.

WILFRED: I suppose you do pretty well out of the motor-buses.

COLLIE: Lot of expenses, you know.

[GERTRUDE *comes out of the house with two tankards of beer on a tray.*

WILFRED: Look what's here.

[*He takes one of the tankards and takes a great pull at it.* EVA *comes back.*

EVA: Father's just coming. He wants to see you, Collie.

COLLIE: Oh, does he?

WILFRED: That doesn't look too good, old man. When a solicitor wants to see you it's generally that he has something disagreeable to say to you.

LOIS: Hurry up and finish your beer and we'll give them their revenge. It'll be getting dark soon.

GWEN: Oh, are you going to play again, Wilfred? Don't you think it's time we went home?

WILFRED: What's the hurry? You take the car. I'll have another set and I'll walk back.

GWEN: Oh, if you're not coming, I'll wait.

WILFRED: [*Trying to hide his irritation behind his joviality.*] Oh, come on, you can trust me out of your sight just this once. I promise to be a good boy.

> [*A little look passes between them. She stifles a sigh and smiles brightly.*

GWEN: Oh, all right. A brisk walk won't do your figure any harm.

> [*She turns towards* MRS. ARDSLEY *to say good-bye.*

MRS. ARDSLEY: I'll come as far as the door with you.

> [*The two of them go out.*

SYDNEY: Where's my stick, Evie? [*She gives it to him and he gets up.*] I think I'll totter down to the court and see how you all play.

ETHEL: I'll come with you, shall I?

EVA: I think I'd better get some fresh tea for father.

LOIS: Hurry up, then, or the light'll be going.

EVA: I shan't be a minute.

> [*She goes into the house.*

LOIS: What should we do in this house without Evie?

SYDNEY: What would Evie do without us? You can't sacrifice yourself unless there's someone about whom you can sacrifice yourself for.

WILFRED: You're a cynical bloke.

LOIS: [*With a smile.*] And ungrateful.

SYDNEY: Not at all. It's jam for Evie to have an invalid to look after. If she could make me see by saying a magic

word, d'you think she'd say it? Not on your life.
Nature destined her to be a saint and it's damned lucky
for her that I'm around to give her the opportunity of
earning a heavenly crown.

ETHEL: [*With a chuckle.*] Come on, give me your arm.

SYDNEY: [*Putting on a cockney accent.*] Spare a copper for a
poor blind man, sir.

[*They go out.*

LOIS: I'll just go and hunt for that ball. I think I know
more or less where it is.

WILFRED: I'd come with you if I weren't so lazy.

LOIS: No, stay there. You'll only wreck the flower beds
with your big feet.

WILFRED: I like that. I flatter myself not many men of my
size have smaller feet than I have.

LOIS: Modest fellow, aren't you? Give me a shout when
Evie comes.

[*She disappears into the garden.*

WILFRED: Good-looking girl that. Nice too. And she's got
a head on her shoulders.

COLLIE: Plays a good game of tennis.

WILFRED: Funny she shouldn't have been snapped up
before now. If I was a young fellow and single I
shouldn't hesitate.

COLLIE: She hasn't got much chance here, poor thing. Who
the devil is there she can marry in a place like this?

WILFRED: I wonder you don't have a cut in yourself.

COLLIE: I'm fifteen years older than she is. And I haven't
got a bean.

WILFRED: Girls nowadays who live in the country have to
take what they can get.

COLLIE: Nothing doing as far as I'm concerned.

WILFRED: [*With a shrewd look at him.*] Oh!

COLLIE: Why d'you want to know?

WILFRED: Only that she's a nice girl and I'd like to see her settled.

COLLIE: I say, old man, I suppose you wouldn't do me a favour.

WILFRED: Of course, I will, old boy. What is it?

COLLIE: Well, to tell you the truth, I'm in a bit of a hole.

WILFRED: Sorry to hear that. What's it all about?

COLLIE: Business has been rotten lately.

WILFRED: I know it has. And I don't know when things are going to improve. I can tell you I'm damned glad I got out when the going was good.

COLLIE: I expect you are.

WILFRED: Everyone told me I was a fool to retire. But I smelt a rat. I said, no, I've worked a good many years and I've made a packet. Now I'm going to live like a gentleman. I sold out at the top of the market. Just in time.

COLLIE: Lucky.

WILFRED: Lucky be damned. Clever, I call it.

COLLIE: Look here, old man, I hate asking you, but I'm terribly hard up just now. I should be awfully grateful if you could lend me a bit.

WILFRED: [*Very heartily.*] Why, my dear old boy, of course I will. I'm always glad to oblige a friend. How much d'you want?

COLLIE: That's awfully kind of you. Could you manage two hundred pounds?

WILFRED: Oh, I say, that's real money. I thought you were going to say a tenner. Two hundred pounds is quite another story.

COLLIE: It's not very much for you.

WILFRED: I'm not made of money, you know. My investments have gone down like everybody else's. Believe me, I haven't got more than I can spend.

COLLIE: I'm in a most awful jam.

WILFRED: Why don't you go to the bank?

COLLIE: I'm overdrawn already. They won't lend me a bob.

WILFRED: But haven't you got any security?

COLLIE: Not that they'll accept.

WILFRED: Then what d'you expect me to lend you the money on?

COLLIE: I'll give you my word of honour to return it as soon as ever I can.

WILFRED: My dear old boy, you're a damned good chap and a D.S.O. and all that sort of thing, but this is business.

COLLIE: You've known me for six months now. You must know I'm honest.

WILFRED: I took a furnished house down here for my wife's health, and when I heard you'd been in the navy of course I came to you for my petrol and tyres and repairs. I know it's hard for you fellows who've been axed. I've paid all my bills on the nail.

COLLIE: I've given you good service.

WILFRED: I know you have. I'm very sorry your garage hasn't proved a good proposition. If you'd been a business man you'd have known it was crazy to settle down in a little tin-pot place like this. But I really don't see that I'm called upon to make you a present of two hundred pounds.

COLLIE: I'm not asking it as a present.

WILFRED: It comes to the same thing. I've lent dozens of fellows money and they never pay it back. I think it's a bit thick to ask me to lend you a sum like that.

COLLIE: You don't think I like it. I tell you I'm absolutely up against it. It means life and death to me.

WILFRED: I'm awfully sorry, old boy, but there's nothing doing. . . . I wonder if Lois has found that ball yet.

[*He gets up and goes into the garden.* COLLIE *sits on dejectedly. In a moment* EVA *comes in with the teapot.*

EVA: What's the matter? You're looking terribly depressed.

COLLIE: [*Trying to collect himself.*] I'm sorry.

EVA: Are they waiting for us?

COLLIE: [*With a slight sigh.*] I suppose so.

EVA: Tell me what the matter is.

COLLIE: [*Forcing a smile.*] It wouldn't interest you.

EVA: Why do you say that? Don't you know that anything that concerns you interests me.

COLLIE: That's very sweet of you.

EVA: I suppose I'm rather reserved. It's difficult for me to show my feelings. I should like you to look upon me as a friend.

COLLIE: I do.

EVA: Tell me what it is then. Perhaps I can help you.

COLLIE: I'm afraid not. I think you've got troubles enough of your own without sharing mine.

EVA: You mean looking after Sydney. I don't look upon that as a trouble. I'm glad to do what I can for the poor boy. When I think of what the war did to him, it's only right that I should sacrifice myself.

COLLIE: It's very good of you, all the same.

EVA: You see, Ethel was married and Lois was so young. Mother isn't very strong. Looking after Sydney helped me to bear the loss of poor Ted.

COLLIE: That was the man you were engaged to?

EVA: Yes. I was terribly unhappy when he was killed.

I'm afraid I was rather morbid about it. One can't afford to give in, can one? I mean, life is given to us, and it's our duty to make the best we can out of it.

COLLIE: [*Rather vaguely.*] Naturally one gets over everything in course of time.

EVA: I suppose one ought to consider oneself fortunate that one can. And I think a girl ought to marry, don't you? I mean, it's a woman's province to have a home of her own and children to look after.

COLLIE: Yes, I suppose it is.

[*There is a moment's pause.*

EVA: It's rather strange that you should never have married, Collie.

COLLIE: [*With a grin.*] I never had anything to marry on.

EVA: Oh, money isn't everything. A clever woman can manage on very little. [*Brightly.*] I must have a look round and see if I can't find someone to suit you.

COLLIE: I'm afraid I'm too old now.

EVA: Oh, what nonsense. You're just the same age as I am. Every woman loves a sailor. Between you and me and the gate-post I don't believe there's a girl here who wouldn't jump at the chance if you asked her.

COLLIE: [*A trifle embarrassed.*] I'm not likely to do that.

EVA: Are you waiting for her to ask you? That's wanting almost too much.

COLLIE: I suppose it is really.

EVA: After all, a nice girl can't do much more than show a man she's not indifferent to him and leave him to draw what conclusions he pleases.

COLLIE: I've got an awful headache. I wonder if you'd tell the others that I can't play tennis again to-day. Perhaps Ethel will make a four.

EVA: Oh, my dear, I am sorry. Of course you mustn't play. That's quite all right.

> [LEONARD ARDSLEY *comes out from the house. He is a red-faced, hearty man of sixty-five, with blue eyes and white hair. He looks more like the old-fashioned sporting squire than the country solicitor. He is on familiar terms with the local gentry and in the season enjoys a day's shooting.*

Oh, there you are, father. We've all had tea.

ARDSLEY: I had somebody with me. [*With a nod to him.*] How are you, Stratton? Run along, Evie, I'll help myself. I want to have a word with our young friend.

EVA: Oh, all right.

> [*She goes out into the garden.*

ARDSLEY: I've just seen Radley.

COLLIE: Yes.

ARDSLEY: I'm afraid I haven't got very good news for you.

COLLIE: He won't wait?

ARDSLEY: He can't wait.

COLLIE: Then what's to be done?

ARDSLEY: The only sensible thing is to file your petition.

COLLIE: It's ridiculous. It's only a matter of a hundred and eighty-seven pounds. I'm sure if I can hang on a little longer I can manage. When does Radley want to be paid?

ARDSLEY: The first of the month.

COLLIE: I've just got to get the money before then, that's all.

ARDSLEY: You've had a hard struggle and you've deserved to succeed. Believe me, no one will be sorrier than I if you're beaten. You know, you needn't worry about my fees. We'll forget about them.

COLLIE: That's very kind of you.

ARDSLEY: Not a bit of it. I think it's very tough on you

fellows who've been kicked out of the navy. A man with your record. You put all your eggs in the one basket, didn't you?

COLLIE: Everything. If I go bust I haven't a shilling. I'll be thankful if I can get a job driving a motor bus.

ARDSLEY: [*Cheerily.*] Oh, I hope it won't come to that. It would be rather a come-down for a man who's commanded a destroyer and has all the ribands you have.

> [MRS. ARDSLEY *comes out of the house with* DR. PRENTICE. *He is a thin, elderly man with iron-grey hair, a stern face and searching eyes.*

Hulloa, Charlie.

PRENTICE: How are you? Oh, Stratton.

ARDSLEY: Just in time for a cup of tea. [*To* COLLIE.] Don't you bother about us if you want to go and play tennis.

COLLIE: No, I'm not playing any more. I'll hop it. Good-bye, Mrs. Ardsley.

MRS. ARDSLEY: Are you going already?

COLLIE: I'm afraid I must.

MRS. ARDSLEY: Well, good-bye. Come again soon.

COLLIE: Good-bye.

> [*He nods to the two men and goes out through the house.*

MRS. ARDSLEY: [*To* PRENTICE.] Will you have some tea?

PRENTICE: No, thank you.

MRS. ARDSLEY: Collie looks rather worried. Is anything the matter?

PRENTICE: I'm told his garage isn't doing any too well.

ARDSLEY: It's the same old story. All these ex-officers. They go into business without knowing anything about it. And by the time they've learnt how many beans make five they've lost every bob they'd got.

MRS. ARDSLEY: It's very hard on them.

ARDSLEY: Of course it is. But what's to be done about it?

The nation can't afford itself the luxury of supporting an army of officers it has no use for.

PRENTICE: The unfortunate thing is that the lives they've led in the service has unfitted them for the rough and tumble of ordinary life.

ARDSLEY: Well, I must get back to my office. Is this just a friendly call, Charlie, or are you hunting a patient? Personally, I am in robust health, thank you very much.

PRENTICE: [*With grim humour.*] That's what you say. I expect your blood pressure's awful.

ARDSLEY: Get along with you. I've never had a day's illness in my life.

PRENTICE: Well, don't blame me if you have a stroke. I always have my suspicions about a man who looks as well as you do.

MRS. ARDSLEY: As a matter of fact, I wanted to have a little talk with Charlie about Eva. She's been very jumpy lately.

ARDSLEY: Oh, that's only your fancy, my dear. She's getting a little old maidish. The great thing is to give her occupation. Fortunately Sydney gives her plenty to do.

PRENTICE: Sydney keeping pretty fit?

MRS. ARDSLEY: As fit as can be expected.

ARDSLEY: Poor old Sydney. The only thing we can do is to make things as easy for him as we can. It's been a great blow to me. I was hoping he'd go into the business. He'd have been able to take a lot of the work off my hands now. I've paid for the war all right.

PRENTICE: [*With a twinkle in his eye.*] He has too, in a way.

ARDSLEY: Of course. But he's got used to it. Invalids do, you know. Well, it's lucky I've got my health and strength. Anyhow, I must go back and do a job of work.

[*He nods to the doctor and goes into the house.*

PRENTICE: Leonard's a wonderful fellow. He always looks at the bright side of things.

MRS. ARDSLEY: It's a strength.

PRENTICE: You've spoilt him.

MRS. ARDSLEY: I've loved him.

PRENTICE: I wonder why.

MRS. ARDSLEY: [*With a smile.*] I can't imagine. I suppose because he can never see further than the end of his nose and I've always had to take care that he didn't trip over the obvious and hurt himself.

PRENTICE: You've been a good wife and mother, Charlotte. There aren't many left like you now.

MRS. ARDSLEY: Times are difficult. I think one should make allowances for all these young things who are faced with problems that we never dreamed of.

PRENTICE: What did you want to say to me about Evie?

MRS. ARDSLEY: I want her to come and see you. She's been losing weight. I'm rather uneasy about her.

PRENTICE: I daresay she wants a holiday. I'll have a talk to her. But you know I'm more concerned about you. I don't like this pain you've been complaining of.

MRS. ARDSLEY: I don't think it's very important. It's just pain, you know. I suppose most women of my age have it now and then.

PRENTICE: I've been thinking about it. I want you to let me make a proper examination.

MRS. ARDSLEY: I'd hate it.

PRENTICE: I'm not a bad doctor, you know, even though I am your brother.

MRS. ARDSLEY: You can't do anything for me. When the pain gets bad I take some aspirin. It's no good making a fuss.

PRENTICE: If you won't let me examine you I shall go to Leonard.

MRS. ARDSLEY: No, don't do that. He'll have a fit.

PRENTICE: Come along, then.

MRS. ARDSLEY: Now?

PRENTICE: Yes, now.

MRS. ARDSLEY: I disliked you when you were a little boy and used to make me bowl to you, and every year that has passed since then has made me dislike you more.

PRENTICE: You're a wrinkled old hag, Charlotte, and women ought to be young and pretty, but upon my word there's something about you that I can't help liking.

MRS. ARDSLEY: [*Smiling.*] You fool.

[LOIS *and* WILFRED CEDAR *saunter in from the garden.*

LOIS: Hulloa, Uncle Charlie. Tennis is off. Evie says Collie's got a bad head.

MRS. ARDSLEY: He's gone home.

PRENTICE: I'm just taking your mother off to have a look at her.

LOIS: Oh, mother, you're not ill?

MRS. ARDSLEY: No, darling, of course not. Uncle Charlie's an old fuss-pot.

[*They go into the house.*

WILFRED: D'you want me to take myself off?

LOIS: No, sit down. Would you like a drink?

WILFRED: Not at the moment. Let's have a talk.

LOIS: The days are drawing in. Oh, how I hate the winter.

WILFRED: It must be pretty grim down here.

LOIS: The wind! When d'you go south?

WILFRED: Oh, not for another month.

LOIS: Shall you take a house here again next year?

WILFRED: I don't know. Would you like me to?

LOIS: Naturally. It's awful when there's no one at the Manor.

WILFRED: D'you know, you're a very pretty girl.

LOIS: It doesn't do me much good.

WILFRED: I wonder you don't go on the stage.

LOIS: One can't go on the stage just like that.

WILFRED: With your looks you could always get a job in the chorus.

LOIS: Can you see father's face if I suggested it?

WILFRED: You haven't got much chance of marrying in a place like this.

LOIS: Oh, I don't know. Someone may turn up.

WILFRED: I believe you'd be a success on the stage.

LOIS: One has to have training. At least a year. I'd have to live in London. It costs money.

WILFRED: I'll pay.

LOIS: You? What *do* you mean?

WILFRED: Well, I'm not exactly a poor man. I can't bear the thought of your going to seed in a rotten little hole like this.

LOIS: Don't be silly. How can I take money from you?

WILFRED: Why not? I mean, it's absurd at this time of day to be conventional.

LOIS: What do you think Gwen would say?

WILFRED: She needn't know.

LOIS: Anyhow, it's too late. I'm twenty-six. One has to start at eighteen. . . . It's extraordinary how the years slip by. I didn't realise I was grown up till I was twenty. I vaguely thought of becoming a typist or a hospital nurse. But I never got beyond thinking of it. I suppose I thought I'd marry.

WILFRED: What'll you do if you don't?

P*

LOIS: Become an old maid. Be the solace of my parents' declining years.

WILFRED: I don't think much of that.

LOIS: I'm not complaining, you know. Life's so monotonous here. Time slips by without your noticing it.

WILFRED: Has no one ever asked you to marry him?

LOIS: Oh yes. An assistant of Uncle Charlie's did. An odious little man. And there was a widower with three children and no money. I didn't think that much catch.

WILFRED: I don't blame you.

LOIS: What made you suggest that just now? Paying for my training?

WILFRED: Oh, I don't know. I was sorry for you.

LOIS: You don't give me the impression of a philanthropist.

WILFRED: Well, if you must know, I'm crazy about you.

LOIS: And you thought I'd show my gratitude in the usual way.

WILFRED: I never thought about it.

LOIS: Oh, come off it.

WILFRED: You're not angry with me? It's not my fault if I'm just dotty about you.

LOIS: After all, you are old enough to be my father.

WILFRED: I know. You needn't rub it in.

LOIS: I think it's just as well that you're going away in a month.

WILFRED: I'd do anything in the world for you, Lois.

LOIS: Thank you very much, but there's nothing you can do.

WILFRED: You don't know what you're talking about. You're just mouldering away here. I can give you a better time than you've ever dreamed of. Paris. You've never been there, have you? By God, you'd go mad over the clothes. You could buy as many as you liked. Cannes and Monte. And what price Venice? Gwen and I spent the summer before last at the Lido. It was a riot, I can tell you.

LOIS: You're a monstrous old man. If I were a properly brought up young woman I should ring for a flunkey and have you shown the door.

WILFRED: I'm not a bad sort. I'm sure I could make you happy. You know, you could turn me round your little finger.

LOIS: [*Looking at her fingers.*] Blazing with jewels?

WILFRED: Rather.

LOIS: [*With a laugh.*] You fool.

WILFRED: God, how I love you. It's a relief to be able to say it at all events. I can't make out how you never guessed it.

LOIS: It never occurred to me. Does Gwen know?

WILFRED: Oh, no, she never sees anything. She hasn't got the brains of a louse.

LOIS: You're not going to make a nuisance of yourself, are you?

WILFRED: No, I'm going to leave you to think about it.

LOIS: That's not necessary. There's nothing doing. I can tell you that at once. Take care, there's someone coming.

[HOWARD BARTLETT *comes in from the house. He is a big, fine man of forty, somewhat on the stout side, but still with the dashing good looks that had attracted* ETHEL *during the war. He wears rather shabby plus-fours and a golf coat of rather too loud a pattern. He is altogether a little showy. He does not drop his aitches often, but his accent is slightly common. At the moment he is not quite sober. You would not say he was drunk, but the liquor he has had during the day has made him jovial.*

HOWARD: Well, here I am.

LOIS: Hulloa, Howard.

HOWARD: I've caught you, have I? What are you doing with my sister-in-law, Cedar? Eh? You be careful of that man, Lois. He's up to no good.

LOIS: [*With a laugh.*] Oh, shut up, Howard.

HOWARD: I know him. He's just the kind of fellow to lead a poor girl astray.

LOIS: [*Coolly.*] Howard, you've had a couple.

HOWARD: I know I have, and I'm feeling all the better for it. [*Harking back.*] Don't you listen to a word he says. He's a wicked old man.

WILFRED: Go on. I like flattery.

HOWARD: You know, his intentions aren't honourable. [*To* WILFRED.] Now, as one man to another, are your intentions honourable?

WILFRED: If you put it like that . . .

HOWARD: One man to another, mind you.

WILFRED: I don't mind telling you they're not.

HOWARD: There, Lois, what did I tell you?

LOIS: At all events I know where I am now.

HOWARD: Don't say I didn't warn you. When you're walking the streets of London, with a baby on your arm and no home to go to, don't say, Howard never warned me.

LOIS: Ethel's waiting for you, Howard. She wants to go home.

HOWARD: No place like home and home's a woman's place.

LOIS: You'll find her somewhere in the garden.

HOWARD: A good woman. You always know where to find

her. She's not one of your gad-abouts. One of the best. And a lady, mind you. [*To* WILFRED.] I don't mind telling you I'm not a gentleman by birth.

WILFRED: Aren't you?

HOWARD: The King made me a gentleman. His Majesty. I may be only a farmer now, but I've been an officer and a gentleman. And don't you forget it.

LOIS: You're drivelling, Howard.

HOWARD: What I mean to say is, leave the girl alone, Cedar. A poor motherless child. An innocent village maiden. I appeal to your better nature.

WILFRED: D'you know what's the matter with you, Bartlett?

HOWARD: I do not.

WILFRED: You're tight.

HOWARD: Me? I'm as sober as a judge. How many drinks d'you think I've had to-day?

WILFRED: More than you can count.

HOWARD: On the fingers of one hand, maybe. [*With triumph.*] But not on the fingers of two. It wants more than that to make me tight.

WILFRED: You're getting older. You can't carry your liquor like you used to.

HOWARD: Do you know, when I was an officer and a gentleman, I could drink a bottle of whisky at a sitting and not turn a hair. [*He sees* MRS. ARDSLEY *and* DR. PRENTICE *coming through the drawing-room.*] Here's the Doctor. We'll ask him.

[*They come out.*

MRS. ARDSLEY: Oh, Howard, I didn't know you were here.

HOWARD: As large as life.

DR. PRENTICE: Been in to Stanbury?

HOWARD: Market-day to-day.

DR. PRENTICE: Do any business?

HOWARD: Business is rotten. Just wasting my time, I am. Farming's gone all to hell.

MRS. ARDSLEY: You look tired, Howard. Would you like me to have a cup of tea made for you?

HOWARD: Tired? I'm never tired. [*Pointing to* WILFRED.] Do you know what this chap says? He says I'm tight.

WILFRED: I was only joking.

HOWARD: [*Solemnly.*] I'm going to get a professional opinion. Uncle Charlie and Dr. Prentice, as one man to another, tell me, am I tight? Don't mind hurting my feelings. I'll bear it, whatever you say, like an officer and a gentleman. 'Shun.

DR. PRENTICE: I've seen men a lot tighter.

HOWARD: You examine me. I want to get to the bottom of this. Tell me to say British Constitution.

DR. PRENTICE: Say British Constitution.

HOWARD: I've already said it. You can't catch me that way. Now what about the chalk line?

DR. PRENTICE: What about it?

HOWARD: Look here, do you want me to teach you your business? Draw a chalk line and make me walk along it. That'll prove it. Go on. Draw a chalk line. Draw it straight, mind you.

DR. PRENTICE: I don't happen to have any chalk.

HOWARD: You haven't got any chalk?

DR. PRENTICE: No.

HOWARD: Then I shall never know if I'm tight or not.
        [SYDNEY *comes from the garden, accompanied by* ETHEL. *A moment later* EVA *follows them.*

ETHEL: Howard. Had a good day?

SYDNEY: Hulloa.

HOWARD: Yes, I met a lot of good chaps, white men, fine upstanding fellows. Straight as a die. Pick of the British nation.

> [ETHEL *gives a little start as she realises that he is tipsy, but pretends to notice nothing.*

ETHEL: [*Brightly.*] How was business?

HOWARD: Rotten. Everybody's broke. Farming—what a game. What I ask you is, why the Government don't do something.

ETHEL: Well, they've promised to.

HOWARD: Are they going to keep their promises? You know they're not, I know they're not, and they know they're not.

ETHEL: Then the only thing is to grin and bear it as we've grinned and borne it all these years.

HOWARD: Are we the backbone of the country or not?

SYDNEY: I've never heard a Member of Parliament who didn't say so.

HOWARD: [*About to get angry.*] I know what I'm talking about.

ETHEL: [*Soothingly.*] Of course you do.

HOWARD: Then why does he contradict me?

SYDNEY: I wasn't contradicting you. I was agreeing with you.

HOWARD: [*Mollified.*] Were you, old boy? Well, that's damned nice of you. You're a sport. I've always liked you, Sydney.

SYDNEY: Good.

HOWARD: I was born on a farm. Born and bred. Except when I was an officer and a gentleman, I've been a farmer all me life. Shall I tell you what's wrong with farming?

SYDNEY: No.

HOWARD: No?

SYDNEY: No.

HOWARD: All right, I won't.

> [*He sinks back, comatose, into his chair. At that moment*
> GWEN CEDAR *comes in from the drawing-room. She
> has a fixed, bright smile on her face.*

MRS. ARDSLEY: [*A little surprised.*] Oh, Gwen.

GWEN: I'm like a bad penny. I was just passing your door
and the maid told me Wilfred was still here, so I thought
I'd step in for him.

MRS. ARDSLEY: Of course.

> [WILFRED'S *face is sullen with anger.*

WILFRED: What's the idea, Gwen?

GWEN: I didn't think you'd want to walk all that way.

WILFRED: You said you were going home.

GWEN: I remembered I had some things to do.

WILFRED: I prefer to walk.

GWEN: [*With a bright smile.*] Why?

WILFRED: Good God, surely I don't have to explain why I
want a walk.

GWEN: It seems so silly when the car is there.

WILFRED: I need the exercise.

GWEN: You've had lots of exercise.

WILFRED: You're making a fool of yourself, Gwen.

GWEN: How rude you are, Wilfred.

WILFRED: It's maddening that you can never trust me out of
your sight for ten minutes.

GWEN: [*Still very bright.*] You're so fascinating. I'm
always afraid some bold bad woman will be running
after you.

WILFRED: [*Surly.*] Come on, then. Let's go.

GWEN: [*Turning to shake hands with* MRS. ARDSLEY.] Tiresome creatures men are, aren't they?

WILFRED: Good-bye, Mrs. Ardsley. Thank you very much

GWEN: It's been a lovely afternoon. So kind of you to ask us.

MRS. ARDSLEY: I hope you'll come again very soon.

> [WILFRED *gives a sullen nod to the others. He waits at the window for his wife and when she flutters out he follows her.*

SYDNEY: What's the trouble?

LOIS: What a fool of a woman.

SYDNEY: I bet he gives her hell in the car.

> [HOWARD *gives a little snore. He has fallen into a drunken sleep.* ETHEL *gives a start.*

ETHEL: Listen to Howard. He's tired out, poor dear. One of the cows has something the matter with her and he was up at five this morning.

MRS. ARDSLEY: Let him sleep for a little, Ethel. Sydney, hadn't you better come in. It's beginning to get quite chilly.

SYDNEY: All right.

> [MRS. ARDSLEY, DR. PRENTICE *and* SYDNEY *go into the house.*

DR. PRENTICE: [*As they go.*] How has the neuralgia been lately?

SYDNEY: Bearable, you know.

> [MRS. ARDSLEY'S *three daughters are left with the drunken, sleeping man.*

ETHEL: Poor Howard, he works so hard. I'm glad to see him get a few minutes rest.

EVA: You work hard too and you get no rest.

ETHEL: I love it. I'm so interested in it, and Howard's a wonderful person to work with.

EVA: Would you marry him over again if you could put the clock back?

ETHEL: Why, of course. He's been a wonderful husband.

> [MRS. ARDSLEY *comes to the door of the drawing-room.*

MRS. ARDSLEY: Evie, Sydney would like a game of chess.

EVA: All right, mother. I'll come.

> [MRS. ARDSLEY *withdraws into the room.* EVA *gets up.*

LOIS: Don't you hate chess?

EVA: I loathe it.

ETHEL: Poor Evie.

EVA: It's one of the few games Sydney can play. I'm glad to do anything I can to make life a little easier for him.

ETHEL: That horrible war.

LOIS: And the chances are that it'll go on like this till we're all weary old women.

> [HOWARD *gives another snore.*

EVA: I'll go.

> [*She makes her way into the house.*

LOIS: At all events you've got your children.

ETHEL: I've got nothing to complain of.

> [LOIS *gets up and bending over* ETHEL *kisses her on the cheek. Then she saunters away into the darkening garden.* ETHEL *looks at her husband and the tears flow down her cheeks. She takes out her handkerchief and nervously pulls it about as she tries to control herself.*

END OF THE FIRST ACT

ACT II

The scene represents the dining-room of the ARDSLEYS' *house. It is furnished in an old-fashioned style, with a mahogany sideboard, mahogany chairs with leather seats and backs, and a solid mahogany dining-table. On each side of the fireplace are two easy chairs, one with arms for the master of the house and one without for the mistress. On the walls are large framed engravings of academy pictures.*

There is a bow window, looking on the High Street, and here EVA *and* SYDNEY *are seated, playing chess. Luncheon is just over and* GERTRUDE, *the maid, is clearing away.*

MRS. ARDSLEY *is sitting in her easy chair reading the paper.*

EVA: Uncle Charlie's car has just driven up.

SYDNEY: Do attend to the game, Evie.

EVA: It's your move.

MRS. ARDSLEY: You'd better go and open the door, Gertrude.

GERTRUDE: Very good, ma'am.

[She goes out.

EVA: He's been here rather often lately.

MRS. ARDSLEY: You know what he is. He will fuss.

SYDNEY: You're not ill, mother, are you?

MRS. ARDSLEY: No, only old.

SYDNEY: I doubt whether even Uncle Charlie can do much about that.

MRS. ARDSLEY: That's what I tell him.

*[*GERTRUDE *shows in* DR. PRENTICE.

GERTRUDE: Dr. Prentice.

[*He comes in, kisses* MRS. ARDSLEY *and waves to the others.*

DR. PRENTICE: How are you? Don't let me disturb your game.

SYDNEY: D'you want us to leave you?

DR. PRENTICE: No. This isn't a doctor's visit. I'm only stopping a minute.

SYDNEY: Queen's knight to queen's bishop third.

[EVA *moves the piece he indicates. The* DOCTOR *sits down and holds out his hands to the fire.*

DR. PRENTICE: Chilly to-day.

MRS. ARDSLEY: Have you arranged something?

DR. PRENTICE: Yes, three o'clock to-morrow afternoon.

MRS. ARDSLEY: That'll suit very well.

DR. PRENTICE: Where's Lois?

MRS. ARDSLEY: She's playing golf. She thought it would be a rush to get back, so she lunched at the club house.

SYDNEY: She's playing with Wilfred. She said she'd bring him back with her and Collie's coming in so that we can have a rubber or two of bridge.

MRS. ARDSLEY: Oh, that'll be nice for you, Sydney.

SYDNEY: Is there a fire in the drawing-room?

MRS. ARDSLEY: I'll have one lit. Gertrude.

[GERTRUDE *has been clearing the rest of the things away and now has finished.*

GERTRUDE: Very good, ma'am.

[*She puts the table-cloth away in the sideboard drawer and goes out.*

MRS. ARDSLEY: [*To* DR. PRENTICE.] Can't you stay and have a man's four.

DR. PRENTICE: I wish I could. I'm too busy.

EVA: King's knight to queen's third.

SYDNEY: That's an idiotic move, Evie.

EVA: There's no reason why I shouldn't make it if I want to.

SYDNEY: You must protect your bishop.

EVA: Play your own game and let me play mine.

MRS. ARDSLEY: Evie.

SYDNEY: You won't look ahead.

EVA: [*Violently.*] Good God, don't I spend my life looking ahead. And a damned cheerful prospect it is.

SYDNEY: My dear, what on earth's the matter with you?

EVA: [*Regaining her self-control.*] Oh, nothing. I'm sorry. I'll protect my bishop. Queen's bishop's pawn to bishop's fourth.

SYDNEY: I'm afraid that's not a very good move.

EVA: It'll do.

SYDNEY: There's not the least use playing chess unless you're prepared to give it some attention.

EVA: Oh, can't you stop nagging. It's enough to drive one insane.

SYDNEY: I didn't mean to nag. I won't say another word.

EVA: Oh, I'm sick of it.

[*She takes the board and throws all the pieces on the floor.*

MRS. ARDSLEY: Evie.

EVA: Damn it. Damn it. Damn it.

MRS. ARDSLEY: Evie, what's the matter with you? You mustn't lose your temper because you're losing a game. That's childish.

EVA: As if I cared whether I lost or won. I hate the filthy game.

DR. PRENTICE: [*Soothingly.*] I think it's very boring myself.

MRS. ARDSLEY: Sydney has so few amusements.

EVA: Why should I be sacrificed all the time?

SYDNEY: [*With an amused smile.*] My dear, we thought you liked it.

EVA: I'm sick of being a drudge.

MRS. ARDSLEY: I'm sorry, I never knew you looked at it like that. I thought you wanted to do everything you could for Sydney.

EVA: I'm very sorry he's blind. But it's not my fault. I'm not responsible for the war. He ought to go into a home.

MRS. ARDSLEY: Oh, how cruel. How callous.

EVA: He took his chance like the rest of them. He's lucky not to have been killed.

SYDNEY: That of course is a matter of opinion.

EVA: It's monstrous that he should try to prevent anyone else from having a good time.

MRS. ARDSLEY: I thought it was a privilege to be able to do what we could to make life easier for him when he gave so much for us. And I felt that it wasn't only for him we were doing it, but also for all those others who, for our sakes, and for what at least they thought was honour, have sacrificed so much of what makes life happy and good to live.

EVA: I've given enough. I gave the man I was going to marry. I adored him. I might have had a home of my own and children. I never had another chance. And now . . . now. Oh, I'm so unhappy.

> [*Bursting into tears, she rushes out of the room. There is a moment's awkward pause.*]

MRS. ARDSLEY: What is the matter with her?

SYDNEY: She wants a man, that's all.

MRS. ARDSLEY: Oh, Sydney, don't. That's horrible.

SYDNEY: But not unnatural.

MRS. ARDSLEY: You mustn't take any notice of what she said to you.

SYDNEY: [*With an indulgent smile.*] Oh, my dear, I knew it

already. The day's long past since I was a wounded hero for whom nothing was good enough. Fifteen years is a long time.

MRS. ARDSLEY: If you could bear it there's no reason why others shouldn't.

SYDNEY: It was easier for me, you know. Being blind is an occupation in itself. It's astonishing how quickly the time passes. But of course it's hard on the others. At first it gives them a sort of exaltation to look after you, then it becomes a habit and they take you as a matter of course, but in the end, human nature being what it is, you become just a damned bore.

MRS. ARDSLEY: You'll never be a bore to me, Sydney.

SYDNEY: [*Affectionately.*] I know. You've got that queer, incomprehensible thing that's called the mother instinct.

MRS. ARDSLEY: I can't live for ever. It was a comfort to me to think that you'd always be safe with Evie.

SYDNEY: [*Almost gaily.*] Oh, don't bother about me, mother. I shall be all right. They say suffering ennobles. It hasn't ennobled me. It's made me sly and cunning. Evie says I'm selfish. I am. But I'm damned artful. I know how to get people to do things for me by working on their sympathy. Evie'll settle down. I shall be as safe as a house.

MRS. ARDSLEY: Her not marrying and all that. It seemed so natural that she should look after you. Ethel's got her husband and children. Lois is so much younger. She doesn't understand. She's hard.

SYDNEY: [*With a good-natured shrug of the shoulders.*] Oh, I don't know. She's got the healthy, normal selfishness of youth. There's no harm in that. She doesn't see why she should be bothered with me, and she damned well isn't going to. I don't blame her. I know exactly where I am with her.

MRS. ARDSLEY: I suppose I ought to go to Evie.

DR. PRENTICE: I'd leave her alone for a little longer.

> [GERTRUDE *comes in with a note.*

GERTRUDE: Mrs. Cedar asked me to give you this, ma'am.

MRS. ARDSLEY: Oh. [*She opens the letter and reads it.*] Is she in the drawing-room?

GERTRUDE: No, ma'am. She's waiting in her car.

MRS. ARDSLEY: Ask her to come in.

GERTRUDE: Very good, ma'am.

> [GERTRUDE *goes out.*

MRS. ARDSLEY: How very strange.

DR. PRENTICE: What is it?

MRS. ARDSLEY: It's from Gwen. She asks if she can see me alone for a few minutes.

SYDNEY: I'll get out then.

> [*He rises, takes his stick and stumps out of the room.*

DR. PRENTICE: I'll go, too.

MRS. ARDSLEY: I wonder what she wants.

DR. PRENTICE: Probably an address or something.

MRS. ARDSLEY: She could have telephoned.

DR. PRENTICE: Am I right in thinking she's a very silly woman?

MRS. ARDSLEY: Quite right.

> [DR. PRENTICE *has been watching* SYDNEY *go and as soon as the door is closed on him he changes his manner.*

DR. PRENTICE: I've had a long talk with Murray.

MRS. ARDSLEY: I hate this consultation that you've forced me into.

DR. PRENTICE: My dear, it's essential. I don't want to alarm you, but I must tell you I'm not satisfied with your condition.

MRS. ARDSLEY: Oh, well. It's at three o'clock to-morrow afternoon?

DR. PRENTICE: Yes. He's promised to ring me up after he's seen you.

MRS. ARDSLEY: [*Giving him her hand.*] You're very nice to me.

DR. PRENTICE: [*Kissing her cheek.*] I'm very fond of you.

> [*He goes out. In a minute* GERTRUDE *shows* GWEN CEDAR *into the room, and after announcing her, goes out.*

GERTRUDE: Mrs. Cedar.

MRS. ARDSLEY: How d'you do.

GWEN: I hope you don't think it very strange my sending in a note like that. I simply had to see you.

MRS. ARDSLEY: Do sit down. We shan't be disturbed.

GWEN: I thought I'd better talk it over with you. I mean, I thought it only fair to you.

MRS. ARDSLEY: Yes?

GWEN: I think I'd better come straight to the point.

MRS. ARDSLEY: [*With a little smile.*] It's always a good plan.

GWEN: You know that I'm Wilfred's second wife.

MRS. ARDSLEY: No, I didn't.

GWEN: He's my second husband. We fell very much in love with one another. And there were divorce proceedings. We've been married for twelve years. It's all so long ago, I didn't see any reason to say anything about it when we came down here.

MRS. ARDSLEY: It was nobody's business but your own.

GWEN: We've been awfully happy together. It's been a great success.

MRS. ARDSLEY: I imagine he's a very easy man to get on with.

GWEN: Of course he's always been very attractive to women.

MRS. ARDSLEY: That's a thing I'm no judge about.

GWEN: He's got a way with him that takes them. And he pays them all kinds of little attentions that flatter them. But of course it doesn't mean anything.

MRS. ARDSLEY: It seldom does.

GWEN: All women don't know that. It's the kind of thing that's quite likely to turn a girl's head. It would be silly to take him seriously. After all he's a married man and *I* would never divorce him whatever he did. Never.

MRS. ARDSLEY: My dear, you said you were coming straight to the point. Aren't you beating about the bush a good deal?

GWEN: Don't you know what I mean?

MRS. ARDSLEY: I haven't an idea.

GWEN: I'm very relieved to hear it.

MRS. ARDSLEY: Won't you explain?

GWEN: You won't be angry with me?

MRS. ARDSLEY: I shouldn't think so.

GWEN: He's been paying a lot of attention to your Lois.

MRS. ARDSLEY: [*With a chuckle.*] Oh, my dear, don't be so ridiculous.

GWEN: I know he's attracted by her.

MRS. ARDSLEY: How can you be so silly?

GWEN: They're together all the time.

MRS. ARDSLEY: Nonsense. They play tennis and golf together. They're playing golf now. There are very few men for your husband to play with during the week. It's been nice for both of them. You don't mean to say you're jealous of that?

GWEN: But you see, I know he's madly in love with her.

MRS. ARDSLEY: Oh, my dear, that's only fancy.

GWEN: How do you know that she isn't in love with him?

MRS. ARDSLEY: He's old enough to be her father.

GWEN: What does that matter?

MRS. ARDSLEY: A lot, I should say. I don't want to hurt your feelings, but you know, a girl of Lois's age looks upon you and me, your husband and mine, as older than God.

GWEN: It isn't as if there were a lot of men here. A girl can't pick and choose in a place like this.

MRS. ARDSLEY: Now I'm afraid I think you're not being very polite.

GWEN: I'm sorry. I don't mean to be rude. I'm so utterly miserable.

MRS. ARDSLEY: [*With kindness.*] You poor dear. I'm sure you're mistaken. And in any case you're going away soon and that'll end it.

GWEN: [*Quickly.*] Then you think there's something to end?

MRS. ARDSLEY: No, no. End your fear, I mean. I know very little about men like your husband. I daresay men of that age are often rather taken by bright young things. I think a sensible wife just shrugs her shoulders and laughs. Her safety is that the bright young things look upon her husband as an old fogey.

GWEN: Oh, I hope you're right. If you only knew the agony I've been through since I found out.

MRS. ARDSLEY: I'm sure I'm right. And if there is any truth in what you think, I'm convinced that a fortnight after you've left here he'll have forgotten all about her.

> [*She gets up to put an end to the conversation.* GWEN *rises too. She glances out of the window and sees a car stopping at the door.*

GWEN: Here they are.

MRS. ARDSLEY: [*Looking out of window.*] Who? Oh, your husband and Lois.

GWEN: He's coming in.

MRS. ARDSLEY: He promised Sydney to play bridge. You don't object to that, do you?

GWEN: I don't want him to see me. He'll think I'm spying on him. He'll be furious.

MRS. ARDSLEY: He won't come in here. He'll go into the drawing-room.

GWEN: You won't say anything to Lois, will you? I don't want to put her back up.

MRS. ARDSLEY: Of course I won't say anything. I'm sure she's absolutely unconscious of what you've been talking about. It would only make her shy and uncomfortable.

GWEN: I'll slip away the moment the coast is clear.

[*The door is burst open and* LOIS *comes in. She is radiant with health and spirits.*

LOIS: Hulloa! Are you here, Gwen?

GWEN: Yes, your mother wanted to see me about the sale of work. I'm just going.

LOIS: Wilfred is here.

GWEN: Is he? Give him my love and tell him not to be late for dinner. You're going to play bridge, aren't you?

LOIS: Yes. Collie and Howard are coming. They'll have a man's four.

GWEN: Wilfred says your brother plays just as well as if he could see.

LOIS: Yes, it's rather marvellous. Of course we have special cards.

GWEN: [*Catching sight of a pearl necklace* LOIS *has on.*] Pretty chain that is you're wearing. I've never seen it before.

LOIS: [*Instinctively putting her hand to her neck and fingering the beads.*] I bought it the other day when I went into Stanbury.

GWEN: How extravagant of you. I didn't know anyone could afford to buy pearls now.

LOIS: It only cost a pound.

GWEN: Aren't they real?

LOIS: Of course not. How could they be?

GWEN: [*Going up to* LOIS *and feeling the pearls.*] I think I know something about pearls. I would have sworn they were real.

LOIS: I wish they were.

GWEN: It's the most wonderful imitation I've ever seen.

LOIS: They do make them marvellously now. I wonder anyone bothers to have real pearls at all.

> [GWEN *is taken aback. She still looks at the pearls doubtfully, Then she makes an effort over herself.*

GWEN: Good-bye, Mrs. Ardsley. I'll have everything ready in good time.

MRS. ARDSLEY: Good-bye, my dear. Lois will see you out.

> [GWEN *and* LOIS *go out.* MRS. ARDSLEY *is left reflective. She is a little puzzled.* LOIS *comes in again.*

MRS. ARDSLEY: Lois dear, I've been thinking you looked rather peaked. Don't you think it would be a good idea if you went to stay at Aunt Emily's for a week or two?

LOIS: I should hate it.

MRS. ARDSLEY: She does love having you there.

LOIS: It's so incredibly boring.

MRS. ARDSLEY: You'll have to go before the end of the year. Much better go now and get it over.

LOIS: I loathe the idea.

MRS. ARDSLEY: Think about it a little. I can't have you not looking your best, you know, or I shall never get you off my hands.

> [*She goes out. Her voice is heard through the still open door:* Oh, here's Collie. You'll find Sydney in the

drawing-room. *As* COLLIE *passes the door he sees* LOIS.

COLLIE: Hulloa, Lois.

LOIS: You're early.

[*He pauses at the door.*

COLLIE: I had an appointment with your father, but he's had to go out. I've left a message with the clerk to say I'm here when I'm wanted.

LOIS: Oh, good.

COLLIE: I'll go along to the drawing-room.

LOIS: Right-ho.

[*He passes on.* LOIS *goes to the looking-glass and looks again at the little string round her neck. She feels the pearls.* WILFRED'S *voice is heard:* Lois.

LOIS: Hulloa.

WILFRED: [*Still outside.*] Where are you?

LOIS: In the dining-room.

[*He comes to the door.*

WILFRED: As Collie's here why shouldn't we start?

LOIS: Howard's coming.

WILFRED: I know. But there's no reason why you shouldn't play a rubber or two before he does.

LOIS: Come in a minute, will you.

WILFRED: Why?

LOIS: Shut the door.

WILFRED: [*Closing the door behind him.*] It's shut.

LOIS: These pearls you gave me, they are false, aren't they?

WILFRED: Of course.

LOIS: How much did they cost?

WILFRED: I told you. A pound.

LOIS: Gwen's just been here.

WILFRED: Why?

LOIS: Oh, I don't know. She came to see mother about the sale of work.

WILFRED: Oh, is that all? She's been very funny lately.

LOIS: She says they're real.

WILFRED: What does she know about it?

LOIS: She says she knows a great deal. She has pearls of her own.

WILFRED: And a pretty packet they cost me.

LOIS: Is she right?

WILFRED: [*Smiling.*] I wouldn't swear she wasn't.

LOIS: Why did you say they were false?

WILFRED: I didn't think you'd take them if you thought they were real.

LOIS: Naturally.

[*She puts her fingers to the clasp.*

WILFRED: What are you going to do?

LOIS: I'm going to give them back to you.

WILFRED: You can't do that now. You'll give the whole show away.

LOIS: There's nothing to give away.

WILFRED: Oh, isn't there? You don't know Gwen. She's got the tongue of a serpent.

LOIS: I can't accept a valuable pearl necklace from you.

WILFRED: At all events you must go on wearing it till we go away.

LOIS: How much did you pay for it?

WILFRED: My dear, it's not very good manners to ask what a present costs.

LOIS: Several hundred pounds?

WILFRED: I shouldn't wonder.

LOIS: D'you know, I've never had a valuable thing in my life. I shall be scared stiff of losing it.

WILFRED: Don't give it a thought. I'm not a very poor man, and if you do I shall survive it.

LOIS: But I might never have known. I might have worn it for years under the impression it was worth nothing.

WILFRED: That's what I hoped.

LOIS: [*With a smile.*] You know, that's rather sweet of you. I would never have thought you capable of that.

WILFRED: Why?

LOIS: Well, I've always looked upon you as rather a show-off. I should have thought you the sort of man who, when he gave a present that cost a lot of money, made pretty sure that you knew it.

WILFRED: That's not very flattering.

LOIS: You couldn't expect me to be so awfully grateful. I mean, a string of false pearls. Howard might have bought me that when he'd won a fiver on a horse.

WILFRED: I liked to think of you wearing pearls I'd given you. It gave me rather a thrill to think of them round your pretty neck.

LOIS: It seems a lot to pay for it.

WILFRED: You see, I'm so terribly in love with you. Give me a kiss, Lois.

> [*He puts his arm round her waist. He tries to kiss her lips, but she turns her face away, and he kisses her cheek.*] You do like me a little, don't you?

LOIS: [*Coolly.*] Yes.

WILFRED: D'you think you could ever love me?

LOIS: It wouldn't be much use, would it?

WILFRED: I'd do anything in the world for you. You know Gwen and I don't get on. We'd be much happier apart.

I know I could make you happy. After all you don't want to stay in this deadly little place all your life.

LOIS: What are you asking me to do now? Run away with you?

WILFRED: Why not?

LOIS: And be chucked the moment you were sick of me? Thank you.

WILFRED: I'll settle twenty thousand pounds on you to-morrow, and if you don't like to run away with me you needn't.

LOIS: Don't be such a donkey.

WILFRED: Gwen would divorce me if I made it worth her while and then we'd be married.

LOIS: I've always understood that when the gay seducer had worked his wicked will on the village maiden he screamed like a hyena at the thought of making an honest woman of her.

WILFRED: Oh, Lois, don't laugh at me. I love you with all my heart. Oh, I know I'm as old as the hills. I wish to God I was twenty years younger. I want you so awfully. I want you for keeps.

> [LOIS *looks at him for a moment seriously.*

LOIS: Let's go and play bridge.

> [ETHEL *comes in.*

ETHEL: Sydney's getting impatient. [*To* WILFRED, *humorously.*] And Howard says, if you don't come along at once you'll have to marry the girl.

LOIS: I didn't know you were here.

ETHEL: We've only just come.

LOIS: Oh, well, if Howard's here you don't want me.

WILFRED: All right, we'll start a rubber. But come and cut in later, won't you.

LOIS: I must go and powder my nose.

> [WILFRED *goes out.*

Ω

ETHEL: I hear Evie's been making a scene.

LOIS: Has she? What about?

ETHEL: Oh, I don't know.   Nerves.   She ought to get married.

LOIS: Who can she marry, poor dear?

ETHEL: Collie. They're just about the same age. I think it would be very suitable.

LOIS: Wilfred says he's going smash.

ETHEL: They could manage. Nobody's got any money nowadays, but one gets along somehow. Even a marriage that isn't quite satisfactory is better than not being married at all.

LOIS: Is that your experience?

ETHEL: I wasn't talking of myself. I haven't got anything to grumble at.

LOIS: Wilfred wants me to run away with him.

ETHEL: Wilfred? What do you mean? Why?

LOIS: He says he's in love with me.

ETHEL: The dirty old man. I don't understand. What does he suggest?

LOIS: Well, I suppose his idea is to keep me till he gets his divorce and then I suppose his idea is to marry me.

ETHEL: The beast.

LOIS: I'm getting on, you know. I'm twenty-six.

ETHEL: [*Aghast.*] Lois.

LOIS: What have I got to look forward to exactly? Getting jumpy like Eva or making the best of a bad job like you.

ETHEL: I have my children. Howard has his faults like everybody else. But he's fond of me. He looks up to me.

LOIS: My dear, you've got a wonderful character. I haven't. D'you think I haven't seen what a strain it is on you sometimes?

ETHEL: Of course it's a hard life. I ought to have known it would be when I married a tenant farmer.

LOIS: But you didn't expect he'd drink.

ETHEL: I don't suppose he drinks any more than most men of his class.

LOIS: Have you ever really quite got used to him?

ETHEL: [*Defiantly.*] I don't know what you mean?

LOIS: Well, he's common, isn't he?

ETHEL: [*Smiling.*] Are you quite sure that you and I are any great shakes?

LOIS: At all events we do talk the King's English. We have decent table manners and we wash.

ETHEL: I don't believe you'd wash much if you had to get up at six and milk the cows. All that's convention. One oughtn't to let oneself be upset by things like that.

LOIS: But aren't you?

ETHEL: Sometimes. I blame myself.

LOIS: What have you got in common with him really?

ETHEL: A recollection. That first year or two when I loved him so madly. He was gallant and young. He was manly. I loved him because he was of the soil and his strength had its roots in it. Nothing mattered then. Nothing that he did offended me.

LOIS: My dear, you're so romantic. I'm not. Romance doesn't last. When it's dead what is left but dust and ashes?

ETHEL: And the consciousness that you've done your best.

LOIS: Oh, that.

ETHEL: It's something. I've made my bed and I'm ready to lie on it. Have you ever heard me complain?

LOIS: Never.

ETHEL: I've carried my head high. I've tried to make Howard a good wife. I've tried to be a good mother to my children. Sometimes I'm inclined to be a little proud of myself.

LOIS: I suppose it's never occurred to you that it would have been better for Howard really if he'd married someone in his own class?

ETHEL: Oh yes, often. That's why I feel I must always have patience with him. I ought to have known. I oughtn't to have been carried away.

LOIS: My dear, you're so noble it makes me positively sick.

ETHEL: I'm not noble at all. I merely have a good deal of common sense . . . Lois, you're not really thinking of going away with that man?

LOIS: No, not really. It's only that it's rather exciting to have the chance.

ETHEL: Oh, I'm so glad.

[LEONARD ARDSLEY *comes in.*

ARDSLEY: What are you two girls doing in here? Discussing frocks and frills, I'll be bound.

ETHEL: [*Kissing him.*] How are you, father?

ARDSLEY: Chatter, chatter, chatter all day long. I know you. It's a marvel to me that you never get tired of talking about clothes. Collie's here, isn't he?

LOIS: Yes, he's playing bridge.

ARDSLEY: Well, run along both of you and send him in here. I want to see him.

LOIS: All right.

ARDSLEY: Kiddies well?

ETHEL: Oh yes. They always are.

ARDSLEY: Fine thing for them living on a farm like that. Grand thing a country life.

ETHEL: They've gone back to school now.

ARDSLEY: Of course. I remember. Best thing in the world for them. Happiest time in their lives. [*The two girls go out.* ARDSLEY *catches sight of a ladies' paper and takes it up.*] I knew it.

> [*He gives a complacent smile at his own perspicacity. The door opens and* COLLIE *comes in.* ARDSLEY *at the sight of him assumes his professional air.*] How d'you do?

COLLIE: You weren't in when I turned up at the office just now.

ARDSLEY: No. I've got someone waiting that I thought you'd better not meet, and I wanted to see you before I saw him. So I came through my private door.

COLLIE: I'm just as glad. I'm not used to solicitors' offices and I'm always rather intimidated.

ARDSLEY: I'm afraid I've got something very serious to say to you.

COLLIE: Oh, Lord.

ARDSLEY: In the three years you've been here we've seen a good deal of you. We all liked you.

COLLIE: It's been a snip for me having this house to come to. Except for all of you I should have had a pretty thin time.

ARDSLEY: I'm sure you'll realise that it's not very pleasant for me to find myself in my present position.

COLLIE: I suppose that means the game's up. I've made a damned good fight for it. Have I got to file my petition?

ARDSLEY: The bank wrote to you last month telling you that you were overdrawn and that they wouldn't cash any further cheques you drew until your account was put in order.

COLLIE: Yes.

ARDSLEY: And after that you gave several post-dated cheques in payment of various accounts.

COLLIE: I was being pestered for money all over the shop. I couldn't help myself.

ARDSLEY: You were hopelessly insolvent. How did you expect to meet them?

COLLIE: I thought something would turn up.

ARDSLEY: Don't you know that's a criminal offence?

COLLIE: Oh, what rot. It's the sort of thing anyone might do when he was up against it.

ARDSLEY: Not without going to gaol.

COLLIE: Good God, you don't mean to say they're going to prosecute?

ARDSLEY: You can't expect the injured parties to take it lying down.

COLLIE: But it's absurd. They know I didn't mean any harm.

ARDSLEY: It's almost incredible that you should be so unbusinesslike.

COLLIE: What should I know about business? I'm a sailor. I was in the navy for twenty years.

ARDSLEY: I'm afraid you've been very unwise.

COLLIE: Then what's going to happen?

ARDSLEY: The bank-manager is in my office now. You must be prepared for the worst, Collie. A warrant will be applied for.

COLLIE: Does that mean I shall be arrested?

ARDSLEY: Of course you'll be released on bail. I'll arrange that. If you elect to be tried by a jury the justices will refer the case to quarter sessions. It's early days yet to decide, we'll see what counsel has to say. My own opinion at the moment is that the best thing you can do is to plead guilty and throw yourself on the mercy of the court.

COLLIE: But I'm not guilty.

ARDSLEY: Don't be such a fool. You're just as guilty as the thief who sneaks ten bob from your till when no one is looking.

COLLIE: What will they do to me?

ARDSLEY: In consideration of your previous good character and your record in the navy, I have little doubt that the judge will be lenient. I should be very disappointed if you got more than from three to six months in the second division.

COLLIE: [*With a flash of anger at the casual way he takes it.*] You don't care, do you?

ARDSLEY: My dear boy, don't think I'm happy about it. In my profession one often finds oneself in very disagreeable situations, but I don't remember ever having found myself in a more painful one than this.

COLLIE: Fortunately most people get over seeing the other fellow come a cropper.

ARDSLEY: It's not only the pleasant social relations we've always had with you, but that you should have got the D.S.O. and been in command of a destroyer—it all makes your fall so much more distressing. I'm afraid it makes it also much more disgraceful.

COLLIE: They'll take my D.S.O. away from me.

ARDSLEY: I suppose so.

COLLIE: I suppose it doesn't occur to you that when a fellow has served the country for twenty years in a job that's unfitted him for anything else, it's rather distressing and rather disgraceful that he should be shoved out into the world with no means of earning his living and nothing between him and starvation but a bonus of a thousand pounds or so?

ARDSLEY: I can't go into that. Though of course it's a good point to take up at the trial. I'll make a note of that. Of course the answer is that the country was up against it and had to economise and if a certain number of individuals had to suffer it can't be helped.

COLLIE: When I was torpedoed during the war and they fished me out, God, what a bit of luck I said. I never knew.

ARDSLEY: Do me the justice to admit that I begged you six months ago to file your petition. You wouldn't take my advice.

COLLIE: I'd had it drummed into me for so many years that nothing is impossible in the British Navy. It was hard to give in while I still had some fight in me.

ARDSLEY: You mustn't despair.

COLLIE: There's not much of a future for an ex-naval officer, forty years of age, after six months in gaol.

ARDSLEY: I've been a hunting man. It's a very good plan not to take your fences before you come to them. Now look here, I must be off. There's whisky and soda on the sideboard. You help yourself to a drink. I'm sure you want it.

COLLIE: Thank you.

ARDSLEY: [*Giving him his hand.*] Good-bye, my boy. I'll let you know about things as soon as I hear.

COLLIE: Good-bye.

> [ARDSLEY *goes out.* COLLIE, *sinking into a chair, buries his face in his hands; but hearing the door open he looks up and pulls himself together.* EVA *comes in.*

EVA: Oh, I beg your pardon. I was looking for my bag. I didn't know anyone was here.

COLLIE: I was just going.

EVA: Please don't. I won't disturb you.

COLLIE: What are you talking about? Surely you can come into your own dining-room.

EVA: I wasn't speaking the truth. I knew you were here

and my bag's upstairs. I heard father go. I wanted to see you. I'm so frightfully anxious.

COLLIE: What about?

EVA: Everyone knows you're in difficulties. Father let fall a hint at luncheon. I knew he was seeing you this afternoon.

COLLIE: It's kind of you to bother, Evie. I've had rather a rough passage, but at all events I know where I am now.

EVA: Can nothing be done?

COLLIE: Not very much, I'm afraid.

EVA: Won't you let me help you?

COLLIE: [*With a smile.*] My dear, how can you?

EVA: It's only a matter of money, isn't it?

COLLIE: Only is good.

EVA: I've got a thousand pounds that my god-mother left me. It's invested and I've always dressed myself on the interest. I could let you have that.

COLLIE: I couldn't possibly take money from you. It's out of the question.

EVA: Why? If I want to give it you.

COLLIE: It's awfully generous of you, but . . .

EVA: [*Interrupting.*] You must know how frightfully fond I am of you.

COLLIE: It's very nice of you, Evie. Besides, your father would never hear of it.

EVA: It's my own money. I'm not a child.

COLLIE: Can't be done, my dear.

EVA: Why shouldn't I buy an interest in your garage? I mean, then it would be just an investment.

COLLIE: Can you see your father's face when you suggested it? It looked all right when I bought it. Things were

Q*

booming then. But the slump has killed it. It isn't worth a bob.

EVA: But surely if you can get more capital you can afford to wait till times get better?

COLLIE: Your father doesn't think much of me as it is. He'd think me a pretty mean skunk if he thought I'd induced you to put your money into an insolvent business.

EVA: You keep on talking of father. It's nothing to do with him. It's you and I that are concerned.

COLLIE: I know you're a damned good sort and you're always going out of your way to do things for people, but there are limits. Perhaps you'll want to get married one of these days and then you'll find your thousand pounds devilish useful.

EVA: I shall never have a better use for it than to give it to someone who means so much to me as you do.

COLLIE: I'm awfully sorry, God knows I want the money, but I really can't take it from anyone like you.

EVA: I thought you liked me.

COLLIE: I like you very much. You're a jolly good friend.

EVA: I thought perhaps some day we might be more than friends. [*There is a moment's silence. She is very nervous, but forces herself to go on.*] After all, if we were engaged, it would be very natural that I should come to the rescue when you were in a hole.

COLLIE: But we're not engaged.

EVA: Why shouldn't we pretend to be? Just for a little while, I mean. Then I could lend you the money and father would help you to get straight.

COLLIE: Oh, my dear, that's absurd. That's the sort of thing they do in novels. You mustn't be so romantic.

EVA: You could always break it off when you got straight.

COLLIE: That's not a very pretty rôle you're asking me to play.

EVA: [*In a husky voice.*] Perhaps when you got used to the idea you wouldn't want to break it off.

COLLIE: My dear, what on earth ever put such an idea in your head?

EVA: You're alone and I'm alone. There's no one in the world that cares twopence for either of us.

COLLIE: Oh, what nonsense. Your family's devoted to you. They depend on you so enormously. Why, the whole house centres round you.

EVA: I want to get away. I'm so unhappy here.

COLLIE: I can't believe that. You're just nervous and run down. I daresay you want a bit of change.

EVA: You won't understand. How can you be so cruel?

COLLIE: I'm not cruel. I'm awfully grateful to you.

EVA: I can't say any more than I have. It's so humiliating.

COLLIE: I'm dreadfully sorry. I don't want to hurt your feelings.

EVA: After all I'm not so old as all that. Plenty of men have wanted to marry me.

COLLIE: I don't doubt that for a minute. I'm quite convinced that one of these days you'll find someone that you really like and I'm sure you'll make him a perfectly grand wife. [*She begins to cry and he looks at her with troubled eyes.*] I'm sorry.

> [*She does not answer and quietly he leaves the room. She sobs. But she hears the door open and starts to her feet, turning her face away so that her tears should not be seen. The newcomer is* HOWARD. *He is quite sober.*]

HOWARD: Where's Collie?

Eva: How should I know?

Howard: We want him for bridge.

Eva: Well, you can see he isn't here, can't you?

Howard: He was here.

Eva: [*Stamping her foot.*] Well, he isn't here now.

Howard: Temper, temper. What price the angel of mercy now?

Eva: You're very funny, aren't you? Terribly amusing.

Howard: I know what you've been doing. You've been asking him to marry you.

Eva: [*Furiously.*] You drunken brute. Damn you. Blast you.

> [*She flings out of the room.* Howard *purses his lips and grins. Then he goes over to the sideboard and helps himself to a whisky and soda. While he is sipping it* Lois *comes in.*

Lois: Hulloa, I thought you were playing bridge.

Howard: No. Your father wanted to see Collie, and Sydney and Wilfred are having a game of piquet.

Lois: So you seized the opportunity to have a drink on the quiet.

Howard: My dear girl, I had to have something to pull myself together. Evie's been swearing at me. Such language, my dear. Called me a drunken brute. I mean, it shakes a chap's morale when a properly brought-up young lady forgets herself like that.

Lois: Are you obliged to drink?

Howard: Well, in a manner of speaking I am. My poor old father died of drink and his poor old father died of drink. So it's in the family. See?

Lois: It is rotten for Ethel.

Howard: She has a lot to put up with, poor girl. You

don't have to tell me. I know it. Fact is, she's too good for me.

LOIS: Much.

HOWARD: That's what I say. She's a lady. I mean you only have to look at her to know that. And mind you, she never lets up. I can be a gentleman when I want to, but I don't want to all the time. I mean to say, I like to have a good old laugh now and again. She never does. Truth is, between you and me, she has no sense of humour.

LOIS: I daresay after being married to you for fifteen years it's worn rather thin.

HOWARD: I like a girl as has a bit of fun in her. Let's have a good time while we're alive, I say; we can do all the sitting quiet we want when we're dead and buried.

LOIS: There's something in that.

HOWARD: Mind you, I'm not complaining of Ethel. Too much of a gentleman to do that. She's class. I know that. And I'm only a common farmer. Only, you know what I mean, you don't always want to be looking up to your wife, do you?

LOIS: No one asked you to marry Ethel.

HOWARD: Pity you wasn't old enough then. I'd have married you instead.

LOIS: Complimentary, aren't you?

HOWARD: You're not half the lady what Ethel is. And you're a bit of a devil I shouldn't wonder. You and me'd get on like a house on fire.

LOIS: You're drunk.

HOWARD: No, I'm not. I'm cold stone sober.

LOIS: Then I like you better drunk.

HOWARD: Give me a kiss, honey.

LOIS: D'you want your face slapped?

HOWARD: I don't mind.

LOIS: The nerve of it.

HOWARD: Come on. Be a sport.

LOIS: Go to hell.

HOWARD: I would with you.

> [*With a sudden movement he catches hold of her and gives her a kiss full on the lips. She tears herself away from him.*

LOIS: How dare you?

HOWARD: Oh, come off it. You didn't mind. You liked it.

LOIS: It almost made me sick. You stink of cows.

HOWARD: A lot of girls like that. Makes them go all funny.

LOIS: You filthy beast.

HOWARD: Want another?

LOIS: If it weren't for Ethel I'd go straight to father.

HOWARD: Don't make me laugh. D'you think I don't know about girls? And if you don't know about men it's high time you did. A good-looking girl like you. You ought to be ashamed of yourself. I mean, think what you're missing.

LOIS: You've got a pretty good opinion of yourself, haven't you?

HOWARD: And not without cause. Of course I don't say it's like the war. God, I wish it had gone on for ever. Those were the days. If you liked the look of a girl you just walked her up the garden path. Of course the uniform had a lot to do with it and being a blasted hero.

LOIS: Brute.

HOWARD: [*Confidentially.*] Look here, why don't you come up to the farm for a few days? We could have a grand old time.

LOIS: I don't know what you take me for, Howard.

HOWARD: Don't talk that sort of rot to me. You're human, same as I am, aren't you? What's the good of mouldering away without having a bit of fun in your life? You come up to the farm. Now the kids have gone to boarding-school their room's empty.

LOIS: If you're not drunk you're crazy.

HOWARD: No, I'm not. You'll come, my girl.

LOIS: [*Contemptuously.*] And what makes you think that?

HOWARD: I'll tell you. Because I want you and you know I want you and there isn't a thing that takes a girl like that. By God, I want you.

> [*He looks at her and the violence of his desire seems heavy in the room.* LOIS *instinctively puts her hand to her breast. Her breathing is oppressed. There is a silence.* MRS. ARDSLEY *comes in.*

LOIS: [*Recovering herself.*] Oh, mother.

HOWARD: I've just been telling this young woman she ought to come up to the farm for a few days. She looks to me as if she wanted a change.

MRS. ARDSLEY: I'm glad you agree with me. Only a little while ago I was suggesting that she should go and stay with Aunt Emily for two or three weeks.

LOIS: I've been thinking it over, mother. I daresay you're quite right. When d'you think I'd better go?

MRS. ARDSLEY: The sooner the better. To-morrow.

LOIS: All right. I'll send the old girl a wire and tell her I'm coming.

MRS. ARDSLEY: You needn't do that. I've just written to her to say that you'll arrive in time for dinner.

LOIS: Have you? You domineering old lady.

MRS. ARDSLEY: You're a very good girl, Lois. I didn't think you'd disregard my wishes.

Lois: I don't think I'm a very good girl. But you're a darling old mother.

> [*She kisses her tenderly.* Mrs. Ardsley, *smiling, pats her hand.*

END OF THE SECOND ACT.

ACT III

The drawing-room at the ARDSLEYS' *house. It is a large low room, with french windows leading on to the terrace that was the scene of the first act. It is furnished in an old-fashioned, commonplace and comfortable way. Nothing much has been added since it was all new when the* ARDSLEYS *married. The walls are overcrowded with framed engravings and water colours, copies of Florentine bas-reliefs, weapons on wooden shields and plates in old English china. The occasional tables are laden with knick-knacks. The armchairs and sofas are covered with loose-covers of faded cretonne.*

It is a rainy, windy day and there is a fire burning on the hearth. The light is failing. It is about half-past four.

WILFRED *is standing at the fire warming his hands.* LOIS *comes in. She is wearing a coat and skirt.*

LOIS: [*Coming towards him with outstretched hand.*] How d'you do? Mother's out. She'll be back to tea. She's gone to Stanbury.

WILFRED: I know. I asked the maid if I could see you. Is it true you're going away to-day?

LOIS: Yes, I'm spending a fortnight with an aunt near Canterbury.

WILFRED: But in a fortnight I shall be gone.

LOIS: Will you?

WILFRED: Were you going without saying good-bye to me?

LOIS: I thought mother would say it for me.

WILFRED: [*In a husky, agitated tone.*] Don't go, Lois.

LOIS: [*Indifferently.*] Why not?

WILFRED: Why are you going?

LOIS: Mother thought I wanted a change. I generally spend a fortnight with Aunt Emily once or twice a year. She's my god-mother and she says she's going to leave me something in her will.

WILFRED: I was going up to London to-morrow to settle that money on you.

LOIS: Don't be so silly. As if I wanted that. If I ran away with you I wouldn't take it. I'd rather have my independence.

WILFRED: You might have given me the last fortnight. It means nothing to you. And so much to me.

LOIS: How did you know I was going?

WILFRED: Gwen told me.

LOIS: How did she know?

WILFRED: Your mother rang up.

LOIS: Oh!

WILFRED: Are you quite sure it was about the sale of work that Gwen came to see your mother yesterday?

LOIS: She wouldn't have dared. You don't know mother. She'd never let anyone say a word against any of us. You've only seen her when she's being nice. She can be as stiff as a poker if one tries to take a liberty with her.

WILFRED: Gwen spotted the pearls all right.

LOIS: [*Beginning to unclasp them.*] Oh, I forgot. I can give them back to you now.

WILFRED: Won't you keep them? Please. It can't hurt you and it'll give me so much pleasure.

LOIS: I don't see how. The chances are that we shall never see one another again. As far as you're concerned it's just throwing money away.

WILFRED: I want to be able to think that you're wearing something I gave you. I've held them in my hands. I want to think that they have the warmth of your body and they touch the softness of your neck.

LOIS: [*Tempted.*] I've never had anything so valuable. I suppose I'm half a strumpet.

WILFRED: They only cost a pound, Lois.

LOIS: Oh, you liar. Does Gwen know you gave them to me?

WILFRED: She hasn't said so. She knows there's no one else who could.

LOIS: Has she been making a scene?

WILFRED: Oh, no, she's been holding herself in. She's afraid.

LOIS: Why? Are you so terrifying?

WILFRED: I don't think you'd find me so.

LOIS: Are you awfully in love with me?

WILFRED: Awfully.

LOIS: Strange, isn't it? I wonder why.

WILFRED: I'm broken-hearted, Lois. I know you don't love me. There's no reason why you should. But you might. If I were very kind to you. And patient. I'd do anything in the world to make you happy.

LOIS: It's curious, it does give one rather a funny feeling to know someone's in love with you.

WILFRED: When Gwen told me you were going, the whole world went black. She tried to say it casually, but she knew she was thrusting a dagger in my heart and she watched my face to see me writhe.

LOIS: Poor Gwen. I suppose people can be rather foul when they're jealous.

WILFRED: Oh, damn Gwen. I can only think of myself. You're everything in the world to me, and every one else can go to hell. It's my last chance, Lois.

[*She slowly shakes her head. He looks at her for a moment with despair.*

WILFRED: Is there nothing I can say to persuade you?

LOIS: Nothing.

WILFRED: I'm done. I'm finished.

LOIS: I don't think so. You'll get over it. When are you going to the Riviera?

WILFRED: It's only a joke to you. [*Violently.*] Oh, I hate being old.

[EVA *comes in.*

EVA: Why haven't the curtains been drawn? Oh, Wilfred.

WILFRED: [*Trying to seem naturally casual.*] How are you to-day?

EVA: I'll turn on the lights.

[*She switches on the electricity while* LOIS *draws the curtains.*

LOIS: It is a foul day.

WILFRED: I'll be getting along.

EVA: Oh, aren't you going to stay to tea? Sydney's just coming. He'd love to play piquet with you.

WILFRED: I'm sorry, I must be off. I only came to say good-bye to Lois.

EVA: We shall be seeing you again soon, I suppose?

WILFRED: I expect so.

[*They shake hands.* LOIS *gives him her hand.*

LOIS: Good-bye. Give my love to Gwen.

WILFRED: Good-bye.

[*He goes out quickly.*

EVA: What's the matter with him? He seems all funny to-day.

LOIS: I didn't notice that he was any different.

EVA: Are you all packed up and everything?

LOIS: Yes.

EVA: Are you taking the five-fifty?

LOIS: Yes.

EVA: That gives you nice time to have tea. Ethel's coming in.

LOIS: I know. She wants me to take some partridges to Aunt Emily.

[SYDNEY *comes in.*

SYDNEY: Tea ready?

EVA: It's not five yet.

SYDNEY: Thank God for the fire. I hate that gas stove in my room. Mother's not back yet, I suppose?

EVA: No. She said she'd be in to tea.

LOIS: Howard says he's expecting a very hard winter.

SYDNEY: Cheerful.

LOIS: Oh, I hate the winter.

EVA: If it weren't for the winter we shouldn't enjoy the spring.

SYDNEY: Are you obliged to say things like that, Evie?

EVA: It happens to be true.

SYDNEY: It happens to be true that two and two are four, but one needn't make a song and dance about it.

LOIS: I'll put on a record, shall I?

EVA: Oh, for goodness' sake don't, it drives me mad.

LOIS: Oh, all right.

[*They both give her a little look of surprise.*

EVA: I'm rather jumpy to-day. I suppose it's the east wind.

SYDNEY: Give me my tatting, Lois, will you?

LOIS: I will.

[*She gives it to him and while he talks he proceeds mechanically with his work.*

SYDNEY: I wonder if Collie will turn up?

EVA: I rang up to ask him to come in to tea. He hasn't been at the garage all day.

[ETHEL *and* HOWARD *come in.*

ETHEL: How's everybody?

SYDNEY: Hulloa.

HOWARD: We've brought the partridges. They'd better be hung for a couple of days. They were only shot yesterday.

SYDNEY: Got many birds this year, Howard?

HOWARD: A few. What's that you're doing?

SYDNEY: Tatting.

EVA: Put on the gramophone if you want to.

HOWARD: I'll put it on.

[*He goes over, gives the machine a wind and starts a record.*

ETHEL: I'm afraid it won't be very amusing for you at Aunt Emily's.

LOIS: I shall read a lot.

SYDNEY: Let's hope she'll die soon and leave you a packet.

LOIS: She's got very little to leave.

[*Suddenly* MR. ARDSLEY *bursts into the room.*

ETHEL: Oh, father.

ARDSLEY: Turn off the gramophone.

EVA: What's the matter?

[HOWARD *who is still at the gramophone stops the record.*

ARDSLEY: Something dreadful's happened. I thought I'd better come in and tell you at once.

EVA: [*With a cry.*] Collie.

ARDSLEY: How d'you know?

SYDNEY: What is it, father?

ARDSLEY: They've just telephoned to me from the police station. There's been an accident. Collie's been shot.

HOWARD: Shot? Who by?

ARDSLEY: I'm afraid he shot himself.

HOWARD: Good God.

EVA: He isn't dead?

ARDSLEY: Yes.

> [EVA *gives a loud, long shriek. It is a sound that is only just human.*

ETHEL: Evie.

> [EVA *goes up to her father with arms raised high in the air and clenched hands*.

EVA: You killed him, you fiend.

ARDSLEY: I? What *are* you talking about?

EVA: You fiend. You beast.

ETHEL: [*Putting a restraining hand on her.*] Evie.

EVA: [*Shaking her off angrily.*] Leave me alone. [*To* ARDSLEY.] You could have saved him. You devil. I hate you. I hate you.

ARDSLEY: Are you mad, Eva?

EVA: You hounded him to his death. You never gave him a chance.

ARDSLEY: Good heavens, we all gave him chance after chance.

EVA: It's a lie. He begged for money. He begged for time. And not one of you would help him. Not one of you remembered that he'd risked his life for you a hundred times. You brutes.

ARDSLEY: Oh, what rubbish.

EVA: I hope you're shamed before the whole world. Let everyone know that a brave and gallant gentleman went to his death because there wasn't a soul in this bloody place who would lend him two hundred pounds.

ARDSLEY: Pretty language, Eva. In point of fact two hundred pounds wouldn't have helped him. It would have saved him from going to gaol, but that's all.

EVA: Gaol?

ARDSLEY: Yes, a warrant for his arrest was issued this morning.

EVA: [*With anguish.*] Poor Collie. I can't bear it. Cruel. Cruel.

[*She begins to sob desperately.*

ARDSLEY: Now, my dear, don't take it so much to heart. Go and lie down in your room. Ethel will come and bathe your forehead with eau-de-Cologne. Of course the whole thing is very unfortunate. No one regrets it more than I do. The poor fellow was in a hopeless mess and perhaps he took the best way out of a situation that could only have thrown discredit on the uniform he'd worn.

[*While he says this* EVA *raises her head and looks at him with eyes of horror.*

EVA: But he was alive and he's dead. He's gone from us for ever. He's been robbed of all the years that were before him. Haven't you any pity for him? He used to come here almost every day.

ARDSLEY: He was a very nice fellow and a gentleman. Unfortunately he wasn't a very good business man.

EVA: As if I cared if he was a good business man.

ARDSLEY: There's no reason why you should. But his creditors did.

EVA: He was everything in the world to me.

ARDSLEY: My dear, what an exaggerated way to speak. You ought to have more sense at your age.

EVA: He loved me and I loved him.

ARDSLEY: Don't talk such nonsense.

EVA: We were engaged to be married.

ARDSLEY: [*With astonishment.*] What's that? Since when?

EVA: Since ages.

ARDSLEY: Well, my dear, you're well out of that. He was in no position to marry.

EVA: [*With anguish.*] It was my only chance.

ARDSLEY: You have a good home. You'd much better stay here.

EVA: And make myself useful?

ARDSLEY: There's no harm in that.

EVA: I've got just as much right to life and happiness as anyone else.

ARDSLEY: Of course you have.

EVA: You've done everything you could to prevent me from marrying.

ARDSLEY: Rubbish.

EVA: Why should I be sacrificed all the time? Why should I be at everybody's beck and call? Why should I have to do everything? I'm sick of being put upon. I'm sick of you, I'm sick of Sydney, I'm sick of Lois. I'm sick of you all.

> [*During the speech her agitation has become quite uncontrolled. There is a table covered with ornaments by her, and now with a violent gesture she throws it over so that everything is scattered on the floor.*

ETHEL: Evie.

EVA: Damn you. Damn you. Damn you.

> [*Shrieking she throws herself down and hysterically beats upon the floor with her fists.*

ARDSLEY: Stop it. Stop it.

HOWARD: Better get her out of here.

> [*He picks her up and carries her out of the room. ARDSLEY opens the door. He and ETHEL follow her out. LOIS and SYDNEY are left alone. LOIS, pale and trembling, has watched the scene with terror.*

LOIS: What's the matter with her?

SYDNEY: Hysterics. Upset you?

LOIS: I'm frightened.

SYDNEY: I'll telephone for Uncle Charlie. I think she wants a doctor.

> [*He makes his way out of the room.* LOIS *stands stock still. She cannot control the nervous trembling that seizes her.* HOWARD *comes in.*

HOWARD: I've put her on the dining-room sofa.

LOIS: Are Ethel and father with her?

HOWARD: Yes. [*He looks at her and sees the condition she is in. He puts his arm round her shoulders.*] Poor old girl, gave you quite a turn, didn't it?

LOIS: [*Unconscious of his touch.*] I'm frightened.

HOWARD: It's not serious, you know. Do her good to let off steam like that. You mustn't take it to heart.

> [*He bends down and kisses her on the cheek.*

LOIS: Why do you do that?

HOWARD: I don't like to see you miserable.

> [*She turns round a little and gives him a thoughtful look. He smiles rather charmingly.*

HOWARD: I'm quite sober.

LOIS: You'd better take your arm away. Ethel can come in any minute.

HOWARD: I'm terribly fond of you, Lois. Don't you like me?

LOIS: [*Miserably.*] Not much.

HOWARD: Shall I come over and see you when you're staying at Aunt Emily's?

LOIS: Why should you?

HOWARD: [*In a low passionate whisper.*] Lois.

> [*She looks at him curiously and with a cold hostility.*

LOIS: Isn't human nature funny? I know with my mind that you're a rotter. And I despise you. Isn't it lucky you can't see into my heart?

HOWARD: Why, what should I see there?

LOIS: Desire.

HOWARD: What for? I don't know what you mean.

LOIS: I didn't think you would or I shouldn't have told you. How shameful and ugly. I see that all right. It's funny, it doesn't seem to make any difference.

HOWARD: Oh, I see what you mean now. That's quite O.K. Give it time, girlie. I'll wait.

LOIS: [*Coolly, indifferently.*] You swine.

[SYDNEY *comes in.*

SYDNEY: Uncle Charlie's on his way round now.

LOIS: Mother will be back in a minute.

SYDNEY: How are you going to get to the station?

HOWARD: I'll drive you if you like.

LOIS: Oh, it's all arranged.

[ARDSLEY *comes in.*

ARDSLEY: Prentice has come. They're putting Evie to bed.

LOIS: I'll go and see if I can do anything.

[*She goes out.*

ARDSLEY: [*To* SYDNEY.] Sydney, did you know anything about her being engaged to Collie?

SYDNEY: I don't believe she was.

ARDSLEY: D'you mean to say you think it was pure invention?

SYDNEY: I shouldn't wonder. But I think she'll stick to it. After all no one can now prove she wasn't.

ARDSLEY: It's a terrible thing about poor Collie. No one can be more distressed than I.

SYDNEY: It seems a bit hard that after going through the war and getting a D.S.O., he should have come to this end.

ARDSLEY: He may have been a very good naval officer. He was a very poor business man. That's all there is to it.

SYDNEY: We might put that on his tombstone. It would make a damned good epitaph.

ARDSLEY: If that's a joke, Sydney, I must say I think it in very bad taste.

SYDNEY: [*With bitter calm.*] You see, I feel I have a certain right to speak. I know how dead keen we all were when the war started. Every sacrifice was worth it. We didn't say much about it because we were rather shy, but honour did mean something to us and patriotism wasn't just a word. And then, when it was all over, we did think that those of us who'd died hadn't died in vain, and those of us who were broken and shattered and knew they wouldn't be any more good in the world were buoyed up by the thought that if they'd given everything they'd given it in a great cause.

ARDSLEY: And they had.

SYDNEY: Do you still think that? I don't. I know that we were the dupes of the incompetent fools who ruled the nations. I know that we were sacrificed to their vanity, their greed and their stupidity. And the worst of it is that as far as I can tell they haven't learnt a thing. They're just as vain, they're just as greedy, they're just as stupid as they ever were. They muddle on, muddle on, and one of these days they'll muddle us all into another war. When that happens I'll tell you what I'm going to do. I'm going out into the streets and cry: Look at me; don't be a lot of damned fools; it's all bunk what they're saying to you, about honour and patriotism and glory, bunk, bunk, bunk.

HOWARD: Who cares if it is bunk? I had the time of my life in the war. No responsibility and plenty of money. More than I'd ever had before or ever since. All the girls you wanted and all the whisky. Excitement. A roughish time in the trenches, but a grand lark afterwards. I tell you it was a bitter day for me when they signed the armistice. What have I got now? Just the same old thing day after day, working my guts out to keep body and soul together. The very day war is declared I join up and the sooner the better if you ask me. That's the life for me. By God!

ARDSLEY: [*To his son.*] You've had a lot to put up with, Sydney. I know that. But don't think you're the only one. It's been a great blow to me that you haven't been able to follow me in my business as I followed my father. Three generations, that would have been. But it wasn't to be. No one wants another war less than I do, but if it comes I'm convinced that you'll do your duty, so far as in you lies, as you did it before. It was a great grief to me that when the call came I was too old to answer. But I did what I could. I was enrolled as a special constable. And if I'm wanted again I shall be ready again.

SYDNEY: [*Between his teeth.*] God give me patience.

HOWARD: You have a whisky and soda, old boy, and you'll feel better.

SYDNEY: Will a whisky and soda make me forget poor Evie half crazy, Collie doing away with himself rather than go to gaol, and my lost sight?

ARDSLEY: But, my dear boy, that's just our immediate circle. Of course we suffered, perhaps we've had more than our fair share, but we're not everyone.

SYDNEY: Don't you know that all over England there are families like ours, all over Germany and all over

France? We were quite content to go our peaceful way, jogging along obscurely, and happy enough. All we asked was to be left alone. Oh, it's no good talking.

ARDSLEY: The fact is, Sydney, you think too much.

SYDNEY: [*Smiling.*] I daresay you're right, father. You see, I have little else to do. I'm thinking of collecting stamps.

ARDSLEY: That's a very good idea, my boy. If you go about it cleverly there's no reason why it shouldn't be a very sound investment.

[MRS. ARDSLEY *comes in. She is still wearing her hat and coat.*

SYDNEY: Hulloa, mother.

[*As she sits down, a trifle wearily, her eye catches the litter on the floor of all the things* EVA *threw over when she upset the table.*

MRS. ARDSLEY: Been having a picnic?

ARDSLEY: Evie upset the table.

MRS. ARDSLEY: In play or anger?

HOWARD: I'd better pick the things up.

MRS. ARDSLEY: It does look rather untidy.

[*He picks up one piece after the other and sets the table straight.*

ARDSLEY: Poor Collie's killed himself.

MRS. ARDSLEY: Yes, I've heard. I'm sorry.

ARDSLEY: Evie's in rather a state about it.

MRS. ARDSLEY: Poor thing, I'll go to her.

ARDSLEY: Charlie Prentice is with her.

SYDNEY: Why don't you wait till you've had a cup of tea, mother? You sound tired.

MRS. ARDSLEY: I am rather. [DR. PRENTICE *comes in and*

she gives him a smile.]   Oh, Charlie. I was just coming upstairs.

PRENTICE: I wouldn't. I've given Evie a hypodermic. I'd rather she were left alone.

ARDSLEY: Take a pew, Charlie. I'm going back to my office. One or two things I want to finish up. I'll be along for tea in a quarter of an hour.

MRS. ARDSLEY: Very well.

[*He goes out.*

HOWARD: [*Having finished.*] There. That's all right, I think.

MRS. ARDSLEY: Thank you.

HOWARD: I say, I think I'll just go along to Collie's garage. There are one or two bits and pieces that I've got my eye on. I'd just as soon make sure that nobody sneaks them.

SYDNEY: Oh, yeah.

HOWARD: Tell Ethel I'll come back for her. I shan't be long.

[*He goes out.*

SYDNEY: What did the specialist say, mother?

MRS. ARDSLEY: What specialist, Sydney?

SYDNEY: Come off it, darling. You don't generally favour your family with a very detailed account of your movements. When you took such pains to tell us exactly why you were going into Stanbury this afternoon, I guessed that you were going to see a specialist.

MRS. ARDSLEY: I never believe a word doctors say to me.

PRENTICE: Don't mind me.

MRS. ARDSLEY: Tell me about Evie.

PRENTICE: I hardly know yet. It may be it would be better if she went into a home for a few weeks.

MRS. ARDSLEY: She isn't mad?

PRENTICE: She's very unbalanced. . . I was just coming round when Sydney telephoned. Murray rang me up after he'd seen you.

MRS. ARDSLEY: Why didn't he mind his own business?

PRENTICE: It was his business.

SYDNEY: Would you like me to leave you?

> [MRS. ARDSLEY *gives him a little, thoughtful look.*

MRS. ARDSLEY: No, stay if you like. But go on with your tatting and pretend you don't hear.

SYDNEY: All right.

> [*He takes his work and goes on as though absorbed in it.*

MRS. ARDSLEY: Don't interrupt.

PRENTICE: I'm afraid Murray could only confirm my diagnosis, Charlotte.

MRS. ARDSLEY: [*Cheerfully.*] I had an idea he would, you know. You stick together, you doctors.

PRENTICE: He agrees with me that an immediate operation is necessary.

MRS. ARDSLEY: I believe he does.

PRENTICE: When I spoke to him on the telephone he said you were—hesitating a little.

MRS. ARDSLEY: Not at all. I didn't hesitate for a minute.

PRENTICE: I'm delighted to hear it. I know your courage. I was confident in your good sense.

MRS. ARDSLEY: I'm glad.

PRENTICE: I'll make all the arrangements and we'll have it done as soon as possible.

MRS. ARDSLEY: I'm not going to be operated on, Charlie.

PRENTICE: My dear, I must be frank with you. It's the only chance we have of saving your life.

MRS. ARDSLEY: That's not true, Charlie. It's the only chance you have of prolonging my life. For a few months or a year perhaps. And then it'll start all over again. Do you think it's worth it? I don't.

PRENTICE: You have your husband and your children to think of.

MRS. ARDSLEY: I know. It would be a frightful expense. If I got over the operation I should always be an invalid. I should have to have a nurse. I should be much more bother than I was worth.

PRENTICE: That's unkind, Charlotte. And it's untrue.

MRS. ARDSLEY: You've known me a great many years, Charlie. Haven't you noticed that when once I make up my mind I don't change it?

PRENTICE: Don't be a damned fool, Charlotte.

MRS. ARDSLEY: I have nothing to complain of. I haven't had an unhappy life. I'm prepared to call it a day.

PRENTICE: I don't know if Murray made himself quite clear.

MRS. ARDSLEY: I asked him to.

PRENTICE: Listen to me. I mean every word I say. If you won't consent to an operation I'm afraid you have only a few months to live.

MRS. ARDSLEY: [*Coolly.*] How odd! Those were his very words.

PRENTICE: Well?

MRS. ARDSLEY: I've often wondered in the past how I should take it when I was told that I was going to die. I've wondered if I'd scream or faint. You know, I didn't do either. It gave me a funny sort of thrill. I felt as if I'd drunk a glass of port on an empty stomach. I had some shopping to do at Stanbury afterwards. I'm afraid I was rather extravagant. I felt so gay and light-hearted.

PRENTICE: That's more than I do.

MRS. ARDSLEY: It shows how right Leonard is when he

R

says it's silly to take your jumps before you come to them.

PRENTICE: Oh, damn Leonard.

MRS. ARDSLEY: I'm free. Nothing matters very much any more. It's a very comfortable feeling.

PRENTICE: And the rest?

MRS. ARDSLEY: Oh, the rest, my dear, is between me and the pale, distant shadow that is all you clever people have left me of God.

PRENTICE: [*After a moment's reflection.*] If you take that view of it, if you know the facts and are prepared to take the consequences, I have no more to say. Perhaps you're right. I admire your courage. I should like to think that I should have enough to follow your example.

MRS. ARDSLEY: There is one thing I'm going to ask you to do for me.

PRENTICE: My dear, anything in the world.

MRS. ARDSLEY: I don't want to suffer more than I need. We've always had a great deal of affection for one another, Charlie.

PRENTICE: I suppose we have.

MRS. ARDSLEY: You doctors are a brutal lot and there's no end to the amount of pain you can bear in other people.

PRENTICE: I will do everything medical practice permits me to save you from suffering.

MRS. ARDSLEY: But I'm going to ask you to do something more.

[*A long, intent look passes between them.*

PRENTICE: I'll do even that.

MRS. ARDSLEY: [*With a change of manner, cheerfully.*] Then that's all right. And now let's forget that I have anything the matter with me.

[SYDNEY *gets up and coming over to his mother bends down and kisses her on the forehead.*

MRS. ARDSLEY: As you're up you might ring the bell, Sydney. I'm simply dying for a cup of tea.

[*As he rings* ETHEL *comes in.*

ETHEL: I didn't know you were back, mother.

MRS. ARDSLEY: Yes, I got in a few minutes ago. [ETHEL *kisses her.*] I was going up to see Evie, but Uncle Charlie thought I'd better wait.

ETHEL: She's quite comfortable.

MRS. ARDSLEY: Asleep?

ETHEL: No, but resting.

MRS. ARDSLEY: Where's Lois?

ETHEL: She's in her room. She's just coming.

[*The* MAID *comes in with a tray, which she puts on a little table.*

MRS. ARDSLEY: [*To her.*] Oh, Gertrude, if anyone calls I'm not at home.

GERTRUDE: Very good, ma'am.

MRS. ARDSLEY: I don't feel inclined to cope with visitors this afternoon.

PRENTICE: I'll take myself off.

MRS. ARDSLEY: Don't be so stupid. You're going to stay and have a cup of tea.

PRENTICE: I have other patients, you know.

MRS. ARDSLEY: They can wait.

[LOIS *comes in.*

MRS. ARDSLEY: You ought to be starting soon, Lois, oughtn't you?

LOIS: I've got time yet. It won't take me five minutes to get to the station.

ETHEL: You won't forget the partridges?

LOIS: No.

MRS. ARDSLEY: Give Aunt Emily my love.

PRENTICE: You might remember me to her, Lois.

LOIS: I will.

MRS. ARDSLEY: Her chrysanthemums ought to be coming on just now.

> [GERTRUDE *has gone out of the room after bringing in the tray and now comes back.*

GERTRUDE: Mrs. Cedar has called, ma'am.

MRS. ARDSLEY: I told you to say I wasn't at home.

GERTRUDE: I said you wasn't, ma'am, but she says it's very important.

MRS. ARDSLEY: Tiresome woman. Tell her I've just come back from Stanbury and I'm very tired. Say, will she forgive me, but I don't feel up to seeing anybody to-day.

GERTRUDE: Very good, ma'am.

> [*She is about to go, when the door is burst open and* GWEN *comes in. She is wrought up.*

GWEN: I'm sorry to force myself on you. It's a matter of life and death. I must see you.

MRS. ARDSLEY: I'm not very well, Gwen. Don't you think you can wait till to-morrow?

GWEN: No, no, no, to-morrow it'll be too late. Oh, God, what shall I do?

MRS. ARDSLEY: Well, since you're here, perhaps the best thing would be to sit down and have a cup of tea.

GWEN: [*In a strangled voice.*] Lois and Wilfred are going to elope.

MRS. ARDSLEY: Oh, my dear, don't be so silly. You're making a perfect nuisance of yourself.

GWEN: It's true, I tell you, it's true.

MRS. ARDSLEY: Lois is going to spend a fortnight with my sister-in-law. I didn't think there was anything in what you said to me, but I didn't want any unpleasantness, so I arranged that she should be away till after you'd gone.

GWEN: She's not going to your sister-in-law's. Wilfred's meeting her at Stanbury. They're going to London.

LOIS: What are you talking about, Gwen?

GWEN: I heard every word you said on the 'phone.

LOIS: [*Trying to hide that she is startled.*] When?

GWEN: Just now. Ten minutes ago. You didn't know I'd had an extension put up into my room. I'm not such a perfect fool as you thought me. Can you deny that you spoke to Wilfred?

LOIS: No.

GWEN: You said, Wilfred, it's a go. And he said, what d'you mean? And you said, I'm trusting myself to your tender mercies. You're for it, my boy. I'm going to elope with you.

ETHEL: She was joking with him.

GWEN: A funny joke. He said, my God, you don't mean it. And she said, I'll get out of the train at Stanbury. Meet me in the car and we'll talk it over on the way to London.

MRS. ARDSLEY: Is it true, Lois?

LOIS: Yes.

SYDNEY: You damned fool, Lois.

GWEN: Oh, Lois, I've never done you any harm. I've been a good friend to you—you can't take my husband from me.

LOIS: I'm not taking him from you. You lost him years ago.

GWEN: You're young, you'll have plenty of chances before you're through. I'm old and he's all I've got. If he leaves me I swear to you that I'll kill myself.

MRS. ARDSLEY: But why have you come here? Why didn't you go to your husband?

GWEN: He won't listen to me. Oh, what a fool I've been. I ought to have known when I saw the pearls.

MRS. ARDSLEY: What pearls?

GWEN: She's wearing them now. She pretends they're false, but they're real, and he gave them to her.

MRS. ARDSLEY: Take them off, Lois, and give them to Gwen.

> [*Without a word* LOIS *undoes the clasp and throws the string on the table.*

GWEN: Do you think I'd touch them? He hates me. Oh, it's so awful to love someone with all your heart and to know that the very sight of you maddens him beyond endurance. I went down on my knees to him. I begged him not to leave me. He said he was sick to death of me. He pushed me over. I heard the door slam. He's gone. He's gone to join her.

> [*She falls to her knees and bursts into a passion of tears.*

MRS. ARDSLEY: Gwen, Gwen, don't give way like that.

> [GWEN, *still on her knees, drags herself up to* MRS. ARDSLEY.

GWEN: Don't let her go to him. You know what it feels like to be old. You know how defenceless one is. She'll regret it. You don't know what he's like. He'll throw her aside when he's tired of her as he's thrown all the others aside. He's hard and cruel and selfish. He's made me so miserable.

MRS. ARDSLEY: If that's true, if he's all you say I should have thought you were well rid of him.

GWEN: I'm too old to start fresh. I'm too old to be left alone. Alone. [*She struggles up to her feet.*] He's mine. I went through the divorce court to get him. I won't let him go. [*Turning on* LOIS.] I swear to you before God that you shall never marry him. He forced his first wife to divorce him because she hadn't money, but I've got money of my own. I'll never divorce him.

LOIS: Nothing would induce me to marry him.

GWEN: Take him if you want to. He'll come back to me. He's old. He tries to keep up. It's all sham. I know the effort it is. He's tired to death and he won't give in. What good can he be to you? How can you be so stupid? You ought to be ashamed.

MRS. ARDSLEY: Gwen. Gwen.

GWEN: Money. Oh, curse the money. He's a rich man and you haven't got a bob between you. You're all in it. All of you. You all want to get something out of it. You brutes. You beasts.

[DR. PRENTICE *gets up and takes her by the arm.*

PRENTICE: Come, Mrs. Cedar, we've had enough of this. You go too far. You must get out of this.

GWEN: I won't go.

PRENTICE: If you don't, I shall put you out.

[*He urges her towards the door.*

GWEN: I'll make such a scandal that you'll never be able to hold up your heads again.

PRENTICE: That's enough now. Get out.

GWEN: Leave me alone, damn you.

PRENTICE: I'm going to take you home. Come on.

[*They both go out. There is a moment's awkward silence when the door is closed on them.*

LOIS: I'm sorry to have exposed you to this disgusting scene, mother.

SYDNEY: You may well be.

ETHEL: You're not really going off with that man, Lois?

LOIS: I am.

ETHEL: You can't be in love with him.

LOIS: Of course not. If I were, d'you think I'd be such a fool as to go?

ETHEL: [*Aghast.*] Lois.

LOIS: If I loved him I'd be afraid.

ETHEL: You don't know what you're doing. It would be awful and unnatural if you loved him, but there would be an excuse for you.

LOIS: Has love done very much for you, Ethel?

ETHEL: Me? I don't know what you mean. I married Howard. I took him for better, for worse.

LOIS: You've been a good wife and a good mother. A virtuous woman. And a lot of good it's done you. I've seen you grow old and tired and hopeless. I'm frightened, Ethel, frightened.

ETHEL: I wasn't obliged to marry. Mother and father were against it.

LOIS: You could have stayed on at home like Evie. So can I. I'm frightened, Ethel. I'm frightened. I don't want to become like Evie.

ETHEL: Mother, can't you do something? It's so awful. It's such madness.

MRS. ARDSLEY: I'm listening to what Lois has to say.

ETHEL: [*With a catch in her breath.*] You're not running away from anybody here?

LOIS: [*Smiling.*] Oh, my dear, that isn't at all in my character.

ETHEL: [*Ashamed and awkward.*] I thought that perhaps someone had been trying to make love to you.

LOIS: Oh, Ethel, don't be so silly. Who is there to make love to me in this God-forsaken place?

ETHEL: I didn't know. Perhaps it was only my fancy. It's just the money?

LOIS: Yes, and what money brings. Freedom and opportunity.

ETHEL: Those are mere words.

LOIS: I'm sick of waiting for something to turn up. Time is flying and soon it'll be too late.

MRS. ARDSLEY: When did you decide, Lois?

LOIS: Half an hour ago.

MRS. ARDSLEY: Have you considered all the consequences?

LOIS: Oh, mother dear, if I did that I should stay here twiddling my thumbs till my dying day.

MRS. ARDSLEY: It's not a very nice thing that you're doing.

LOIS: I know.

MRS. ARDSLEY: It's cruel to Gwen.

LOIS: [*With a shrug.*] I or another.

MRS. ARDSLEY: It'll be a dreadful blow to your father.

LOIS: I'm sorry.

MRS. ARDSLEY: And the scandal won't be very nice for us.

LOIS: I can't help it.

ETHEL: It would be bad enough if you were going to be married. Gwen says she won't divorce.

LOIS: I don't want to marry him.

ETHEL: What's to happen to you if he chucks you?

LOIS: Darling, you're years older than I am and a married woman. How can you be so innocent? Has it never occurred to you what power it gives a woman when a man is madly in love with her and she doesn't care a row of pins for him?

R*

[*Gertrude comes in with the teapot and the hot water on a tray.*

MRS. ARDSLEY: [*To* ETHEL.] Go and tell your father tea is ready, Ethel.

[*With a disheartened gesture* ETHEL *goes out.*

LOIS: I'll go and put on my hat. [GERTRUDE *goes out.*] I'm sorry to disappoint you, mother. I don't want to cause you pain.

MRS. ARDSLEY: Have you quite made up your mind, Lois?

LOIS: Quite.

MRS. ARDSLEY: That is what I thought. Then perhaps you *had* better go and put on your hat.

LOIS: What about father? I don't want him to make a scene.

MRS. ARDSLEY: I'll tell him after you've gone.

LOIS: Thank you.

[*She goes out.* MRS. ARDSLEY *and* SYDNEY *are left alone.*

SYDNEY: Are you going to let her go, mother?

MRS. ARDSLEY: How can I stop her?

SYDNEY: You can tell her what the surgeon told you this afternoon.

MRS. ARDSLEY: Oh, my dear, with one foot in the grave it's rather late to start blackmail.

SYDNEY: She wouldn't go, you know.

MRS. ARDSLEY: I don't think she would. I can't do that, Sydney. I shouldn't like to think of her waiting for my death. I should feel like apologising for every day I lingered on.

SYDNEY: She might change her mind.

MRS. ARDSLEY: She's young, she has her life before her, she

must do what she thinks best with it. I don't belong to life any longer. I don't think I have the right to influence her.

SYDNEY: Aren't you afraid she'll come an awful cropper.

MRS. ARDSLEY: She's hard and selfish. I don't think she's stupid. She can take care of herself.

SYDNEY: She might be a stranger, to hear you speak.

MRS. ARDSLEY: Does it sound unkind? You see, I feel as if nothing mattered very much any more. I've had my day. I've done what I could. Now those who come after me must shift for themselves.

SYDNEY: You're not frightened at all?

MRS. ARDSLEY: Not a bit. I'm strangely happy. I'm rather relieved to think it's over. I'm not at home in this world of to-day. I'm pre-war. Everything's so changed now. I don't understand the new ways. To me life is like a party that was very nice to start with, but has become rather rowdy as time went on, and I'm not at all sorry to go home.

[ETHEL *comes back.*

ETHEL: I've told father. He's just coming.

MRS. ARDSLEY: I'm afraid we've let the tea stand rather a long time.

SYDNEY: Father likes nothing better than a good strong cup.

[LOIS *comes in. She has her hat on.*

LOIS: [*Startled and anxious.*] Mother, Evie is coming down the stairs.

MRS. ARDSLEY: Isn't she asleep?

SYDNEY: Uncle Charlie said he'd given her something.

[*The door is opened and* EVA *comes in. Her eyes are bright from the drug the doctor has given her. She has a queer, fixed smile on her face. She has changed into her best frock.*

MRS. ARDSLEY: I thought you were lying down, Evie. They told me you didn't feel quite up to the mark.

EVA: I had to come down to tea. Collie's coming.

LOIS: [*Shocked.*] Collie.

EVA: He'd have been so disappointed if I hadn't come.

MRS. ARDSLEY: You've put on your best dress.

EVA: It is rather an occasion, isn't it? You see, I'm engaged to be married.

ETHEL: Evie, what do you mean?

EVA: I'm telling you beforehand so that you should be prepared. Collie's coming here this afternoon to talk to father about it. Don't say anything about it till he comes.

> [*There is a moment's awkward pause. They none of them know what to say or do.*]

MRS. ARDSLEY: Let me give you your tea, darling.

EVA: I don't want any tea. I'm too excited. [*She catches sight of the string of pearls that* LOIS *had put on the table.*] What are these pearls doing here?

LOIS: You can have them if you like.

MRS. ARDSLEY: Lois.

LOIS: They're mine.

EVA: Can I really? It'll be an engagement present. Oh, Lois, that is sweet of you. [*She goes up to her and kisses her, then, standing in front of the glass puts them on.*] Collie always says I have such a pretty neck.

> [MR. ARDSLEY *and* HOWARD *come in.*

ARDSLEY: Now what about this cup of tea?

HOWARD: Hulloa, Evie. All right again?

EVA: Oh, yes. There's nothing the matter with me.

ARDSLEY: All ready to start, Lois?

LOIS: Yes.

ARDSLEY: Don't cut it too fine.

HOWARD: I may look you up one of these days, Lois. I've got to go over to Canterbury to see a man on business. I don't suppose I shall be able to get back for the night, Ethel.

ETHEL: No?

HOWARD: I'll come over and fetch you in the car, Lois, and we'll do a picture together.

LOIS: [*Mocking him.*] That would be grand.

ARDSLEY: Well, I must say it's very nice to have a cup of tea by one's own fireside and surrounded by one's family. If you come to think of it we none of us have anything very much to worry about. Of course we none of us have more money than we know what to do with, but we have our health and we have our happiness. I don't think we've got very much to complain of. Things haven't been going too well lately, but I think the world is turning the corner and we can all look forward to better times in future. This old England of ours isn't done yet and I for one believe in it and all it stands for.

[EVA *begins to sing in a thin cracked voice.*

EVA: God save our gracious King!
             Long live our noble King!
                God save our King!

[*The others look at her, petrified, in horror-struck surprise. When she stops* LOIS *gives a little cry and hurries from the room.*

THE END

SHEPPEY

A PLAY
in Three Acts

CHARACTERS

SHEPPEY
ERNEST TURNER
BRADLEY
MR. BOLTON
ALBERT
COOPER
DR. JERVIS
TWO CUSTOMERS
A REPORTER
A HAIRDRESSER
MRS. MILLER
FLORRIE
BESSIE LEGROS
MISS GRANGE
MISS JAMES

SHEPPEY

ACT ONE

The Scene is BRADLEY'S *Hairdressing and Barber's Saloon in Jermyn Street.*

At the back is the front shop in which the cashier sits, and the door from the street leads into it. From this a doorway, closed by a curtain, gives entrance to the saloon. This is lined with mirrors, with basins, and in front of each basin is a barber's chair. In the middle of the room is a table on which are papers and magazines, two or three chairs for customers to sit on if they have to wait, and a round coat and hat rack and umbrella stand. A door in one of the side walls leads to the room where the assistants sit when they are not occupied.

When the curtain rises TWO CUSTOMERS *are being served. One of them has just had his hair cut by* ALBERT, *and* MISS GRANGE, *the manicurist, is finishing his nails. The other customer is in process of being shaved by* SHEPPEY. SHEPPEY *is a stoutish, middle-aged man, with a red face and twinkling eyes. He has a fine head of black wavy hair. He has a jovial, well-fed look. He is a bit of a character and knows it.* MISS GRANGE *is very refined.*

ALBERT: Anything on the 'air, sir?

CUSTOMER: As long as it's not greasy.

ALBERT: Number three, sir?

CUSTOMER: All right.

> [ALBERT *sprinkles some hair wash on the customer's head. During the next few speeches he brushes and combs the hair.*

ALBERT: Anything you're wanting to-day, sir?

CUSTOMER: No.

ALBERT: 'Air's very dry, sir.

CUSTOMER: That's how I like it.

ALBERT: Getting a bit thin on top, sir.

CUSTOMER: I think it's rather becoming.

ALBERT: Matter of taste, sir. I can thoroughly recommend our number three. We sell a rare lot of it.

CUSTOMER: You're not going to sell any to me.

ALBERT: Very good, sir. All I meant to say is, it can't 'elp but do the 'air good. Mr. Bradley makes it 'imself. It's made of the very best materials. I can guarantee that.

CUSTOMER: Shut up!

MISS GRANGE: You don't want a high polish on them, do you?

CUSTOMER: Just ordinary.

MISS GRANGE: I'll put a high polish on them if you like.

CUSTOMER: I don't want to see my face in them, you know.

MISS GRANGE: I never like to see a gentleman's nails too highly polished.

CUSTOMER: I daresay you're right.

MISS GRANGE: I mean to say, I always think it makes one look like a foreigner.

CUSTOMER: Oh, do you think it does?

MISS GRANGE: I'm positive of it. And one doesn't want to look like one of them Argentines, does he?

CUSTOMER: They look terribly rich, you know.

MISS GRANGE: I can put as much polish on your nails as you like, you know.

CUSTOMER: Oh no, don't trouble.

MISS GRANGE: Oh, it's no trouble. I mean, you've only got to say the word.

CUSTOMER: As long as they're neat and clean that'll do me.

MISS GRANGE: That's what I always say, neat but not gaudy

SHEPPEY: [*To the customer he is shaving.*] Razor all right, sir?

SECOND CUSTOMER: Yes.

SHEPPEY: Very mild to-day, sir.

SECOND CUSTOMER: Yes.

SHEPPEY: I shouldn't be surprised if we 'ad a bit of rain to-night, sir.

SECOND CUSTOMER: Yes?

SHEPPEY: I 'ear the French 'orse won the three-thirty, sir.

SECOND CUSTOMER: Yes.

SHEPPEY: 'Ave anything on, sir?

SECOND CUSTOMER: Yes.

SHEPPEY: Bit of luck for you, sir.

SECOND CUSTOMER: Yes.

SHEPPEY: I backed Varsity Boy meself, sir. Shilling each way.

SECOND CUSTOMER: Yes?

SHEPPEY: 'E 'ad a pretty good chance.

SECOND CUSTOMER: Yes.

SHEPPEY: You 'ave to be pretty smart to spot a winner every time.

SECOND CUSTOMER: Yes.

SHEPPEY: It's a mug's game, backing 'orses.

SECOND CUSTOMER: Yes.

SHEPPEY: That's what I say. But one must 'ave a bit of excitement. Sport of Kings, they call it.

SECOND CUSTOMER: Yes.

SHEPPEY: Pity so many owners giving up.

SECOND CUSTOMER: Yes.

SHEPPEY: 'Ard times for all of us.

SECOND CUSTOMER: Yes.

> [MR. BOLTON *comes in. He is a smart-looking, middle-aged man.* BRADLEY, *the proprietor, precedes him through the curtains.*

BRADLEY: This way, sir.

BOLTON: I'm not too late, am I?

BRADLEY: No, sir, we don't shut till seven. I told my other young lady she might go, but Miss Grange is here. [*Calling.*] Number Three.

BOLTON: I'll wait for Sheppey.

BRADLEY: Just as you like, sir.

SHEPPEY: I shan't be above two minutes, sir.

> [No. 3 *comes through the door.*

BRADLEY: All right, Victor. Mr. Bolton's going to wait for Sheppey.

> [No. 3 *nods and goes back again.*

> [*Taking* MR. BOLTON's *hat and stick.*] Evening paper, sir?

BOLTON: Afternoon, Miss Grange.

MISS GRANGE: Afternoon, sir. You're quite a stranger. I'm just finished.

BOLTON: I don't know that I want a manicure to-day.

MISS GRANGE: It's nearly a fortnight since you had them done last, Mr. Bolton.

BOLTON: I'm only going to have a shave.

MISS GRANGE: That'll give me plenty of time. I can finish by the time Sheppey does.

SHEPPEY: Don't you put me on my mettle, Miss Grange. I can shave a customer in four and a 'alf minutes if I want to.

BOLTON: You needn't try to make any records on me, Sheppey.

MISS GRANGE: I don't say I can make an absolutely first-rate job of it in the time it takes you to give a gentleman a shave, but I *can* make his nails look decent.

BRADLEY: That's right, Mr. Bolton. I've 'ad to do with a good many young ladies in my time. I can't off 'and remember one as was quicker than Miss Grange.

MISS GRANGE: Well, practice makes perfect, they say. I like a gentleman's hands to look as if they were a gentleman's hands, and I don't mind who knows it. [*To the customer she is serving.*] There, sir, I think that's all right.

CUSTOMER: Grand.

　　[*He gets up.* ALBERT *removes his gown, and takes up a brush and gives him a rapid brush down.*]

ALBERT: Allow me, sir.

CUSTOMER: Oh, that's all right.

MISS GRANGE: [*Archly.*] We must send you out of the shop nice and tidy, you know.

CUSTOMER: How much do I owe?

ALBERT: Pay at the desk, sir.

　　The CUSTOMER *takes a shilling out of his pocket and gives it to* MISS GRANGE.

CUSTOMER: Here you are.

MISS GRANGE: Thank you, sir.

BRADLEY: [*Helping him on with his coat.*] Allow me, sir.

ALBERT: [*Producing a bottle of hair wash.*] This is our number three, sir.

CUSTOMER: Very pretty.

BRADLEY· We sell a rare lot of it, sir.

CUSTOMER: So the gentleman who was cutting my hair said. The information left me speechless.

BRADLEY: There isn't a preparation on the market to come up to it. And it's not because I make it myself that I say that.

ALBERT: You'd be surprised what it would do for your 'air, sir.

CUSTOMER: I hate surprises. [*He nods.*] Afternoon.

[*The* CUSTOMER *is ushered out by* ALBERT.]

SHEPPEY: A little off the ears, sir?

SECOND CUSTOMER: No.

SHEPPEY: Very good, sir. Shall you be wanting any 'air wash to-day, sir?

SECOND CUSTOMER: No.

SHEPPEY: Razor blades?

SECOND CUSTOMER: No.

SHEPPEY: There's a new safety razor just been put on the market. Beautiful bit of work. I suppose you wouldn't like just to 'ave a look at it.

SECOND CUSTOMER: No.

SHEPPEY: Very good, sir. Shall I just give the 'air a brush, sir?

SECOND CUSTOMER: No.

SHEPPEY: Very good, sir. Then I think that'll be all, sir.

[*The* CUSTOMER *gets up and* SHEPPEY *takes his gown off him. The* CUSTOMER *tips him.*]

Thank you, sir. [*To* MR. BOLTON.] Now I'm ready for you, sir.

BRADLEY: I'll just give you a brush, sir.

MR. BOLTON *sits down in* SHEPPEY'S *chair and* MISS GRANGE *brings up her little stool.* SHEPPEY *fetches a clean gown. Meanwhile* BRADLEY *brushes down the second customer and gives him his hat.*

MISS GRANGE: Now let me have a look at those nails of yours, Mr. Bolton. Oh, Mr. Bolton. I do believe you've been unfaithful to me.

BOLTON: What makes you think that, Miss Grange?

MISS GRANGE: Well, I can see with half an eye that someone

has been messing about with your hands. Oh, Mr. Bolton, that is too bad of you.

BOLTON: I broke a nail playing golf down in the country. I had to do something about it.

MISS GRANGE: Well, I am disappointed. I never thought you'd do a thing like that. I shall have no end of a job getting your nails nice again. The fact is you can't trust anyone in this world.

BOLTON: I apologise, Miss Grange.

MISS GRANGE: Oh, I didn't mean you, sir. You're a gentleman and that nobody can deny. I meant that girl that done your nails. Well, I ask you.

[SHEPPEY *comes back with a gown and puts it on* MR. BOLTON.

BOLTON: Sheppey, I regret to inform you that Miss Grange is upset.

MISS GRANGE: I am and I'm not going to deny it.

SHEPPEY: Why, what's the trouble?

MISS GRANGE: Mr. Bolton's been unfaithful to me.

SHEPPEY: You know what men are, Miss Grange. You can't trust them out of your sight.

MISS GRANGE: And no one knows that better than me, Sheppey.

[SHEPPEY *begins to lather* MR. BOLTON's *face*. ALBERT *comes in again*.

BOLTON: You didn't seem to be doing very well with your last customer, Sheppey.

SHEPPEY: Not what you'd call a brilliant conversationalist was he? I knew there was nothing doing the moment he sat down. I only asked 'im if he was wanting anything to-day so as he shouldn't feel slighted.

BOLTON: [*To* ALBERT.] You didn't have much luck with your number three either, Albert.

ALBERT: You're right there, sir. He was one of them tight ones and no mistake.

MISS GRANGE: I'll say this for you, Albert. You had a good try.

SHEPPEY: I was listening to you. You didn't try the right way.

ALBERT: When a gent says he likes being bald—well, I ask you.

MISS GRANGE: He was aggravating, I must say. He had an answer to everything.

SHEPPEY: When a customer tries to be funny 'e's easy.

MISS GRANGE: Well, Sheppey, I don't believe even you could have got him to buy anything.

BOLTON: Is Sheppey a good salesman?

MISS GRANGE: You ask Mr. Bradley.

BRADLEY: Best I've ever had.

BOLTON: How d'you do it, Sheppey?

SHEPPEY: Oh, it's just knack, sir. Of course you want a lot of tact.

BOLTON: You needn't mind telling me, you know. You'll never catch me if you try till doomsday. All these preparations of yours. A lot of damned nonsense. I wouldn't take one of them as a gift.

[SHEPPEY, *unseen by* BOLTON, *gives* BRADLEY *and* ALBERT *a wink.* BRADLEY *presently goes out.*

SHEPPEY: I know I couldn't sell you anything not in a hundred years. You 'ave to be a judge of character in my business and I know it would be just waste of time to try.

BOLTON: Thank you for those kind words.

SHEPPEY: You see, we make our money out of the vanity of the 'uman race. And I don't mind telling you that men are every bit as vain as women.

MISS GRANGE: Vainer, if you ask me.

SHEPPEY: Now I don't think I'm wrong in stating that you 'aven't got a spark of vanity in your composition.

BOLTON: I daresay you're right.

SHEPPEY: I know I'm right. I mean, if you was vain you wouldn't want to look any older than you need, would you?

BOLTON: I'm only just over forty, you know.

SHEPPEY: Is that a fact, sir? Of course, being so grey over the temples makes you look more.

MISS GRANGE: Oh, I like the grey over the temples, Sheppey. I always think it makes a gentleman look so distingay.

SHEPPEY: I don't say it don't look distingay. I only say it adds a good five years to one's age. If Mr. Bolton 'adn't got that grey 'e wouldn't look a day over thirty-five.

MISS GRANGE: He wouldn't look that, Sheppey.

BOLTON: I'm not going to dye my hair to please you, Sheppey.

SHEPPEY: I don't blame you. I'd never recommend a gentleman to dye his hair. It seems unnatural somehow.

MISS GRANGE: I always think it makes a face look so hard.

SHEPPEY: What I mean to say is, I don't suppose you mind if you look thirty-five or forty-eight. Why should you?

BOLTON: I don't know that I want to look as though I had one foot in the grave, you know.

SHEPPEY: You know what I'm thinking of, Miss Grange?

MISS GRANGE: That German stuff.

SHEPPEY: Mind you, sir, I'm not trying to sell it to you.

BOLTON: That's a good job because you won't succeed.

SHEPPEY: I'm all for British goods. I don't 'old with

foreigners or their doings. When the traveller come in with it I was all against it meself, but 'e persuaded Mr. Bradley to give it a trial. And you'd be surprised at the amount we've sold of it.

MISS GRANGE: Especially when you think what it costs.

SHEPPEY: What with the duty and one thing and another we can't sell it for less than twenty-five shillings a bottle.

BOLTON: What is it, a dye?

SHEPPEY: No, that's what it isn't. It just makes the 'air grow its natural colour. The result is so gradual that nobody notices. I can tell you this, if you give it a trial, at the end of three weeks you wouldn't 'ave a grey 'air on your 'ead.

BOLTON: You don't really expect me to believe that?

SHEPPEY: What reason 'ave I got for saying it? I know you're not going to try it, sir. Why should you? I know you're not the sort of gentleman as minds what 'e looks like.

BOLTON: You're not pulling my leg, are you?

SHEPPEY: How d'you mean, sir?

BOLTON: I thought you might be up to some hanky-panky.

SHEPPEY: Trying to sell you that stuff? That's not the way I'd go about it. Look here, sir, I don't mind telling you a secret. If you want to sell something to a customer you've got to keep your eye on 'im all the time. You've got to watch 'im like as if you was a boxer in the ring. Now, 'ave I been looking at you?

BOLTON: I haven't noticed it.

SHEPPEY: Well, then. A funny thing 'appened the other day. I expect you know the Marquess of Twickenham, sir.

BOLTON: No, I don't.

SHEPPEY: 'E's one of our customers and so's 'is brother,

Lord John. He absolutely insisted on trying this preparation. He was getting terribly grey and it upset 'im like. Well, one morning a gentleman come in and sat down in my chair. Good-morning, Lord John, I said to 'im. He began to laugh. I'm not Lord John, 'e said, I'm the Marquess of Twickenham. Would you believe it, I'd taken 'im for 'is younger brother. 'E 'adn't got a grey 'air in 'is 'ead.

MISS GRANGE: I couldn't help laughing at the sight of Sheppey's face.

SHEPPEY: Well, his lordship told me there was fifteen years between them.

MISS GRANGE: Almost a miracle, I call it.

BOLTON: What's the stuff called?

SHEPPEY: Get a bottle, Albert, and let Mr. Bolton 'ave a look at it.

BOLTON: Don't bother. It doesn't matter at all.

SHEPPEY: [*With a wink at* ALBERT.] Just as a matter of curiosity. 'Ave anything on the race to-day, sir?

BOLTON: No, I didn't.

SHEPPEY: I wish I 'adn't.

[ALBERT *goes into the front shop.*

BOLTON: Mug's game, betting.

MISS GRANGE: Sheppey doesn't think so. You'd be surprised the winners he picks.

SHEPPEY: Of course I never 'ave more than a shilling each way. With a wife and daughter to provide for I can't afford to take risks. I must say I like to 'ave a bit on.

BOLTON: You must be pretty smart if you don't lose more than you win.

SHEPPEY: Well, I'll tell you, I'm lucky. I always 'ave been.

MISS GRANGE: They say it's better to be born lucky than rich, don't they?

BOLTON: Did you have a ticket for the Irish Sweep?

SHEPPEY: Yes, I wouldn't miss that for anything. I've always 'ad one, ever since they started.

BOLTON: You've never won anything, I suppose?

SHEPPEY: Not yet, but I'm in 'opes.

BOLTON: The draw was yesterday, wasn't it?

SHEPPEY: Yes. They're drawing the consolation prizes to-day. I might win one of them.

MISS GRANGE: It would be a nice thing if you opened your paper to-morrow morning and saw your name there.

SHEPPEY: I shouldn't be surprised.

[ALBERT *comes in.*

ALBERT: Captain Fortescue's on the 'phone, Sheppey. He wants to know if you're free to-morrow morning at eleven-thirty.

SHEPPEY: Yes. I'm free. Book him, will you?

ALBERT: All right.

[*He goes out.*

MISS GRANGE: He was in this morning, Sheppey. He *was* in a way when he found you wasn't here.

SHEPPEY: Well, it wasn't my fault, was it?

MISS GRANGE: Cursing and swearing all over the place, he was.

SHEPPEY: I know. Only a captain and thinks 'imself a colonel.

[ALBERT *comes in again.*

ALBERT: He says, he ain't going to put up with any of your damned impudence again, and if you're not ready and waiting at eleven-thirty sharp he won't be responsible for the consequences.

SHEPPEY: I suppose they've made 'im commander-in-chief all of a sudden.

BOLTON: How is it that you weren't here this morning? I

thought you'd never missed a day for fourteen years.

SHEPPEY: No more I 'ave. Except for me fortnight's 'oliday in the summer. I was at Lambeth Police Court all the morning.

BOLTON: Drunk or disorderly?

SHEPPEY: Not me. 'Alf a pint of bitter to my dinner, and 'alf a pint when I go off work in the evening, that's all the liquor that ever passes my lips.

MISS GRANGE: He was witness in a case.

SHEPPEY: I caught a chap stealing the doctor's overcoat out of 'is car. It was standing outside the next 'ouse to mine and I come out of my front door just in the nick of time.

BOLTON: You can't leave a thing in your car now. It's rotten. You gave him in charge?

SHEPPEY: Yes. I almost wished I 'adn't afterwards. Out of work. Told the magistrate 'e 'adn't 'ad a bite for two days. You couldn't 'ardly 'elp feeling sorry for him really.

MISS GRANGE: You're too soft-hearted, Sheppey. All this unemployment. I believe if you really want a job you can always find one.

SHEPPEY: You wouldn't say that if you'd 'eard all I did this morning. My case didn't come on till near the end and I sat there and listened. It made me quite uncomfortable.

BOLTON: Why?

SHEPPEY: Well, you know, I'd 'ad a good breakfast before I left 'ome, and I was enjoying meself. It was a bit of a treat for me not 'aving to come to the shop for once in a way. A lot of cases there was.

BOLTON: Anything interesting?

SHEPPEY: Well, I don't know if you'd call 'em interesting. There was one woman who'd been caught stealing a bit of steak off a barrer. She 'ad eighteen bob a week to keep 'erself and three children. A respectable-looking woman she was too.

BOLTON: Of course there's a good deal of distress abou nowadays, but there's nothing to do about it.

MISS GRANGE: That's what I say, there always have been rich and poor in the world and there always will be.

SHEPPEY: It seems funny in a country like this there should be a lot of people starving.

MISS GRANGE: If you have three good meals a day and a roof over your head, be thankful, I say, and don't worry about anybody else.

SHEPPEY: Well, I don't, not as a rule. Only you see, 'aving it brought 'ome to me all of a sudden, like it was this morning, it did give me a bit of a turn. There they was standing in the dock. They didn't look any different to anybody else. They looked just like you and me, if you understand what I mean. I couldn't 'elp saying to meself, not one of them'd be 'ere if they earned what I do.

BOLTON: You earn good money because you're steady and industrious.

SHEPPEY: I know that. But p'raps if they'd 'ad my chances they'd 'ave been just as good as me.

MISS GRANGE: You *are* morbid to-day, Sheppey. You can't be well.

BOLTON: Well, it's just on seven. You'll feel better after you've had your glass of beer.

SHEPPEY: Perhaps I shall. I generally 'ave a steak and veg. for my dinner, but some'ow to-day I didn't fancy it.

MISS GRANGE: I hope you haven't caught something sitting with all those dirty, unhealthy people.

SHEPPEY: You don't 'ave much 'eart to keep yourself clean when you don't know where your next meal is coming from and I don't expect it's so easy to keep 'ealthy when you don't get 'ardly enough nourishment to keep body and soul together.

MISS GRANGE: Oh, don't harp so. Why, you might be a Socialist to hear you talk. I always thought you were a good Conservative.

SHEPPEY: I'm a Conservative all right. I'll tell you what, Miss Grange, you let me take you to a police court one morning when we're slack and you see for yourself.

MISS GRANGE: Not me. I'm not going to upset myself. What the eye doesn't see the heart doesn't grieve over, I say. We've all got troubles enough of our own without bothering about other people's.

BOLTON: That's the only sensible way to look at it, you know, Sheppey. Everyone knows there's a lot of poverty in this world, but it can't be helped. It's just one of those things that you have to accept, like influenza or a run of bad luck at cards. And the fact remains that no one need starve to death in this country. There are institutions where he can always get a meal and there are shelters where he can always get a bed.

MISS GRANGE: My belief is that a lot of those people who sleep out on the Embankment sleep there because they really like it.

BOLTON: What did your fellow get?

SHEPPEY: Remanded for a week, sir.

BOLTON: Well, I wouldn't mind betting they'll find out that's not the only thing he's done. A man doesn't steal because he's hungry, he steals because he's a thief.

MISS GRANGE: And if he's hungry I should have thought he was better off in prison than outside.

BOLTON: It's no good fashing oneself about things one can't help. Better brains than yours have tried to find a way out, and if they haven't it's not likely you will.

S

MISS GRANGE: Everyone for himself and the devil take the hindmost, I say.

SHEPPEY: I'm a very ignorant man, I know that. All the same it does make me a bit uncomfortable to think it was me as gave the poor devil in charge.

BOLTON: You did quite right. Society must be protected, and it's a citizen's duty to uphold the law. A pretty state of things it would be if a fellow was justified in helping himself to whatever he fancied.

[ALBERT *comes through the curtains.*

ALBERT: You're wanted on the 'phone, Sheppey.

SHEPPEY: Say I'm busy and ask 'em to leave a message.

ALBERT: It's your wife and she says it's urgent.

SHEPPEY: I don't care who it is. My wife knows very well I won't 'ave 'er ringing me up when I'm working.

BOLTON: Never mind about me, Sheppey. You go to the telephone. I don't mind waiting.

SHEPPEY: I wouldn't think of it. You know what women are, sir, give 'em an inch and they'll take an ell.

MISS GRANGE: Perhaps it's important, Sheppey. She's never rung you up before all the time I've been here.

SHEPPEY: I should think not indeed. When I'm at 'ome I'm at 'er beck and call, within reason, you know, but when I'm at the shop I'm me own master, as far as she's concerned.

[ALBERT *comes in again.*

ALBERT: She says she can't leave a message and you've got to go to the 'phone yourself.

SHEPPEY: You tell 'er if it was the King of England ringing up from Buckingham Palace to give me the Order of the Garter I wouldn't go not while I was in the middle of shaving a customer.

[ALBERT *goes out.*

BOLTON: How long have you been married, Sheppey?

SHEPPEY: Twenty-three years, sir, and if I may quote the words of our national bard it don't seem a day too much.

BOLTON: [*Smiling.*] Well, if this is the first time your wife has ever rung you up in working hours I don't think it would hurt you to see what she wants.

SHEPPEY: When you've been at the job as long as I 'ave, sir, you'll know there's one thing you must never do in married life, and that's create a precedent.

MISS GRANGE: The way you talk, Sheppey. A nicer woman than Mrs. Miller I never did know.

BOLTON: Who's Mrs. Miller?

SHEPPEY: That's my old lady. My name's Miller really.

BOLTON: Is it? I never knew that.

SHEPPEY: They call me Sheppey because I was born there. Isle of Sheppey. Kent, you know. They kid me because they say I've got Sheppey on the brain.

MISS GRANGE: To hear him talk you'd think there was no place like it.

SHEPPEY: No more there is. I always go there for me 'olidays and when I retire I'm going to settle down there.

MISS GRANGE: I went there one bank holiday. I didn't think so much of it.

SHEPPEY: The garden of England, that's what it is. I know the very 'ouse I'm going to buy when my ship comes home. Two acres of land. View of the sea. Just the place for me and my old woman.

> [BRADLEY *comes in followed by* ALBERT *and the young lady who acts as cashier*, MISS JAMES *by name*.

BRADLEY: Put that razor down, Sheppey.

SHEPPEY: Why, what's the trouble?

BRADLEY: You've won a prize in the Sweep.

SHEPPEY: Is that all? That's no reason to leave a job unfinished.

[*He is about to go on with his shaving when* MR. BOLTON *holds his arm.*

BOLTON: No, you don't. I don't want my throat cut.

SHEPPEY: A little thing like that's not going to affect my 'and. Is that what you're frightened of? Why, I could shave a gentleman if they was dropping bombs over St. James's Palace and Jermyn Street was burning like a load of straw.

BOLTON: I don't mind telling you I'm not a gentleman who'd be wanting a shave just at that moment.

BRADLEY: I'll finish Mr. Bolton myself. Give me your razor.

BOLTON: [*Passing his hand over his chin.*] No, that's all right. That'll do.

[BRADLEY *sponges and wipes his face.*

ALBERT: There's a wire for you from Dublin, and they've rung up your house from the *Daily Echo.* They wanted your business address.

BRADLEY: You haven't lost the ticket, Sheppey?

SHEPPEY: Not me. I've got it on me now. [*He takes out his pocket book and produces the ticket.*]

MISS GRANGE: How much is it, Mr. Bradley?

ALBERT: Mrs. Miller didn't say. She was all excited. Crying and laughing she was. The consolation prizes are a hundred pounds.

BOLTON: Well, even that's worth having.

SHEPPEY: I can do with it.

MISS GRANGE: You don't seem a bit excited, Sheppey.

SHEPPEY: Well, to tell you the truth I've been sort of expecting it. I was born lucky.

MISS GRANGE: If it was me I'd be doing Catherine-wheels all over the shop.

SHEPPEY: I don't believe Mr. Bradley would like that, Miss

Grange. Besides, it might put ideas in Albert's 'ead. 'Im not being a married man and all that.

MISS GRANGE: Oh, don't be so coarse, Sheppey. You know I don't like that sort of joke.

[MR. BOLTON, *now ready, gets up from his chair*.

BOLTON: You'd better ring up the *Echo* and ask how much it is.

BRADLEY: A hundred pounds.

BOLTON: What about the ten residuary prizes? How do you know it's not one of them?

SHEPPEY: I never thought of that.

BRADLEY: Couldn't be.

ALBERT: There'll be a special edition. Perhaps it's out by now.

BRADLEY: You nip along round the corner, Albert, and see if it is.

ALBERT: All right, sir.

[*He goes out*.

BOLTON: [*Giving* SHEPPEY *a tip*.] Here you are, Sheppey, and my best congratulations.

SHEPPEY: Thank you very much, sir.

BOLTON: Whatever it is don't blue it.

SHEPPEY: Not me, sir. I've made up my mind exactly what I'm going to do with it.

MISS GRANGE: How can you when you don't know how much it is yet? I mean, supposing it *is* one of the residuary prizes? [*Pocketing* BOLTON'S *tip*.] Thank you, sir.

SHEPPEY: Anything up to thirty thousand pounds I've got all fixed up.

BOLTON: I'll tell you what I'll do, Sheppey: to celebrate the occasion I'll have a bottle of that German stuff you were talking about.

SHEPPEY: Very good, sir. Shall I send it or will you take it with you?

BOLTON: Mind you, I don't believe in it, but to oblige you I'll try it.

SHEPPEY: Well, sir, I'm sure you'll be surprised.

BOLTON: I may just as well take it with me.

SHEPPEY: A bottle of Grayline for Mr. Bolton, please, Mr. Bradley.

BRADLEY: I'll just do it up for you, sir. Cash, please.

BOLTON: Good-night.

THE OTHERS: Good-night, sir.

> [MISS JAMES *steps out and* BOLTON *follows.* BRADLEY *has held open the curtain for him and goes out after him.*

MISS GRANGE: You are a caution, Sheppey.

SHEPPEY: I know I am. I don't believe there's another man in the business could 'ave sold Mr. Bolton a bottle of 'air-dye. They can say what they like, that's all it is. If it's anything at all, that's to say.

MISS GRANGE: Oh, I wasn't thinking of that.

SHEPPEY: You wasn't? But it was a masterpiece the way I kidded him. 'E put me on my mettle, saying I'd never sell 'im anything not if I tried till doomsday. 'E's no fool either. Not like some of these young fellows as'll believe anything you tell them. You know, I was listening meself to what I was saying and I said to meself, you're a wonder, Sheppey, there's no doubt about it, you're a little wonder.

MISS GRANGE: Oh, you make me sick, Sheppey, patting yourself on the back because you sell a mug a bottle of hair restorer, when you've just won a prize in the Irish Sweep.

SHEPPEY: [*Taking off his long white working coat.*] Well, I'll tell you, Miss Grange, seeing's believing. I don't ever believe anything till I see it in the papers.

MISS GRANGE: There's Albert.

[ALBERT *comes in.*

ALBERT: The papers 'aven't come yet.

MISS GRANGE: Oh, bother.

BRADLEY: [*Coming in.*] I've told Miss James to try and get the *Echo*. It's just on seven. Draw the blind down, Albert.

ALBERT: Right you are, sir.

BRADLEY: I expect you'll be glad to be getting along home, Sheppey.

MISS GRANGE: Mrs. Miller and your daughter will be in a state.

[*The bell rings as the door opens.*

BRADLEY: Hulloa, who's that?

MISS GRANGE: My word, people think they can come at any old time.

BRADLEY: Oh, that's all right. Albert 'll say we're closed.

[ALBERT *re-enters.*

ALBERT: [*In a whisper.*] It's a fellow from the *Echo*. Wants to see Sheppey.

MISS GRANGE: [*Overwhelmed.*] No?

BRADLEY: Tell him to come along.

MISS GRANGE: Gracious! And me all anyhow.

[*She takes out her powder and begins to make up.*

SHEPPEY: Where do you come in?

MISS GRANGE: I don't want to disgrace the shop.

ALBERT: [*Through the curtains.*] Step this way, sir.

[*A young pasty-faced man with a camera enters.*

REPORTER: Mr. Miller?

SHEPPEY: That's my name. Sheppey for short.

REPORTER: [*Shaking hands with him.*] Best congratulations.

SHEPPEY: Don't mention it.

REPORTER: Paper sent me along to get a brief interview.

SHEPPEY: You've just come in time. Another five minutes and you'd have found us all gone.

REPORTER: Feeling pretty good, I suppose?

SHEPPEY: Not so bad.

REPORTER: Ever won anything before?

SHEPPEY: Never.

REPORTER: I suppose you've had tickets?

SHEPPEY: Never missed since they started.

REPORTER: Well, you don't mind if I say it's the first time you ever had one. I mean, it makes a better story.

SHEPPEY: No, I don't object to that.

BRADLEY: We were just trying to get on to your paper when you came in.

REPORTER: Oh, what about?

MISS GRANGE: It's one of the hundred-pound prizes, I suppose?

REPORTER: D'you mean to say you didn't know? It's one of the residuary prizes. Eight thousand five hundred pounds.

SHEPPEY: Is that what it is? That's real money that is.

[MISS JAMES, *who has followed the reporter in, suddenly bursts into tears.*

BRADLEY: Hulloa, what's the matter with you, Miss James?

MISS JAMES: [*Sobbing.*] I do apologise. I can't help it. Eight thousand five hundred pounds. It makes me feel quite sick.

MISS GRANGE: If you're going to be sick you'd better go to the lavatory, I think.

MISS JAMES: Oh, it's all right. Excitement always takes me like that.

SHEPPEY: It's 'er stomach, poor girl.

REPORTER: What'll you do with the money? I suppose you've hardly had time to decide yet.

SHEPPEY: What makes you think a silly thing like that? I decided that when I bought the ticket. I'm going to pay off the rest of the money on my 'ouse. And there's a little place on the Isle of Sheppey I've got my eye on, two acres of land and just the sort of dinky little 'ouse I've always thought would suit me.

MISS GRANGE: Fancy you a landed proprietor, Sheppey. We shall have to call you squire.

SHEPPEY: Then there's my daughter wants to get married. I'll give her a slap-up wedding. Champagne and caviare. And I'll keep a girl to 'elp my wife. No more rough work for that old lady.

ALBERT: I'd buy a baby Austin if I was in your place.

SHEPPEY: And who says I won't buy a baby Austin? It would save me a lot of expense getting down to my property in the country.

REPORTER: You won't go on working, then?

SHEPPEY: Me? I wouldn't know what to do with myself if I stopped working. I'm what you might call an artist. Isn't that right, Governor?

BRADLEY: I wouldn't swear you weren't, not in a court of law.

SHEPPEY: No, young fellow, I'm not one to waste the gifts the Almighty has given me.

REPORTER: What about a photograph of you at work? I think the paper'd like that. Pity it's so late and no customers.

MISS GRANGE: Mr. Bradley can pretend he's a customer.

BRADLEY: That's right. Give me a gown, Albert.

ALBERT: Here you are, Governor.

s*

BRADLEY: You put on your coat, Sheppey.

SHEPPEY: Half a tick. Shave or hair-cut?

REPORTER: Shave, I think. Looks more natural.

BRADLEY: I'll just put a bit of lather on my face.

MISS GRANGE: I'll get my stool and pretend I'm doing your nails.

SHEPPEY: 'Ere, who's being photographed, Miss Grange, you or me?

MISS GRANGE: Don't be a dog in the manger, Sheppey. I only want it to make a good picture.

SHEPPEY: You might be one of them Society beauties shoving yourself in like that. Albert 'll be wanting to come in next.

REPORTER: She's all right. I like that.

> [*They all get into attitudes. The* REPORTER *looks through his camera.*

BRADLEY: Don't stand like that, Sheppey. They won't see anything but my legs.

SHEPPEY: They want to see my face, don't they?

REPORTER: Get on the other side of him.

SHEPPEY: You won't be able to see me.

REPORTER: Yes, I shall. That's a good position. Let me see the razor.

BRADLEY: Not too near my face, Sheppey.

REPORTER: Hold it right out.

> [SHEPPEY *stretches out his arm.*

REPORTER: That's right. Fine.

BRADLEY: [*Noticing that* ALBERT *has edged in.*] What are you doing there, Albert? You get the hell out of there, see?

SHEPPEY: You don't want to break the camera, do you?

ALBERT: [*Sulkily.*] All right. One'd think you'd never been photoed before. Fuss you make of it.

REPORTER: Now look at me. Pleasant, now. This isn't a funeral. He's just won a prize in the Irish Sweep. Smile. That's right. Hold it. Thank you.

> [*They put on frozen smiles and when he says thank you return to their natural state.* BRADLEY *wipes the soap off his face and gets out of the chair.* MISS GRANGE *gathers up her stool and her box of utensils.*

MISS GRANGE: Will it be in the paper to-morrow?

REPORTER: It should be.

MISS GRANGE: I shall be excited.

SHEPPEY: It'll be in the papers to-night, won't it? I mean about the draw, the names and all that?

REPORTER: Yes. Haven't you seen a paper yet? I've got one on me. For the address, you know.

SHEPPEY: Mind letting me 'ave a squint? You know, I've never seen my name in print before. Fact is, I can't quite believe it's all true till I see it in black and white.

REPORTER: [*Taking the newspaper out of his pocket.*] Here you are. Front page.

> [SHEPPEY *takes the paper and looks at it.*

SHEPPEY: That's right. Eight thousand five hundred pounds, Isle of Sheppey. That's my synonym. Joseph Miller. The Rosary, Moore Street, Camberwell, S.E. 17. Well, well, well, who'd 'ave thought it. [*Without thinking he takes off his wig and discloses a very bald head. He meditatively scratches it.*]

REPORTER: [*Taken aback.*] Is that a wig you're wearing?

SHEPPEY: [*Coming down to earth.*] Me? Yes. I 'ave to in working hours. Customers are that funny. If you try and sell them a 'air tonic and you're bald like I am, they say it don't seem to 'ave done you much good.

REPORTER: It gave me quite a turn to see you take it off all of a sudden.

SHEPPEY: 'Ere, you're not going to say anything about it in the paper?

REPORTER: [*With a smile.*] That's asking something.

SHEPPEY: You wouldn't do that. I mean, you and me are in the same trade, so to speak. I mean, we 'ave to kid the public a bit, don't we? And you know what the public is, it wants to be kidded.

REPORTER: [*Good-naturedly.*] All right. I'll forget about it. Thank you very much. Good evening.

BRADLEY: Good evening, sir. Give us a look in when you want a hair-cut. Sheppey 'll attend to you himself.

SHEPPEY: I will with pleasure.

REPORTER: But I tell you what, you'll never sell me a hair restorer.

SHEPPEY: I wouldn't be too sure, sir.

REPORTER: Good night.

ALL: Good night, sir.

> [*He goes out.* ALBERT *accompanies him to the door and soon after comes back.*

MISS GRANGE: Well, that's what I call luck.

SHEPPEY: Yes, I'll admit that.

MISS JAMES: And you so calm about it all. That's what I can't get over.

SHEPPEY: Well, I'm used to it, as you might say. I been lucky all my life.

BRADLEY: I wish I knew how it was done.

SHEPPEY: I'll tell you. You must believe in it. When I was a young fellow I was a rare one for the girls. And d'you know how I used to get 'em? Bounce. It's the same with luck, you've got to bounce it.

MISS GRANGE: [*With a toss of her head.*] I like that. No one will get me with bounce. The fellow who gets me has got to have a good situation and a bit put by in the savings bank.

MISS JAMES: Men are not what they were. There's no denying that.

SHEPPEY: That's your poor stomach again, Miss James.

BRADLEY: Well I'll be getting off. *Tempus fugit*, as they say.

SHEPPEY: 'Alf a mo, governor. You must all drink my 'ealth first. I tell you what, I'll pop over to the Bunch of Keys and get a bottle of champagne.

MISS GRANGE: Oh, Sheppey, if there's anything I like it's a glass of fizz.

SHEPPEY: I shan't be a minute.

[*He hurries out.*

MISS GRANGE: It's funny when you think about it; I'm almost as excited as if I'd won something myself.

BRADLEY: That shows you have a nice nature, Miss Grange.

MISS GRANGE: One has to have a nice nature in this business or you couldn't listen to the silly things gentlemen say to one all day long.

ALBERT: I never pay any attention. It just goes in at one ear and out at the other with me.

MISS GRANGE: It's easy for you. Gentlemen expect a manicurist to be bright and snappy. And you've got to laugh at their silly jokes or else they say you've got no sense of humour.

BRADLEY: That's all part of the job.

MISS GRANGE: I know it is. I'm not complaining. And of course you get a dinner and a theatre out of it now and again.

ALBERT: To say nothing of a kiss and cuddle in the taxi on the way home.

MISS JAMES: You are vulgar, Albert.

MISS GRANGE: Well, if a girl won't give a gentleman a kiss in return for dinner and a theatre more fool her, I say. I mean she must know when to stop, of course. But if you're a lady you can always keep a gentleman in his place.

ALBERT: I suppose they take you to the stalls, don't they?

MISS GRANGE: Well, it all depends. If they're bachelors, yes. But if they're married it's generally dress circles. They don't think it's so conspicuous.

BRADLEY: Of course we have a lot of tip-top swells coming to this establishment and naturally they have to be careful.

MISS GRANGE: Oh, I'm not blaming them. If they mention it, I always say I quaite understand. *Noblesse oblige*, if you know what I mean.

> [*The whole staff is gathered in the shop when* SHEPPEY *comes in with a bottle of champagne in his hand. He is accompanied by a pretty, painted woman, no longer very young, and flashily dressed in rather shabby clothes. This is* BESSIE LEGROS.

SHEPPEY: Here I am and here's the champagne. I got the best. Fourteen and nine.

ALBERT: Whew! It ought to be good at the price.

BRADLEY: Who's the lady, Sheppey?

SHEPPEY: A friend of mine. Well, not exactly a friend, but I know 'er, see? I always go in to the Bunch of Keys to 'ave my beer when I shut up of a evening and she's generally 'aving one at the same time.

BRADLEY: [*With a nod to* BESSIE.] Pleased to meet you.

BESSIE: The pleasure's mine.

SHEPPEY: So we got talking like. And so when I saw 'er just now, I said to 'er, no beer for you to-day, miss. You come along with me and 'ave a glass of fizz.

BESSIE: I didn't say yes and I didn't say no. You know the song, don't you?

BRADLEY: But you came along, I see.

BESSIE: I didn't want to, not really. I said to Mr. Miller, Oh, they won't want me, I shall only be in the way. But he said, Get along with you, it's months since you tasted fizz, I lay. And he was right there.

BRADLEY: Well, you're welcome as far as I'm concerned, and it's Sheppey that's standing the champagne.

ALBERT: Better let me open it, Sheppey. I'm more used to it than you are.

SHEPPEY: 'Ark at 'im. All right, only be careful. Now then, you girls, what about glasses?

MISS JAMES: We can manage.

MISS GRANGE: There's a glass in the lavatory, Victor.

> [VICTOR goes out and comes in again in a moment with a glass. MISS JAMES goes round the shop and collects whatever there is that can be used to drink out of.

BESSIE: [To BRADLEY.] You have got a beautiful place here.

BRADLEY: You have to have these days. Lots of competition, you know.

BESSIE: It's the same in everything. There ought to be a law against it, I think.

BRADLEY: You'd be surprised the amount of stuff we have to carry. You come and have a look at my show-cases.

> [They walk into the front shop.

MISS GRANGE: Come over here a minute, Sheppey. I want to say something to you.

SHEPPEY: [Going over to her.] What is it?

MISS GRANGE: She's a tart.

SHEPPEY: I know that.

MISS GRANGE: You didn't ought to have brought her in here, Sheppey.

SHEPPEY: Why?

MISS GRANGE: You ought to have more respect for me and Miss James.

SHEPPEY: Now look 'ere, my dear, you may be in the ladies' 'air-dressing yourself one day. If you think a ladies' salon can get along without tarts you're crazy.

MISS GRANGE: I don't say I've got any objection to them in business; it's meeting them socially I object to.

SHEPPEY: Oh, be a sport, Miss Grange. After all one doesn't win eight thousand five 'undred pounds in a sweep every day of one's life. To oblige me.

MISS GRANGE: Well, as long as you know, I don't mind so much. And they do say, to the pure all things are pure.

[*By this time* ALBERT *has opened the bottle, and* BRADLEY *and* BESSIE *stroll in again.*

ALBERT: Come on, all of you. First come first served.

[*They gather round and take the tumblers he fills.*

BRADLEY: Well, Sheppey, here's your very good health. If I couldn't win a prize myself there's no one I'd rather see win it than you.

ALBERT: And so say all of us.

ALL: [*Chanting.*] And so say all of us. For he's a jolly good fellow. For he's a jolly good fellow.

SHEPPEY: I'm very much obliged to you, ladies and gentlemen. This spontaneous effusion of good will has touched me to the bottom of me 'eart. Ladies and gentlemen, I drink your very good 'ealth.

MISS GRANGE: I must say, I like a glass of champagne.

BESSIE: It's class. That's what it is.

MISS GRANGE: Mind you, I wouldn't want it every day.

BESSIE: Oh, no, I mean if you drunk it every day it wouldn't be a treat, would it?

ALBERT: A1, Sheppey. Reminds me of the fizz we 'ad at my sister's wedding.

SHEPPEY: It ought to be good for the money. They 'ad some at twelve and six, but I said, No, on a day like this I want the best.

BRADLEY: Now, Sheppey, just because you've won a nice bit of money, don't you go wasting it on a lot of foolishness.

SHEPPEY: Not me. I've got me 'ead screwed on me shoulders all right.

BRADLEY: I'm very glad to hear you say it. Now I must be getting along home or my wife'll think I'm up to some hanky-panky. You'll shut up all right, Sheppey, won't you?

SHEPPEY: You can trust me.

ALBERT: I'll be going too. I'm taking my young lady to the pictures.

[*He and* VICTOR *go out to take off their white coats.*

MISS GRANGE: Are you coming, Miss James?

MISS JAMES: I'm quite ready.

BRADLEY: Good night, all. See you to-morrow.

ALL: Good night, sir.

[BRADLEY *goes out.*

MISS GRANGE: Are you going anywhere to-night, dear?

MISS JAMES: No, I'm going to run up that *crêpe de Chine* I bought yesterday.

[MISS GRANGE *and* MISS JAMES *go out.*

BESSIE: I'll be getting along too.

SHEPPEY: Don't you hurry. Here, there's a drop more in the bottle. Pity to waste it.

BESSIE: I won't say no.

[ALBERT *and* VICTOR *come through.*

ALBERT: Good night.

SHEPPEY: Good night.

BESSIE: Hope you have a nice time with your young lady.

ALBERT: Trust me.

> [ALBERT *and* VICTOR *go out as* MISS JAMES *and* MISS GRANGE *come in with their hats on.*

SHEPPEY: You ain't been long.

MISS GRANGE: I haven't got too much time. It's partnership evening at my bridge club and I don't want to keep them waiting.

SHEPPEY: Well, good night.

MISS GRANGE: Night, Sheppey. [*She gives* BESSIE *a stiff bow.*] Good naight.

BESSIE: Good night, miss.

[*The two girls go out.*

SHEPPEY: I'll just put the catch on the door.

> [*He goes out. When* BESSIE *is left alone she crumples up wearily on her chair. Her face is screwed up into a grimace and a sob is wrung from her. She clenches her hands in the effort to control herself, but the tears come and she takes her handkerchief out of her bag.* SHEPPEY *returns.*

SHEPPEY: 'Ulloa, what are you crying for?

BESSIE: I'm not crying. It's only tears running out of me eyes.

SHEPPEY: What's the trouble?

BESSIE: Nothing. Only it's cosy here. And you all being so friendly. I shall be all right in a minute.

SHEPPEY: Here, drink your champagne.

BESSIE: No, I daren't. Not on an empty stomach. I expect that's what upset me.

SHEPPEY: Didn't you have no tea?

BESSIE: No, nor dinner either. I'm banting.

SHEPPEY: Well, that's a silly thing to do.

BESSIE: Not if you've got no money. I only had tenpence. I spent threepence on my bus up west and I must keep threepence for me bus home if I don't click to-night. And I was going to spend the other fourpence on a beer when you come in.

SHEPPEY: Well, I saved you that anyway.

BESSIE: I felt I just couldn't walk up and down and round and round for hours if I didn't have my beer.

SHEPPEY: You must be pretty peckish, aren't you?

BESSIE: Oh, I don't mind that. I'm getting used to it by now. It's me room I'm worrying about. I'm three weeks behind with me rent and if I don't get a job to-night she'll turn me out.

SHEPPEY: Oh, I say.

BESSIE: Oh, well, the night's young yet. Never say die, that's my motto. It's fine and dry, that's something. It's when it's wet I don't like it.

SHEPPEY: It ain't exactly my idea of a life of pleasure, I must say.

BESSIE: Pleasure? Believe me or not, it's no pleasure to me.

SHEPPEY: What'll you do if you're turned out of your room?

BESSIE: I don't know. Salvation Army Shelter. But you have to sing hymns there. If it don't rain you're better off on the Embankment, they tell me, and the river's nice and close if you happen to feel like jumping in.

SHEPPEY: Ain't you got any family?

BESSIE: Not in London. And then they think I'm doing well. I wouldn't humiliate myself by going to them.

SHEPPEY: I don't want to hurt your feelings, and of course

I never mentioned it when we 'ad our little chats at the Bunch of Keys, but you've always seemed a very respectable woman to me, it surprised me that you was, well, as you might say, on the streets.

BESSIE: And well you might be. It's a rare come-down for me, I can tell you. If you'd told me eighteen months ago I'd come to this, I'd have said, Why, you're dreaming.

SHEPPEY: I knew I was right. The very first time we 'ad a talk, afterwards I said to meself, That's a superior class of woman. I mean, you're not silly. You can talk sensibly. The dogs and football and politics.

BESSIE: I'm no fool. I know that.

SHEPPEY: Seems funny you should be doing this, if you understand what I mean.

BESSIE: It's the slump done it. I was all right before that come. I had a nice little flat in Kennington. And I had three or four gentlemen used to visit me regular. Respectable tradesmen, you know, with wives and families, one was a J.P., nice class of men. I used to make my seven or eight pounds a week. And they liked me because they knew they could trust me. If you're a married man and in a good position, you have to be careful, don't you?

SHEPPEY: Yes, I suppose so. Speaking for meself, from the day I married me wife I've never looked this way or that way.

BESSIE: I don't blame you. But you don't find many like that. My experience is, most men want a little bit of fun now and again and somehow they don't want to have it with their wives.

SHEPPEY: Well, what 'appened then?

BESSIE: I had a bit of bad luck. I got double pneumonia and I had to go away for a bit. And when I come back one of my gentlemen had been sold up and another said he couldn't afford luxuries any more. I dare say I wasn't as good-looking as I had been. Well, to cut a long story short, things just went from bad to worse, and the end of it was I had to put me pride in me pocket and come up west.

SHEPPEY: I say, what's your name? You never told me.

BESSIE: Bessie Legros.

SHEPPEY: Oh, French.

BESSIE: Not really. But gentlemen think it is and when they ask me me name and I tell them Bessie Legros, they get all excited. Paris and all that. That's why I took the name. When I had my little flat in Kennington I used to call myself Mrs. Gloucester, because my first situation when I come to London was in Gloucester Place. Very nice lady, she was, not like some I could name, and I thought I owed her something.

SHEPPEY: Sort of compliment you paid her, as you might say.

BESSIE: [*Getting up.*] Well, I must be getting on the job if I want to earn my rent. No rest for the weary. My God, what a life.

SHEPPEY: It's slavery, that's what it is.

BESSIE: So's domestic service for the matter of that. And in my business, well, it is a bit of a gamble, you know.

SHEPPEY: That 'elps, of course.

BESSIE: You may click and you may not. And that keeps you going.

SHEPPEY: Look 'ere. I don't 'alf like the idea of you walking about on an empty stomach. It can't be good for you. 'Ere's five bob. You can get a good meal on that and there'll be something over in case you want it. [*He takes two half-crowns out of his pocket and gives them to her.*]

BESSIE: I scarcely like to take it.

SHEPPEY: Why not?

BESSIE: Well, from a friend. I mean, it's not like as if it was from a gentleman. I'll pay it back as soon as ever I can. I promise you. I always have paid my way and except the rent I've never owed sixpence to nobody.

SHEPPEY: D'you know what I recommend? A nice bit of steak with a baked potato.

BESSIE: I'll have that, Mr. Miller, and thank you for the idea.

SHEPPEY: I'll come out with you. I expect my old woman's terribly excited. Crying and laughing, they said she was. Good old Ada. [*He gets up. He puts his hand to his forehead.*] Oh, my 'ead. I do feel funny.

BESSIE: Aren't you well, Mr. Miller? Sit down, do.

SHEPPEY: All muzzy.

> [*He sinks down on the chair and immediately falls over on the ground.*

BESSIE: My God! [*She sinks down on her knees beside him and shakes him.*] Mr. Miller. Mr. Miller. Sheppey. Pull yourself together. Don't be silly. Oh, my God, I believe he's fainted. Sheppey. Come on now. Wake up. Oh dear! Oh dear!

SHEPPEY: [*Coming to.*] I'm choking.

BESSIE: Half a mo'. I'll loosen your collar. My word, it is tight. The things men wear.

SHEPPEY: Where am I?

BESSIE: My God, you did give me a turn. I thought you was dead and I'd be had up for murder. How are you feeling?

SHEPPEY: Like a bit of fish that's gone wonky.

BESSIE: Well, lie still a minute.

SHEPPEY: I must have fainted. Thing I never done in my life before.

BESSIE: Looked more like a fit to me.

SHEPPEY: Never been fits in my family.

BESSIE: I expect it was the champagne.

SHEPPEY: Fourteen and nine a bottle. Couldn't 've been that. You saw me pay for it yourself.

BESSIE: You not being used to it and all.

SHEPPEY: I'm feeling better now. I'll just 'ave a set down for a minute.

BESSIE: I'll help you.

[*He gets up on his feet and sits down again in the chair.*

SHEPPEY: I'll be all right in two shakes now. Don't you bother about me. I can look after meself.

BESSIE: How are you going to get home?

SHEPPEY: Bus from Piccadilly Circus.

BESSIE: You're not fit to go by bus. You ought to take a taxi.

SHEPPEY: My old woman 'll think me off me nut if she sees me driving up in a taxi.

BESSIE: Well, a taxi you'll take, my boy. I don't think you're fit to go alone either. Like me to come with you?

SHEPPEY: I shall be all right. I don't want you to neglect your work for my sake.

BESSIE: Oh, that's all right. Trade's slack at this sort of time anyhow. I shall get back before things get busy.

SHEPPEY: Well, I don't mind telling you I do feel a bit queer.

BESSIE: The sooner you get home the better. Where's your hat?

SHEPPEY: Through that door, and me coat's with it. [*She goes out and comes in again immediately with his hat and coat.*] That's very good of you, I'm sure.

BESSIE: I'll just help you on. [*She helps him on with his coat.*] What about shutting up?

SHEPPEY: Only got to slam the gate behind us. There's the lights.

BESSIE: I'll put them out. [*They go to the door,* SHEPPEY *leaning on her arm.*] Feeling all right?

SHEPPEY: Feeling fine. All light inside. And 'appy.

BESSIE: That's a good thing. There ain't too much happiness in the world, I always say.

SHEPPEY: I'd like everybody to be happy.

BESSIE: Well, they can't be. There ain't enough happiness to go round.

SHEPPEY: [*Pointing.*] There are the switches.

BESSIE: Which do I turn? All of them?

SHEPPEY: That's right.

> [*As he says this she switches off the lights and they disappear through the curtains into the front shop.*

END OF ACT ONE

ACT TWO

The Scene represents the living room of SHEPPEY'S *house at Camberwell. It is furnished with a suite in fumed oak bought many years ago on the hire-purchase system. There is a shabby old cottage piano with yellow keys and a large grandfather's chair covered with faded twill. On an overmantel above the fireplace are china ornaments. In the place of honour in the middle of the mantelshelf is an old silver-gilt snuff-box. The curtains are of plush. The walls are decorated with hand-painted plates, photogravures in gilt frames and enlarged photographs of family groups. It is stuffy and overcrowded.*

It is latish on Saturday afternoon. Just over a week has passed since the events shown in the preceding act.

MRS. MILLER *is sitting on a chair, darning socks, and her daughter* FLORRIE *is at the dining-table, studying a French grammar and writing an exercise.*

MRS. MILLER *is a stout, middle-aged woman, with a good-natured, homely face. She has kind eyes and a pleasant smile. She is neat enough in her person, but she has been married too long to bother much how she looks.* FLORRIE *is rather smart. She wears a frock bought at the sales, artificial silk stockings and very high-heeled shoes. Her short hair is permanently waved. She is pretty, alert and self-assured. She has been a typist in the city, and is confident that there is little worth knowing that she doesn't know.*

MRS. MILLER: I shall 'ave to be thinking about getting supper on the way soon.

FLORRIE: Oh, mum, how can I be expected to work if you keep on talking?

MRS. MILLER: Sorry. It's a bit of a change 'aving you 'ome on a Saturday afternoon.

FLORRIE: Ernie had to umpire. The first eleven are playing Cricklewood.

MRS. MILLER: Teaching in the Council School all the week, it seems a shame 'e shouldn't 'ave 'is Saturday afternoons.

FLORRIE: Oh, dry up, mother.

MRS. MILLER: Sorry. You'll strain your eyes reading too much.

FLORRIE: I'm not reading. I'm writing. Don't say anything to Ernie.

MRS. MILLER: How can I? I don't know what you're writing any more than the man in the moon.

FLORRIE: Exercises. I'm learning French. Only it's a secret.

MRS. MILLER: Whatever are you learning French for, Florrie? I don't believe any good can come of that.

FLORRIE: Now Dad's got this money, me and Ernie have made up our minds to spend our honeymoon in Paris.

MRS. MILLER: Oh, 'ave you? Well, it remains to be seen what your Dad and me 'ave got to say to that. Paris, indeed. A nice place for a young married couple to go to.

FLORRIE: [*With a grin.*] You mean it's a nice place for a young unmarried couple to go to.

MRS. MILLER: Don't be common, Florrie. You know I can't abide anything common.

FLORRIE: You're so old-fashioned, mum. Why, it's an education to go to Paris. You know how keen Ernie is on culture.

MRS. MILLER: I know he's an educated man. I mean, he wouldn't 'ave got a job as master in one of the County Council schools if he wasn't.

FLORRIE: You see, I want to surprise him. You look such
a fool if you can't say a word. I can see his face wnen
I start jabbering away at parlez-vous français, garçong,
apportez moi une café-au-lait, a quelle heure parti le
traing, oui, oui.

MRS. MILLER: Wonders will never cease.

FLORRIE: I've got a gift for languages. I know that. D'you
remember the gipsy last summer on the pier? That's
one of the things she said, that I had a gift for languages.

MRS. MILLER: I wasn't thinking of that. What amuses me
is, you was always going to the pictures and flattening
your nose against the shop windows, thinking of nothing
but dress, and now you read Ernie's books and you're
studying French and I don't know what all.

FLORRIE: Well, it's natural, isn't it? I don't want Ernie to
think I'm just an ignoramus.

MRS. MILLER: A what?

FLORRIE: An ignoramus. He says he knows I've got a good
brain, but I haven't had the chance to develop it that
he has; he says he's quite ready to make allowances.

MRS. MILLER: That's very kind of 'im, to be sure. I think
a young fellow's very lucky if 'e can find a girl as can
make her own clothes and cook his dinner for him and
not spend more money than 'e gives 'er. I know it was
in my time.

FLORRIE: Oh, well, things are different now. Now a girl's
got to be educated same as a fellow. Education's everything. I mean, it's only by having education that we
can make the world what it ought to be.

MRS. MILLER: Who's going to do that? You and Ernie?

FLORRIE: You see, I know Ernie looks upon it as a bit of
a come-down marrying me. Of course he hasn't said
so, but I know he feels it, Dad being only a hairdresser and
not even having a saloon of his own. Being an employee.

MRS. MILLER: Your Dad earns better money than many as are their own masters and 'e 'asn't got the responsibility.

FLORRIE: It's not the money, it's the position. Ernie's father was a clerk in the City. Quite a gentleman by all accounts and naturally that means a lot to Ernie. Mum, you won't ever let on that before you married Dad you were in service, will you?

MRS. MILLER: I'm not ashamed of it. If Ernie thinks I learnt to make them meat pies he likes so much without being a professional cook he's a bigger fool than I take 'im for.

FLORRIE: He never notices what he's eating. I mean, he knows it's good, but his mind is busy with his thoughts. What you don't understand is that Ernie's got a wonderful brain.

MRS. MILLER: [*With a fond smile.*] Perhaps not. But what I do understand is that you're more in love with 'im than I ever thought to see you with anybody.

FLORRIE: [*Charmingly.*] I know, mum, I can't help it, I'm just silly about him.

MRS. MILLER: I don't blame you, my girl. It only comes once in a lifetime, love like that. I daresay 'e's all right. You love 'im all you can. You've been a good daughter to me and a good daughter to your Dad. I 'ope you'll be as 'appy together as your Dad and me 'ave been and I can't say more than that.

FLORRIE: Dear old mum.

[*There is a knock at the front door.*

MRS. MILLER: There's Ernie, I expect.

FLORRIE: [*Getting up and going to the window.*] No, it isn't. I'd know his knock in a thousand. It's more masterful than that. [*Looking out.*] It's a gentleman. He's come in a car.

MRS. MILLER: Go and see who it is.

FLORRIE: All right.

> [*She goes out.* MRS. MILLER *goes to the window and looks out.* FLORRIE *comes in again.*

FLORRIE: It's Mr. Bradley, mum. He's asking for Dad. Seems quite surprised he's out.

MRS. MILLER: Ask 'im to come in.

> [FLORRIE *goes to the door and opens it and speaks.*

FLORRIE: Will you come in, sir?

> [BRADLEY *enters.*

BRADLEY: My name's Bradley. I just came to see how your husband was getting on, Mrs. Miller.

MRS. MILLER: Won't you sit down, sir?

BRADLEY: I don't mind if I do.

MRS. MILLER: He's out just at the minute.

BRADLEY: Seems to be out a lot.

MRS. MILLER: I 'ad the doctor to 'im and the doctor said 'e ought to stay in bed. I tried to make 'im, but would 'e listen to me? Seems as though 'e couldn't sit still. Out all day long.

BRADLEY: Where does he go?

MRS. MILLER: Well, that's just what I don't know. 'E 'ardly seems to know 'imself.

BRADLEY: If he's well enough to go gadding about all over the place, I should have thought he was well enough to do a job of work.

MRS. MILLER: The doctor wouldn't 'ear of 'im working. 'E's not 'imself. Friday, not yesterday, Friday a week ago, the day we 'eard about the Sweep 'e come 'ome in a taxi. 'E said 'e'd fainted in the shop.

BRADLEY: I know. He told me when he came on the Saturday morning.

MRS. MILLER: I didn't want 'im to go to work that morning.

But 'e would go. Said 'e 'ad an appointment with the Commander-in-Chief.

BRADLEY: [*With a smile.*] That's right. Captain Fortescue. Sheppey calls him that because of the side he puts on.

MRS. MILLER: Well, on the Saturday afternoon, after dinner, I could see 'e wasn't well and suddenly 'e came all over queer. 'E just fell like a stone. My word, I was frightened. Fortunately Florrie was 'ere.

BRADLEY: Your daughter, I suppose?

FLORRIE: That's right.

BRADLEY: Pleased to meet you.

MRS. MILLER: She phoned for the doctor. The doctor said it looked more like a stroke to 'im than a faint.

BRADLEY: Lucky he's not paralysed if that's the case.

MRS. MILLER: The doctor says the shock and the excitement of winning all that money and Sheppey 'aving such a 'igh blood pressure and all, 'e's convinced it wasn't just an ordinary faint in the shop, but that was a sort of stroke too.

BRADLEY: I don't wonder you're anxious. If he's had two strokes. They always say three's fatal.

MRS. MILLER: The doctor says not to worry. 'E's only got to get 'is blood pressure down and 'e'll be good for another twenty years.

BRADLEY: Doctors don't know everything.

MRS. MILLER: 'E's going back to work on Monday morning.

BRADLEY: Oh, is he? That's just what I wanted to see him about.

MRS. MILLER: It would break 'is 'eart if 'e couldn't go on working. He takes such a pride in his profession.

BRADLEY: [*With a shrewd look at her.*] He wrote me a letter last night.

MRS. MILLER: Did 'e? 'E never told me.

BRADLEY: He must have left it himself. It hadn't got a stamp on.

FLORRIE: What did he say?

BRADLEY: I don't know that I'm quite at liberty to divulge the contents. Perhaps I ought to have a talk to him about it first.

MRS. MILLER: 'E's bound to be in soon. 'E knows we're 'aving supper early because Florrie and the gentleman she's engaged to are going to the pictures.

BRADLEY: [To FLORRIE.] Oh, yes. Sheppey told me you were engaged to be married. And when is the happy event going to take place, may I ask?

FLORRIE: [Becoming very refined.] July. My fiancé's in the scholastic profession and of course we've got to wait till the boys break up for the summer holidays.

BRADLEY: Almost the first thing Sheppey said when he knew he'd won a prize was, now I shall be able to give my daughter a slap-up wedding.

FLORRIE: My fiancé's father was on the Stock Exchange, you know, and sometimes my fiancé says he wonders if he didn't make a mistake not going into the City, on account of the money, you know, but I say to him, money isn't everything, if you're in the scholastic profession you do have decent hols.

MRS. MILLER: [To BRADLEY.] 'Olidays, you know. Well, if it wasn't for the money your Dad's getting for the Sweep I don't know when you'd 'ave married. In them County Council schools the pay's terrible.

BRADLEY: Oh? Teacher in a board school, is he?

FLORRIE: Of course, if you're a professional man you don't expect to make the money you do in trade.

MRS. MILLER: How they expect a fellow to keep a wife and two or three children on it, I don't know, especially when you consider the position they have to keep up.

[*There is a tat-tat-tat on the door.*

FLORRIE: There's Ernie.

[*She bolts out of the room.*

BRADLEY: Bit of luck Sheppey winning all that money, Mrs. Miller.

MRS. MILLER: I know. Florrie was crazy to get married. She was in the City, you know, typewriting. She didn't take long to give in her notice, I can tell you.

BRADLEY: It'll make a difference to you too.

MRS. MILLER: I expect it will. I shan't be sorry to 'ave a girl to do the rough work for me. Funny thing, you know, I never 'ave liked washing-up, and God knows I've done enough of it. But when you've been in the 'ouses I 'ave, with always a kitchen-maid to do the rough work, it goes against the grain to do it yourself, and that nobody can deny.

[FLORRIE *comes in with* ERNEST TURNER. *He is a very young man, twenty-two or twenty-three, and extremely good-looking in a somewhat romantic way, with long wavy hair, fine eyes and the profile of a film-star. He is dressed in grey flannel trousers and a brown tweed coat, loose, easy and shabby, because it is his pose not to pay any attention to the minor matter of clothes. He is alert, vibrant, as they say, and charming.*

ERNIE: Hulloa, Mrs. Miller.

MRS. MILLER: Come in, Ernie. This is Mr. Bradley, Dad's employer.

ERNIE: [*Shaking hands with him cordially.*] I'm very glad to meet you.

BRADLEY: Same here. I hear I've got to congratulate you on being engaged to this young lady.

ERNIE: We've been engaged for two years. What you can

congratulate me on is that I'm going to make a blushing bride of her now.

BRADLEY: Send me an invite and I'll roll up with a wedding present.

MRS. MILLER: Of course we'll send you an invite, Mr. Bradley. It'll be an honour to 'ave you come.

BRADLEY: Well, Sheppey's been in my employment for fifteen years and I look upon him as a friend. I really do. You know we all call him Sheppey at the shop?

ERNIE: Yes, I know. I call him Sheppey too. Seems to suit him somehow.

MRS. MILLER: I've got in the 'abit of it meself now.

BRADLEY: He's wonderfully popular with my customers. Lot of them won't let anybody touch them but him, and if he's busy they'll wait or come another day.

MRS. MILLER: I never asked you if you'd like a cup of tea, Mr. Bradley.

BRADLEY: No, thank you. I wouldn't trouble you.

MRS. MILLER: It's no trouble. I've got to go into the kitchen anyway to get my supper going.

FLORRIE: If you want to please mum you'll ask her to show you the kitchen. She's as proud of that.

MRS. MILLER: Sheppey give me one of them new Eagle stoves for my birthday. You wouldn't believe the difference it makes.

BRADLEY: I know. He was talking about it in the shop. I should like to see that, I must admit. If all I hear is true, I've half a mind to buy one myself.

MRS. MILLER: I'll show it you with pleasure.

BRADLEY: [*To* FLORRIE.] You'll excuse me, won't you?

    [*They go out.* FLORRIE *turns and faces* ERNIE, *smiling.*

ERNIE: You've got a nerve, shooing him off like that.

FLORRIE: I saw at a glance that he was that sort of man, interested in contraptions.

ERNIE: Wonderful eye for character you've got.

[*He goes up to her and leans his face forward. She leans hers forward too and gradually their lips meet. Then he takes her in his arms and a long kiss is exchanged. She breaks away with a sigh.*

FLORRIE: Oh! I feel all the better for that.

ERNIE: I don't think it's done me any harm either.

FLORRIE: Did you win your match?

ERNIE: What do you think? With me umpiring. As a matter of fact I had a few words with their umpire. But I wasn't going to let my boys be licked by any Cricklewood chaps. You can't blame me.

FLORRIE: I don't. You'd do anything for your boys, wouldn't you?

ERNIE: Well, I like them, I don't deny that, and they like me. They're getting up a subscription, a penny each, to give me a wedding present.

FLORRIE: That is nice of them.

ERNIE: It's voluntary, of course, but I shouldn't like to be in any boy's shoes who didn't subscribe. It's a grand thing, teaching. Getting a hold on all those young minds and training them. I mean, it must mean something to a man when he sees the way they look up to him.

FLORRIE: I should be very much surprised if they didn't look up to you.

ERNIE: That's as it may be, but it does give one a sort of sense of responsibility. After all, they're the citizens of the future. And what sort of citizens they'll be depends on me. You might almost say that what I think to-day Camberwell'll think to-morrow.

FLORRIE: It is a responsibility, I see that.

ERNIE: Kiss me.

[*They kiss again.*

FLORRIE: Oh, Ernie, I do love you so.

ERNIE: I'm not going to blame you for that.

FLORRIE: I wish you loved me as much as I love you.

ERNIE: I love you more than anyone in the world. I can't say more than that. But you mustn't forget that man's love is of man's life a thing apart; 'tis woman's whole existence.

FLORRIE: You're so ambitious.

ERNIE: Well, don't you want me to be?

FLORRIE: Yes. I won't stand in your way, Ernie. I know you want to get on.

ERNIE: There's no reason why I shouldn't, that I can see. I mean, think of the advantages I've got. And this money you'll have now. That'll make a difference. I don't see why I shouldn't stand for Parliament.

FLORRIE: Oh, Ernie, that would be lovely.

ERNIE: It's a chance in a lifetime. The old men are finished. Youth is the only thing that counts now. The world's in a mess and who's going to put it right? Youth. It's people like you and me who've got to get busy if we don't want to see civilisation crumbling under our feet. What the people want is a leader.

FLORRIE: You couldn't expect to be a leader right away, Ernie.

ERNIE: Perhaps not, but just as a matter of historical information I don't mind telling you that Pitt was Prime Minister at twenty-four. You wouldn't mind living in Downing Street, would you? Convenient, you know.

FLORRIE: Ernie.

ERNIE: Well, why not? Look at Snowden and Ramsay MacDonald. If they could do it, why can't I? With my brains and your beauty we can do anything.

FLORRIE: With the light behind you're not bad-looking yourself, Ernie.

ERNIE: Looks don't matter for a man. What a man wants is personality. That's one of the reasons I'd like to go to Paris for our honeymoon. One's got to develop one's personality.

FLORRIE: I was telling mum just now. She doesn't like the idea much. I think Dad's going to give us a hundred pounds, and I don't see why we shouldn't do what we like with it.

ERNIE: We could go to Switzerland on that.

FLORRIE: Oh, Ernie, I'd simply love to climb Mont Blanc.

ERNIE: I wouldn't mind myself. And Switzerland does seem the right place for a schoolmaster to go to in August. We'd meet lots of my colleagues.

FLORRIE: And then there's lovely Lucerne.

ERNIE: There's only one thing; it seems a bit thick doing all that on your money.

FLORRIE: That's silly. It won't be my money, it'll be our money.

ERNIE: Of course it's really an investment. It's not as if we were going just for pleasure. We're going to enlarge our minds. What can they know of England that only England know?

FLORRIE: That's right.

ERNIE: We've got to train ourselves so that when the opportunity comes we shall be ready to take it. We don't want to live for ourselves. We want to live for others. A life of service, that's what I look forward to.

FLORRIE: Well, I'll do all I can, Ernie.

ERNIE: I know you will. But look here, I think we ought to begin as we mean to go on. It's struck me, when we're in a big position, it'll sound silly you calling me Ernie and me calling you Florrie. I think we ought to stop it before it gets so much of a habit we can't break it.

FLORRIE: Whatever do you mean, Ernie?

ERNIE: Well, I think I ought to call you Florence and you ought to call me Ernest.

FLORRIE: It would make me laugh.

ERNIE: Well, try. To oblige me. You couldn't call a Prime Minister Ernie. People wouldn't have any respect for him.

FLORRIE: All right. I don't mind trying. But not till after the honeymoon. As long as we're on our honeymoon I want you to be just Ernie.

ERNIE: Have it your own way.

FLORRIE: Oh, isn't life lovely?

ERNIE: Of course it's lovely. I'm an optimist, I am. I mean, what's the good of taking a gloomy view of things? I know the world isn't perfect. But you can't have everything all at once. I believe in life and I believe in my fellow-men. You must believe.

FLORRIE: Kiss me.

[*Just as he is about to kiss her* BRADLEY *comes in.*

BRADLEY: Your ma wants you a minute, Miss Florrie.

FLORRIE: Oh, does she? All right.

[*She goes out.*

BRADLEY: Well, aren't you going to say thank you?

ERNIE: What for?

BRADLEY: Leaving you alone with your young lady. I saw you couldn't get rid of me fast enough. I've been a young fellow myself, you know.

ERNIE: I see you've got tact.

BRADLEY: You want it in my business. A hairdresser that hasn't got tact is no more use than a canary that can't sing. I just wanted to have a word or two with you.

ERNIE: Fire away.

BRADLEY: I flatter myself I'm not a bad judge of character, and the moment I saw you I said to myself, that young fellow's got his head screwed on his shoulders all right.

ERNIE: I know how many beans make five, if that's what you mean.

BRADLEY: You'll never guess why I've come here to-day. Now Sheppey's got all this money it's all wrong that he should only be an assistant. [*Impressively.*] I've come here to-day to offer him a partnership in my business.

ERNIE: You haven't?

BRADLEY: I have. And mind you, it's a fine business. The accounts are in apple-pie order, and anyone can see them who wants to. I'll give him ten per cent on his money and a share of the profits.

ERNIE: That sounds pretty good to me.

BRADLEY: I expect he'll jump at it, but he's a funny fellow, Sheppey; he may not like the idea of the responsibility. I want you to back me up.

ERNIE: I certainly will. I don't think anyone can call me a snob, but there is a difference between having a father-in-law who's a hairdresser and a father-in-law who runs a high-class saloon in Jermyn Street.

BRADLEY: All the difference in the world. Then that's settled. But there's something else I wanted to say to you.

ERNIE: Yes?

BRADLEY: Sheppey was up in the West End last night. He left a letter at my place. There's a pub just opposite. The Bunch of Keys it's called. He always has his dinner there.

ERNIE: I know. A cut off the joint, veg. and half a pint of bitter. Every day of his life as regular as clockwork.

BRADLEY: And every night after shutting up he goes there and has another half-pint. A creature of habit, that's what he is. You can always depend on him. Well, I just happened to hear that he was in there last night.

ERNIE: Nothing strange in that.

BRADLEY: No. Only he's got to know a tart there. He brought her in to my place to have a drink the evening he heard about the Sweep. Well, to cut a long story short, he went off with her last night.

ERNIE: You don't mean to tell me that.

BRADLEY: Of course it's no business of mine. All I mean to say is, if he's coming into partnership with me, he can't go about with common tarts, can he? It would be a pity if just because he's got a bit of money he went off the rails.

ERNIE: You do surprise me. That's the last thing I should ever have thought he'd do.

BRADLEY: You know what these women are.

ERNIE: He's so steady.

BRADLEY: I know he is. Mind you, I'm not accusing him. I only say it looks fishy.

ERNIE: What do you expect me to do about it?

BRADLEY: I thought if you gave your young lady a hint— girls know a lot nowadays—she'll understand, and if she gave her ma a hint to keep an eye on him . . . A good woman's influence can do a lot, and my experience is, if a fellow's wife once gets suspicious he has to be pretty smart to put anything over on her.

> [SHEPPEY *comes in. His cheeks are flushed and his eyes are shining, but otherwise he looks just as he did when we last saw him. Of course he does not wear the official wig of his business hours.*

SHEPPEY: Good evening, gentlemen.

BRADLEY: There you are.

SHEPPEY: Mrs. Miller told me you was 'ere, sir. Sorry I've kept you waiting.

BRADLEY: That's all right. I'm glad to see you looking so fit.

SHEPPEY: I'm fine. The doctor says I've made a wonderful recovery.

ERNIE: You'd better not let him find out you've been out and about when he said you were to stay in and keep quiet.

BRADLEY: Now, young fellow, if you wouldn't mind. I'd just like to have a talk with Sheppey.

ERNIE: I'll hop it. See you later.

[*He goes out.*

BRADLEY: I wasn't a bit surprised to get your letter, Sheppey.

SHEPPEY: Won't you sit down, sir?

BRADLEY: No, I'll stand if you don't mind. You sit down.

SHEPPEY: I think I will. I'm a bit tired. I been doing a lot to-day.

BRADLEY: Naturally it was a bit of a shock to me when you said you were leaving. After fifteen years. But in a manner of speaking I was expecting it. I said to myself at once, now Sheppey's got all this money he won't want to go on being an assistant. I mean, it's not in human nature.

SHEPPEY: I've always been very 'appy with you, sir. You've been a good master. And I know I've tried to give satisfaction.

BRADLEY: You're the best assistant I've ever had, Sheppey, and I don't mind who knows it. No one's got the way you have with a customer. And they like you. You've got a sense of humour.

SHEPPEY: I suppose I 'ave. Sometimes the things I say almost make me laugh myself.

BRADLEY: I suppose it's no good offering you more wages?

SHEPPEY: No, sir, it isn't. When I wrote that letter resigning my position it wasn't because I wanted a rise. I've always been satisfied with what I got.

BRADLEY: It's no good beating about the bush. Fair and square's my motto. I'm prepared to put my cards on the table. I don't want to lose you, Sheppey.

SHEPPEY: They say the best of friends must part.

BRADLEY: I know what you want, Sheppey, and I'm prepared to give it to you.

SHEPPEY: What do you mean by that, sir?

BRADLEY: Oh, go on. I wasn't born yesterday. And look here, you needn't go on calling me sir. From now on I'm Jim to you. The moment I read your letter I saw what the game was. Well, all right. I'm on.

SHEPPEY: I give you my word I don't know what you're talking about.

BRADLEY: Oh, yes, you do. And I'm quite agreeable. I'll take you in. Of course we shall have to discuss terms. We must keep the old name. The public's used to it and it's worth something.

SHEPPEY: You're not offering me a partnership in Bradley's?

BRADLEY: Yes, I am.

[SHEPPEY *gives him a little startled look, hesitates for a moment, and then speaks in a low, harsh voice.*

SHEPPEY: Get thee behind me, Satan.

BRADLEY: [*Startled.*] Sheppey! What d'you mean?

SHEPPEY: You know there's nothing I wanted more than to be a partner at Bradley's. It's been the ambition of my life. I never shut up the shop, not a night, without saying to meself, I'd give a lot to be Jim Bradley's partner.

BRADLEY: Well, now you can be.

T*

SHEPPEY: No, I can't. It's come too late. I've got other fish to fry.

BRADLEY: You haven't fixed up with another firm? Sheppey, you wouldn't play me a dirty trick like that, without saying a word to me about it? Not after fifteen years. Look here, Sheppey, I tell you what I'll do. I'll put your name up beside mine. Bradley and Miller it'll be. What do you say to that? It'll be a wonderful moment for you when you see it over the window.

SHEPPEY: It's not that, Mr. Bradley. I'm giving up the 'airdressing.

BRADLEY: You're not going to lead an evil life, Sheppey?

SHEPPEY: [*Smiling.*] I 'ope not. It would be rather late in the day for that.

BRADLEY: They say there's no fool like an old fool. You've got money now, I know. But it won't last for ever. Wine, women and song, and you'll run through it in no time.

SHEPPEY: I'm going to invest it.

BRADLEY: You'll never find a better investment than what I offer you.

SHEPPEY: That's a matter of opinion.

BRADLEY: A man that's got a real gift for hairdressing. I mean, it's such a waste. What do you expect to get for your money?

SHEPPEY: [*Casually.*] Treasure in 'eaven.

BRADLEY: Now, my boy, don't you go into any wild-cat schemes. You talk to your wife about it. She's a sensible woman. I know this offer of mine comes sudden. I'm not going to take no for an answer now. You think it over.

SHEPPEY: Thanks. But I've quite made up my mind.

BRADLEY: My experience is that no married man's ever made up his mind till he's heard what his wife has got to say about it. I'll tell you what I'll do. I'll be off now. You'll be working next week, I suppose?

SHEPPEY: Yes. I must work out my notice.

BRADLEY: I'll give you the week to think it over. Say good-bye to Mrs. Miller for me, won't you?

SHEPPEY: I will. I'll just see you to the door.

BRADLEY: I'll find my way out all right. Don't trouble.

SHEPPEY: O.K. Good evening, sir. Thank you for coming.

> [BRADLEY *goes out.* SHEPPEY *goes over to the window and looks out into the street.* MRS. MILLER, FLORRIE *and* ERNIE *come in.*

ERNIE: We heard him go.

SHEPPEY: Nice-looking car, that is. My word, the governor's proud of it.

FLORRIE: You'll be having one just as good yourself now, dad.

MRS. MILLER: Ernie's told us, dad.

SHEPPEY: Told you what?

FLORRIE: Oh, dad, don't try and make a secret of it.

MRS. MILLER: I'm so glad for your sake, dear. I know there's nothing you wanted so much. I almost feel like crying.

SHEPPEY: Now what are you all talking about?

ERNIE: It's like this, Sheppey, Bradley gave me a hint. In fact he told me in so many words that he was going to offer you a partnership.

SHEPPEY: Oh, that?

FLORRIE: Don't take it so calm, dad. Aren't you excited?

MRS. MILLER: It'll be a grand day for me when I walk up Jermyn Street and see your name in great big letters alongside of Mr. Bradley's.

FLORRIE: Whoops, dearie.

MRS. MILLER: And of course there's the position too. I must 'ave a girl to do the rough work now.

FLORRIE: You don't want a girl. You must have a general and a char in twice a week to do the scrubbing.

MRS. MILLER: [*With a happy little grin.*] I shall be quite the lady before I'm finished.

ERNIE: And why not?

SHEPPEY: [*Quietly.*] I'll tell you why not. Because I've declined the governor's invitation with thanks.

FLORRIE: Dad.

MRS. MILLER: Whatever for? Your 'eart's been set on being your own master.

SHEPPEY: I know it 'as.

ERNIE: You haven't turned it down flat?

SHEPPEY: I 'ave.

ERNIE: Naturally he wasn't going to make his final offer straight away. He said to me terms would have to be discussed.

MRS. MILLER: It's not the responsibility you're afraid of, Sheppey?

SHEPPEY: No.

ERNIE: But it's a chance in a thousand.

FLORRIE: You don't want to be ordered about when you can order other people about, surely.

SHEPPEY: I gave in my notice last night. Of course I shall 'ave to work out the week. Then I'm through.

MRS. MILLER: D'you mean you're giving up work altogether? You'd never be 'appy without something to do, dad.

ERNIE: You can't get more than three and a half per cent on your money now, you know. What with income tax and one thing and another you won't find you'll have so much. I mean, it'll be a tight squeeze to make both ends meet.

FLORRIE: Especially with me and Ernie getting married so soon. We counted on your being able to help us a bit at first.

SHEPPEY: I'm not going to invest my money at three and a half per cent. I'm not going to invest it to bring that sort of return at all.

ERNIE: What's the idea?

SHEPPEY: Well, you know, I been worried lately. You know that day I had to go to the police court. The prisoners, you know, they was just the same as you and me, I mean, if you'd passed them in the street you'd 'ave thought them exactly like anybody else, and d'you know what put them in the dock, three out of four? Just that they 'adn't enough to eat. It give me quite a turn.

ERNIE: The Government's to blame.

MRS. MILLER: Quiet, Ernie.

SHEPPEY: And that same evening I met a woman I know up west, and I discovered accidentally that she 'adn't 'ad a bite of food in twenty-four hours.

ERNIE: Times are bad, of course.

SHEPPEY: Now, this money I've got. I could do with it, of course, but I don't really need it, not in comparison, I mean, with the people 'as 'aven't got enough to eat and no coal to put in their grates.

ERNIE: Perhaps not. But you've got it and they haven't. That's the luck of the game. You were born lucky. I've heard you say that dozens of times.

SHEPPEY: I know it. And perhaps the luckiest thing that's ever 'appened to me is 'aving the chance I've got now.

MRS. MILLER: What d'you mean exactly, dad?

SHEPPEY: Well, I don't feel justified some'ow in keeping this money.

FLORRIE: Then give it to Ernie and me. We'll be glad to take it.

SHEPPEY: [*With a smile.*] You don't want it either.

ERNIE: What are you going to do with it then?

SHEPPEY: Ever read the Gospel, Ernie?

ERNIE: Of course I have. It's got some damned good lines in it. And the style's fine. Of course you wouldn't want to write like that now.

SHEPPEY: I been reading it a lot this last week. Not being able to go to the shop, you know. But I'm not an educated man like you, Ernie. I read it for the story.

ERNIE: It's a good story. I don't think anyone would deny that.

SHEPPEY: I came across one bit that knocked me all of a heap. It seemed as if it 'ad been written for me.

ERNIE: What was that?

SHEPPEY: Sell all that thou 'ast, and distribute it to the poor, and thou shalt 'ave treasure in 'eaven: and come and follow me.

ERNIE: I know. And it goes on: it's easier for a camel to go through the eye of a needle than for a rich man to enter the Kingdom of Heaven. The rich have been trying to get round that for the last two thousand years.

SHEPPEY: It was like a great white light. I saw my way plain before me. I'm going to give this money of mine away to them as needs it more than I do.

[*They are thunderstruck. They speak on each other's words.*

MRS. MILLER: Sheppey, what do you mean?

ERNIE: You're crazy. You can't do a thing like that.

FLORRIE: I should think mum would have something to say to that.

MRS. MILLER: You don't mean it, dad?

SHEPPEY: Yes, I do.

ERNIE: It's ridiculous.

FLORRIE: Criminal, I call it.

ERNIE: After all, what's eight thousand pounds? A drop in the ocean. You might as well throw the money down a drain-pipe for all the good it will do.

MRS. MILLER: But, Sheppey, you can't afford to do a thing like that. It would be all very well for some of them rich people in the West End.

SHEPPEY: They can't do anything. They 'aven't got more money than they know what to do with.

ERNIE: Never heard that before.

SHEPPEY: That's why I'm telling you. Now I do know what I'm talking about. We've always 'ad a tip-top trade at Bradley's. Some of the most important men in the country. Why, only the other day I 'ad a gentleman in as said if things didn't look up soon 'e'd 'ave to give up either his yacht or 'is racing stable.

ERNIE: He isn't obliged to have a racing stable, is he?

SHEPPEY: It's not for 'imself 'e 'as it. 'E's told me over and over again. It's for the good of the country.

ERNIE: And do you believe that?

SHEPPEY: 'E's a gentleman. There's no reason for 'im to tell me a lie, is there? And you wouldn't believe 'ow much it costs to run a pack of 'ounds. I was shaving Lord Mereston one day last week and 'e said to me, Sheppey, 'e said, you wouldn't believe 'ow expensive life is, my daughter's coming out and I've got to give a ball, seven 'undred people and champagne at eighteen bob a bottle. My boy's nursing a constituency and it's costing me fifteen 'undred a year, and to put the lid on, Sheppey, 'e says, I've 'ad to fork out a couple of thousand quid for a diamond bracelet to give my wife for our silver wedding. I tell you what, Sheppey, 'e says, if things don't take a turn for the better soon I'll 'ave to give up being shaved and damned well shave meself. The rich ain't got more money than they can spend on themselves.

I know that for a fact. And besides, they don't know
about the poor.

ERNIE: They can find out, can't they? They can read the
papers.

SHEPPEY: Well, by the time they've read the court and
society news, the divorces and the sporting intelligence,
they've read enough. They don't want to be depressed
by reading about unpleasant things. You can't 'ardly
blame them. It's the poor as must 'elp the poor.

ERNIE: And they do, don't they? Everyone knows that the
poor are splendid to one another. Everyone who writes
about them says that. But when all's said and done
charity begins at home.

FLORRIE: That's right. I mean, one must think of those who
are near and dear to one first.

ERNIE: Mind you, I don't deny that things are pretty rotten
in the state of Denmark. But it's no job for an individual. It's a problem and a very grave one, but it's a
problem for the community. And the community's
tackling it. I don't say charity doesn't want organising.
It does. But there's one thing I'm quite sure about, that
the indiscriminate charity of private individuals does
more harm than good. That's been proved over and
over again. I mean, there's not a charity organisation in
England that won't tell you that to give a penny to a
beggar in the street is a crime.

SHEPPEY: You may be right. But when you see an old
fellow with one leg selling matches in the bitter cold it
seems almost against 'uman nature not to give 'im a
copper.

ERNIE: Well, one ought not to. One's only encouraging
them. One's got to take a broad view of things. The
law of life is simple as A B C. Get on or get under. If a
man can't earn his own living he's no good, to the state
or anybody else, and he must be eliminated. That's

natural selection. If you molly-coddle the unfit you only make it harder for the rest of us.

SHEPPEY: I'm not an educated man, but I 'ave got two eyes in my 'ead. And I can't see much difference between the fit and the unfit. It seems to me that good and bad are pretty much alike. I think it's just a toss up which you are. You remember that story about the seed that was thrown on stony ground and the seed that was thrown on good rich ground.

ERNIE: You've got that all wrong, Sheppey. That seed never did any good because it couldn't adapt itself to its surroundings. That's the struggle for life and the survival of the fittest. It just proves what I say.

SHEPPEY: I read it different. I thought perhaps if it'd been watered a bit and given a bit of shade it might 'ave been all right. You see, these organisations are all very well, but there's a lot of red-tape about them, you know that, and they don't realise a lot of people are proud and don't like asking, and some of them ain't got the nerve to, and there's a lot as are downright stupid, you can't deny that.

ERNIE: Well, what can you do about it?

SHEPPEY: I'll tell you. I'll just keep my eyes open and talk to people, and I'll give 'alf a crown 'ere and five bob there, just as man to man, you know, and a sack of coals to someone as 'asn't got any, and if I see a kid wants a pair of boots I'll buy him a pair.

ERNIE: Of course you know you'll have every rotter and sponger after you. And those half crowns and five bobs, where do you think they'll go? On drink.

SHEPPEY: I dare say I shall make mistakes sometimes. I don't think that matters. Besides, if a chap's down and out and thinks he'd rather spend 'alf a crown on beer than on food and lodging, that's 'is look out.

ERNIE: And what do you expect to get out of it for yourself?

SHEPPEY: Oh, I don't know. Peace of mind. The Kingdom of Heaven, perhaps.

ERNIE: And what'll be the result? In a year or two your money'll be gone. D'you think anything'll be different?

SHEPPEY: You never can tell. Perhaps someone'll come and take my place. If I can only get people to see what I mean. I might be an example to others. Someone's got to start a thing like this.

ERNIE: D'you think a hairdresser's the right man to start it?

SHEPPEY: I don't know why not. Jesus was only a carpenter, wasn't he?

FLORRIE: I think it's awful comparing yourself to Jesus, dad. I wonder you're not afraid a thunderbolt'll come down from Heaven and smite you.

ERNIE: [*Sulkily.*] Well, it's not my money, and it's no business of mine what you do with it, but if you'll take my advice you'll look before you leap.

SHEPPEY: [*With a twinkle in his eye.*] I'm always glad to take advice from those younger than myself.

FLORRIE: What about me and Ernie getting married? We were going to wait, but when you won that Sweep, we settled to marry now. I've given notice at the office and everything.

SHEPPEY: There's no reason I can see why you shouldn't get married. You'll 'ave as much as mum and me 'ad when we married.

FLORRIE: Things are different now. And besides, Ernie's got to keep up a position that you didn't have to. We were counting on your paying the rent of our flat.

SHEPPEY: You can live here.

FLORRIE: Can I? Well, I'm marrying to have a home of my own. Say something, mum, do. You can't let him play ducks and drakes with our money like that.

MRS. MILLER: I don't know if I'm standing on me 'ead or me 'eels.

ERNIE: [*Crossly.*] Well, it's not the first time a man has loved the human race so much he's left his own family to starve.

FLORRIE: Don't blame me, Ernie.

SHEPPEY: I knew it would be a sort of disappointment to you.

ERNIE: The mistake you make, Sheppey, is taking things too literally. The New Testament must be looked upon as fiction, a beautiful fiction if you like, but a fiction. No educated man accepts the Gospel narrative as sober fact. In fact a great many people believe that Jesus never existed at all.

SHEPPEY: I don't know that that matters so much.

ERNIE: Just now, when I asked you what you expected to get out of it, you said the Kingdom of Heaven.

SHEPPEY: I know I did. But sometimes I think the Kingdom of 'Eaven's in me own 'eart.

FLORRIE: You're barmy.

SHEPPEY: [*Smiling.*] Because I want to live like Jesus?

FLORRIE: Well, who ever heard of anyone wanting to live like Jesus at this time of day? I think it's just blasphemous.

ERNIE: And there's another thing you must remember. Everyone knows the Gospels were written by ignorant men. I mean they were just ordinary working chaps. And the parables and all that were addressed to the same sort of crowd you might see at Woolworth's of a Saturday night.

SHEPPEY: Well, perhaps that's why it all come 'ome to me so much, because I'm an ignorant working man meself.

ERNIE: Yes, but don't you see, they've got to be explained. Why do **you** suppose they have professors of theology and doctors of divinity? They're there to explain to people that whatever Jesus said he didn't really mean it, but something quite different.

SHEPPEY: You may be right, of course. But I don't see why 'e shouldn't 'ave.

ERNIE: It stands to reason. Those precepts, the sermon on the Mount and all that, may have been very well for a small peasant community, but they're just not applicable to our great world states. They're impracticable.

SHEPPEY: I don't know so much about that. Personally I don't know anyone as 'as tried to put them in practice.

FLORRIE: Well, that's a proof they're impracticable, dad. I mean, if they were, clergymen and ministers and that like, would do them.

SHEPPEY: Perhaps they don't believe in them.

FLORRIE: I don't know why they shouldn't. I believe in them. But there's all the difference in believing a thing just as a thing you believe . . .

ERNIE: Theoretically, she means.

FLORRIE: Yes, and believing it so that you act on it. I mean, when you believe a horse can't lose, you don't believe it in the same way as you believe that if you go out in the rain you'll get wet.

ERNIE: [*To* SHEPPEY.] I see what you mean, of course. It's an ideal. But you've always got to remember this, an ideal's something you aim at; as soon as you reach it, it stops being an ideal.

SHEPPEY: It don't seem like an ideal to me. It seems to me like plain commonsense.

ERNIE: Well, I think it's the damnedest nonsense I ever heard.

SHEPPEY: I'm not quite sure that what you think is gospel truth either.

FLORRIE: Ernie's an educated man, dad, and you're not.

[A knock at the door is heard.

MRS. MILLER: See who that is, Florrie. Who ever can be coming here at this hour?

*[*FLORRIE *goes to the window.*

FLORRIE: Oh, mum, it's a lady. She's got a silk dress on. Her shoes don't look none too good.

SHEPPEY: I know who it is. It's someone I was expecting. I'll go.

[He goes out.

FLORRIE: Did you know anything about this, mum?

MRS. MILLER: Not a word. It's come as a complete surprise to me.

ERNIE: [*To* FLORRIE.] You got it in one, Florrie. You hit the nail on the head.

FLORRIE: How do you mean?

ERNIE: He's barmy.

MRS. MILLER: Oh, Ernie, that's a horrible thing to say.

ERNIE: I don't say it's permanent. But he's barmy. I mean, that's obvious. Look here, what do you say to me running for the doctor?

FLORRIE: That's a good idea, Ernie.

MRS. MILLER: I don't know what to say. I mean it's so unlike him.

FLORRIE: Go on, Ernie. Here's my key.

ERNIE: [*Taking it.*] I shan't be two ticks.

[He goes out.

MRS. MILLER: And him that's always been so sensible. He's never been near, that's not in 'is nature, but 'e's never been one to throw money about neither.

FLORRIE: Ernie's upset.

MRS. MILLER: I don't know what he's got to be upset for.

FLORRIE: Oh, don't you? Mum, this has got to be stopped. I won't lose Ernie. I won't.

MRS. MILLER: Oh, don't be so silly, Florrie. Why should you lose Ernie?

FLORRIE: You don't know men like I do.

MRS. MILLER: I like that. I suppose I didn't know men before you were born.

FLORRIE: When a woman's been married a year or two she forgets. I can see Ernie's upset.

[SHEPPEY *comes in with* BESSIE LEGROS.

SHEPPEY: Come in, my dear. Mum, I've brought a friend to see you. This is my wife and that's my daughter Florrie.

MRS. MILLER: Oh, Sheppey, and me not dressed or anything. [*To* BESSIE.] Good evening. Won't you sit down?

BESSIE: Pleased to meet you. [*To* FLORRIE *with a smile.*] Good evening.

FLORRIE: Good evening. [*She looks her up and down and with her cockney sharpness sums her up and purses her lips.*]

SHEPPEY: She's going to stay and 'ave a bit of supper with us.

MRS. MILLER: Oh, dad, you might 'ave warned me.

SHEPPEY: You don't mind pot-luck, do you?

BESSIE: Me? A pleasure, I'm sure.

SHEPPEY: There's always plenty and my wife's a wonderful good cook. You'd be surprised 'ow tasty she makes things.

FLORRIE: [*To* BESSIE.] You known dad long?

BESSIE: Well, in a manner of speaking I have and in a manner of speaking I haven't.

SHEPPEY: I knew 'er by sight first. She was always at the Bunch of Keys when I went in to 'ave my beer after I'd shut up. And so we got talking, see? And then last week when I fainted she brought me round. She came in the taxi with me as far as the door.

BESSIE: I thought he wasn't fit to take a taxi by himself.

MRS. MILLER: That was very kind of you, I'm sure. I'll give you a nice supper. I'm very glad Sheppey asked you to drop in.

FLORRIE: [*Suspiciously.*] But I thought you fainted *after* the shop shut.

SHEPPEY: So I did. We'd just been 'aving a bottle of fizz to celebrate the occasion and the others 'ad gone.

FLORRIE: [*Acidly.*] Oh, I see.

SHEPPEY: Now look 'ere, Florrie, I want you and 'er to be friends. I want you to be a sister to 'er. And I want mum to be a mother to 'er.

FLORRIE: The acquaintance is a bit short for that, isn't it?

SHEPPEY: She's in trouble, mum, and I want you to 'elp 'er. That evening when I fainted she 'adn't 'ad a bit of food all day and I don't believe she's 'ad much to-day either. She ain't got a place to sleep to-night, so I said we'd give 'er a shake-down here.

MRS. MILLER: Sheppey, we 'aven't got room.

SHEPPEY: Yes, we 'ave. There's the attic and we can rig up that old bed you said you was going to sell.

MRS. MILLER: I wouldn't like to ask anybody to sleep in that.

BESSIE: Didn't I tell you? I knew they wouldn't like it. It's all right. I'll manage somehow.

SHEPPEY: [*To his wife.*] To oblige me, my dear. If you say no, it means the Embankment or the streets.

FLORRIE: Well, she'd be at home there, wouldn't she?

SHEPPEY: You speak when you're spoken to, Florrie. [*To his wife.*] She's a nice woman and a good woman. You can't deceive me. It's not often I ask you to do me a favour.

MRS. MILLER: [*Giving in.*] I'll be glad to 'ave you to stay the night, Miss.

BESSIE: That is kind of you. It's a relief to me. I tell you that straight. I didn't know which way to turn.

[ERNIE *comes in. He gives* FLORRIE *a little nod to indicate that he has executed his commission.*

SHEPPEY: 'Ullo, Ernie, where 'ave you been?

ERNIE: I just went out to get a packet of fags.

SHEPPEY: There are some in the snuff-box.

ERNIE: I thought they were only for show. [*Seeing* BESSIE.] Got a visitor?

SHEPPEY: This is Ernie, our Florrie's intended. And this is Bessie.

ERNIE: Bessie what?

BESSIE: Legros.

SHEPPEY: She ain't really French.

BESSIE: No, it's the name I go by for business purposes.

FLORRIE: Dad met her at the Bunch of Keys.

ERNIE: [*Remembering what* BRADLEY *had said to him.*] Oh, did he? I see.

MRS. MILLER: Well, I'll just go and 'ave a look and see 'ow my supper's getting on.

[*She goes out.*

FLORRIE: I'll be getting the table laid.

BESSIE: If I can lend a hand I'll be glad to, I'm sure.

FLORRIE: [*With a little sniff.*] I can manage.

SHEPPEY: [*To* BESSIE.] I'd like to show you my snuff-box. [*He goes over to the chimney-piece and takes it up.*] One of my customers left it me in 'is will. A very nice gentleman 'e was. I shaved 'im when 'e was dead.

BESSIE: It's lovely.

SHEPPEY: 'E told me it was given to 'is grandfather by King George the Fourth.

BESSIE: It must be worth a packet.

SHEPPEY: It's not that so much. It's the sentiment. I mean, 'aving it left me, see? I wouldn't sell it for a thousand pounds.

FLORRIE: [*Getting out the tablecloth.*] I suppose you haven't asked anyone else to drop in, dad?

SHEPPEY: Well, now you come to mention it, I 'ave.

FLORRIE: Oh, you haven't, dad?

SHEPPEY: Yes, you know that chap what I caught sneaking the doctor's overcoat. I told 'im to come round.

FLORRIE: Dad!

ERNIE: Isn't he in gaol?

SHEPPEY: No, the magistrate said 'e'd give 'im another chance this time, 'im 'aving been out of work so long, and not 'aving 'ad anything to eat for two days.

ERNIE: But the copper told you he'd been in jug two or three times before.

SHEPPEY: Yes, 'e's 'ad bad luck. That's right. 'E's never 'ad a chance really.

FLORRIE: Oh, and are you going to give him one?

SHEPPEY: That's the idea.

> [*The door is opened and the* DOCTOR *comes in. He is a middle-aged, red-faced man, and very hearty.*

DOCTOR: May I come in?

SHEPPEY: Why, doctor, where 'ave you sprung from?

DOCTOR: I was just passing and I thought I'd look in and see how you were getting along.

SHEPPEY: I've never been better in my life. I'm going back to work next Monday.

DOCTOR: You mustn't try and do too much. When are they going to pay you your Sweep money?

SHEPPEY: In a week or two, I believe.

DOCTOR: Why don't you go down to the Isle of Sheppey for

a bit, and have another look at that cottage you've had your eye on?

SHEPPEY: I'm not going to buy that now.

DOCTOR: Oh, why not? I thought your heart was set on it.

SHEPPEY: [*With a sigh.*] I know. I can't. Not now. I should never 'ave a moment's peace.

DOCTOR: You'll have to be looking out for a nice safe investment then. Don't put too many eggs in one basket, that's all.

SHEPPEY: I've just been talking about that to my family. I'd be very much obliged if you'd tell them I'm in full possession of my senses.

DOCTOR: Why? What's the trouble?

SHEPPEY: Well, you see, it's my money, isn't it? I don't see why I shouldn't do what I like with it.

DOCTOR: And what do you want to do with it?

SHEPPEY: Clothe the naked and visit the sick, give food to 'im that is a'ungered and drink to 'im that is athirst.

DOCTOR: Very praiseworthy of course, within reason. What put the idea into your head?

SHEPPEY: It came. A great white light.

DOCTOR: Oh, yes. I see. Of course it's a thing to think over. What we've got to do before we go any further is to get you fit and strong. At your age one can't take liberties with one's constitution. I don't mind telling you I don't like this high blood pressure of yours. Often has funny effects. D'you see things?

SHEPPEY: I see you.

DOCTOR: Yes, of course. I mean, do you see things other people don't see?

SHEPPEY: I see wickedness and vice beating the land with their wings.

[*The* DOCTOR *looks at him meditatively, wondering what he shall ask him next, when* MRS. MILLER *comes in.*

MRS. MILLER: Sheppey, there's a man at the door says you told him to come here.

SHEPPEY: That's right.

[COOPER *appears at the open door. He is a ragged-looking fellow in a cap, with a scarf round his neck.*

SHEPPEY: Come in, old man. Pleased to see you. Found your way all right?

COOPER: I 'ave good reason to remember.

SHEPPEY: You'll stay to supper, won't you?

COOPER: I don't mind if I do.

MRS. MILLER: Who is 'e, dad?

SHEPPEY: He's your brother.

MRS. MILLER: That! That's no brother of mine. I 'aven't got a brother and no one knows that better than what you do.

SHEPPEY: 'E's your brother and my brother.

MRS. MILLER: I never 'ad but one brother. 'Is name was Percy, and 'e died of meningitis when 'e was seven years of age. [*To* COOPER.] What's your name?

COOPER: Cooper, mum. Jim Cooper.

MRS. MILLER: I never even known a Cooper. [*To* SHEPPEY.] What are you going to do with him?

SHEPPEY: 'E's 'ungry and I'm going to give 'im food. 'E's 'omeless and I'm going to give 'im shelter.

MRS. MILLER: Shelter? Where?

SHEPPEY: 'Ere. In my 'ouse. In my bed.

MRS. MILLER: In my bed? And where am I to sleep, then?

SHEPPEY: You can sleep with Florrie.

FLORRIE: I can tell you who he is, mum. He's the chap dad caught sneaking the doctor's coat and he's been in and out of prison half a dozen times. He's a thief.

COOPER: 'Ere, who are you a'calling a thief?

FLORRIE: Well, you are, aren't you?

COOPER: I may be. But if you was a man I'd like to see you say it.

FLORRIE: [*To* BESSIE.] And as for you. You're a tart.

BESSIE: You can call me that if you like, but when I had my little flat in Kennington I described myself as an actress.

MRS. MILLER: Supper's ready. If you don't want it to spoil you'd better finish laying the cloth, Florrie.

[FLORRIE *sinks down on a chair and gives a sob.*

FLORRIE: What a humiliation! What a humiliation for people in our position!

MRS. MILLER: I thought this Sweep money was going to bring us all peace and 'appiness. It don't look much like that now.

SHEPPEY: Peace and 'appiness, that's what we're all looking for, but where are we going to find it?

END OF ACT TWO

ACT THREE

The Scene is the same as in the preceding Act.

Florrie *is at the window, looking out.* Bessie *comes in. She has an exercise book in her hand.*

Bessie: Your ma says, what's this doing in the kitchen? She very nearly throwed it away.

Florrie: I shouldn't have cared if she had. It's my exercise book. Fat chance I've got of going to France now.

Bessie: It's a long lane that has no turning.

Florrie: What's the time? [*She looks out of window again.*]

Bessie: Getting on for six. Expecting somebody?

Florrie: Yes and no.

Bessie: Dead-and-alive street this. You never see anything going on.

Florrie: It's a very good class of street, that's why.

Bessie: I don't say it isn't.

Florrie: How much longer are you going to stay here?

Bessie: It depends on your pa. I mean, as far as I'm concerned, I'm sure I don't want to stay where I'm not wanted. You don't like me, do you?

Florrie: Oh, I don't mind you. After the first shock, I mean you being an immoral woman and me being virtuous, I can't see you're any different from anybody else.

Bessie: I don't feel different.

Florrie: Of course at first I thought you were after dad.

Bessie: Me? I like your pa as a friend. But that's all.

FLORRIE: Ernie says he wouldn't be surprised if it hadn't been going on ever so long.

BESSIE: He doesn't know what he's talking about.

FLORRIE: Ernie's very respectable. And when you're very respectable you always believe the worst of people.

BESSIE: You're worried about Ernie, aren't you?

FLORRIE: Well, all this has been an upset to him.

BESSIE: I can quite understand that. Men don't like surprises. They always want things to go on in the same old way. They're not like women. Anything for a change. Men are awfully conventional, you know.

FLORRIE: You see, we were going to be married next month, and now I don't know when it'll be.

BESSIE: Oh, I say. I know what it is when you've made all your plans and then something happens.

FLORRIE: He wants to break it off.

BESSIE: He hasn't said so?

FLORRIE: No. But I know he's got it in his mind. Only he's got his self-respect to think of, he's got to find an excuse. Mum says if he wants to break it off it shows he doesn't really love me. But she doesn't know men like I do.

BESSIE: They want knowing. There's no mistake about that.

FLORRIE: I wish you'd give me some advice. You ought to know more about men than most people.

BESSIE: Well, I'll tell you. They're near, they'll spend money if they can make a splash, but if they think no one'll know, they're as mean as cat's meat. They're timid, you know, make a scene in public and they'll just go all to pieces. Some of them don't like to see a woman cry. But you have to be careful not to cry too much, you may drive them away, and my experience is, if a man once goes, he don't come back.

It'd be a tough job dealing with them if they didn't like flattery. You can't lay it on too thick, my dear, they can never have enough of it. Flattery's meat and drink to them. They'll listen to it for hours. You get sick and tired, but there they are, as fresh as a daisy, just eating it.

FLORRIE: It's easy for you. I'm so much in love with Ernie. I'd forgive him anything.

BESSIE: It's bad when it takes you like that. It makes you so helpless.

FLORRIE: When you're in love with a man like I am with Ernie he does aggravate you so.

BESSIE: I know. It does seem as if they've got no sense sometimes.

FLORRIE: Ernie's stuck on politics for some reason.

BESSIE: You have to put up with a man's ideas. My experience is they don't amount to anything, really, but you must never let on you think that.

> [*There is a knock at the door.*

FLORRIE: That's his knock. Oh, my heart. It's thumping so I can hardly bear it.

BESSIE: I'll go and open the door for him. You stay here.

FLORRIE: Thanks. My knees are wobbling so I'd have a job to get to the door.

BESSIE: Pull yourself together, dear. If you let a man see he means all that to you, he'll lead you a dog's life.

> [*She goes out. In a moment* ERNIE *comes in. He has an evening paper in his hand.*

FLORRIE: [*Bright and eager.*] Ernie! I never recognised your knock. This is a surprise.

ERNIE: [*On the surly side.*] I told you I was coming along about now.

FLORRIE: I didn't know it was so late. Time slips by so quickly when you're busy.

ERNIE: I see that woman's here still. What about the fellow?

FLORRIE: Cooper? Oh, he's here. I wonder we haven't all been murdered in our beds by now.

ERNIE: Where's your dad?

FLORRIE: Out somewhere. I don't know. [*She can't keep it up any longer.*] Haven't you forgotten something, Ernie?

ERNIE: Me?

FLORRIE: You haven't kissed me.

ERNIE: Sorry. [*He goes towards her.*]

FLORRIE: You need not if you don't want to.

ERNIE: Don't be so silly. [*He kisses her.*]

FLORRIE: [*Clinging to him.*] Oh, Ernie, I'm so miserable.

ERNIE: Of course you're worried. That's only natural. You can't expect anyone to like seeing their father make a damned fool of himself.

FLORRIE: I wish he'd never won that beastly money. We were all as happy as could be.

ERNIE: I should have thought your mum could have done something.

FLORRIE: That's what I tell her. She says he won't listen.

ERNIE: It seems almost a pity you should have given up your job.

FLORRIE: [*With a quick look at him.*] I suppose the best thing I can do is to look out for another.

ERNIE: It's no good not looking facts in the face. I don't see how we can marry just yet, Florrie.

FLORRIE: Of course it's for you to say.

ERNIE: Naturally it's a disappointment. But we were prepared to wait before and I suppose we can wait now.

FLORRIE: [*Clutching her hands in her wretchedness.*] If you want to break it off you've only got to say so.

ERNIE: Me? Whatever put an idea like that in your head?

FLORRIE: Only that I saw it was in yours.

ERNIE: I wouldn't let you down, Florrie. Not for anything in the world.

FLORRIE: It's not much good being engaged if nothing's ever going to come of it.

ERNIE: Who says nothing's ever going to come of it?

FLORRIE: You don't love me like you did a month ago.

ERNIE: That's a lie.

FLORRIE: Listen, Ernie, I love you so much, I've got to know one way or the other. This uncertainty's killing me.

ERNIE: My dear, you must be reasonable. We decided we wouldn't be married till I was in a position to provide for you. I didn't want you to have to work. You'd have enough to do looking after the home. And you ought to have a kid or two.

FLORRIE: Oh, don't, Ernie. It makes me feel awful, hearing you talk like that.

ERNIE: You must look at my side of it too.

FLORRIE: What d'you mean?

ERNIE: Well, I'm ambitious. I know I've got ability. I've got a good brain.

FLORRIE: No one's ever denied that, Ernie.

ERNIE: If I've got exceptional powers I ought to use them. I don't want to stick in the common rut. They say you can't keep a good man down, but it's no use hanging a millstone round your neck.

FLORRIE: Meaning me?

ERNIE: Of course not. I wasn't thinking of you. I love you no end, Florrie. I've never seen a girl I could think of marrying except you and my firm conviction is that I never shall.

FLORRIE: You're not just saying that to please me?

ERNIE: No, I swear I'm not. And you mustn't think that what I'm going to say now doesn't mean I don't love you as much as ever I did. If things come right and we could be married to-morrow there wouldn't be a happier chap in London.

FLORRIE: Well, what is it you're going to say?

ERNIE: It's just this: what your father does is his business, and he can do what he likes with his own money. But I'm not going to be made to look a fool by any man.

FLORRIE: What's going to make you look a fool?

ERNIE: If I have a father-in-law who lives like Jesus of course I shall look a fool. How do you expect me to keep my authority over the boys I teach when they know my father-in-law's a funny old buffer mixing with the lowest of the low, and giving his money away? They'd rot the life out of me.

FLORRIE: It's not very nice for mum or me.

ERNIE: I think it's awful for your poor mother. Of course it won't really be so bad for you, having your work in the City, and naturally, people there won't know anything about it.

FLORRIE: All the same, I don't see how I can help feeling the disgrace of it.

ERNIE: There you are, you see. Now, put yourself in my place.

FLORRIE: What do you propose?

ERNIE: Well, I'd rather leave it to you.

FLORRIE: I see.

[MRS. MILLER *comes in.*

FLORRIE: Here's mum.

ERNIE: Oh, good evening.

MRS. MILLER: Why, Ernie, you're quite a stranger.

ERNIE: I've had a lot of school work to do yesterday and the day before.

MRS. MILLER: The place 'as been all upside-down with Bessie and that there Cooper being 'ere.

ERNIE: A shame, I call it.

MRS. MILLER: The extra work keeps me from thinking and that's something.

FLORRIE: It isn't our house any more. It's a home for waifs and strays.

ERNIE: Where's Sheppey, now?

MRS. MILLER: 'E 'ad an appointment to see the doctor at four. I'm surprised 'e's not back. It's gone six.

FLORRIE: You never told me he was going to the doctor's, mum.

MRS. MILLER: I thought I'd better not say anything about it. It's not very pleasant.

ERNIE: Why, what's up?

MRS. MILLER: I'd rather not speak about it.

FLORRIE: Oh, go on, mum. We shall have to know sooner or later.

MRS. MILLER: Well, the fact is, Dr. Jervis is making an examination as to the state of his mind. I didn't like the idea myself, but 'e said 'e thought 'e ought to. It seems so under'and somehow.

ERNIE: How do you mean?

MRS. MILLER: Well, Dr. Jervis got Sheppey up there pretending 'e wanted to make a thorough examination of 'is 'eart. Said 'e could do it better in 'is consulting-room, where 'e 'ad all 'is instruments, than what he could 'ere.

ERNIE: Well, Sheppey's got a high blood pressure, we know that, I mean I shouldn't be surprised if his heart wasn't a bit wonky.

MRS. MILLER: Dr. Jervis 'as got a friend of 'is to come up. 'E's a specialist it seems, and 'e's coming as a great favour to Dr. Jervis. 'E's one of the 'eads at Bethlehem.

ERNIE: The lunatic asylum!

[FLORRIE *with clasped hands begins to move her lips, speaking with soundless words.*

MRS. MILLER: 'E's going to pretend 'e's just dropped in for a cup of tea, and then Dr. Jervis is going to ask Sheppey to stay and 'ave a cup. And they're going to get 'im in conversation. Dr. Jervis said it might take an hour or more before they come to a decision. I tell you I can't bear it. I can't bear the idea of letting my poor old man walk into a trap like that.

ERNIE: It's for his own good, isn't it?

MRS. MILLER: [*Noticing* FLORRIE.] Florrie, whatever are you doing of?

FLORRIE: Praying to God.

MRS. MILLER: Not in the sitting-room, Florrie. I'm sure that's not right.

FLORRIE: O God, make them say he's potty. O God, make them say he's potty. O God, make them say he's potty.

MRS. MILLER: Oh, Florrie, how can you ask God to do a thing like that?

FLORRIE: If God makes them say he's potty he'll be shut up. Then he can't throw all that money away and he can't make an exhibition of himself. [*Going on in a whisper.*] O God, make them say he's potty. O God, make them say he's potty.

MRS. MILLER: They won't shut him up. I shouldn't like them to do that. Oh, do stop it, Florrie.

FLORRIE: I won't stop it. It means life and happiness to me. O God, make them say he's potty, and I'll give up sugar in my tea all through Lent.

MRS. MILLER: That's not giving up very much. You're trying to break yourself of sugar as it is because you think it's fattening.

FLORRIE: Well, it's giving up something you like, isn't it? O God, make them say he's potty, and I promise I won't go to the pictures all next month. [*She goes on muttering to herself with her hands clasped and her eyes turned to the ceiling.*]

MRS. MILLER: I wish I 'adn't let Dr. Jervis persuade me. I never thought they might want to shut 'im up.

ERNIE: It's quite evident he can't manage his own affairs.

MRS. MILLER: 'Ow do you know?

ERNIE: Well, it's obvious, isn't it? Wanting to give his money away.

FLORRIE: [*Interrupting herself for a moment.*] And filling the house with riff-raff. O God, make them say he's . . . [*Her voice dwindles away, but her lips keep on moving.*]

ERNIE: It's not the behaviour of a sane man. Nobody can deny that.

MRS. MILLER: 'Ow do you know 'e's not sane, and it ain't all the rest of us as are potty?

ERNIE: That's absurd. Sanity means doing what everybody else does, and thinking what everybody else thinks. That's the whole foundation of democracy. If the individual isn't prepared to act the same way as everybody else there's only one place for him and that's the lunatic asylum.

FLORRIE: Don't argue with her, Ernie. O God, make them say . . .

MRS. MILLER: Jesus didn't do what everybody else did.

FLORRIE: Oh, mum, don't talk about Jesus. It's blasphemous, it really is. Can't you see I'm praying?

ERNIE: All that was a long time ago. As I was saying to Sheppey only the other day, circumstances alter cases. We're civilised now. Besides—mind you, I don't want to say anything offensive, live and let live is my motto, and I'm all for toleration—but looking at the facts impartially I can't help seeing there was a lot to be said on the other side and if I'd been in Pontius Pilate's position I dare say I'd have done just what he did.

MRS. MILLER: I was brought up different from you. Living in the country and all, I never 'ad the opportunity to get the education girls get now. I began to earn my own living when I was fifteen.

FLORRIE: [*Sharply.*] Mum. We don't want to go into ancient history. [*Her lips go on moving as she repeats and repeats her prayer.*]

MRS. MILLER: But we was church-going people, and I used to go to Sunday school. Nothing of what Sheppey says was new to me, as you might say.

FLORRIE: [*Aghast.*] Whatever do you mean by that, mum?

MRS. MILLER: Well, I knew it all, I mean. I'd 'eard it al^l over and over again when I was a girl. I never paid any attention to it of course, but when Sheppey brought it up again it all come back to me.

ERNIE: I may be dense, but really I don't follow.

MRS. MILLER: Sheppey's right about what Jesus said. About giving to the poor and all that. And loving your neighbour as yourself. I remember all that.

ERNIE: I dare say you do. But you never knew anyone that acted on it, did you?

MRS. MILLER: They was young ladies as took Sunday school at 'ome, and I don't think they'd 'ave liked it if one acted on it. They'd 'ave thought it presuming.

ERNIE: And so it is presuming. It's always presumption to think you know better than other people.

MRS. MILLER: I'm sure Sheppey doesn't mean it like that. No one knows 'is place better than what he does. Why, I've 'eard 'im say twenty times, I like a joke as well as any man, but I wouldn't take a liberty with one of my customers any more than I'd like 'im to take a liberty with me.

FLORRIE: [*Almost with agony.*] You're not going to take dad's side? You can't do that, mum. I mean, think of Ernie and me.

MRS. MILLER: It's not a matter of taking sides. I want to do what's best for everybody. But it's like this, if the doctors say 'e's not quite right in 'is 'ead, well, that settles it. But if they say 'e is, then I don't feel justified in preventing 'im from doing what 'e thinks is right.

FLORRIE: Mum. Mum. I think that's awful. [*Almost in tears.*] O God, make them say he's potty. O God, make them say he's potty.

MRS. MILLER: I don't say that I don't think the idea's peculiar. And I know it won't be very pleasant for any of us. But 'ow do I know 'e's not right?

ERNIE: I should have thought your common sense would have told you that.

MRS. MILLER: I'm not clever like you, Ernie. I feel a lot that I can't exactly say. There's something in my 'eart that says, dear old Sheppey, 'e always was a character.

ERNIE: D'you mean to say you're going to sit there twiddling your thumbs and watch him throwing all that money down the drain?

MRS. MILLER: I shan't like it, of course. I mean, I should 'ave liked to own this 'ouse and it would 'ave been a 'elp to 'ave a girl in to do the rough work. But there's something inside me that says, all that don't matter really; if Sheppey wants to do what Jesus said—well, that's only what you was taught when you was a girl.

FLORRIE: And what's to happen to you when the money's gone? You don't suppose they'd have dad back at the shop after making such an exhibition of himself?

ERNIE: And jobs aren't easy to get these days. Especially for a man of Sheppey's age.

MRS. MILLER: Well, 'e's been a good 'usband to me. Never a 'arsh word. 'E's worked for me a good many years. I can earn my own living and 'is too.

ERNIE: Easier said than done.

MRS. MILLER: When one's as good a cook as what I am, and honest, it's not 'ard to get a job. Why, there's not one of these girls that's a patch on me. I'm not one for praising myself, God knows, but I do know my own value. Put me in front of a decent stove and give me the materials and not even the Queen of England can turn out a better dinner than me. And now, my girl, you'd better come and peel the potatoes.

FLORRIE: All right, mum. Are you coming, Ernie?

ERNIE: Yes, I will in a minute. I just want to take a look at the paper.

> [FLORRIE *quickly bites her finger to choke down the tears that have sprung to her eyes. The two women go out.* ERNIE *opens the paper, but he does not read it, he looks sullenly in front of him.* BESSIE *comes in. He gives her a look, but does not speak. He starts reading.*

BESSIE: Anything in the paper?

ERNIE: No.

BESSIE: What are you reading then?

ERNIE: The news.

BESSIE: Racing?

ERNIE: No, political.

BESSIE: Florrie tells me you want to be a Member of Parliament.

ERNIE: Fat chance I have now.

BESSIE: I suppose you was counting on Sheppey doing something for you.

ERNIE: Wouldn't you have in my place?

BESSIE: Well, whatever happens you're lucky to have got Florrie. She's a nice girl. And with her looks she could marry almost anybody.

ERNIE: I suppose you think she's throwing herself away on me?

BESSIE: There's no accounting for tastes. Working in the City like she does I wonder she hasn't been snapped up by one of them rich men long ago.

ERNIE: I'll thank you not to put ideas in Florrie's head. Her future's settled and if I hear of another fellow running after her I shall have something to say to him.

[BESSIE *smiles quietly to herself. The door is opened softly and* COOPER *slinks in.*

COOPER: 'Afternoon all.

BESSIE: Hulloa! How did you get in? I never heard you knock.

COOPER: The lock's got one of them safety catches. I don't 'ave to 'ave anybody open a door like that for me.

BESSIE: That's good news, I must say.

COOPER: Any fags around?

BESSIE: I haven't got any.

COOPER: Suppose I shall 'ave to smoke me own then.

[*He takes a packet out of his pocket and lights a cigarette.*]

BESSIE: You aren't going to offer me one, I suppose?

COOPER: No, I don't approve of ladies smoking.

ERNIE: [*Taking out a packet and offering it to* BESSIE.] Here's one if you want it.

BESSIE: Thanks.

COOPER: What won the three-thirty?

ERNIE: I haven't looked.

COOPER: What'd you buy a paper for then? Wanton waste, I call that.

ERNIE: If you two are going to have a little chat I'll ask you to excuse me.

BESSIE: [*Mincing.*] Oh, don't mention it.

[ERNIE *goes out.*

COOPER: Quite the gentleman, eh?

BESSIE: He's all right. He's only a kid. Swallowed the multiplication table when he was at school and it won't go up or down. Makes him kind of uneasy like.

COOPER: Where's Sheppey?

BESSIE: Out somewhere.

COOPER: What's he after? I can't make 'im out.

BESSIE: He's a puzzle to me too.

COOPER: Religion, I suppose it is, at the back of it.

BESSIE: I'm not so sure. I know a lot about religion. When I had my little flat in Kennington one of my regulars was a religious man. He was a draper in a very good way of business. A prominent Baptist he was. Used to come every Tuesday and Friday. After he'd had his little bit of fun he used to love a good old talk about religion. But he didn't give much away. He used to say there wasn't a draper in the South of London as could squeeze more profit out of a reel of cotton than what he could.

COOPER: You have to be pretty smart with all the competition there is nowadays.

BESSIE: D'you find that in your business?

COOPER: There's always room at the top.

BESSIE: Swank.

COOPER: Besides, what is my business?

BESSIE: Petty thieving, ain't it?

COOPER: Oh, and who do you think you are? You've got no cause to despise me.

BESSIE: I don't despise you. I shouldn't have thought it was worth it, that's all. I mean, in and out of quod all the time. It can't be pleasant.

COOPER: Well, I'll tell you, it's the excitement. And then again, when you've done a job you feel all keyed up, if you know what I mean. You can't hardly help laughing when you think how blasted clever you are. But it's the excitement that's the chief thing.

BESSIE: I can understand that. You'd think after all I've been through, turned out of my room and everything, now I've got a good bed to sleep in and plenty to eat, I'd be satisfied. But if the truth was only known, when it gets about time for me to get all dolled up and go up West—oh, I feel simply terrible.

COOPER: Do you really?

BESSIE: D'you know what I did last night? I put my dress on and I made up the old face and I put on my usual perfume, and I just stood in my room and fancied myself walking down Jermyn Street.

COOPER: Why didn't you go?

BESSIE: Oh, well, on account of poor old Sheppey, I suppose.

COOPER: It don't look as if he was going to show up.

BESSIE: What d'you want to see him about?

COOPER: Well, if you must know, I get sort of restless when the pubs open. I could do with a bob to get a drop of beer.

BESSIE: Oh, well, I don't blame you.

COOPER: [*Going.*] If he asks for me, say I've gone up the street. I'll be back presently.

> [BESSIE *gives a quick look round and sees the snuff-box is missing. She gets between* COOPER *and the door.*]

BESSIE: Where's that snuff-box?

COOPER: What snuff-box?

BESSIE: You know. The one Sheppey had left him.

COOPER: How should I know?

BESSIE: Sheppey sets a rare store on that. He wouldn't lose it for the world.

COOPER: Perhaps the old girl put it away when you come 'ere. Thought it safer.

BESSIE: It was here a minute ago. I saw it.

COOPER: I can't 'elp that. I don't even know what you're talking about.

BESSIE: Yes, you do. You give it up now.

COOPER: 'Ere, who are you talking to?

BESSIE: I thought you was in a great hurry to get out all of a sudden.

COOPER: Look 'ere, my girl. You mind your own business or something unpleasant will 'appen to you.

BESSIE: I'm not frightened of a dirty little tyke like you.

COOPER: Get out of my way. D'you think I'm going to demean myself by arguing with a common prostitute?

BESSIE: You give up that snuff-box.

COOPER: I tell you I 'aven't got it.

BESSIE: Yes, you have. It's in your pocket. Why, I can see it.

COOPER: [*With an instinctive gesture of his hand towards his hip pocket.*] That's a lie.

BESSIE: [*With a hoarse chuckle of triumph.*] Ah. I've caught you. I knew you had it.

COOPER: [*Trying to push past her.*] Oh, shut your mug.

BESSIE: You're not going out of this room till you give that back.

COOPER: What's it got to do with you, anyway?

BESSIE: He may be a silly old fathead, but he means well, and I'm not going to stand by and see you sneak his bits and pieces.

COOPER: I tell you I've got to 'ave a drink.

BESSIE: What you do outside's got nothing to do with me. But not here you don't do anything.

COOPER: If you don't get out of my way I'll give you such a swipe over the jaw.

BESSIE: [*Peering right into his face.*] You dare to hit me. You filthy little sneak-thief. You snivelling little mongrel cur. You dirty son of a . . . [*With a quick movement she tries to snatch the snuff-box out of his pocket.*]

COOPER: No, you don't.

BESSIE: Damn you.

[*There is a short struggle in the middle of which* SHEPPEY *comes in.*

SHEPPEY: Hulloa, what's this?

[*They separate. They are both a trifle out of breath*

BESSIE: He's got that snuff-box of yours.

SHEPPEY: What about it?

BESSIE: He was just going out to pawn it.

SHEPPEY: What d'you want to do that for, Jim?

COOPER: It's a bleeding lie.

SHEPPEY: It ain't in its usual place.

COOPER: If anyone took it she did. You know what them women are. Just trying to put the blame on me.

BESSIE: You look in his hip-pocket.

SHEPPEY: Empty out your pockets, old man.

COOPER: I won't. I won't be treated like this by any man. D'you think you've got the right to insult me just because I'm your guest?

BESSIE: Oh, dear, 'ark at you.

SHEPPEY: It's no good, old man, I'm afraid you've got to empty them pockets of yours.

COOPER: Who says so?

SHEPPEY: I do and if necessary I can make you.

COOPER: I've 'ad enough of this. I'm going.

> [*He tries to brush past* SHEPPEY, *but* SHEPPEY, *with surprising quickness, seizes him and trips him up, and with his knee on his chest to hold him down gets the snuff-box out of his pocket.*]

SHEPPEY: Get up now. Why didn't you give it quietly?

COOPER: 'Ere, you nearly broke my arm.

BESSIE: Why, Sheppey, I am surprised. I didn't know you was as nippy as that.

SHEPPEY: I was a bit of a wrestler when I was a young feller.

BESSIE: Shall I get a cop?

COOPER: [*Springing to his feet.*] You ain't going to give me in charge, Governor? I didn't really mean to take it. It was a sudden temptation. I didn't know what I was doing really.

BESSIE: Whine. Go on. Whine.

SHEPPEY: No, I'm not going to give you in charge. The judge said 'e'd give you the maximum if you ever come before 'im again.

BESSIE: You ain't going to let him go? After all you done for him.

SHEPPEY: I ain't done anything for 'im. What I done I done for meself. Sorry if I 'urt you, old man. I'm stronger than you'd think for, and sometimes I put more strength into a thing than I should.

COOPER: No one's got a right to leave things like that about.

SHEPPEY: It's not gold, you know, it's only silver-gilt. It's not the worth I value it for, it's the sentiment. It was left me by a gentleman I'd attended for years and all through 'is last illness 'e would 'ave me go to his 'ouse and shave 'im every day. 'E said to 'is daughter only the day before 'e died, if I appear before my Maker looking like a gentleman it'll be to Sheppey I owe it. 'Ere take it. [*He hands the snuff-box to* COOPER.]

COOPER: What d'you mean?

SHEPPEY: I'm giving it you.

COOPER: Why?

SHEPPEY: You want it, don't you?

COOPER: No.

SHEPPEY: Why did you pinch it, then?

COOPER: That's quite another matter. I didn't mind pinching it. I'm not going to take it as a present. I only pinched it because I wanted a bob or two for a few beers. I'd 'ave give you back the ticket. Straight, I would.

SHEPPEY: If you wanted a bob why didn't you say so? [*Putting his hand in his pocket and taking out a shilling.*] 'Ere you are.

[COOPER *looks at the shilling in his hand and then at* SHEPPEY. *He is full of suspicion.*

COOPER: 'Ere, what's the meaning of this?

SHEPPEY: If a chap can only see God in a pint of beer 'e may as well look there as not see 'im at all.

COOPER: Is it a trap?

SHEPPEY: Don't talk so silly.

[COOPER *is puzzled and uneasy. He looks at the shilling, and he looks at* SHEPPEY.

COOPER: I don't like this. There's something funny about it all. What are you getting at? What's the idea? 'Ere, take your bob. I won't 'ave it. It'll bring me bad luck.

I'm off. I've 'ad enough of this place. I like to know where I am with people. This gives me the creeps. I wish I'd never come 'ere.

[He goes out quickly.

BESSIE: Well, that's a good riddance to bad rubbish.

SHEPPEY: Whoever would 'a thought it'd 'ave taken 'im like that?

BESSIE: What did you want to give him that there box for?

SHEPPEY: Well, I just couldn't 'elp meself.

BESSIE: You know, you ought to be a bit more careful. You're going to get a nasty knock one of these days if you go on treating good and bad alike.

SHEPPEY: The fact is, I can't see there's much to choose between them.

BESSIE: Come off it, Sheppey. Why, that Cooper, he's just a dirty tyke.

SHEPPEY: I know 'e is. Some'ow I don't mind.

BESSIE: Fact is, Sheppey, you've got no moral sense.

SHEPPEY: I suppose that's it. Lucky I was born lucky.

BESSIE: You're a caution and no mistake.

SHEPPEY: Sorry 'e's gone. I'd got quite used to seeing 'im about the 'ouse.

BESSIE: I'm going too, Sheppey.

SHEPPEY: Why? Ain't you getting on with mum and Florrie?

BESSIE: It's not that, I want to get back to the West End. I've been glad to have a bit of a rest here. It's done me no end of good. I miss the girls and I miss the street. When you've been used to meeting a lot of people you do come to depend on it somehow. And then, you never know what's going to happen to you. It's not the going with men I like, it's the getting off. I mean, you can't help feeling, well, that's one up to me. And besides— oh, well, I don't know, it's the whole thing. It's got its

ups and downs, I don't say it hasn't, but it's exciting;
even if you don't get off it's exciting. That's what I mean,
see?

SHEPPEY: I thought you was fed up with it.

BESSIE: So I was. I was run down and out of sorts. But
now it's different somehow. I know it's a disappointment to you. I'm sorry. Thank you for all you've done
for me.

SHEPPEY: All right. 'Ave it your own way. There'll always
be a 'ome for you 'ere when you want one.

BESSIE: D'you mean to say you'd take me back?

SHEPPEY: Of course I would. I don't blame you. I only
want people to be 'appy.

BESSIE: I think I know a thing or two about men, but I
don't mind saying you've got me beat. Well, so long.

SHEPPEY: You're not going now?

BESSIE: Yes, I am. I can't stand it another minute. I'll just
get myself dressed and then I'll slip away without saying
anything to nobody.

SHEPPEY: All right. And don't forget when you feel like
coming you're welcome.

BESSIE: It's a strange world and no mistake.

    [*She goes out. In a moment* MRS. MILLER *comes in.*

MRS. MILLER: I 'eard you come in. I couldn't leave my
kitchen. I was just making a nice calves-foot jelly for
Mrs. Robinson.

SHEPPEY: That's right, my dear. She'll enjoy that.

MRS. MILLER: I told you they was twins, didn't I?

SHEPPEY: Yes.

MRS. MILLER: What did the doctor say about you?

SHEPPEY: Oh, we 'ad a rare set to. 'E 'ad a friend there,
another doctor, Ennismore 'is name was, a tip-top swell,
it appears, and Dr. Jervis said as 'e was there we might

just as well profit by it and 'e examined me too.

MRS. MILLER: I see.

SHEPPEY: A very nice gentleman, he was. Intelligent. He was very interested in my plan. He got me to tell him all about it. My word, he did ask me some funny questions. I couldn't 'ardly 'elp laughing. Asked me if I'd ever seen my dad 'ave 'is bath. Yes, I said, every Saturday night, 'e used to make me scrub 'is back for 'im.

MRS. MILLER: You *were* gone a time.

SHEPPEY: I know I was. We must 'ave talked for nearly two hours. I left them at it. Dr. Jervis said they'd 'ave a little chat and 'e'd come 'ere later. [*There is a knock at the front door.*] That might be 'im now.

MRS. MILLER: Oh, I do hate doctors.

SHEPPEY: Why, you're not anxious, are you?

MRS. MILLER: Yes.

SHEPPEY: That's silly. There's nothing the matter with me. I never felt better in my life.

[FLORRIE *opens the door.*

FLORRIE: Mum, will you come a minute?

SHEPPEY: Is it the doctor? [*He goes to the door.*] Come in, doctor.

[DR. JERVIS *comes in followed by* ERNIE.

DR. JERVIS: Good afternoon, Mrs. Miller.

MRS. MILLER: Good afternoon, sir.

DR. JERVIS: Your husband told you? By a piece of good luck a friend of mine, a West End specialist, happened to be there when Sheppey came.

SHEPPEY: I was just telling about 'im. 'E made quite an impression on me.

DR. JERVIS: We've had a talk about you. Heart a bit weak, you know. We think a rest would do you good.

SHEPPEY: Me?

DR. JERVIS: We want you to go into a home for a while where you'll be comfortable and looked after properly.

  [MRS. MILLER, FLORRIE *and* ERNIE *at once see what this means.* MRS. MILLER *can hardly restrain a start of dismay.*

SHEPPEY: I'm not going to no 'ome. Can't spare the time. I'm a busy man.

MRS. MILLER: Couldn't we look after 'im 'ere?

DR. JERVIS: It's not the same thing. My doctor friend is at the head of a very good hospital. You'll be under his direct care. I don't say you're seriously ill, but you're ill, and you want proper attention.

SHEPPEY: You know, doctors don't know everything.

DR. JERVIS: They don't pretend to.

FLORRIE: It's silly to talk like that, dad. If Dr. Jervis says you're ill, you are ill.

SHEPPEY: I know more about me own 'ealth than 'e does.

DR. JERVIS: Why do you say that? I'd never pretend to know as much as you do about the care of the hair.

SHEPPEY: Sit down, and just let me 'ave a look at your 'air.

DR. JERVIS: Oh, my hair's all right.

SHEPPEY: That's what people say. There's many a man walking about London now with a bald 'ead who'd 'ave a good 'ead of 'air if he'd taken my advice in time.

DR. JERVIS: [*Humouring him.*] All right, you have a look at it.

  [*He sits down and* SHEPPEY *steps over to him. He takes a glass out of his pocket and inspects the doctor's hair.*

SHEPPEY: Been falling out a bit lately?

DR. JERVIS: A bit, you know. I'm getting on.

SHEPPEY: It's just as I thought. If you don't do something

about it you'll be as bald as I am in six months.

DR. JERVIS: Oh, I can't believe that.

SHEPPEY: It's true. And it's a pity. You've got beautiful 'air. I mean, it's not often one comes across a gentleman with 'air of this texture.

DR. JERVIS: Funny you should say that. My wife always says I have nice hair.

SHEPPEY: She won't be able to say it much longer.

DR. JERVIS: Well, I don't know what can be done about it.

SHEPPEY: I do. If you'll massage your 'ead for five minutes night and morning with our number three I guarantee that in six months you'll 'ave as fine a 'ead of 'air as you've ever 'ad in your life.

DR. JERVIS: D'you expect me to believe that?

SHEPPEY: No.

DR. JERVIS: [Good-naturedly.] Well, I'll tell you what I'll do: when I'm passing down Jermyn Street I'll drop in and buy myself a bottle.

SHEPPEY: You needn't do that. I always keep a small stock 'ere, in case any of my friends want any. I'll just pop along and put you up a little. Eight and six or thirteen and four?

DR. JERVIS: Thirteen and four. I may as well be hanged for a sheep as a lamb.

SHEPPEY: You'll never regret it. It won't take me more than five minutes.

[He goes out.

DR. JERVIS: Of course I only did that to humour him, you know.

MRS. MILLER: Oh, doctor, whatever do you mean?

DR. JERVIS: My friend, Dr. Ennismore, is one of the greatest authorities in England on diseases of the mind and he's made a thorough examination of your husband. He has no doubt at all that he's suffering from acute mania.

MRS. MILLER: Oh, dear.

DR. JERVIS: We want you to persuade him that it's for his own good to go into a home. I'll have another talk with him to-morrow myself. If he won't consent we're prepared to certify him.

MRS. MILLER: Is that really necessary? I mean, I can't bear the thought of 'im being put away.

DR. JERVIS: I must tell you that the prognosis in these cases is not favourable. It's much better that he should be put under restraint before he commits some act that may have unfortunate consequences to himself or to others.

ERNIE: I don't want to say I told you so, but the fact remains, I said he was crazy from the beginning.

DR. JERVIS: It's quite obvious that a sane man is not going to give all his money away to the poor. A sane man takes money from the poor. He runs chain stores, founds building societies, or engages in municipal work.

MRS. MILLER: Sheppey always 'as liked people. I mean, you might almost say 'e loved 'is fellow-men.

DR. JERVIS: That's not a healthy sign, you know. The normal man is selfish, grasping, destructive, vain and sensual. What is generally termed morality is forced upon him by the herd, and the obligation he is under to repress his natural instincts is undoubtedly the cause of many of the disorders of the mind. Dr. Ennismore said to me just now that he had little doubt that philanthropy in general could always be ascribed to repressed homosexuality.

ERNIE: Is it really? I call that very interesting.

DR. JERVIS: He is of opinion that with rational education of the young, philanthropy could be entirely stamped out of this country.

ERNIE: I should like to meet him. He sounds clever.

DR. JERVIS: He asked Sheppey some very searching questions and it looks very much as if there was a distinct father-complex at the bottom of his trouble.

ERNIE: Œdipus and all that. I know.

DR. JERVIS: [*To* MRS. MILLER.] He was asking me when you first noticed anything peculiar.

MRS. MILLER: I never noticed anything peculiar, not till all of a sudden 'e said 'e wanted to live like Jesus.

DR. JERVIS: Has he always been a religious man?

MRS. MILLER: No, that's just it. I mean, 'e never went to church or anything like that. 'E liked to spend 'is Sunday mornings doing odd jobs about the 'ouse. If 'e'd been a bad man it would be different. It seems so funny for a good man to become religious.

DR. JERVIS: Didn't you suspect something was wrong when you saw him reading the Bible?

MRS. MILLER: I'll tell you exactly what 'appened. 'E always reads the *Morning Post*, on account of the Society news, you know. 'E finds it useful with 'is customers to know who's engaged to be married and all that.

DR. JERVIS: I see.

MRS. MILLER: Well, when 'e was ill I went out and got it for 'im. And on the Monday morning when I took it in to 'im, 'e said, mum, 'ave we got a Bible in the 'ouse? Yes, I said, and I give it 'im. I meant no 'arm. Náturally I thought 'e wanted it for a cross-word puzzle.

DR. JERVIS: That's the peculiar cunning of the insane. It's often very difficult indeed to get them to say what you want them to. Now I don't know if you remember, last week when I saw him I asked him if he saw things. He said he saw sin and wickedness beating with their wings. It struck me at the time. That beating with the wings—very suggestive. And then he talked of a great white light. Dr. Ennismore is convinced he has visual hallucinations, but will he admit it? He's as obstinate as a mule.

MRS. MILLER: 'E never 'as been. 'E was a man as would always listen to reason.

DR. JERVIS: His general state is typical. The bright eyes and flushed cheeks. The restlessness and insomnia. Ennismore is a very careful man and he wouldn't say what wasn't a fact. He says he's never seen a prettier case of religious paranoia in all his practice.

MRS. MILLER: I've never 'eard of there being any madness in 'is family. It's like a stigma on all of us.

DR. JERVIS: Get that idea out of your head at once, Mrs. Miller. Ennismore's opinion is that everybody's mad. He says we couldn't live in this world if we weren't.

[SHEPPEY *comes in with a bottle neatly made up into a paper parcel.*

SHEPPEY: 'Ere you are, doctor. I've made it into a nice little package for you.

DR. JERVIS: Would you like cash?

SHEPPEY: No, take it off my bill. I know our number three. After you've once used it you'll never be able to do without it.

DR. JERVIS: Well, I must be getting along.

SHEPPEY: I'll just show you out.

DR. JERVIS: Good-bye, Mrs. Miller. [*He nods to the others.*] Good evening.

MRS. MILLER: Good evening, sir.

[DR. JERVIS *goes out accompanied by* SHEPPEY.

ERNIE: I sympathise with you, Mrs. Miller. I do indeed. But you must say it's the best that could have happened for all parties.

FLORRIE: It would have been a shame to throw all that good money away.

ERNIE: What d'you say to going to the pictures, Florrie? Early show.

FLORRIE: Right ho. You don't want me, mum, do you?

MRS. MILLER: [*A little doubtfully.*] No, dear.

FLORRIE: Why, what's the matter?

MRS. MILLER: Well, I shouldn't 'ave thought you'd want to go to the pictures to-night, when your poor old dad . . .

FLORRIE: I can't do him any good by staying at home. And I want to go all I can these next few days, as I shan't be able to go all next month.

ERNIE: Why not?

FLORRIE: I promised God I wouldn't, not if he made the doctors say poor dad was potty.

ERNIE: You're not going to pay any attention to that? That's only superstition.

FLORRIE: I don't care what it is. I've promised and I'm going to keep my promise. I may want something else one of these days, and then where should I be if I hadn't kept it.

ERNIE: You don't suppose it had any effect really?

FLORRIE: No one can say that, Ernie. I promised I'd do something for God if he'd do something for me. Well, he has, and I'm going to keep my word.

ERNIE: Oh, well, darling, have it your own way.

FLORRIE: Besides, what with getting ready for the wedding and poor dad being in an asylum, we shan't have much chance of going to the pictures next month anyway.

ERNIE: You're a grand girl, Florrie. I don't know what I should do without you.

FLORRIE: You wouldn't have liked breaking it off, would you?

ERNIE: Me? Why, the thought never entered my head.

FLORRIE: Oh, yes it did. And I don't blame you.

ERNIE: Well, I don't mind telling you now that I was having a bit of a struggle between my inclinations and my duty to myself. And when I say my duty to myself, of course I mean my duty to the community.

MRS. MILLER: [*With a sigh, tolerantly.*] Oh, go on with you. After all one's only young once.

FLORRIE: Come on, Ernie. We don't want to get there when it's half over.

                    [*As they are going out* SHEPPEY *comes in.*

SHEPPEY: 'Ulloa, where are you two off to?

FLORRIE: Going to the pictures. See you later.

                                        [*They go out.*

MRS. MILLER: You look a bit tired, dear. Why don't you go to our room and 'ave a lay down?

SHEPPEY: No, I don't fancy that. I'll just sit in my chair and perhaps I'll 'ave forty winks. I don't feel very grand, really. I've 'ad a busy day.

MRS. MILLER: You won't be going out again, will you? Let me take off your boots.

    [*She goes down on her knees and begins to take them off.*

SHEPPEY: You've been a good wife to me, Ada.

MRS. MILLER: Oh, don't be so silly. If you talk like that I shall think you're ill and I shall put you right to bed with a 'ot-water bottle.

SHEPPEY: You 'ave, you know. I expect I've often been aggravating and unreasonable like.

MRS. MILLER: Oh, go on. If you want me to 'ave a good cry, say so.

SHEPPEY: I expect this 'as been a disappointment to you, about the money, I mean. I know you wanted to finish paying for the 'ouse and a girl to do the rough work.

MRS. MILLER: Don't let's talk about that, Sheppey.

SHEPPEY: We must, my dear. It'll be all right for Florrie. She's got Ernie. 'E's a bit conceited, but that's because 'e's young. 'E's a good boy really. Florrie 'll lick 'im into shape all right. She'll turn 'im round 'er little finger like you 'ave me, dear.

MRS. MILLER: I like that.

SHEPPEY: But it's going to be different for you. I know that. That's why I want you to look at it like I do. It's the pain of the world that gets me.

MRS. MILLER: Oh, Sheppey, don't you think that's just because you're run down?

SHEPPEY: I tell you I never felt better in me life. I feel so light in myself if it wasn't for me 'eavy boots I believe I'd float right away.

MRS. MILLER: You would look funny, Sheppey, flying around like a butterfly.

SHEPPEY: I'm going to 'ave a grand time, Ada.

MRS. MILLER: Are you, dear?

SHEPPEY: Don't think I'm not grateful for all you done for me, Ada. Don't think I'm not sorry to disappoint you. But I've got to do this.

MRS. MILLER: I know you wouldn't do anything but what you thought was right, Sheppey.

SHEPPEY: You won't 'old it up against me, dear?

MRS. MILLER: As if I'd ever 'old anything up against you, Sheppey. Aggravating as you may be.

SHEPPEY: It's many a day since you kissed me, Ada.

MRS. MILLER: Go on with you. What would anyone want an old woman like me kissing them for?

SHEPPEY: First time I kissed you, you slapped my face good and proper.

MRS. MILLER: I thought you was a bit too free and easy.

SHEPPEY: Come on, Ada. To show there's no ill feeling.

> [*He leans forward and she puts up her face. They kiss one another gently on the lips.*

MRS. MILLER: It makes me feel quite foolish.

SHEPPEY: What 'ave you got for supper to-night?

MRS. MILLER: Well, I've made a cottage pie.

SHEPPEY: D'you know what I'd fancy?

MRS. MILLER: No.

SHEPPEY: I'd fancy a couple of kippers. You know I always 'ave liked kippers.

MRS. MILLER: I know you 'ave. I'll tell you what I'll do. I'll run out in a little while and get them for you.

SHEPPEY: You're sure it's not too much trouble?

MRS. MILLER: It's no trouble at all. Now you just sit down in your chair. See if you can 'ave forty winks.

SHEPPEY: All right.

MRS. MILLER: I won't disturb you till supper's ready. We'll 'ave it the moment Florrie and Ernie come back.

SHEPPEY: I don't mind telling you that I shall enjoy a bit of a rest.

MRS. MILLER: I'll draw the blind.

> [*She goes to the window and does this. She goes out.* SHEPPEY *sits down in the winged grandfather's chair, so that he is hidden from sight. The stage is darkened to show the passage of a couple of hours.*

> [*When the scene grows a little lighter, night has fallen. Through the blind is seen the light of an arc lamp in the street. The chair in which* SHEPPEY *is sleeping is vaguely discernible. There is a knock at the door. No answer comes from* SHEPPEY *and the knock is repeated.*

SHEPPEY: Come in. [*The door is not opened.*] Come in. [*He gets up.*] I thought I 'eard a knock.

[*The door is opened wide, silently; and as it opens it gives the impression that it has not been pushed but has swung open of its own accord.* BESSIE *stands in the door. She wears a long black cloak, but no hat.*

SHEPPEY: Oh, it's you, is it? I thought I 'eard a knock.

BESSIE: I didn't knock.

SHEPPEY: Didn't you? I suppose I was dreaming. Come in, dear.

[*She comes in and the door closes behind her.*

SHEPPEY: Got somebody with you?

BESSIE: No.

SHEPPEY: Who shut the door then? It's funny. I must be half asleep. [*He goes to the door, opens it and looks out.*] There's nobody there.

BESSIE: [*With the shadow of a smile.*] No.

SHEPPEY: You 'aven't been gone long.

BESSIE: Have you been expecting me?

SHEPPEY: Thought better of it, I suppose. Well, I can't say I'm sorry. I'll put on some light. [*He switches on a standard lamp. The room is now dimly lit.* BESSIE *stands near the door, motionless.*] What are you standing like that for? Come in.

BESSIE: Thanks.

[*She enters into the room. There is something about her that seems strange to him. He cannot quite make it out. It makes him vaguely uneasy.*

SHEPPEY: Did my old woman let you in?

BESSIE: The house is empty.

SHEPPEY: I suppose she's popped out to get them kippers. We wasn't expecting you in to supper.

BESSIE: I generally come before I'm wanted.

SHEPPEY: No, you don't, not 'ere. I said you was always welcome and I meant it.

BESSIE: It's pleasant to hear that for once.

SHEPPEY: I say, why are you speaking so funny all of a sudden?

BESSIE: Am I? I didn't know.

> [*The cockney accent with which* BESSIE *spoke has in fact disappeared, and this woman speaks now in ordinary English.*

SHEPPEY: All posh. [*Imitating her.*] The house is empty. It's pleasant to hear that for once. No good trying to be the perfect lady with me, you know.

BESSIE: I'm afraid you must take me as I am.

SHEPPEY: Oh, go on, speak natural. 'Ave you been drinking? [*She does not answer and he gives her a quick suspicious look.*] What's the matter with you to-night? You are Bessie Legros, aren't you? You're just like 'er. [*He goes up to her.*] And yet there's something different. [*Puzzled and astonished.*] You're not Bessie Legros.

WOMAN: No.

SHEPPEY: Who are you?

WOMAN: Death.

SHEPPEY: [*With his usual friendly good humour.*] Well, I'm glad you've told me. I shouldn't have known otherwise. Sit down, won't you?

DEATH: No, I won't do that.

SHEPPEY: In a hurry?

DEATH: I have no time to waste.

SHEPPEY: Are you on your way to Mrs. Robinson's? My wife was making her some calves-foot jelly only this afternoon. If it's the twins I don't suppose they'll be sorry. They've got four already and Robinson's been out of work for eight months.

DEATH: Has he? No, I wasn't thinking of going there.

SHEPPEY: Well, you know your own business best.

DEATH: I have my whims and fancies.

SHEPPEY: Being a woman.

DEATH: You like your little joke, don't you?

SHEPPEY: I always 'ave. 'Aving a sense of 'umour 'as been an asset to me. I've often 'eard my customers say to the governor, No, I'll wait for Sheppey. 'E always gives me a good laugh.

DEATH: That's more than my customers can say of me.

SHEPPEY: [*Gently chaffing her.*] I suppose on the whole people would just as soon 'ave your room as your company.

DEATH: I'm not often welcome. And yet sometimes you'd think they'd be glad to see me.

SHEPPEY: Well, I don't know. It's not a very nice thing to say to a lady, but I think your looks are a bit against you.

DEATH: I felt there must be something.

SHEPPEY: Funny me taking you for Bessie Legros. Now I come to talk to you you're not a bit like her. Of course she's what they call a common prostitute, but there's something you can't 'ardly 'elp liking about 'er. [*He pinches his arm.*]

DEATH: Why do you do that?

SHEPPEY: I was only pinching my arm. I wanted to see if I was awake. I'm dreaming, but I know I'm dreaming. That's funny, isn't it?

DEATH: What makes you think you're dreaming?

SHEPPEY: Well, I know I am. I'm sitting in my chair 'aving a nap really. I've been 'aving the most extraordinary dreams lately. I was telling the doctor about them only this afternoon. Our own doctor thought I was potty. [*With glee.*] I got back on 'im all right. Sold 'im a bottle of our number three.

DEATH: That was clever of you.

SHEPPEY: I know it was. 'E tried to pretend 'e was only buying it to 'umour me. My eye and Betty Martin. He bought it because I 'ypnotised 'im. And 'e'll use it night and morning like I told 'im to. There's no one I couldn't sell our number three to. I could sell you a bottle if I wanted to.

DEATH: I don't think it would do me much good.

SHEPPEY: Now don't say that. When people say a thing like that it puts me on my mettle. Just let me 'ave a look at your 'air.

DEATH: I haven't got time just now.

SHEPPEY: I don't say you 'aven't got a good 'ead of 'air, but 'ow d'you know you're going to keep it? 'Ulloa, who's this?

[*The door opens and* COOPER *slinks in.*

COOPER: It's me, governor.

SHEPPEY: You've come back then?

COOPER: Been waiting on the opposite side of the street till the coast was clear. They're all out.

SHEPPEY: Yes, I know they are.

COOPER: As I was going out I 'eard them talking. I was 'iding just outside the kitchen and I 'eard every word they said. They're going to shut you up, governor.

SHEPPEY: Me? What for?

COOPER: 'Cause you're barmy.

SHEPPEY: Don't be so silly.

COOPER: God's truth, governor. I swear it is. Florrie and that bloke of 'ers. They're going to shut you up so they can get 'old of your money. Your old woman's in it too.

SHEPPEY: You make me laugh. Why, my old woman wouldn't let them touch a 'air of my 'ead.

COOPER: They're going to try and make you go to the asylum peaceful, but if you won't they're going to sign you up.

SHEPPEY: Oh, is that what you think? And what are you going to do about it?

COOPER: Well, I've come to warn you.

SHEPPEY: That's very kind of you, I'm sure.

COOPER: When I thought you was in your right mind you give me the creeps. That's why I skipped. Now I know you're barmy—well, that's another story altogether. I'm used to people like that. My mother's uncle was barmy. Used to live with us. Thought 'e was a loaf of sugar. Wouldn't wash, because 'e thought 'e'd melt.

SHEPPEY: That's a funny idea.

COOPER: You've been a good sport to me. Saved me from a stretch. One good turn deserves another. You slip out of the 'ouse now with me when there's nobody about. I'll take care of you, see? Never mind about the money.

SHEPPEY: [*To the woman.*] What do you think about that? I knew 'e was no worse than anybody else, really.

COOPER: [*Startled.*] Who are you talking to?

SHEPPEY: That lady there.

COOPER: Where? I don't see no lady.

SHEPPEY: Look again.

COOPER: There's no one there.

SHEPPEY: That's a good one. Looking straight at you and says there's no one there.

DEATH: I'm not surprised.

SHEPPEY: [*To* COOPER.] Hear that?

COOPER: What?

SHEPPEY: She says she's not surprised.

COOPER: Nobody's spoke but you and me.

SHEPPEY: 'E don't seem to 'ear either.

DEATH: Why should he? I have nothing to say to him yet.

SHEPPEY: I was just going to sell her a bottle of our number three when you come in. Women think they're artful. They're just as easy as men really.

COOPER: Look 'ere, governor, if you want to get away you'd better look nippy. They'll be back in 'alf a mo'.

SHEPPEY: Not me. I ain't going to trust myself to a fellow that's as blind as a bat and as deaf as a post.

COOPER: Don't I tell you if you stay 'ere they'll shut you up?

SHEPPEY: Maybe you mean well and maybe you don't. Maybe you're the devil in disguise. I'm a respectable member of society and I'm not going on any 'arum-scarum adventures.

COOPER: Don't say the gipsy never warned you.

SHEPPEY: That's all right. I'm in the middle of an interesting conversation with this lady. I don't want to be disturbed.

COOPER: Oh, all right, 'ave it your own way.

[*He slips out of the room.* SHEPPEY *turns to* DEATH *with a smile.*

SHEPPEY: Funny 'im not being able to see you.

DEATH: The hemp's not picked yet to make the rope that's waiting for him.

SHEPPEY: That's not a very nice thing to say about anybody.

DEATH: It all comes to the same thing in the end, you know.

SHEPPEY: But I say, if you ain't there really, 'ow is it *I* see you?

DEATH: Can't you guess?

SHEPPEY: [*With a sudden movement of dismay.*] Look 'ere, you ain't come 'ere on my account?

DEATH: Yes.

SHEPPEY: You're joking. I thought you'd just come to 'ave a little chat. I'm sorry, my dear, there's nothing doing to-day. You must call again some other time.

DEATH: I'm too busy for that.

SHEPPEY: I don't think that's treating me right. Coming in all friendly and pleasant. If I'd known what you was after I'd 'ave nipped off with Cooper when 'e asked me.

DEATH: That wouldn't have helped you much.

SHEPPEY: I wish now I'd gone down to the Isle of Sheppey when the doctor advised it. You wouldn't 'ave thought of looking for me there.

DEATH: There was a merchant in Bagdad who sent his servant to market to buy provisions and in a little while the servant came back, white and trembling, and said, Master, just now when I was in the market-place I was jostled by a woman in the crowd and when I turned I saw it was death that jostled me. She looked at me and made a threatening gesture; now, lend me your horse, and I will ride away from this city and avoid my fate. I will go to Samarra and there death will not find me. The merchant lent him his horse, and the servant mounted it, and he dug his spurs in its flanks and as fast as the horse could gallop he went. Then the merchant went down to the market-place and he saw me standing in the crowd and he came to me and said, Why did you make a threatening gesture to my servant when you saw him this morning? That was not a threatening gesture, I said, it was only a start of surprise. I was astonished to see him in Bagdad, for I had an appointment with him to-night in Samarra.

SHEPPEY: [*With a little shudder.*] D'you mean there's no escaping you?

DEATH: No.

SHEPPEY: [*Trying to wheedle her.*] I don't fancy the idea of leaving this world. I know my way about and I'm at 'ome 'ere. Seems silly at my age to go on a wild-goose chase like this.

DEATH: Are you afraid?

SHEPPEY: What of? The Judgment Day? [*With a little smile.*] No, not really. You see, the way I look at it is this: I've 'ad dozens of apprentices under me, and often they was silly and inattentive and broke things, you know what boys are, fond of a lark; well, of course I told 'em off, but I never 'eld it up against them. I'm not going to believe in a God that's not got as much common sense and as much sense of 'umour as I 'ave.

DEATH: Are you ready then?

SHEPPEY: What for?

DEATH: To start.

SHEPPEY: Now? This minute? I never knew you meant that. Why, what's the 'urry? I must talk it over with my wife first. I never do a thing without consulting 'er.

DEATH: She can't help you now.

SHEPPEY: Besides, she's giving me kippers for my supper. She'd be terribly upset if I wasn't 'ere to eat them after she's taken all that trouble.

DEATH: Others will eat them in your place.

SHEPPEY: To tell you the truth, I'm feeling rather tired. I don't feel like making a journey to-night.

DEATH: It's an easy one.

SHEPPEY: And then there's another thing. I daresay you don't read the papers and 'aven't 'eard about it. I won over eight thousand pounds in the Irish Sweep and I've made up my mind to use it in a particular way. It would be ridiculous for me to pop off just when I'm going to do a bit of good in the world.

DEATH: It does happen like that sometimes. The world will get on quite well without you. You men, you find it hard to realise that.

[*There is the sound of the street door being closed.*

SHEPPEY: There's my wife just come in. I'll call her, shall I?

DEATH: She wouldn't hear you if you did.

SHEPPEY: You know, we've never been separated since we married. I don't think she'll like me going off like this without 'er.

DEATH: She can't come with you on this journey.

SHEPPEY: She'll be quite lost in the 'ouse without 'aving me to look after. Of course I suppose in a way it'll be a rest for 'er. Cooking my dinner and washing my clothes. It won't 'urt 'er to take things a bit easy for the rest of 'er life. It'll seem strange to 'er just at first.

DEATH: People get used to it, you know.

SHEPPEY: Especially widows, I've noticed. Seems funny me talking of Ada as a widow. She'll take it terrible 'ard, you know.

DEATH: She'll get over it in time.

SHEPPEY: That's not much consolation to me. Look 'ere, I'll tell you what I'll do, I'll give you a thousand pounds of my Sweep money and you go out the way you came.

DEATH: Money's no use to me.

SHEPPEY: You know, I don't feel at all well. I think I ought to see the doctor.

DEATH: You'll feel better presently.

SHEPPEY: You seem to 'ave an answer to everything. Seems a pity, when you come to think of it, me not being able to do what I'd set me 'eart on. Of course, they kep' on telling me I'd do more 'arm than good. What was that other thing 'e said? Thy will be done. [*With a sigh.*] Fact is, I'm so tired, I don't seem to mind any more.

DEATH: I know. It's often surprised me. People are so frightened beforehand, and the older they are the more frightened, but when it comes to the point they don't really mind.

SHEPPEY: There's just one thing I'd like to ask you before we go. What's on the other side really?

DEATH: I've often wondered.

SHEPPEY: Do you mean to say you don't know? [*She shakes her head.*] Are you going to tell me you go about taking people away, one after the other, young and old, whether they like it or not, and you don't know where it is they're going?

DEATH: It's no business of mine.

SHEPPEY: I don't think you're justified for a minute. I mean, you 'aven't got the right to take a responsibility like that.

DEATH: To tell you the truth, I've sometimes wondered if it isn't all a terrible misunderstanding.

SHEPPEY: [*Indignantly.*] All right, then. I'll just go and see for myself. Which way do we go?

DEATH: Out of the door.

SHEPPEY: That seems rather tame. I thought we'd fly out of the window or pop up the chimney. Something spectacular, you know.

DEATH: No.

SHEPPEY: Well, I'll just put on my boots. [*He looks round for them.*] There now. That artful old woman, she was afraid I'd go out and she's taken them away and 'id them.

DEATH: You'll have to come without.

SHEPPEY: I shall look funny walking about without my boots on.

DEATH: Nobody will notice.

SHEPPEY: I'll just put out the light. No good running up an electric light bill.

> [*He switches off the electric light at the door. The door is opened and they pass out. In the empty room a rattle, the death rattle, is heard. It seems to come from the chair in which* SHEPPEY *was sleeping.*

> [*The door is opened again and* FLORRIE *and* ERNIE *come in. He switches on the light.* ERNIE *turns back and speaks to* MRS. MILLER *in the passage.*

ERNIE: No, he's not here.

FLORRIE: Perhaps he's gone out.

MRS. MILLER: [*In the door.*] No, 'is 'at's in the 'all. I expect 'e's 'aving a lay down in our room. I'll let 'im be till supper's ready. You lay the table, Florrie.

FLORRIE: Right you are, mum.

> [MRS. MILLER *disappears from sight.* FLORRIE *gets the tablecloth and the knives and forks from the sideboard.* ERNIE *helps her to lay the cloth.*

ERNIE: No lodgers to-night, it appears.

FLORRIE: Thank goodness.

ERNIE: What's happened to them?

FLORRIE: I don't know and I don't care. Though I don't mind Bessie really.

ERNIE: Sorry I didn't have a talk to her. Oldest profession in the world, they say. It would have been interesting to clarify my views on the subject.

> [MRS. MILLER *comes in with the tray on which are glasses, a loaf of bread and a jug of water.*

MRS. MILLER: What was the picture like?

FLORRIE: Lovely.

ERNIE: Bit sloppy for me. I hate all this sentiment.

FLORRIE: I saw you crying all right.

ERNIE: What a lie.

MRS. MILLER: It's nothing to be ashamed of. I like a good
   cry myself.

[She goes out.

ERNIE: Good-looking chap, the gangster. I'll admit that.

FLORRIE: He wasn't as good-looking as you.

ERNIE: The rot you talk, Florrie.

FLORRIE: I mean it.

ERNIE: Oh, do you?

   *[They are standing together, close to the gramophone. He
      puts his arms round her and kisses her. Their lips
      linger.*

FLORRIE: Love me, Ernie?

ERNIE: I couldn't love anyone like I love you.

   *[With his disengaged hand he switches on the gramophone.
      They begin to dance cheek to cheek.*

FLORRIE: Mum's a bit low to-night.

ERNIE: Worried about your dad, I suppose.

FLORRIE: Naturally she's anxious. The doctor told her the
   other day he might pop off any minute.

ERNIE: Don't you believe it. They live for ever in asylums.
   He's good for another twenty years.

FLORRIE: Isn't it lovely to think of everything coming out
   all right?

ERNIE: Must you talk?

   *[He kisses her on the lips as they dance on. MRS. MILLER
      comes in again with the tray. There is a cottage pie
      on it, and on a plate SHEPPEY's two kippers.*

MRS. MILLER: Really you're a disgrace, you two. Is that
   what you call laying the table?

   [They stop and ERNIE turns off the music.

ERNIE: The woman tempted me and I fell.

FLORRIE: That's right, blame me.

ERNIE: I don't know what it is, but there's something about her I can't help liking.

MRS. MILLER: Oh, dear, don't be so silly. One of you's just as bad as the other. D'you think nobody's ever been in love before? Run up and tell your dad supper's ready, my girl.

[ERNIE's *glance falls on the grandfather's chair.*

ERNIE: You needn't do that. Here he is ready and waiting.
[*He swings round the chair sideways so that an arm and a hand are seen to fall over the arm of the chair.*

FLORRIE: Why, he's asleep.

[MRS. MILLER *takes a step forward and stops suddenly.*

MRS. MILLER: That's not sleep. [*She looks at him for a moment.*] He always said 'e was born lucky. He's died lucky too.

THE END